Network Intrusion Detection

Third Edition

Contents At a Glance

Network Intrusion Detection

Third Edition

Stephen Northcutt
Judy Novak

New Riders

www.newriders.com

201 West 103rd Street, Indianapolis, Indiana 46290
An Imprint of Pearson Education
Boston • Indianapolis • London • Munich • New York • San Francisco

Network Intrusion Detection
Third Edition

Trademarks

Warning and Disclaimer

Publisher
David Dwyer

Associate Publisher
Stephanie Wall

Production Manager
Gina Kanouse

Managing Editor
Kristy Knoop

Senior Acquisitions Editor
Linda Anne Bump

Senior Marketing Manager
Tammy Detrich

Publicity Manager
Susan Nixon

Project Editor
Suzanne Pettypiece

Copy Editor
Kelli Brooks

Indexer
Larry Sweazy

Manufacturing Coordinator
Jim Conway

Book Designer
Louisa Klucznik

Cover Designer
Brainstorm Design, Inc.

Cover Production
Aren Howell

Proofreader
Beth Trudell

Composition
Gloria Schurick

Dedication

Network Intrusion Detection, Third Edition is dedicated to Dr. Richard Stevens

Stephen Northcutt: I can still see him in my mind quite clearly at lunch in the speaker's room at SANS conferences—long blond hair, ponytail, the slightly fried look of someone who gives his all for his students. I remember the scores from his comment forms. Richard Stevens was the best instructor of us all. I know he is gone and yet, every couple days, I reach for his book *TCP/IP Illustrated, Volume 1*, usually to glance at the packet headers inside the front cover. I am so thankful to own that book; it helps me understand IP and TCP, the network protocols that drive our world. In three weeks or so, I will teach TCP to some four hundred students. I am so scared. I cannot fill his shoes, not even close, but the knowledge must continue to be passed on. I can't stress "must" enough; there is no magic product that can do intrusion detection for you. In the end, every analyst needs a basic understanding of how IP works so they will be able to detect the anomalies. That was the gift Dr. Stevens left each of us. This book builds upon that foundation!

Judy Novak: Of all the influences in the field of security and traffic analysis, none has been more profound than that of the late Dr. Richard Stevens. He was a prolific and accomplished author. The book I'm most familiar with is my dog-eared, garlic sauce-stained copy of *TCP/IP Illustrated, Volume 1*. It is an absolute masterpiece because he is the ultimate authority on TCP/IP and Unix, and he had the rare ability to make the subjects coherent. I know several of the instructors at SANS consider this work to be the "bible" of TCP/IP. I once had the opportunity to be a student in a course he taught for SANS, and I think I sat with mouth agape in reverence of someone with such knowledge. Last summer, he agreed to edit a course I had written for SANS in elementary TCP/IP concepts. This was the equivalent of having Shakespeare critically review a grocery list. I carry his book with me everywhere, and I will not soon forget him.

TABLE OF CONTENTS

About the Authors

Stephen Northcutt is a graduate of Mary Washington College. Before entering the field of computer security, he worked as a Navy helicopter search and rescue crewman, white water raft guide, chef, martial arts instructor, cartographer, and network designer. Stephen is author/co-author of *Incident Handling Step by Step, Intrusion Signatures and Analysis, Inside Network Perimeter Security*, and the previous two editions of this book. He was the original author of the Shadow intrusion detection system and leader of the Department of Defense's Shadow Intrusion Detection team before accepting the position of Chief for Information Warfare at the Ballistic Missile Defense Organization. Stephen currently serves as Director of Training and Certification for the SANS Institute.

Judy Novak is currently a senior security analyst working for the Baltimore-based consulting firm of Jacob and Sundstrom, Inc. She primarily works at the Johns Hopkins University Applied Physics Laboratory where she is involved in intrusion detection and traffic monitoring and Information Operations research. Judy was one of the founding members of the Army Research Labs Computer Incident Response Team where she worked for three years. She has contributed to the development of a SANS course in TCP/IP and written a SANS hands-on course, "Network Traffic Analysis Using tcpdump," both of which are used in SANS certifications tracks. Judy is a graduate of the University of Maryland—home of the 2002 NCAA basketball champions. She is an aging, yet still passionate, bicyclist, and Lance Armstrong is her modern-day hero!

About the Technical Reviewers

These reviewers contributed their considerable hands-on expertise to the entire development process for *Network Intrusion Detection, Third Edition*. As the book was being written, these dedicated professionals reviewed all the material for technical content, organization, and flow. Their feedback was critical to ensuring that *Network Intrusion Detection, Third Edition* fits our readers' need for the highest-quality technical information.

Karen Kent Frederick is a senior security engineer for the Rapid Response team at NFR Security. She is completing her master's degree in computer science, focusing in network security, from the University of Idaho's Engineering Outreach program. Karen has over 10 years of experience in technical support, system administration, and security. She holds several certifications, including the SANS GSEC, GCIA, GCUX, and GCIH. Karen is one of the authors of *Intrusion Signatures and Analysis* and *Inside Network Perimeter Security: The Definitive Guide to Firewalls, VPNs, Routers, and Intrusion Detection Systems*. Karen also frequently writes articles on intrusion detection for SecurityFocus.com.

David Heinbuch joined the Johns Hopkins University Applied Physics Laboratory in 1998. He has experience in intrusion detection, modeling and simulation, vulnerability assessment, and software development. As a member of the Information Operations group, he works on programs in various areas, including secure computing systems, attack modeling and analysis, and intrusion detection. Mr. Heinbuch has a bachelor of science in computer engineering from Virginia Tech and an master's of science in computer science from the Whiting School of Engineering, Johns Hopkins University.

Acknowledgments

Stephen Northcutt: The network detects and analytical insights that fill the pages of this book are contributions from many analysts all over the world. You and I owe them a debt of thanks; they have given us a great gift in making what was once mysterious, a known pattern.

I thank everyone who has served on, or contributed to, the Incidents.org team. You have found many new patterns, helped minimize the damage from a number of compromised systems, and even managed to teach a bit of intrusion detection along the way. Good work!

Incident handlers would be of little purpose if people weren't reporting attacks. The folks who contribute data to dshield.org are making a real difference. You showed that it was possible to share attack information and analysis and that bit by bit we would get smarter, better able to understand exploits and probes.

Judy Novak, thank you for working with me on this project. Your efforts and knowledge are the reason for the book's success. I truly appreciate the work our technical editors, Karen Kent Frederick and David Heinbuch, have done to catch the errors that can creep in while you are working late into the night, or from an airplane. Suzanne Pettypiece, thank you for your patience and organization in the busiest months of my entire life. A big thanks to Linda Bump for working with us to keep the project on schedule!

I want to take this opportunity to express my appreciation to Alan and Marsha Paller for friendship, support, encouragement, and guidance.

Kathy and Hunter, thank you again for the love and support in a writing cycle. Kathy, I especially thank you for being willing to quit your job to help me keep all the plates spinning. I love you.

"But if any of you lacks wisdom, let him ask of God, who gives to all men generously and without reproach, and it will be given to him." James 1:5

Any wisdom or understanding I have is a gift from the Lord Jesus Christ, God the All Mighty, and the credit should be given to Him, not to me.

I hope you enjoy the book and it serves you well!

Judy Novak: Many thanks to Stephen Northcutt for his tireless efforts in educating the world about security and encouraging me to join him in his efforts. His guidance has literally changed my life and the rewards and opportunities from his influence have been plentiful. While the words to express my thanks seem anemic, the gratitude is truly heartfelt.

I'd like to thank the wonderfully wise technical editors David Heinbuch and Karen Kent Frederick for their patient and astute feedback. They are the blessed souls who save me from total embarrassment! Also, I'd like to extend special thanks to Paul Ritchey, who edited the Snort chapters for technical accuracy. He whipped out the feedback with speed and insight.

Finally, last, but never least, I'd like to thank my family—Bob and Jesse—for leaving me alone long enough when I needed to work on the book, but gently nudging me to take a break when atrophy set in. There is real danger in being left alone too long!

Tell Us What You Think

As the reader of this book, you are the most important critic and commentator. We value your opinion and want to know what we're doing right, what we could do better, what areas you'd like to see us publish in, and any other words of wisdom you're willing to pass our way.

As the Associate Publisher at New Riders, I welcome your comments. You can fax, email, or write me directly to let me know what you did or didn't like about this book—as well as what we can do to make our books stronger.

Please note that I cannot help you with technical problems related to the topic of this book, and that due to the high volume of mail I receive, I might not be able to reply to every message.

When you write, please be sure to include this book's title and author as well as your name and phone or fax number. I will carefully review your comments and share them with the author and editors who worked on the book.

Fax: 317-581-4663
Email: stephanie.wall@newriders.com
Mail: Stephanie Wall
          Associate Publisher
          New Riders Publishing
          201 West 103rd Street
          Indianapolis, IN 46290 USA

Introduction

Our goal in writing *Network Intrusion Detection, Third Edition* has been to empower you as an analyst. We believe that if you read this book cover to cover, and put the material into practice as you go, you will be ready to enter the world of intrusion analysis. Many people have read our books, or attended our live class offered by SANS, and the lights have gone on; then, they are off to the races. We will cover the technical material, the workings of TCP/IP, and also make every effort to help you understand how an analyst thinks through dozens of examples.

   Network Intrusion Detection, Third Edition is offered in five parts. Part I, "TCP/IP," begins with Chapter 1, ranging from an introduction to the fundamental concepts of the Internet protocol to a discussion of Remote Procedure Calls (RPCs). We realize that it has become stylish to begin a book saying a few words about TCP/IP, but the system Judy and I have developed has not only taught more people IP but a lot more about IP as well—more than any other system ever developed. We call it "real TCP" because the material is based on how packets actually perform on the network, not theory. Even if you are familiar with IP, give the first part of the book a look. We are confident you will be pleasantly surprised. Perhaps the most important chapter in Part I is Chapter 5, "Stimulus and Response." Whenever you look at a network trace, the first thing you need to determine is if it is a stimulus or a response. This helps you to properly analyze the traffic. Please take the time to make sure you master this material; it will prevent analysis errors as you move forward.

> **Tip**
> Whenever you look at a network trace, the first thing you need to determine is if it is a stimulus or a response.

The book continues in Part II, "Traffic Analysis" with a discussion of traffic analysis. By this, we mean analyzing the network traffic by consideration of the header fields of the IP and higher protocol fields. Although ASCII and hex signatures are a critical part of intrusion detection, they are only tools in the analyst's tool belt. Also in Part II, we begin to show you the importance of each field, how they are rich treasures to understanding. Every field has meaning, and fields provide information both about the sender of the packet and its intended purpose. As this part of the book comes to a close, we tell you stories from the perspective of an analyst seeing network patterns for the first time. The goal is to help you prepare for the day when you will face an unknown pattern.

Although there are times a network pattern is so obvious it almost screams its message, more often you have to search for events of interest. Sometimes, you can do this with a well-known signature, but equally often, you must search for it. Whenever attackers write software for denial of service, or exploits, the software tends to leave a signature that is the result of crafting the packet. This is similar to the way that a bullet bears the marks of the barrel of the gun that fired it, and experts can positively identify the gun by the bullet. In Part III of the book, "Filters/Rules for Network Monitoring" we build the skills to examine any field in the packet and the knowledge to determine what is normal and what is anomalous. In this section, we practice these skills both with TCPdump and also Snort.

In Part IV, we consider the larger framework of intrusion detection. We discuss where you should place sensors, what a console needs to support for data analysis, and automated and manual response issues to intrusion detection. In addition, this section helps arm the analyst with information about how the intrusion detection capability fits in with the business model of the organization.

Finally, this book provides three appendixes that reference common signatures of well-known reconnaissance, denial of service, and exploit scans. We believe you will find this to be no fluff, packed with data from the first to the last page.

Network Intrusion Detection, Third Edition has not been developed by professional technical writers. Judy and I have been working as analysts since 1996 and have faced a number of new patterns. We are thankful for this opportunity to share our experiences and insights with you and hope this book will be of service to you in your journey as an intrusion analyst.

I

TCP/IP

1

IP Concepts

As you read this chapter, it will become apparent that you belong in one of two categories: the beginner category or that of the seasoned veteran. The Internet Protocol (IP) is a large and potentially intimidating topic that requires a gentle introduction for uninitiated beginners so as not to overwhelm them with foreign acronyms, details, and concepts. Therefore, the purpose of this first chapter is to expose newcomers to terms, concepts, and the ever-present acronyms of IP. The suite of protocols covered here is more commonly known as Transmission Control Protocol/Internet Protocol (TCP/IP). These protocols are required to communicate between hosts on the Internet—the worldwide infrastructure of networked hosts. Indeed, communication protocols other than TCP/IP exist (for instance, AppleTalk for Apple computers). These protocols are typically found on intranets, where associated hosts talk on a private network. Most Internet communications require TCP/IP, which is the standard for global communications between hosts and networks.

Those seasoned veteran readers who dabble in TCP/IP daily might be tempted to skip this chapter. Even so, you should give it a quick skim. If you ever need to explain a concept about IP (perhaps to the individual who signs off on your pay raise or bonus, for example), you might find this chapter's approach useful. Those of you who are getting your feet wet in this area will certainly benefit from this introduction.

This is an around-the-world introduction to TCP/IP presented in a single chapter. Many of the topics discussed in this introductory chapter are covered in much greater detail and complexity in upcoming chapters; those chapters contain the core content, but you need to be able to peel away the theoretical skin to understand them. Specifically, this chapter covers the following topics:

- **The TCP/IP Internet model.** This section examines the foundations of communications over the Internet, specifically communications made possible by using a common model known as the TCP/IP Internet model.

- **Packaging of data on the Internet.** This section reviews the encapsulation of data to be sent through different legs of a journey to its destination.

- **Physical and logical addresses.** This section highlights the different ways to identify a computer or host on the Internet.

- **TCP/IP services and ports.** This section explores how hosts communicate with each other for different purposes and through different applications.

- **Domain Name System.** This section focuses on the importance of host names and IP number translations.

- **Routing.** This section explains how data is directed from the sending computer to the receiving computer.

The TCP/IP Internet Model

Computer users often want to communicate with another computer on the Internet for some purpose or another (to view a web page on a remote web server, for instance). A response from a web server can seem almost instantaneous, but a lot of processes and infrastructures actually support this seemingly trivial act behind the scenes.

Layers

Figure 1.1 shows a logical roadmap of some of the processes involved in host-to-host communications. You begin the process of downloading a web page in the box labeled "Web browser." Before your request to see a web page can get to the web server, your computer must package the request and send it through various processes and layers. Each layer represents a logical leg in the journey from the sending computer to the receiving computer. After the sending computer packages the data through the different layers, it is delivered to the receiving computer over the Internet. The receiving computer unwraps the data layer by layer. An individual layer gets the data intended for it and passes the remainder of the message to upper layers.

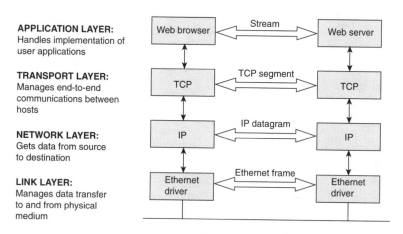

Figure 1.1   The TCP/IP Internet model.

Although discussed in more detail later in this chapter, it is important now to briefly look at each layer. The following four layers comprise the TCP/IP Internet model:

- **Application layer.** The application layer is the topmost layer (the request for a web page in the preceding example). Software on the sending and receiving computers supports the implementation of the application (the web browser and web server, for instance).

- **Transport layer.** Below the application layer lays the transport layer. This layer encompasses many aspects of how the two hosts will communicate. This transport layer is often concerned with providing reliability over other inherently unreliable layers.

    Two transport layers protocols will be covered: TCP, which is referred to as a reliable protocol because mechanisms ensure data delivery, and User Datagram Protocol (UDP), which makes no promise of reliable delivery. In this example application, TCP is required because of the unacceptability of data loss.

- **Network layer.** Below the transport layer is the network layer, which is responsible for moving the data from the source computer to the destination computer (the web server in this case), often one hop or leg of the journey at a time. This hop is between a computer and a router or a router and a router, but it ultimately takes the data closer in routing space to its destination.

- **Link layer.** The bottom layer is the link layer, which is the component that takes care of communications from a host to the physical medium on which it resides. In this case, that component is Ethernet. This layer is concerned with receiving and sending data from the host over a specific interface to the network.

Data Flow

Look at Figure 1.1 again. In theory, the data flow activity is this: The request for a web page "descends" the sender's layers, often referred to as the TCP/IP stack. It gets directed to the destination computer and "ascends" its TCP/IP stack. The vertical arrows between layers represent the up and down flow on the same computer. The horizontal arrows between computers signify that each layer talks to its "peer" layer on the communicating host. The two computers do not directly interact with each other, per se. When the request descends the sending computer's TCP/IP stack, it is packaged in such a manner that each layer has a message for its counterpart layer, and so they appear to be talking directly.

This concept is quite important and crucial to understanding this chapter and the TCP/IP model, in general. Therefore, it is important to reiterate the poignant points and elaborate on terminology. The term TCP/IP stack is used to denote the layered structure of processing a TCP/IP request or response. A process known as encapsulation does the implementation of the layering. This means that data on the sender's host gets wrapped with identifying information to assist the receiving host in parsing the received message layer by layer. Each layer on the sending host adds its own header, and the receiving host reverses the process by examining the message, stripping it of its header, and directing it to the appropriate layer. This process is repeated for the higher layers until the data reaches the uppermost layer, which finally processes the web page request. When the response is sent back, the entire process is repeated; now the web server host packages the data to be sent, it is delivered and received, and the web browser host strips the received message to pass to the application layer supporting the web browser.

Packaging (Beyond Paper or Plastic)

At a very granular level, data exchanged between hosts must be bundled in some kind of standard format. A host is a generic term that can reference a workstation on your desk, a router, or a web server to name just a few examples. The important distinction is that these computers are connected to a network capable of transporting data to and from the computer. In the generic sense, the packaging of associated data is called a packet. The problem in terminology arises because this data package is labeled differently at various layers of communication between the source application and the destination application located on different hosts. This section discusses some of the key concepts related to data packaging, including bits, bytes, packets, data encapsulation, and interpretation of the layers.

Bits, Bytes, and Packets

The atom of computing is a bit, a single storage location that has a value of either 0 or 1 (also known as binary). Although succinct and compact, you cannot actually store or convey a lot of information with a single bit, so bits are grouped into clumps of eight. A unit of eight bits is a byte (or octet, if you prefer). Eight times a very small amount of information is still pretty small, but an octet can contain an American Standard Code for Information Interchange (ASCII) character, such as the letter a or a comma (,). It can also hold a large integer number, as high as 255 (2^8-1).

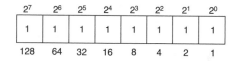

Figure 1.2

Bits, Bytes, and Binary

Figure 1.2 shows a byte. Because this discussion is focusing on bits, binary is the language used— the language of 0s and 1s. Each bit is represented as a power of 2, the base of binary. Notice that a byte spans powers of 2 from 2^0 through 2^7. If all bits have a value of 0, the byte is obviously 0. Now, imagine that all bits are 1s. Add up all the individual bit values, starting with the smallest value (2^0 = 1, any base with an exponent of 0 is 1); you will have 1 + 2 + 4 + 8 + 16 + 32 + 64 + 128. The total value is 255, and that is the maximum value that a given byte can have. This value is examined later when the discussion turns to IP addresses.

You just saw an example of how binary-to-decimal conversion is done. If you are given a byte of data, just re-create this byte with the appropriate powers of 2 and their associated decimal values. Any bit that is set is assigned the accompanying decimal value of that bit. Then, just total up all the decimal values; voila, the conversion is done. This is not really rocket science after all.

Multiple bytes, or octets, are grouped together for shipping across a network by packaging them into packets. Figure 1.3 shows one of the great truths of networking: An overhead cost accrues when slinging packets around the network. You have to go through a lot of trouble to package your content for shipping across a network and then to unwrap it when it gets to the other side (and even more trouble, of course, to finish the job with a tamper-proof seal). A field known as the cyclical redundancy check (CRC), or checksum, is used to validate that the frame (the name given to the packet on the wire) has not been damaged or corrupted in transit.

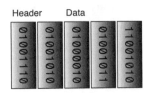

The header provides addressing and type information
much like the outside of a snail-mail envelope.

Figure 1.3   Portrait of a packet.

Like an envelope addressed for mailing, IP packets need to include the addresses of both the sending and receiving hosts (see Figure 1.3). If you live in a house with a street address, you can think of that as your hardware address, the address assigned to your house. In networking, at least with Ethernet networks, this is analogous to a network interface card's (NIC) Media Access Controller (MAC) address. This hardware address is assigned to the NIC when the card is constructed. The MAC address is 48 bits long, which means it can hold a very large number ($2^{48}-1$). The "Addresses" section later in this chapter discusses the differences between MAC addresses and IP addresses.

To create a frame, which is the name the packet acquires when transmitted on physical media, you construct the packet using various protocol layers and then include the physical information. Finally, the frame is placed on the networking medium by the NIC. The frame has a frame header of 14 bytes, with fields such as the source and destination MAC addresses, frame data that can vary in length, and a trailer of 4 bytes that represents the CRC.

Encapsulation Revisited

Figure 1.4 represents the concept of the layered packaging configuration. Different layers of protocols theoretically "talk" to like layers of protocols on the source and destination hosts. The layers are stacked atop one another—

hence, the origin of the term "TCP/IP stack." At each layer of the stack, the packet consists of a header of its own and data, sometimes known as the payload. All the encapsulation is done for the purpose of sending some kind of content, but the encapsulation requires different header information at different levels in its journey from source to destination.

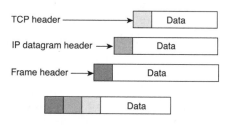

Headers are prepended as the packet descends the stack

Figure 1.4 One layer's header is another layer's data.

Suppose that you have a message or other content to send. It is first collected by the application, which could be a program such as telnet or electronic mail; these TCP applications are discussed in more detail in the section "IP Protocols." The TCP packet is known as a TCP segment and includes the TCP header and TCP data. If this were UDP, the packet would be known as a datagram, which is confusing because it is redundant with the name at the IP layer.

At this point, the TCP segment is handed down from the TCP layer of the TCP/IP stack to the IP layer. The IP layer prepends (that means appends at the front) header information to the TCP segment and becomes known as an IP datagram. Really, the TCP header and data become invisibly enmeshed as data for the IP datagram, which has its own header. The IP datagram is delivered to the link layer of the TCP/IP stack, and it is known as a frame. The link layer prepends the frame header to the IP datagram to carry it across the physical medium, such as Ethernet.

The process is repeated in reverse when the frame arrives at the destination host and all headers are stripped away and passed to the proper upper-layer protocols. Each layer of the TCP/IP stack with its embedded message converses with the similar layer of the receiving host.

Interpretation of the Layers

With all the layering going on, the bottom line is that you have a bunch of adjacent 0s and 1s. How do you know how to interpret them? Suppose that you are looking at the IP header; how do you know what kind of embedded protocol you will find following it? Surely that must be known to properly interpret the protocol. The term *protocol* is meant to denote a set of agreed upon rules or formats. Each protocol (such as IP, TCP, UDP, and ICMP) has its own layouts and formats.

Figure 1.5 shows an example of the organization of the IP header. You can see that a certain number of bits are allocated for each field in the header. A Protocol field identifies the embedded protocol. Each row that you see in the IP header is 32 bits (0 through 31, inclusive), which means four (8-bit) bytes. To complicate matters a little, counting starts with 0 when talking about bit and byte locations. The first row represents bytes 0 through 3; the second row represents bytes 4 through 7; and the third row represents bytes 8 through 11. Notice that the circled Protocol field is in the third row. The preceding time-to-live (TTL) field is 1 byte long, which makes it the 8th byte; and the Protocol field, which is also 1 byte long, represents the 9th byte. This means that the 9th byte (actually, it's the 10th byte, but remember counting starts at 0) is examined to find the embedded protocol. The point is that most packets at their respective levels are positional; fields can be discovered by going to known displacements in the packet.

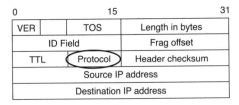

IP header with no options shown, 20 bytes total

Figure 1.5 Positional layouts.

Now that you have counted your way to the Protocol field, what is it and what does it do? The value in this field tells you what protocol is found in the embedded data. Suppose that the value you find in this byte is 17. You might find the protocol value expressed in hexadecimal. A hexadecimal 11 is the same as a decimal 17. This means that a UDP packet is embedded after the IP header. A value of 6 means that the embedded packet is TCP, and a value of 1 means that it is Internet Control Message Protocol (ICMP).

Base 16, Hexadecimal

Okay, so you have learned that binary is base 2 and is made up of 0s and 1s. This is the numbering system used by computers to represent data. So, why complicate the matter with another entirely new numbering system, base 16 (or hexadecimal)? The real dilemma is that it takes a lot of bits to represent any sizable number and, therefore, binary becomes very unwieldy very soon. Hexadecimal assists in referencing binary numbers in a more abbreviated notation. You can replace 4 binary bits with 1 hexadecimal character ($2^4 = 16$).

Consider, for example, the IP header protocol field; it is 8 bits. That can be converted into 2 hex characters. A decimal 17 in the protocol field, as mentioned earlier, means that the embedded protocol is UDP. How do you go from a decimal 17 to a hexadecimal 11?

$$2^7 \; 2^6 \; 2^5 \; 2^4 \qquad 2^3 \; 2^2 \; 2^1 \; 2^0$$
$$0 \quad 0 \quad 0 \quad 1 \qquad 0 \quad 0 \quad 0 \quad 1$$

The binary powers of the 8 bits are shown. To arrive at 17, you need to have the bit corresponding to 16 (or 2^4) set to 1, and the bit corresponding to 1 (2^0) set to 1—that is, 16 + 1 = 17. These have been grouped as two hex digits, two 4-bit clumps. The 4 bits (or hex character) that are leftmost (also known as high-order or most significant bits) have a value of 0001. Likewise, the 4 bits that are rightmost (also known as low-order or least significant bits) have a value of 0001. Each hex character represents values of 0 through 15. And each of these has a low-order bit of 1 set (2^0), and so we arrive at the value of 11 hexadecimal (also known as 0x11, in which the 0x distinguishes this as hex, not decimal).

Addresses

Most likely, you have heard the term IP address. But, what does it really represent and what does it really do? And, exactly how do hosts address each other? These are some of the topics covered in this section.

Physical Addresses, Media Access Controller Addresses

You can scour the headers of IP packets looking for physical layer MAC addresses until you turn blue, and you will not find them. MAC addresses do not mean anything to IP, which uses logical addresses; they are not part of the protocol. For all intents and purposes, they may as well not exist.

By the same token, physical MAC addresses are how the Ethernet card interfaces with the network. The Ethernet card does not know a single thing about IP, IP headers, or logical IP addresses. So, you are faced with the signature line of Cool Hand Luke: "What we have here is a failure to communicate." Clearly, if things are going to work, an operation process is required that facilitates the correspondence between logical IP and physical MAC addresses.

Do you know the IP address of your desktop computer? If you don't, you are not really one down at all; it is absolutely normal not to know it. It is normal for several reasons, one being that in these days most of you don't even own or even get to keep the same IP address. IP address space is a precious commodity. When you connect to the network, many of you are loaned an address for that session, or possibly longer by an Internet service provider (ISP) or network service provider via applications, such as Dynamic Host Configuration Protocol (DHCP).

Leasing an IP Number: Dynamic Host Configuration Protocol

DHCP is a protocol that permits dynamic assignment of IP numbers. This replaces the labor-intensive process of IP address management, in which every host is configured with a static IP number assigned to it. DHCP allows the centralization and automation of the IP assignment process. Hosts are leased an IP number for a given amount of time, and this makes the process of managing and administering large networks more efficient. This is good for the network administrator, but makes the security administrator's job more complicated (for example, when some IP number and associated temporary owner have to be chased down for questionable activity).

Exactly how many possible IP numbers are there? The exact number is 2^{32} (because the address is comprised of 32 bits), which is a number higher than 4 billion. But, every single IP number is not available; reserved ranges decrease the possible numbers. With the explosive growth of the Internet worldwide, the sad realization has dawned that the IP addresses are being rapidly depleted. What are some remedies for the address depletion?

First, a particular site can use DHCP and assign IP numbers temporarily for the duration of their use. This means that not all hosts will be active at any given time and a smaller pool of possible IP numbers is required. The other remedy is something known as reserved private addresses. The governing body of the Internet, the Internet Address Numbers Authority (IANA), has set aside blocks of IP addresses to be used for internal addresses only. For instance, the 192.168 and 172.16 subnets are to be used for hosts talking within a particular network. This traffic should not leave the site's gateway. This allows a site with an insufficient number of IP addresses to use these Class B network addresses for internal purposes and to save the assigned IP addresses for other purposes.

Okay, go ahead and smirk now; some of you did know your IP address. That is good. However, do you know your host's MAC address by heart? The answer would most likely be "no," because almost no one knows his MAC address. There are several reasons for this, but the primary one is that a 48-bit address with no provisions for human memorization is hard to lock into the brain.

The Address Resolution Protocol (ARP) enables you to resolve the translation of physical MAC addresses to logical IP addresses. ARP is not an IP protocol per se; it is the process of sending an Ethernet frame to all systems on the same network segment. This is known as a broadcast. If a message is a broadcast message, it is sent to all the machines on part of or the entire network. A point worth emphasizing is that ARP is for locally attached hosts only on the same network; this cannot be done between hosts on different networks.

The source host broadcasts the ARP request, and then presumably the destination host picks it up and replies with its MAC address. During this transaction, both the source and destination host, and any listening hosts on the network, cache (or save) what they have learned about the other host, thereby storing the IP and MAC addresses. This storage cuts down on the number of new ARP requests required. Ultimately, on the same network segment, the communications will occur between MAC addresses and not IP addresses. They might begin as a TCP/IP transaction with two hosts communicating between the same layers of TCP/IP, but when the actual delivery occurs, communication is between two hosts' MAC addresses.

Why are MAC addresses so huge? After all, 48 bits is a lot of address space. The idea was that they would be unique for all time and space! That sounds good if you say it real fast, but future plans are to expand this value to 128 bits to accommodate its current limitations in allowing each NIC manufacturer to have a unique vendor code embedded in the MAC address.

Logical Addresses, IP Addresses

An IP address has 32 allocated bits to identify a host. This 32-bit number is expressed as four decimal numbers separated by periods (for example, 192.168.5.5). These are not just random or sequential assignments. The initial portion of the IP number tells something about the size of the network on which the host resides. The remainder of the IP number distinguishes hosts on that network. Addresses are categorized by class; classes tell how many hosts are in a given network or how many bits in the IP address are assigned for the unique hosts in a network (see Table 1.1). A grouping known as Class A addresses assigns the initial 8 bits for a network portion of the address, for example, and the final 24 bits for the host portion of the address. Because 24 bits have been allocated for the hosts, more than 16 million (2^{24}-1) hosts can possibly be in the network. An example of a Class A network is the 18.0.0.0 through 18.255.255.255, IP space assigned to Massachusetts Institute of Technology.

Table 1.1 **32 Bits for IP Address Space**

Class	Network Bits	Host Bits	Number of Hosts
A	8	24	16 million+
B	16	16	65,000+
C	24	8	255

The IP address classes range from Class A addresses to Class E. Classes A, B, and C are unicast addresses; when you send a packet to them, presumably you are addressing a single machine. Class D is known as a multicast address used to communicate with a designated set of hosts. Class E is reserved for experimental use. Table 1.2 shows the address range associated with each class.

Table 1.2 **Address Classes and IP Ranges**

Class	Beginning IP	Ending IP
A	0.0.0.0	127.255.255.255
B	128.0.0.0	191.255.255.255
C	192.0.0.0	223.255.255.255
D	224.0.0.0	239.255.255.255
E	240.0.0.0	247.255.255.255

House Rules of CIDR

You might hear a new term, classless inter-domain routing (CIDR) to refer to addresses. For the longest time, addresses were part of a particular class and that meant your network was allocated either 16 million+, 65,000+, or 255 hosts. The most common situation was networks that required between 255 and 65,000 hosts. Because many of these sites were allocated Class B networks, many IP numbers went unassigned. Given that IP numbers are finite commodities, a remedy was needed to allocate networks without class constraints.

CIDR assigns networks, not on 8-bit boundaries, but on single-bit boundaries. This allows a site to receive the appropriate number of IP numbers, and thus reduces waste. CIDR uses a unique notation to designate the range of hosts assigned to a site. If you want to specify the 192.168 address range in CIDR, it would look like 192.168/16. The first part of the notation is the decimal representation of the bit pattern allocated to the network. It is followed by a slash and then the number of bits that represent the network portion of the address. This example is the same as a Class B network, but it can be modified easily enough to represent smaller networks.

Subnet Masks

Another concept you need to be aware of is something known as the subnet mask. This mask informs a given computer system how many bits in its IP address have been relegated to the network and how many to the host. Each bit that is a network bit is "masked" with a 1. A Class A address, for instance, has 8 network bits and 24 host bits. In binary, the 8 consecutive bits (all with a value of 1) translate to a decimal 255. The subnet mask is then designated as 255.0.0.0. Other classes have other subnet masks. A Class B network has a standard subnet mask of 255.255.0.0, and a Class C network has a standard subnet mask of 255.255.255.0. Why is this needed if you can tell what class and how many bits have been reserved for the network by examining the IP address? Some network administrators subdivide their networks. For instance, a Class C network could be divided into four individual subnets by assigning an appropriate subnet mask.

Service Ports

This section is a "bit" easier. TCP and UDP have 16-bit port number fields in their respective header fields. This means they can have as many as 65,536 different ports, or services, and they are numbered from 0 to 65,535. One very important point to register in your long-term memory is that even though a service is usually located at its assigned port number, nothing guarantees this as true. Telnet, for instance, is almost universally found on TCP port 23. There is nothing stopping your nonconformist side from offering it at port 31337. And, what better way for a hacker who has broken into a computer to hide his tracks than by offering a service at an unexpected port? If a hacker were to run telnet at some high-numbered port rather than port 23, it would make his unauthorized connection more difficult to find and identify. Any service can be run at any port. On the other hand, if you want to network with other hosts, it is best to follow the standards. For UNIX hosts, the /etc/services file can be an excellent resource to match TCP or UDP port numbers with the expected, or well-known, services likely to be offered at that port number.

You see some very common port numbers and service examples from the /etc/services file. An excerpt here shows you the format of the file and the associated services. You see that a service known as domain (Domain Name Service, or DNS) can be offered on both TCP and UDP. This is unusual, but not abnormal; most services are offered on either TCP or UDP, but there are some exceptions (such as DNS).

```
ftp          21/tcp
telnet       23/tcp
smtp         25/tcp
domain       53/udp
domain       53/tcp
```

Figure 1.6 shows how the service is specified in the packet. In this case, a UDP header has a 16-bit field known as the destination port. This is where the desired service or port is found. In this example, the value in the UDP header's port number field would be 53, signifying that this datagram is destined for the Domain Name Service.

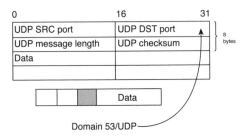

Figure 1.6   Not just any port.

At one time in history, special significance was attached to ports below 1024. Those lower-numbered ports were the so-called trusted ports (chuckle) because only root could use them. The term *trusted port* originated because ports below 1024 were allocated to system processes. Therefore, if a foreign host saw an incoming connection with a source port less than 1024, it was assumed to be trusted because it ostensibly came from a system process. This made much more sense when the Internet was a safer place. This is much less true today, but the ports above 1024 have special significance. These are often called the ephemeral ports, which means they could be used by most any service for most any reason.

IP Protocols

Turn your attention again to the four primary layers of the TCP/IP model (refer back to Figure 1.1). You (as the user) use an application to interact with the IP communications stack. You use a program such as FTP to transfer files, telnet as a terminal emulator, and email to forward tired jokes and stories to 50 of your closest friends. The application takes the message, the information from the user or user process, and prepares it to be sent down through the IP stack. The remaining three layers are transport, network, and link.

Two different transport models are discussed at this point: a connection-oriented model (TCP) and a connectionless model (UDP). Connection-oriented means just what it sounds like: The software does everything that it can to ensure that the communication is reliable and complete and begins the process by establishing a connection known as a handshake. Connectionless, on the other hand, is a send-and-pray delivery that has no handshake and no promise of reliability. Any offered reliability must be built in to the application. Table 1.3 shows some of the TCP and UDP attributes.

Table 1.3   **Attributes of TCP Versus UDP**

TCP	**UDP**
Reliable	Unreliable
Connection-oriented	Connectionless
Slower	Faster

UDP is the easiest communication protocol to comprehend—after all, you just assemble packets and fire them into the network. The destination host scoops them up, demultiplexes (strips the headers off at one layer and sends it to the appropriate upper-layer protocol), and extracts the message. Certainly, a few datagrams might get lost along the way, but that is often okay; for plenty of applications, this is not an issue. If you were broadcasting audio, for instance, and a word got lost, your mind could probably compensate for this and fill in the missing word. If you were sending video, perhaps there would be a little blank spot where some packets got lost. Most of the time, this is acceptable. The data that travels over UDP is not necessarily unreliable; it is just that UDP itself is not responsible for it. The application must ignore the missing pieces or ask for the missing pieces.

What if you have an application that cannot tolerate the loss of packets? That is when TCP is used. It ensures that all data sent is received. Several mechanisms are in place to verify delivery and proper sequencing of TCP data. One means of control is an acknowledgement.

An acknowledgement (ACK) is an important part of the TCP protocol. TCP is so reliable because each packet is acknowledged after the destination host receives it. If a packet is not received (and therefore not acknowledged), it is resent. Thus, TCP ensures that all the packets are received, and so is deemed a reliable service. This is a much slower way of doing business, but you can set certain optimizations to speed up the process. That said, TCP will always be slower than UDP.

The final IP protocol discussed here is the Internet Control Message Protocol (ICMP), which is a fascinating lightweight set of applications originally created for network troubleshooting and to report error conditions. The most well-known ICMP application is certainly the echo request/echo reply (or ping). You can use a ping to determine whether a given network host is reachable. Other ICMP applications are used for such things as flow control, packet rerouting, and network information collection (to name just a few of the functions). Chapter 4, "ICMP," discusses ICMP and its related functions in more detail.

Domain Name System

Naming a thing is not the same as knowing a thing, but it is often the first step. I remember when I first started hearing about the Domain Name System (DNS). At the time, the major database software vendors were all talking about their distributed database products that would be available "real soon now," and then the next thing I knew I was running distributed database software. It didn't cost me a thing, and it worked from day one. DNS is a distributed database because the entire address table is not stored on a single host; instead, it is distributed across many servers.

At one point, the IP addresses and names were kept in tables that were downloaded nightly. As the Internet kept growing, this became impractical for a number of reasons related to the size of the table and issues surrounding single point of failure. Take a look at this excerpt of the static host file /etc/hosts maintained on a UNIX host:

```
/etc/hosts
127.0.0.1       loopback
172.20.1.41     relay relay.sans.org
172.20.31.19    goo goo.sans.org
```

Although UNIX and Windows 2000 hosts still maintain a small local hosts file to identify local and frequently used hosts, this function has been augmented by adding DNS capabilities. Most UNIX and Windows 2000 hosts are configured to search the host's file first and if a host is not found there, to search DNS for the resolution for the host. This offloads most of the maintenance burden from the system administrator to individual administrators who maintain DNS servers.

Before jumping into the DNS, a discussion of DNS domains is needed. A domain is really just a logical division of DNS or the DNS database. The initial seven well-known "generic" domains have the three-letter endings such .com, .org, .edu, .net, and to a lesser extent .int, .gov, and .mil. The list of top-level domains has been expanded to include .aero, .biz, .coop, .info, .museum, .name, and .pro. There are also two-letter domains, which often appear as country codes (.us, .fr, and .uk for the United States, France, and the United Kingdom). Within each of those generic domains are the domains used every day (for example, yahoo.com and sans.org). Each of these domains represents a slice of the entire DNS pie.

Now that you have been introduced to the concept of DNS domains, how does DNS name resolution really work? At a very rudimentary level, there are basically two resolving routines: gethostbyaddr and gethostbyname. When you do some kind of DNS resolution, a host needs to either translate an IP number into a host name or a host name into an IP number. The real issue at hand is that people refer to hosts by their God-given host names, whereas computers refer to hosts by their binary-derived IP numbers. After all, there is no field in an IP datagram for the host name, only the IP number.

The gethostbyaddr call issued by your host delivers an IP number to a DNS server and tells it to resolve the host name and return it. There is much more to the process than meets the superficial eye, and this is discussed in Chapter 6, "DNS." Conversely, a gethostbyname call delivers a host name to a DNS server and requests resolution to an IP number. Understand that this explanation of DNS is a gross oversimplification of the processes and issues involved because it is intended to be a very introductory exposure.

Routing: How You Get There from Here

Do you remember reading about TCP/IP as a four-layer protocol stack: application, transport, network, and link?

Some time was taken to explain what the application and transport layers do, but the explanation stopped at the network layer. Well, the network layer is concerned with routing and how to get from one host to another host regardless of the physical interconnection or the layout of the network. A better name for this layer might be the IP layer because this is the layer at which IP addresses are used and routing occurs. It is significant to understand that IP doesn't concern itself with the underlying physical link.

You have already learned about the mechanism used to direct traffic to a host that resides on a network with the same network ID and subnet mask as the sending host. ARP is used to broadcast a request to all hosts on the local network asking one to respond with a MAC address that matches the desired destination IP number. How then is traffic directed to other networks since ARP is broadcast only on the local network? That is where routing comes in.

Each host has a routing table that knows about a default router. When the destination host is not on the local network, the traffic to be sent is directed to the default router. The router is responsible for forwarding the traffic one hop closer to its destination. This hop can be to another router or to the destination host itself if it resides on a network directly connected to the router's interface. The question then becomes, how do routers know how to correctly direct the traffic and how do they receive updated information? After all, this has to be a dynamic process given that routes change because of problems and growth.

Routers maintain tables of routes that they know about. They use dynamic routing protocols to update their tables.

Routing protocols are divided into two major categories: Interior Gateway Protocols (IGPs) and Exterior Gateway Protocols (EGPs). The Interior Gateway Protocols support routing traffic within a network that is under the same administrative control, also known as an Autonomous System (AS). This is a fancy name for all the routers for which a site has responsibility. The Routing Information Protocol (RIP) is a widely deployed IGP. RIP is a simple protocol, which requires very little configuration and is supported by essentially every device. Another IGP is Open Shortest Path First (OSPF). These two protocols differ in the way that they receive routing updates and their perspective on finding best routes.

Exterior Gateway Protocols are required when packets must travel between different Autonomous Systems. These protocols bridge separate Autonomous Systems into a single network in which all of the computers on the network can interact seamlessly with each other. The Border Gateway Protocol (BGP) is a widely used Exterior Gateway Protocol. Currently, BGP provides the routing protocol that supports the Internet backbone. BGP servers on the Internet backbone must maintain routing tables that include all of the external addresses on the Internet—a pretty daunting task.

Summary

A lot of new and diverse topics have been jam-packed into this introductory chapter. Details aside, you need to take away some core concepts with you to understand the upcoming chapters on TCP/IP.

First, visualize the transfer of data between two networked hosts as a series of layers, much like a stack. On the sending end, the message to be delivered is encapsulated in a series of headers as it is passed down the stack. On the receiving end, the process is reversed and the encapsulating headers are stripped and delivered to the associated layer of the stack for processing. Each layer on the sending host really communicates with its peer layer on the receiving host. Data is exchanged and packaged in different bundles with different names depending on the purpose of the data and the layer at which it is found in the TCP/IP stack.

Hosts are addressed as both IP numbers and MAC numbers at different layers of the TCP/IP stack. Remember that port numbers are used with TCP and UDP to designate a specific application, such as sendmail or telnet. TCP is the connection-oriented protocol that promises delivery, whereas UDP makes no such promise and is considered unreliable. DNS is used to translate host names to IP addresses and vice versa. Finally, routing is responsible for transporting the datagram from source to destination host. TCP/IP is a vast and complex topic. Various aspects of it will be examined in more detail in subsequent chapters of this part of the book.

2

Introduction to TCPdump and TCP

NOW THAT YOU HAVE LEARNED A BIT about Internet Protocol (IP), you can take a closer look at how it works by using a practical analysis tool known as *TCPdump*. Just as you cannot do any kind of intrusion detection or traffic analysis without knowledge of TCP/IP, you cannot do analysis without a tool of some sort. TCPdump, or its Windows cousin Windump, is a popular and widely used piece of software that can give you some insight into the traffic activity that occurs on a given network. This chapter teaches you how to manipulate the tool for your own purposes and explains the output that it displays. The discussion then turns to one of the most important and common protocols, TCP. You are introduced to some theory, but the real goal is to enable you to catch a visual clue about TCP's behavior by examining it using TCPdump.

An excellent free tool for packet sniffing and interpretation is known as Ethereal, which is available for both Windows and UNIX. It provides a GUI interface to interpret all layers of the packet and many times the payload. It is even protocol aware, meaning that it knows how to interpret the payload of many common protocols. For instance, it would know how to decipher a normally coded DNS query. You are probably wondering why Ethereal is not being used as the tool of choice in this book. First, it is more difficult to translate the Ethereal output to readable book format. TCPdump is more succinct and more easily viewed. Second, TCPdump is more primitive because it requires the user to do much of the interpretation of the output. The challenge is to make you think rather than hand you all the answers, as Ethereal does.

The second part of this chapter begins the discussion of network protocols with a discussion of TCP. All the chapters in this book that discuss network protocols follow a similar format. To give you insight into "normal" activity, the protocol is first presented as you would expect to see it under normal circumstances. However, because the Internet has become a wild and unpredictable arena, you are quite likely to see aberrant kinds of activity too. Each protocol chapter discusses some of the deviant departures you might encounter. This chapter follows that basic format.

TCPdump

TCPdump is a UNIX tool used to gather data from the network, decipher the bits, and display the output in a semi coherent fashion. The semi coherent output becomes fully coherent output with a little explanation and exposure to the tool. When I first came to work at the Dahlgren Navy Laboratory, for example, I spent the first week watching a network analyzer. My boss, Bob Hott, came by every couple of hours to ask questions or have me give him a small assignment. At the end of the week, he had learned something about the behavior of IP and the character of his network. I strongly encourage you to spend some time watching your network traffic; your investment will pay off for you many times over in your journey as an analyst.

Although output from commercial tools might differ slightly or be more fashionable than TCPdump, TCPdump runs close to the metal and can help you understand other tools as well. This section demonstrates the use and demystifies the output of TCPdump.

> **Where Do You Get TCPdump and Its Variants?**
>
> You can download TCPdump from `ftp://ftp.ee.lbl.gov/tcpdump.tar.Z`
>
> You need to download software known as libpcap, which implements a portable framework for capturing low-level network traffic. You can find it at `ftp://ftp.ee.lbl.gov/libpcap.tar.Z`

This is the "official" version of TCPdump; Lawrence Berkeley Labs authored it. Yet, more recently, a collective effort has arisen to maintain and improve the code. More feature-rich versions are being developed and can be found at www.tcpdump.org

Windump is a Windows variant of TCPdump. You can download it from http://netgroup-serv.polito.it/windump

It also requires winpcap software to function. You can obtain winpcap from this same site.

TCPdump Behavior

After TCPdump has been installed, most operating systems require root access to run it. This is because reading packets requires access to devices accessible to root-only. TCPdump is run by issuing the command **tcpdump**. By default, this reads all the traffic from the default network interface and spews all the output to the console. This is not always the behavior the user wants; in fact, this is pretty irritating because records are likely to fly by uncontrollably on a busy network. Therefore, many different command-line options are available to alter the default behavior.

Filters

Suppose, for instance, that you don't want to collect all the traffic from the default network interface. Maybe you are interested only in TCP records. TCPdump has a filter that enables you to specify the records that you are interested in collecting. TCPdump comes complete with a filter "language" to denote the field(s) in an IP datagram that should be examined and retained if the specified conditions are met. To collect only TCP records, issue the command **tcpdump 'tcp'**. The filter in this example is **'tcp'**.

Filters get much more complicated and restrictive than this simple one when you use combinations of fields and traits. Just about any field in an IP datagram, including the actual data payload, can be used to limit the purview of collected records. It seems logical that TCPdump should include a way to indicate that the filter is stored in a file so that users don't have to type a long filter complete with ham-handed keystrokes on the command line itself. And true to logic, TCPdump has an **−F** *filename* option to indicate that the filter is located in the file *filename*.

Binary Collection

As mentioned earlier, TCPdump dumps all the collected output to the screen. This is tolerable behavior if you are looking for a specific record. Most times, however, TCPdump is running in unattended mode, gathering records for retrospective analysis. To gather data for retrospective analysis, you want TCPdump to collect the records in a binary format, also known as raw output. When TCPdump displays records on the console, they have been translated from the native raw output format to a human-readable format. For retrospective analysis, the desired format for storage is the binary mode, in which all captured data is stored, not just the data translated for output. To collect in raw output mode, use the command **tcpdump −w** *filename*, in which *filename* is the name of the file to which the records will be written in binary format.

To read this raw output file, another command-line option is necessary: **tcpdump −r** *filename*. This option reads input to TCPdump from *filename* rather than from the default network interface. You can read a file that has been written using the −w option only by using TCPdump with the −r option. If you have ever used the UNIX tar utility, you know that when you create a tar file, often referred to as a tarball, you must read that same tar file using tar. The same principle applies with TCPdump.

Altering the Amount of Data Collected

One final option is discussed before proceeding because it determines the amount of data that TCPdump collects. TCPdump does not attempt to collect the entire datagram sent. The reason for this is due to volume concerns and many times the user's interest is in the header portions of the datagram that are usually collected with the default length. The snapshot length, sometimes known as snaplen, determines the exact number of bytes collected. One of the most common lengths of collected data is 68 bytes.

What exactly do you get with these 68 bytes of data? Figure 2.1 shows a sample breakdown of a packet. The header fields can be different lengths than depicted, based on the protocol and header options. First you have an encapsulating link layer header—if this were Ethernet, it would represent 14 bytes of Ethernet frame header with fields such as source and destination MAC addresses. Next, you have an IP datagram header, which is minimally 20 bytes if there are no IP options. The encapsulated protocol header (TCP, UDP, ICMP, and so on) follows that and can range from 8 bytes to more than 20 bytes for TCP headers with options. The data, or payload in the datagram, is collected after all the headers. As you can see, there might not be much, if any, payload collected because of the default snaplen. To alter the default snaplen, use the **tcpdump –s** *length* command, in which *length* is the desired number of bytes to be collected. If you want to capture an entire Ethernet frame (not including 4 bytes of trailer), use **tcpdump –s 1514**. This captures the 14-byte Ethernet frame header and the maximum transmission unit length for Ethernet of 1500 bytes.

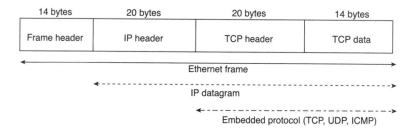

Figure 2.1   Sample packet.

You can use many more command-line options with TCPdump. To learn about them, issue the command **man tcpdump command**. Be warned, however, that the output is copious (change the printer cartridge and restock the paper), but very informative if you have the patience and curiosity to wade through it.

TCPdump Output

Because you will be seeing many TCPdump traces in this book, it is important for you to understand the format. One of the hardest tasks for the novice analyst to master is decrypting TCPdump output. TCPdump output is fairly standard for the different protocols (TCP, UDP, ICMP, for example), but does have some nuances. The first step is to identify the protocol that you are examining. TCP output will be used to explain the general TCPdump format. Here is a TCP record displayed by TCPdump:

```
09:32:43:910000 nmap.edu.1173 > dns.net.21: S 62697789:62697789(0) win 512
```

- **09:32:43:9147882**   This is the time stamp in the format of two digits for hours, two digits for minutes, two digits for seconds, and six digits for fractional parts of a second.

- **nmap.edu**   This is the source host name. If there is no resolution for the IP number or the default behavior of host name resolution is not requested (TCPdump -n option), the IP number appears and not the host name.

- **1173**   This is the source port number, or port service.

- **>**   This is the marker to indicate a directional flow going from source to destination.

- **dns.net**   This is the destination host name.

- **21**   This is the destination port number (for example, **21** might be translated as FTP).

- **s**   This is the TCP flag. The *S* represents the SYN flag, which indicates a request to start a TCP connection.

- **62697789:62697789(0)**   This is the *beginning TCP sequence number:ending TCP sequence number* (data bytes). Sequence numbers are used by TCP to order the data received. For a session establishment such as this, the beginning sequence number represents the *initial sequence number* (ISN), selected as a unique number to mark the first byte of data. The ending sequence number is the beginning sequence number plus the number of data bytes sent within this TCP segment. As you see, the number of data bytes sent for a session establishment request is usually 0. That is why the beginning and ending sequence numbers are the same. Normal session establishments do not send data.

- **win 512**   This is the receiving buffer size (in bytes) of nmap.edu for this connection.

TCP Flags

Normal TCP connections have one or more flags set. Flags are used to indicate the function of the connection. Table 2.1 shows the TCP flags, their representation in TCPdump, and their meanings.

Table 2.1   **TCPdump Flags**

TCP Flag	Flag Representation	Flag Meaning
SYN	s	This is a session establishment request, which is the first part of any TCP connection.
ACK	ack	This flag is used generally to acknowledge the receipt of data from the sender. This might be seen in conjunction with or "piggybacked" with other flags.

Table 2.1 **Continued**

TCP Flag	Flag Representation	Flag Meaning
FIN	F	This flag indicates the sender's intention to gracefully terminate the sending host's connection to the receiving host.
RESET	R	This flag indicates the sender's intention to immediately abort the existing connection with the receiving host.
PUSH	P	This flag immediately "pushes" data from the sending host to the receiving host's application software. There is no waiting for the buffer to fill up. In this case, responsiveness, not bandwidth efficiency, is the focus. For many interactive applications such as telnet, the primary concern is the quickest response time, which the PUSH flag attempts to signal.
URGENT	urg	This flag indicates that there is "urgent" data that should take precedence over other data. An example of this is pressing Ctrl+C to abort an FTP download.
Placeholder	.	If the connection does not have a SYN, FIN, RESET, or PUSH flag set, a placeholder (a period) will be found after the destination port.

TCPdump output for TCP is unique; the flag field and the sequence numbers are distinguishing characteristics. When you see these telltale signs in the TCPdump output, you know the record is TCP. UDP records are likely to have the word *udp* in the TCPdump output. Although true most of the time, just when you think you can rely on this as a steadfast way to identify UDP output, TCPdump throws you a curve ball. TCPdump analyzes some UDP services, such as *Domain Name Service* (DNS) and *Simple Network Management Protocol* (SNMP), at the application level in addition to the protocol level as UDP. Like Ethereal, it is protocol aware and can interpret normally coded payloads of certain protocols. The output might look foreign to you the first few times you see it because it does not have the word *udp* and because there are no TCP trademarks such as flags or sequence numbers. Typically, this is UDP output with more detail. Finally, ICMP is easily identified because the word *icmp* appears, without exception, in the TCPdump output.

Absolute and Relative Sequence Numbers

Not to belabor the discussion of TCPdump output any more than is necessary, but TCP sequence numbers need to be addressed in a little more detail. Sequence numbers are associated only with TCP output, as just discussed. TCP sequence numbers are used by the destination host to reassemble TCP traffic that arrives. Remember that TCP guarantees order, whereas UDP does not. The sequence numbers are decimal number representations of a 32-bit field, so they can be pretty monstrous in size and intimidating to read. TCPdump helps make the output more coherent by changing from the absolute ISNs to relative sequence numbers after the two hosts exchange their ISNs. Look at the following TCPdump output. The time stamp has been omitted for the clarity and space-saving considerations:

```
client.com.38060 > telnet.com.telnet: S 3774957990:3774957990(0) win 8760
<mss 1460> (DF)
telnet.com.telnet > client.com.38060: S 2009600000:2009600000(0) ack
3774957991 win 1024 <mss 1460>
client.com.38060 > telnet.com.telnet: .ack 1 win 8760 (DF)
client.com.38060 > telnet.com.telnet: P 1:28(27) ack 1 win 8760 (DF)
```

The section, "Establishing a TCP Connection," discusses the actual theory of this output. For now, however, look at the numbers in bold. The first two numbers in the first two lines in bold represent the very large ISNs in absolute format that are exchanged from client.com and telnet.com, respectively. The third line has a number in bold that represents a relative sequence number—1. This means that client.com has acknowledged receiving the previous SYN by telnet.com with an ISN of 2009600000. The 1 as the acknowledgement value means that the next expected relative byte to be received by client.com is byte 1. That would have an absolute sequence number of 2009600001, if it were not displayed as a relative sequence number. If this seems confusing, the theory of acknowledgement numbers will be discussed in more detail in the upcoming section "Introduction to TCP."

The final line has the numbers 1 and 28 in bold to indicate that relative to the absolute sequence number of 3774957990, the 1st byte through (but not including) the 28th byte are sent from client.com to telnet.com. The final line also has ack 1.. This acknowledgement number will not change until telnet.com sends more data.

If you ever need to leave the sequence numbers in their absolute form, the TCPdump −S option will alter the default behavior of expressing TCP sequence numbers in relative terms after the exchange of the ISNs.

> **Changing the TCPdump Collection Interface**
> You might find that you want to read TCPdump traffic from a different interface than the default one. The default interface is the lowest number active one, not including the loopback interface. For instance, if you were on a Linux box and had two NIC cards, one might be known as eth0 and the next eth1. To change the default interface, the −i option of TCPdump is used. The following command will select ppp0 as the listening interface:
>
> tcpdump -i ppp0

Dumping in Hexadecimal

TCPdump does not display all the fields of the captured data. For example, the IP header has a field that stores the length of the IP header. How do you display this field if it is not available from the standard TCPdump output? There is a TCPdump command-line option (−x) that dumps the entire datagram captured with the default snaplen in hexadecimal. Hexadecimal output is far more difficult to read and interpret, but it is necessary to display the entire captured datagram.

To interpret TPCdump hexadecimal output, you need some reference material that discusses the format of the IP datagram headers and describes what each of the fields represents. (One such reference title is *TCP/IP Illustrated, Volume 1*, by W. Richard Stevens.) You then must translate hexadecimal to decimal for numeric fields and numeric to ASCII for character fields. Ethereal is probably the best tool to use for translation of TCPdump records that are stored in binary form with the −w tcpdump command line option; it can read TCPdump binary data as input.

Introduction to TCP

TCP is a reliable connection-oriented protocol used with well-known applications such as telnet or smtp. An application such as telnet cannot tolerate the uncertainty of the Internet Protocol that can lose datagrams or deliver them in a different order from which they were sent. TCP is the protocol that orchestrates and ensures reliability. It does so using the following mechanisms:

- **Exclusive TCP connection.** When a TCP session is established, the connection is exclusive and unique between the two hosts. This kind of connection is called a unicast connection. The negotiation of the unique session allows both sides to track the traffic exchanged between the two hosts.

- **TCP sequence numbers.** These provide a sense of chronology to the TCP data sent and received. A telnet command or exchange might take several packets known as TCP segments to transmit all the data. Data is assigned a TCP sequence number to uniquely identify the data in each segment being sent. Because the data might arrive in a different order from which it was sent, TCP sequence numbers are also used to reassemble the data in the correct order.

- **Acknowledgements.** Acknowledgements are used to inform the sender that data has been received. Acknowledgements are made to sequence numbers to identify the exact data received. If the sender does not receive an acknowledgement for specific data in a given time, it assumes that the data has been lost. The sender will retransmit what it believes was lost.

Establishing a TCP Connection

Figure 2.2 shows establishing a TCP connection is almost ceremonial in nature, involving what is commonly known as the three-way handshake. This is normally completed before any data is passed between two hosts. What is depicted is the client or source host initiating a connection to the server or destination host. The term *client* is used to mean the host requesting some kind of service from another host. A server is a host that listens on a well-known port number for requests of a particular service. TCP requires a destination port or service to be specified. Examples of destination ports are 23 (telnet), 25 (smtp), or port 80 (also known as the HTTP or the web server port).

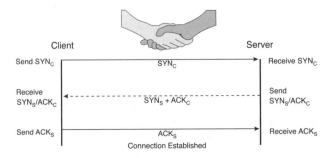

Figure 2.2 The three-way handshake.

The three-way handshake proceeds as follows:

1. The client sends a SYN (SYN_C) to signal a request for a TCP connection to the server.

2. If the server is up and offers the desired service, and can accept the incoming connection, it sends a connection request of its own signaled by a new SYN (SYN_S) to the client and acknowledges the client's connection request with an ACK (ACK_C). This is all accomplished in a single packet.

3. Finally, if the client receives the server's SYN and ACK of the SYN that the client sent and still wants to continue the connection, it sends a final lone ACK (ACK_S) to the server. This acknowledges that the client received the server's request for a connection.

After the three-way handshake has been executed in this manner, the connection has been established. Data can now be exchanged between the two hosts. If you examine the three-way handshake with a little more scrutiny, you will discover that two connections have really been established. The first is between the client and server and the second between the server and the client. This is because TCP is *full duplex*, which means that data exchanges can travel in either direction independently.

The following example shows the three-way handshake, using TCPdump to display the exchange:

```
tclient.net.39904 > telnet.com.23: S 733381829:733381829(0) win 8760 <mss
1460> (DF)
telnet.com.23 > tclient.net.39904: S 1192930639:1192930639(0) ack 733381830
win 1024 <mss 1460> (DF)
tclient.net.39904 > telnet.com.23: . ack 1 win 8760 (DF)
```

In the first record, you see the client, tclient.net, attempt a connection to the telnet server, port 23, of telnet.com. You see the SYN flag set followed by the ISN, 733381829, and the same ending sequence number, 0 payload bytes in the parentheses. After that, you see a window size of 8760 and a *maximum segment size* (mss) that it advertises to the server. The window size of 8760 says that the client has an 8760-byte buffer for aggregated incoming data to this connection. The mss informs the destination host that the physical network on which tclient.net resides should not receive more than 1460 bytes of TCP payload (20-byte IP header + 20-byte TCP header + 1460-byte payload = 1500 bytes, which is the maximum transmission unit, or MTU, for Ethernet) at a time. In this case, even though the client, (tclient.net) can accept 8760 bytes of data, the physical medium on which it resides, most likely Ethernet, cannot accept more than 1460 bytes for a TCP payload size.

In the second record, you see telnet.com send a SYN and an ACK to tclient.net informing it that it is an available and willing participant in this connection and is willing to establish one of its own as well. telnet.com informs tclient.net of its ISN, 1192930639. This is also the ending sequence number because no data is sent; this is normal for the SYN/ACK records. The number following the ACK is the acknowledgement number, in this case, 733381830. Note that this value is the ISN advertised by tclient.net in the first record 733381829 plus 1. telnet.com has just acknowledged that it expects absolute byte number 733381830 as the next sequence number from tclient.net. telnet.com advertises a window size of 1024 and a maximum segment size of 1460.

In the final line, tclient.net sends the final lone ACK to telnet.com and acknowledges receiving the SYN/ACK flags from telnet.com. The value of 1 as the relative acknowledgement number indicates that it next expects the first byte from telnet.com. Also, notice that the sequence numbers have changed from absolute to relative values beginning with this record. Right after the destination part, following the colon, you see a period. Remember this is the placeholder value when none of the PUSH, RESET, SYN, or FIN bits is set.

Server and Client Ports

In the past, more so than today, well-known server ports generally fell in the range of 1–1023. Historically under UNIX, only processes running with root privilege could open a port below 1024. These ports should remain constant on the host for which they are offered. In other words, if you find telnet at port 23 on a particular host one day, you should find it there the next day. You will find many of the older well-established services in this range of 1–1023 (such as telnet on port 23 and smtp on port 25). Today, some of the newer services, such as AOL Instant Messenger, usually associated with TCP port 5190, don't tend to conform to this original convention. This is partially because there are more services than numbers in this range today.

Client ports, often known as *ephemeral ports*, are selected only for a particular connection and are reused after the connection is freed. These are generally numbered greater than 1023. When a client initiates a connection to a server, an unused ephemeral port is selected. For most services, the client and server continue to exchange data on these two ports for the entirety of the session. This connection is known as a *socket pair* and it will be unique. There will be only one connection on the Internet that has this combination of source IP and source port connected to this destination IP and destination port.

Someone from the same source IP might even be connected to the same destination IP and port. This user will be given a different ephemeral port, however, thus distinguishing it from the other connection to the same server and destination port. Two users on the same host might connect to the same web server. Although this is the same source IP, destination IP, and port (80), the web server can maintain who gets what by the ephemeral source ports involved.

Examine the three-way handshake exchange again, but this time in the context of client and server ports:

```
tclient.net.39904 > telnet.com.23: S 733381829:733381829(0) win 8760 <mss
1460> (DF)
telnet.com.23 > tclient.net.39904: S 1192930639:1192930639(0) ack 733381830
win 1024 <mss 1460> (DF)
tclient.net.39904 > telnet.com.23: . ack 1 win 8760 (DF)
```

You see that tclient.net has selected ephemeral port 39904 on which to communicate and to connect to well-known port 23 of telnet.com. Any further exchanges after the three-way handshake are done using these two negotiated ports. After the connection is closed and some time has passed, tclient.net releases port 39904 for use by another connection. Port 23 of telnet.com remains bound to the telnet service for additional telnet requests.

Connection Termination

You can terminate a session in two ways: the graceful method or an abrupt method. The graceful method is the phone conversation equivalent of you saying, "Thanks, but we're not interested," and hanging up on the telemarketer. This informs the telemarketer that the conversation is over and that he should now hang up and place another intrusive dinnertime call to some other hapless victim. The abrupt equivalent of this is just hanging up after you determine someone isn't worth your valuable time.

The Graceful Method

When the graceful TCP session termination method is conducted, one of the hosts, either the client or server, signals with a FIN to the other that it wants to terminate the session. The receiving host signals back with an ACK (to acknowledge the request). This terminates only half the connection. Then, the other host must initiate a FIN as well, and the receiving host needs to acknowledge this. Both sides need to initiate a FIN and acknowledge the other's FIN because TCP is full duplex. Both the client and server send data in an asynchronous manner, so both sides of the connection have to be individually terminated. Look at the following two TCPdump exchanges:

1. Client initiates a close with a FIN, and server does an ACK, as follows:

```
tclient.net.39904 >telnet.com.23: F 14:14(0) ack 186 win 8760 (DF)
telnet.com.23 > tclient.net.39904: . ack 15 win 1024 (DF)
```

2. Server initiates close with a FIN, and client does an ACK, as follows:

```
telnet.com.23 > tclient.net.39904: F 186:186(0) ack 15 win 1024 (DF)
tclient.net.39904 > telnet.com.23: . ack 187 win 8760 (DF)
```

The connection between tclient.net and telnet.com is now closed.

The Abrupt Method

```
The second termination method is an abrupt halting of the connection. This is
done with one host sending the other a RESET. This signals the desire to
abruptly terminate the connection.tclient.net.39904 > telnet.com.23: R
28:28(0) ack 1 win 8760 (DF)
```

This output shows tclient.com as it aborts the connection to telnet.com. It sends a RESET to telnet.net to signal the intent to terminate immediately. There should be no further communication between the two hosts using the negotiated session after the abort.

Data Transfer

Now that you know how TCP establishes and terminates a connection, it is time to take a look at what happens in between. Normally, the whole reason for establishing a session is so data can be exchanged between two hosts. The following data excerpt might be transferred between tclient.net and telnet.com after the three-way handshake and before the termination:

```
tclient.net.39904 > telnet.com.23: P 1:28(27) ack 1 win 8760 (DF)
telnet.com.23 > tclient.net.39904: P 1:14(13) ack 1 win 1024
telnet.com.23 > tclient.net.39904: P 14:23(9) ack 28 win 1024
```

The first line shows tclient.net sending 27 bytes of data (a relative range of 1 to 28 bytes as seen in the parentheses) to telnet.com. This is the first time the new P flag has appeared; it represents PUSH. Because telnet is an interactive application that demands the fastest response time available, the PUSH flag signals to the receiver of the data, in this case telnet.com, to push the data immediately to the telnet application upon receipt of data in the incoming buffer. This line also acknowledges that the next relative sequence number expected by tclient.com from telnet.com is byte 1.

The second line shows telnet.com sending 13 bytes of data to tclient.com and acknowledging receipt of 1 byte of data from tclient.com. It has yet to acknowledge receipt of the 27 new bytes just sent by tclient.net. The final line shows telnet.com sending an additional 9 bytes to client.com. See how the relative bytes begin at 14 (14:23) bytes after the 13 (1:14) preceding bytes sent from telnet.com to tclient.net.

This exchange also acknowledges receipt of 27 bytes of data from tclient.net to telnet.com. You see ack 28 because this is known as an *expectational acknowledgement*: Byte 28 is the next anticipated byte to be received. All traffic exchanges between the two hosts will have the ACK flag set after the three-way handshake has been completed. This is sometimes used as an indication of an established session.

What's the Bottom Line?

What if you need to analyze some traffic for malicious intent? Is it really necessary for you to absorb all the detailed theory about TCP to do any kind of analysis of TCP traffic of normal or anomalous behavior? The bottom line is that you can do elementary analysis without flipping bits. Here are some of the more general behaviors that you might examine:

- **Was the three-way handshake completed between two hosts?** If it was, this means that the server listens at the port at which the client requested and the server accepted the connection. This is fine if the expected behavior is that the server listens at the requested port. However, what if the server port is not one that you expect to listen? This might indicate some service, known to the system administrator and not to you, is running. It might also mean, however, that someone maliciously installed some backdoor application on the server without your knowledge.

- **Was data transmitted?** In TCPdump output, after the TCP sequence numbers, you find the number of data bytes in parentheses that were sent. If you see data transmitted, that means that the two hosts are speaking to each other. When you are doing some kind of retrospective analysis of unexpected activity between two hosts, looking at the number of bytes exchanged can come in handy in assessing the severity of what might have transpired. You might not be able to see the actual data bytes or payload, but numbers can be telling. Lengthy individual exchanges and the number of exchanges in aggregate can readily indicate potential damage by an intruder.

- **Who began and/or ended the connection?** By determining which host initiated and terminated the connection, you get an idea of who is in control. Typically, the client requests the connection and the server responds (as you have already seen). Either host can end the conversation, so observe which one initiates the termination with a RESET or FIN.

Damage Assessment

Using TCPdump as a detective tool to analyze an attempted computer break-in is like investigating a burglary attempt or actual burglary. The first step in damage assessment is determining whether the perpetrator actually got into the computer system (or in the case of a burglary, into the house). Repeated SYN attempts to a system without a reply might be the equivalent of jimmying a door without successful entry. The completion of the three-way handshake is the equivalent of entry; it might just be through the garage door, which also requires a key to get into the house, but it is indicative of some kind of entry. The three-way handshake is the evidence equivalent of finding a previous locked door now unlocked or finding strange fingerprints inside the locked door.

The server port number can indicate the intruder's interest. The use of a conventional port, such as telnet, means that perhaps the burglar might be doing a serious raid of goods (password files, trusted host relationships, and so on), the equivalent of a thief's interest in jewelry and appliances. What about the unconventional port numbers that don't support a known service? Is that the sign of some kind of a joyride through your system just to prove it can be done—kind of like coming home to find that someone drank all the milk in the refrigerator, threw the empty carton on the floor, and did or took nothing else?

Whereas the house burglary damage might be assessed by determining what is blatantly gone (the big-screen TV, for example), what about a burglar who broke into a big, fully stocked warehouse that didn't keep good inventory records? How would you make an assessment of stolen goods? Perhaps a neighbor saw a strange vehicle in the driveway. Was it a moving van or was it a motorcycle? When you examine the number of bytes exchanged in the TCPdump output, you are in effect determining what kind of haul the burglar made off with. You are making best-guess efforts based on the little evidence that you have.

TCP Gone Awry

In subsequent chapters, you will read many examples of the malicious attacks that employ TCP. Appendix A, "Exploits and Scans to Apply Exploits," and Appendix C, "Detection of Intelligence Gathering," discuss scanning methods that use different and sometimes unexpected combinations of TCP flags to perform reconnaissance on networks and circumvent detection or bypass filtering attempts. The following sections introduce some other anomalous TCP activity, such as an ACK scan, a telnet scan, and TCP session hijacking.

An ACK Scan

Scans of ports are done for a variety of reasons, but they usually are used to discover whether a host or hosts are offering a particular service. If a host is found to be offering a service that might be exploitable, the hacker might try to break in using some vulnerability. Often, scans are blatant; the hacker makes no attempt to hide his reconnaissance of your network, except that the computer from which the scans originate might be compromised. The hacker assumes that either no one is monitoring the scanning activity or that by using the compromised host, no one can identify the hacker with the scan. Most likely there will be no attribution because no one can associate the hacker with the scan.

At times, however, the scanner attempts to be more furtive about the reconnaissance efforts in an attempt to evade notice. Examine the following activity, which is TCPdump output of many related connections. The prober can identify live hosts by those responding to the ACK scan. The deletion of time stamps makes it more readable:

```
ack.com.23 > 192.168.2.112.23: . ack 778483003 win 1028
ack.com.23 > 192.168.31.4.23: . ack 778483003 win 1028
ack.com.143 > 192.168.2.112.143: . ack 778483003 win 1028
ack.com.143 > 192.168.31.4.143: . ack 778483003 win 1028
ack.com.110 > 192.168.2.112.110: . ack 778483003 win 1028
ack.com.110 > 192.168.31.4.110: . ack 778483003 win 1028
ack.com.23 > 192.168.14.19.23: . ack 778483003 win 1028
ack.com.143 > 192.168.14.19.143: . ack 778483003 win 1028
ack.com.110 > 192.168.14.19.110: . ack 778483003 win 1028
ack.com.23 > 192.168.33.53.23: . ack 778483003 win 1028
ack.com.23 > 192.168.37.3.23: . ack 914633252 win 1028
ack.com.23 > 192.168.14.49.23: . ack 3631132968 win 1028
```

The preceding scan from ack.com sends an ACK flag to various different hosts on the internal 192.168 network. A lone ACK should be found only as the final transmission of the three-way handshake, an acknowledgement of received data, an acknowledgement of a received FIN, or data that is transmitted where the entire sending buffer has not been emptied. This is not the case in this scan because no other traffic is found from ack.com to indicate that this is a reaction to some natural catalyst.

This might be an attempt to find live hosts, somewhat akin to the function of ping. If a live host receives an ACK for either an open or closed port, it should respond with a RESET. Also, filtering routers that allow only "established" connections into the network (in other words, the ACK bit is set) will not filter this kind of scan. As sites become more security conscious and begin to block more traffic into the network, those who want to do reconnaissance have to become more clever and stealthy in the manner in which they scan, as shown in this example.

Note that the source ports are the same as the destination ports. This is not the expected behavior of the client selecting an ephemeral port with a value greater than 1023. This is another signature that helps to identify this scan. With the lone ACK flag set and identical source and destination ports, we can assume that this traffic has been "crafted." Someone has written a program to execute this particular scan; it is not the result of normal TCP/IP stack traffic generation.

Reserved Private Networks

Throughout the text, you will see references of networks 192.168 and 172.16 as examples. These particular address spaces are part of what the governing body of the Internet, the Internet Address Numbers Authority (IANA), has deemed to be reserved private networks per RFC 1918. In other words, these are address spaces that should be used for internal networks and traffic should not be sent to or from these networks. These address spaces are often used so that a site will not exhaust its actual assigned addresses.

Traffic to these networks is not routable because these are private address spaces. When you see these address spaces used in examples, understand that they are being used to disguise the real address spaces that were scanned or probed. The intent is not to imply that traffic can be routed to theses networks via the Internet.

A Telnet Scan?

Look carefully at the next scan. Short of finding Waldo in the output, do you see anything amiss?

```
scanner.se.45820 > 192.168.209.5.23: S 4195942931:4195942935(4) win 4096
scanner.se.45820 > 192.168.216.5.23: S 4195944723:4195944727(4) win 4096
scanner.se.52526 > 172.16.68.5.23: S 357331986:357331990(4) win 4096
scanner.se.45820 > 192.168.183.5.23: S 4196001810:4196001814(4) win 4096
scanner.se.52526 > 172.16.248.5.23: S 357312531:357312535(4) win 4096
scanner.se.45820 > 192.168.205.5.23: S 4196007442:4196007446(4) win 4096
scanner.se.52526 > 172.16.250.5.23: S 357313043:357313047(4) win 4096
scanner.se.52526 > 172.16.198.5.23: S 357365266:357365270(4) win 4096
scanner.se.52526 > 172.16.161.5.23: S 357355794:357355798(4) win 4096
```

To the naked eye, it is a scan from scanner.se of destination hosts on the 192.168 and 172.16 subnets—specifically to destination port 23, or telnet. You might conclude that this is an attempt to find all hosts on the destination subnets that offer telnet, and that would be mostly correct. A subtle signature might indicate potentially evasive behavior, however. A SYN request usually sends no data bytes, but this scan sends 4 bytes, as you can tell by looking at the number in the parentheses.

You might imagine that the 4 bytes of data sent before the completion of the three-way handshake would be discarded. However, this is not the case. The 4 bytes should be included in the data after the handshake has been completed as noted by RFC 793. Any payload bytes that are sent during the handshake become part of the data stream after the completion of the handshake according to the RFC. This could be a good way to circumvent detection by an *intrusion-detection system* (IDS) that examines data sent only after the three-way handshake.

If you see 64 data bytes sent on a SYN connection to your DNS server to the DNS port 53, this might indicate a different issue altogether. Software known as 3DNS attempts to give users the quickest response time to web requests. One way that this is done is by attempting to measure the response time to your DNS server from one or more web servers that might be used to respond to the user's request. As a representative size of a typical web request, 64 bytes are used. If you see this activity, it should not be considered stealthy; perhaps you might deem it invasive or annoying, or even ineffective because many sites block inbound activity to TCP port 53, but the intent is not malicious.

TCP Session Hijacking

Although TCP appears to be a fairly safe protocol because of all the negotiation involved in session establishment and all the protocol and precision involved in data exchange, don't get complacent. Evil sniffers can be set up on an unsuspecting host to capture TCP or other data that crosses the sniffers' path. Sniffers that are placed on networks that are not switched can snoop clear-text data such as user IDs and passwords that are not encrypted in any way.

Session hijacking software, such as Hunt, uses another approach to exploit an existing TCP session. These attempt to intercept an established TCP session and hijack one end of the connection from the session to an evil host. The problem is that conventional TCP exchanges do not require any authentication or confirmation that they are the actual hosts involved in a previously established connection. After a session has been established between two hosts, those hosts use the following to reconfirm the corresponding host:

- **IP number.** The established IP numbers of the hosts must not change.
- **Port numbers.** Most protocols communicate between established ports only; ports do not change.
- **Sequence numbers.** Sequence numbers must change predictably in respect to the ISN and the aggregate number of bytes sent from one host to another.
- **Acknowledgement numbers.** Acknowledgement numbers must change in respect to delivered sequence numbers and aggregate bytes acknowledged from one host to another.

If a hostile user can observe data exchanges and successfully intercept an ongoing connection with all the authentication parameters properly set, he can hijack a session. Imagine the damage that can be done if this hijacked session is one that has root authority. Many complications and considerations are involved in session hijacking. It is not a trivial endeavor, but it is made simpler using the Hunt software.

Summary

A vast and growing number of security tools are at your disposal. You have many tool choices when it comes to monitoring your network. When you decide which tool to use, make sure that the tool provides at least the level of detail that TCPdump offers. Admittedly, TCPdump does not provide especially aesthetic output, but it does give the required amount of detail to make intelligent assessments about traffic activity. If you select a tool that is easier on the eye, but lighter on content, you might not get the whole story.

TCP is the protocol used for applications that require reliable delivery. TCP exchanges follow a prescribed architecture of session establishment, possible data transfer, and session termination, replete with all the mechanisms to ensure delivery and receipt of data. When you observe TCP activity with TCPdump, you can delve into the details, if desired or necessary, or you can observe broader patterns and make more general assessments of the type of activity that has transpired.

TCP is a very robust protocol, and it has been robustly mutated for malicious uses. Carefully analyze it for the unexpected when monitoring TCP activity. As Intrusion Detection Systems (IDSs) and firewalls become more sophisticated in function, so do the hackers' efforts to circumvent detection and shunning. It is important for an intrusion analyst to have a good understanding of TCP, and TCPdump is an excellent instructional tool.

3

Fragmentation

AT DIFFERENT TIMES, ATTACKERS USE FRAGMENTATION BOTH to mask and facilitate their probes and exploits. Some intrusion-detection systems and packet-filtering devices do not support packet reassembly or perform it correctly and therefore do not detect or block activity where the signature is split over multiple datagrams. Availability or denial-of-service attacks use highly fragmented traffic to exhaust system resources. These are some of the reasons you might want to learn about fragmentation and some of the topics covered in this chapter.

By understanding how this facet of IP works, you will be equipped to detect and analyze fragmented traffic and discover whether it is normal fragmentation versus fragmentation used for other purposes. Fragmentation can be a naturally occurring effect of traffic traveling through networks of varying sized maximum transmission units (MTU). The theory and composition of normal fragmentation is discussed first in this chapter to acquaint you with how it should operate.

Theory of Fragmentation

Fragmentation occurs when an IP datagram traveling on a network has to traverse a network with a maximum transmission unit that is smaller than the size of the datagram. For instance, the MTU or maximum size for an IP datagram for Ethernet is 1500 bytes. If a datagram is larger than 1500 bytes and needs to traverse an Ethernet network, it requires fragmentation by a router directing it to the Ethernet network. Fragmentation can also occur when a host needs to put a datagram on the network that exceeds its own network's MTU.

Fragments continue on to their destination, where the destination host reassembles them. Fragments can even become further fragmented if they cross an MTU smaller than the fragment size. Although fragmentation is a perfectly normal event, it is possible to craft fragments for the purposes of avoiding detection by routers and intrusion-detection systems that don't deal well with fragmentation.

What kind of information must the fragments carry for the destination host to reassemble them back to the original unfragmented state? The following list answers this question:

- All fragments from the same datagram must be associated with each other fragment by using a common fragment identification number. This is cloned from a field in the IP header known as the IP identification number, also called the fragment ID.

- Each fragment must carry what its place or offset is in the original unfragmented packet.

- Each fragment must tell the length of the data carried in the fragment.

- Finally, each fragment must know if more fragments follow it. This is done using the More Fragments (MF) flag.

The Fragment ID Number/IP Identification Number

The IP identification value is a 16-bit field found in the IP header of all datagrams. This uniquely identifies each datagram sent by the host. Typically, this value increases by one for each datagram sent by that host.

When the datagram becomes fragmented, all fragments created from this datagram contain this same IP identification number, or fragment ID. The following TCPdump output shows an IP identification number of 202 for this unfragmented output:

```
ping.com > 192.168.244.2: icmp: echo request (ttl 240, id 202)
```

If this datagram were to become fragmented on the way to its destination, all fragments created from this datagram would share a fragment ID of 202. This TCPdump output was generated using the -vv option. This is a verbose option that says to list the time-to-live (TTL) value and the IP identification values at the end of the standard output.

This information is contained in the IP header. The IP header is placed in an IP datagram followed by an encapsulated fragment. As you have learned, all TCP/IP traffic must be wrapped within IP because IP is the protocol responsible for getting the packet delivered.

Visualizing Fragmentation: Seeing Is Understanding

This discussion uses Ethernet as the example link layer medium to demonstrate the packaging of datagrams. Figure 3.1 depicts the configuration of a datagram that is not fragmented. As previously mentioned, a datagram traveling on Ethernet has an MTU of 1500 bytes. Each datagram must have an IP header, which is typically 20 bytes, but can be more if IP options, such as source routing, are included.

As a quick refresher, recall that the IP header contains information such as the source and destination IP numbers. It is considered the "network" portion of the IP datagram because routers use the information found in the IP header to direct the datagram toward its destination. Some kind of data is encapsulated after the IP header. This data can be an IP protocol such as TCP, UDP, or ICMP. If this data were TCP, for instance, it would include a TCP header and TCP data.

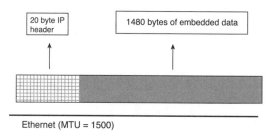

| 20 byte IP header | 1480 bytes of embedded data |

Ethernet (MTU = 1500)

Figure 3.1   Ethernet datagram packaging.

Figure 3.2 shows a datagram of 4028 bytes. This is an ICMP echo request bound for an Ethernet network that has an MTU of 1500. This is an abnormally large ICMP echo request that is not representative of normal traffic, but it is used to illustrate how fragmentation occurs. So, the 4028 byte datagram will have to be divided into fragments of 1500 bytes or less. Each of these 1500-byte fragmented packets will have a 20-byte IP header like the initial fragment, leaving 1480 bytes maximum for data for each fragment. Figure 3.3 examines this same datagram, but shows the allocation of bytes per fragment. The following sections examine the contents of each of the individual three fragments.

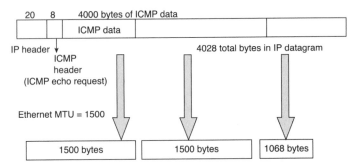

Figure 3.2 Original 4028 byte fragment broken into three fragments of 1500 bytes or less.

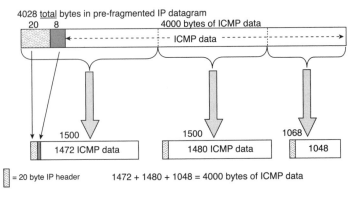

Figure 3.3 Byte allocations per fragment.

All Aboard the Fragment Train

Turn your concentration to the initial fragment in the fragment train shown in Figure 3.4. The "original" IP header will be cloned to contain the identical fragment identification numbers for the first and remaining fragments.

The first fragment is the only one that will carry with it the ICMP message header. This header is not cloned in subsequent associated fragments and this concept of the first fragment alone identifying the nature of the fragment is significant, as you will soon learn. The first fragment has a 0 offset, a length of 1480 bytes of length, 1472 bytes of data, and 8 bytes of ICMP header; and because more fragments follow, the More Fragments flag is set.

Figure 3.5 explains the configuration of the first fragment in the fragment train. The first 20 bytes of the 1500 bytes are the IP header. The next 8 bytes are the ICMP header. Remember that this was an ICMP echo request that has an 8-byte header in its original packet. The remaining 1472 bytes are for ICMP data.

In addition to the normal fields carried in the IP header, such as source and destination IP and protocol (in this instance of ICMP), there are fields specifically for fragmentation. The fragment ID with a value of 21223 is the common link for all the fragments in the fragment train. There is a field known as the More Fragments flag, which indicates that another fragment follows the current one. In this first fragment, the flag is set to 1 to indicate that more fragments do follow. Also, the offset of the data contained in this fragment relative to the data of the whole unfragmented datagram must be stored. For the first record, the offset is 0. Finally, the length of the data carried in this fragment is stored as the fragment length—in this fragment, the length is 1480. This is the 8-byte ICMP header followed by the first 1472 bytes of the ICMP data.

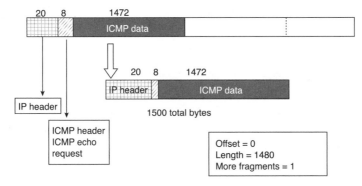

Figure 3.4   The fragment engine.

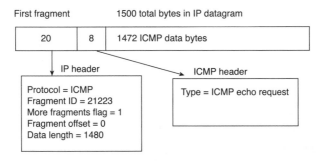

Figure 3.5   The guts of the fragment engine.

The Fragment Dining Car

Take a look at Figure 3.6 to focus on the next fragment in the fragment train. An IP header is cloned from the "original" header with an identical fragment identification number, and most of the other data in the IP header (such as the source and destination numbers) is replicated for the new header. Embedded after this new IP header is 1480 ICMP data bytes. As you can see, the second fragment has an offset of 1480 and a length of 1480 bytes; and because one more fragment follows, the More Fragments flag is set.

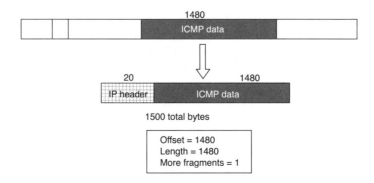

Figure 3.6   The fragment dining car.

Continuing with fragmentation in Figure 3.7, you can examine the IP datagram carrying the second fragment. As with all fragments in this fragment train, it requires a 20-byte IP header. Again, the protocol in the header indicates ICMP. The fragment identification number remains 21223. And, the More Fragments flag is turned on because another fragment follows. The offset is 1480 bytes into the data portion of the original ICMP message data. The preceding fragment occupied the first 1480 bytes. This fragment is 1480 bytes long as well, and it is composed entirely of ICMP data bytes.

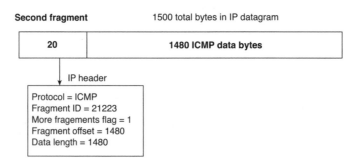

Figure 3.7   The guts of the fragment dining car.

It is worth repeating that the ICMP header in the first fragment does not get cloned along with the ICMP data. This means that if you were to examine this fragment alone, you could not tell the type of the ICMP message—in this case, an ICMP echo request. This becomes an important issue with regard to packet-filtering devices (as discussed later in this chapter).

The Fragment Caboose

Examine the final fragment in the fragment train in Figure 3.8. Again, an IP header is cloned from the "original" header with an identical fragment identification number, and other fields are replicated for the new header. The final 1048 ICMP data bytes are embedded in this new IP datagram. You see the third fragment has an offset of 2960 and a length of 1048 bytes; and because no more fragments follow, the More Fragments flag is 0.

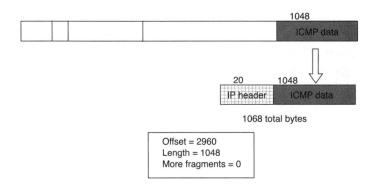

Figure 3.8   The fragment caboose.

Figure 3.9 depicts the last fragment in the fragment train. Again, 20 bytes are reserved for the IP header. The remaining ICMP data bytes are carried in the data portion of this fragment. The fragment ID is 21223, and the More Fragments flag is not set because this is the last fragment. The offset is 2960 (the sum of the two 1480-byte previous fragments). Only 1048 data bytes are carried in this fragment comprised entirely of the remaining ICMP message bytes. This fragment, like the second one, has no ICMP header and therefore no ICMP message type to reflect that this is an ICMP echo request.

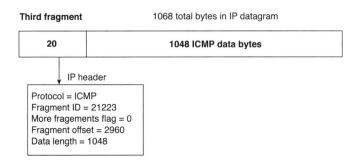

Figure 3.9   The guts of the fragment caboose.

Viewing Fragmentation Using TCPdump

Take a look at the following TCPdump output. As you can see, the three different records represent the three fragments discussed earlier. This means that the host running TCPdump has collected the ICMP echo request after the fragmentation occurred. Here are the records:

```
ping.com > myhost.com: icmp: echo request (frag 21223:1480@0+)
ping.com > myhost.com: (frag 21223:1480@1480+)
ping.com > myhost.com: (frag 21223:1048@2960
```

The first line shows ping.com sending an ICMP echo request to myhost.com. The reason that TCPdump can identify this as an ICMP echo request is because the first fragment contains the 8-byte ICMP header that identifies this as an ICMP echo request. Now, look at the fragmentation notation at the right side of the record. TCPdump convention for displaying fragmented output is that the word *frag* appears, followed by the fragment ID (21223, in this example), followed by a colon. The length of data in the current fragment follows, 1480, followed by an at (@) sign, and then you see the offset into the data (0, because this is the first fragment). The plus (+) sign indicates that the More Fragments flag is set. This fragment knows the purpose of the traffic, knows it is the first fragment, knows that more fragments follow, but doesn't know what or how many follow.

The second record differs somewhat. Notice that there is no ICMP echo request label. This is because there is no ICMP header to tell what kind of ICMP traffic this is. The IP header will still have the protocol field set to ICMP, but that is all you can tell looking at this fragment alone. You see the TCPdump output lists the fragment ID of 21223, the current data length of 1480, and the offset of 1480. The plus sign signifies that the More Fragments flag is set. This fragment has an affiliation, a follower, and a sense of placement, but is essentially clueless about its purpose—sounds like freshman year at college.

The last line is very similar to the second one in format. It shows the same fragment ID of 21223, it has a length of 1048, and a displacement of 2960. No More Fragments flag appears in the final record, however, as you would expect. This fragment has an affiliation, no sense of purpose, and no followers.

How the Fragment Offset Is Stored

Although TCPdump nicely computes the fragment offset for you, it is stored in the packet differently. Be forewarned that if you ever examine a fragment offset in a packet—perhaps from a TCPdump hex dump—you will need to do some manipulation before arriving at the actual byte offset.

The fragment offset is found in part of the sixth byte and the entire seventh byte offset of the IP header. It is a 13-bit field that can represent a maximum value of 8191 ($2^{13} - 1$). Yet, theoretically, though rarely indicative of normal fragmentation, the offset can be greater than 8191 because the maximum datagram size is 65,535 ($2^{16} - 1$) bytes. To represent the offset value found in the packet as bytes, multiply it by 8. For those of you who want to know the mathematical origin of this, 65,536 (2^{16}) divided by 8192 (2^{13}) is 8.

Fragmentation and Packet-Filtering Devices

This section covers fragmentation and how a packet-filtering device, such as a router or firewall, might deal with it. The problem arises when such a device attempts to block fragmented traffic.

Because only the first fragment of a fragment train will contain any kind of protocol header such as TCP, UDP, or ICMP, only this fragment is prevented from entry into the network guarded by a packet-filtering device incapable of examining state of a header field. What I mean by *state* is it appears obvious to you that any fragment sharing the fragment ID of the blocked one should also be blocked. But, some packet-filtering devices don't maintain this information. They myopically look at each fragment as an individual entity and don't connect it with previous or subsequent packets. Intuitively enough, this is not a particularly good architecture, so why is it used? Think about the overhead required to maintain state. It means that each fragment must be examined and stored; this is expensive in terms of time, processing, and memory. Eventually, fragments must be allowed or rejected access and that too consumes more resources. It is far simpler to have an atomic architecture that scrutinizes on a per-packet basis.

If a particular packet doesn't match the blocking criteria, in this instance, because of the absence of a protocol header, it is allowed into the network. Fragmented TCP or UDP datagrams might contain their respective header information in the first fragment only. Blocking decisions are often based on header information, such as TCP or UDP destination ports. This means that fragmented TCP and UDP are susceptible to the same shortcomings of a stateless packet-filtering device.

One final point to remember is that IP is not a reliable protocol, and it is very possible for the first fragment that contains the protocol header information to be lost. When this occurs, the packet-filtering device has an even more difficult job of allowing or denying traffic. In fact, if one of the fragments does not arrive at the destination, all must be resent.

The Don't Fragment Flag

In some of the TCPdump output you have looked at, you might have seen the letters DF in parentheses. This means the Don't Fragment flag is set. No surprises here; as the name implies, if this flag is set, fragmentation will not be done on the datagram. If this flag is set and the datagram crosses a network where fragmentation is required, the router discovers this, discards the datagram, and sends an ICMP "unreachable—need to frag" error message back to the sending host.

The ICMP error message contains the MTU of the network that required fragmentation. Some hosts intentionally send an initial datagram across the network with the DF flag set as a way to discover the path MTU for a particular source to destination host. If the ICMP error message is returned with the smaller MTU, the host then packages all datagrams bound for that destination in small enough units to avoid fragmentation. This is often used with TCP because TCP requires a lot of overhead. Fragmentation can introduce inefficiency because if one fragment is lost, all must be sent again; that is one reason it is desirable to avoid fragmentation. As you can surmise, a malicious user also can use this mechanism to discover the MTU of a segment of your network to be used later for fragmentation exploits. The user could craft datagrams with different lengths and the DF flag set and observe when an ICMP error message is received. This assumes that the targeted network doesn't disable the ICMP error message from being sent. The following TCPdump output shows an ICMP message in which a router discovered that fragmentation was necessary, but the Don't Fragment flag was set.

```
router.ru > mail.mysite.com: icmp: host.ru unreachable - need to frag (mtu
308) (DF)
```

The stimulus for this reply was that mail.mysite.com attempted to send a datagram larger than 308 bytes to host.ru with the DF flag set before this packet was sent. router.ru finds that the datagram must traverse a smaller network with an MTU of 308 bytes and fragmentation is necessary.

When router.ru examines the record, it finds that the Don't Fragment flag is set and an ICMP message is sent back to mail.mysite.com informing it of the problem. Now, mail.mysite.com either must package the datagrams to be smaller than the MTU of 308 so that fragmentation doesn't occur or it must remove the DF flag so that fragmentation can occur and then resend the datagram.

Malicious Fragmentation

There is no rest for the weary analyst when it comes to malicious fragmentation. Fragmentation, it seems, has provided a field day of play and plunder for the hackers, and they have produced a bevy of attacks.

This advice is repeated for other protocols and at other times in this book, but be especially alert and watchful when analyzing fragmentation. Some of the best analysts I know have been mockingly accused of paranoia by envisioning everyone attacking their networks in every different way. Well, I would like to invite you to join the misfits' bandwagon of paranoia when it comes to fragmentation. If your IDS cannot be tuned to give special scrutiny to fragmentation, you might be missing a chunk of the action. If your IDS can correctly maintain state, reassemble fragments, and then make some kind of intelligent assessment, you appear to be well-armed.

One of the most infamous denial-of-service attacks associated with fragmentation, Ping of Death, is discussed in Appendix B, "Denial of Service." The next sections examine a couple of other fragmentation attacks.

TCP Header Fragments

nmap is an excellent scanning tool that runs on many UNIX platforms and is available from www.insecure.org/nmap. It does conventional port scanning to discover what ports are open on a target host and does stealth scanning that looks for open ports, but also makes an attempt to elude detection by intrusion-detection systems. An nmap command-line option (-f) fragments the 20-byte TCP headers in multiple fragments in an attempt to avoid detection. The following TCPdump output was generated using the command:

```
nmap -f -sS -p 53 target.com
```

This sends a fragmented SYN connection to port 53 of target.com:

```
truncated-tcp 16 (frag 25096:16@0+)
fragger.org > target.com: (frag 25096:4@16)
truncated-tcp 16 (frag 4265:16@0+)
fragger.org > target.com: (frag 4265:4@16)
truncated-tcp 16 (frag 34927:16@0+)
fragger.org > target.com: (frag 34927:4@16)
```

The preceding TCPdump output shows a scan that fragmented the TCP header. This is a scan from fragger.org that scanned port 53 on target.com using a standard TCP SYN request. This is not obvious, however, because of the small fragments involved.

Looking at the first line of data, you see a fragment with 16 bytes of truncated TCP data. The minimum TCP header is 20 bytes with no options. Because this is not a complete TCP header, TCPdump reports this as `truncated-tcp`. In the next record, the additional 4 bytes of TCP header are sent. It is possible that an intrusion-detection system might not capture or report this kind of stealth scan.

Teardrop

Now that you are familiar with the way fragmentation should work, take a look at the following TCPdump output. See if you can detect a problem with the fragmentation generated by a malicious program known as Teardrop:

```
evilfrag.com.139 > target.net.139: udp 28 (frag 242:36@0+)
evilfrag.com > target.net: (frag 242:4@24)
```

The first fragment delivered is a UDP datagram that has a fragment ID of 242, a length of 36 data bytes, and an offset of 0. This is represented in Figure 3.10 by the patterned rectangles. It spans bytes 0 through 35, inclusive.

Now, the second fragment comes along. It is associated with the first fragment because of fragment ID of 242, it has a length of 4, and it begins at an offset of 24 bytes into the data portion. It is depicted in Figure 3.10 in the solid color in the middle. As you can see, it actually overlaps bytes 24 through 27 of the first fragment.

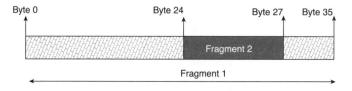

Figure 3.10   Teardrop fragment mutation.

The Teardrop attack exploits weaknesses in the reassembly process of fragments. The Teardrop program creates fragments with overlapping offset fields. When these fragments are reassembled at the destination host, some systems will crash, hang, or reboot. This attack was first reported in 1997, yet it provides a good example of how malformed fragments can wreak havoc on a target host.

A malformed or an incomplete set of fragments still presents problems for some hosts. More recently, a program known as Jolt2 that will be discussed in more detail in Chapter 5, "Stimulus and Response," can cause a denial of service via resource starvation simply by repeatedly sending a non-zero offset fragment to Windows hosts as recent as Windows 2000.

So many problems exist because hosts, routers, and intrusion-detection systems have to deal with many aspects of fragmentation. First, they have to make sure that all the fragments in a fragment train are received. Second, they have to make sure that they are properly formatted—none may overlap—and in aggregate, they may not exceed the maximum datagram size of 65,535. Finally, they must check that no shenanigans are attempted by fragmenting protocol headers. This is a tall order because it requires fragment reassembly and detection of mutations. To do this correctly, this requires a commitment of memory and allocation of CPU power, and if not implemented correctly, it can cause denial of service or other problems.

Analyzing Fragmentation

Believe it or not, fragmentation is not really so complicated after you understand a little theory and get comfortable with the notation associated with it. Many times as a network analyst, in the process of examining TCPdump output, I have gone through the mental exercise of "what's wrong with this fragmentation?" It is more than an academic skill; it is required theory in your arsenal of knowledge to analyze traffic on your network and safeguard it against fragmentation types of exploits.

If you do discover some kind of genuine mutant fragmentation, you might experience an initial and well-deserved feeling of triumph. But, realize that the discovery is just the first step in unraveling the mystery. Next, you have to figure out what the intended purpose of the weird fragmentation is, and this is not always obvious. One common explanation is some kind of denial of service, either a degradation of service or an outright disabling of the target host. Other explanations are to evade detection or circumvent shunning by monitoring or filtering devices incapable of fragment reassembly. Take a look at what is happening on the network in general and the target host specifically to make your assessment.

Finally, if you think that your site is well-protected at the perimeter and you don't have a firewall or filtering router that is stateful, think again! With such a gaping hole, it is almost trivial for even an inexperienced intruder to bypass your weak defense.

Summary

Normal fragmentation involves separating and packaging the original datagram into new packets less than or equal to the size of a smaller MTU. Each new fragment becomes a packet of its own with a new IP header consisting of many cloned fields (IP numbers, IP identification number, and so on) from the IP header of the original unfragmented datagram. However, each new fragment will contain some unique identifying information such as the offset into the fragment train, the number of data bytes in the fragment, and whether more fragments follow.

Malicious fragmentation comes in many different forms. Ultimately, the purpose might be a denial of service or an opportunity to sneak some traffic into a network that might normally block an unfragmented incarnation of this traffic. Some packet-filtering devices do not handle fragmentation well, if at all, allowing these fragments entry into the network. By having an appreciation and understanding of fragmentation, in general, you will be better able to detect malicious fragmentation and recognize normal fragmentation.

4

ICMP

INTERNET CONTROL MESSAGE PROTOCOL (ICMP) WAS CONCEIVED as an innocuous method of reporting error conditions and issuing and responding to simple requests. Perhaps because of its seemingly benign origins, some of the current mutations of ICMP for less-than-upstanding purposes seem all the more out-rageous. In its pure state, ICMP is supposed to be a relatively simple and chaste protocol, but it has been altered to act as a conduit for evil purposes. Therefore, it is important to understand how this protocol is used both for its intended purposes and for malicious purposes.

This chapter examines several aspects of ICMP. First, you are introduced to some background about ICMP followed by how ICMP is used to find live hosts on a target network. Next, you learn about both the expected and unex-pected uses of ICMP that you might see in your own network. You then put this ICMP theory into action by analyzing some unusual detected ICMP activity. Finally, the discussion focuses on protecting your network by blocking inbound ICMP activity and the accompanying repercussions of doing so.

ICMP Theory

Before delving into examples of ICMP traffic, let's flesh out ICMP a little by giving it some foundation and perspective. If you are already familiar with the theory of ICMP, or if the sound of ICMP theory isn't high on your quiver quotient, you can skip to the section, "Mapping Techniques," and ping away.

Why Do You Need ICMP?

As you will recall from Chapter 2, "Introduction to TCPdump and TCP," TCP is a connection-oriented protocol with lots of overhead involved in ensuring reliable delivery. *User Datagram Protocol* (UDP) is a connectionless protocol that doesn't promise reliable delivery. Both UDP and TCP require a server port with which a client can communicate.

A simple request such as determining whether a host is alive, commonly known as ping, doesn't need ports to communicate and doesn't require reliable delivery. This request and several more use ICMP to deliver and respond to such traffic.

In addition, what if some kind of error condition is discovered by a router or a host, and that router or host needs to inform a sending source host of the problem? Because TCP is a more robust protocol, it handles some error conditions such as a nonlistening port by sending back a TCP response with the TCP flags of RESET/ACK set. If a TCP client or server receives too much information, it also has a mechanism to close down the receiving buffer by setting a window size of 0. This indicates that the receiving host cannot accept any more data until the current buffered data is processed.

However, UDP and IP aren't robust enough to communicate error conditions. If a UDP port is not listening or too much data is sent to a listening port, UDP has no way to convey these conditions. That is where ICMP comes in: It provides a simple means of communicating between hosts or a router and a host to alert them to some kind of problem situation.

Where Does ICMP Fit In?

The TCP/IP Internet layering model discussed in Chapter 1, "IP Concepts," is one representation of the different layers that form data and pass the data between hosts. Figure 4.1 illustrates this.

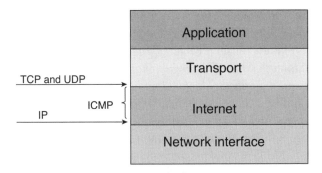

Figure 4.1   TCP/IP Internet model.

Starting at the top, you can see the high-level application layer activity that might represent a TCP/IP application such as telnet. Next is the transport layer, with such protocols as TCP and UDP that provide the end-to-end communication between hosts. Beneath that is the Internet layer, which is responsible for getting the datagram from source to destination. Finally, there is the network layer, which transmits the datagrams over the network.

You can see from this that ICMP is in the same network layer as IP. ICMP is encapsulated in the IP datagram after the IP header, but it is still considered to be in the same layer as IP.

Understanding ICMP

ICMP differs from TCP and UDP in several ways. For starters, ICMP has no port numbers like those found in the transport layer protocols UDP or TCP. The closest thing that ICMP has to a differentiation in services is an ICMP message type and code, the first 2 bytes in the ICMP header. These bytes tell the function of the particular ICMP message.

ICMP Types

Listing and exploring all the variations of ICMPs is beyond the scope of this book. However, **www.iana.org/assignments/icmp-parameters** is a great reference for those who want to know more about this topic.

Next, there is really no such thing as a client and server. In fact, when ICMP error messages are delivered, the receiving host might respond internally but might not communicate anything back to the informer. ICMP also gives no guarantees about the delivery of a message.

One of the unusual traits about ICMP is that services or ports do not have to be activated or listening. Just about every operating system can respond to an ICMP echo request (ping). The hard part is turning off the default behavior of responding to an ICMP echo request.

Another unique trait about ICMP is that it supports broadcast traffic. TCP required an exclusive client/server unicast relationship, but ICMP isn't nearly as exclusive. As the "Smurf Attack" section of this chapter shows, ICMP's willingness to respond to broadcast traffic sometimes can cause problems.

A host uses ICMP for simple replies and requests, and it uses ICMP to inform another host of some kind of error condition. For instance, a receiving host might have a problem keeping up with the traffic that the sending host is delivering to it. One of the ways that a host can inform a sending host to throttle down the delivery rate is to send it an ICMP source quench message.

ICMP is used as a mechanism by routers to inform a sending host of some kind of problem. A router might deliver an ICMP "admin prohibited" message to a sending host. This means that the sending host attempted to send some kind of traffic that was forbidden by an access control list statement of a router interface.

In a situation such as this, you would expect the router to be the sender of the message because it is the one forbidding the activity. However, a router also might intervene to inform a sending host about a condition when a destination host cannot respond. If the destination host is unreachable, for example, the destination host can obviously not respond. In this instance, the router might reply instead.

Although a router might try to be helpful by informing the sending host of a problem, it also is providing information that could be used for reconnaissance purposes. The sender then could glean some knowledge about the type of activity that the router reports. A good security practice is to silence a router by preventing it from issuing ICMP unreachable messages to preclude the dissemination of unnecessary information. This will be discussed in more detail in the section, "Host Unreachable."

Summary of ICMP Theory

Let's quickly summarize what you've learned in this short section on ICMP theory. You have learned that ICMP is a means of delivering error messages between hosts. It is encapsulated in an IP header, but is considered part of the IP or Internet layer.

ICMP is a unique protocol because it doesn't use ports to communicate like the transport protocols do. ICMP messages can get lost and not be delivered. In addition, ICMP can be broadcast to many hosts because there is no sense of an exclusive connection.

Finally, hosts and routers are the senders of ICMP messages. Hosts listen for ICMP, and most will respond unless they deliberately have been altered for silence.

Mapping Techniques

Mapping a target network is a very strategic part of most intelligently planned attacks. This initial step in reconnaissance attempts to discover the live hosts in a target network. An attacker then can direct a more focused scan or exploit toward live hosts only.

If mapping is not done and a malicious user or program attacks a network, the attack can become very noisy by generating a lot of traffic on the target network and not be very productive. The latter quarter of 1999 saw an example of this kind of bull-in-a-china shop reckless scan. A Trojan named RingZero that infected Windows hosts appeared to scan foreign hosts for open Web proxy ports. One of the shortcomings of the RingZero scanning activity was that it appeared to scan random hosts on many networks. In doing so, many IP addresses that were not active were scanned along with the active ones. This was a noisy scan for intrusion-detection systems that saw it. Also, a lot of work had to be done to receive any valuable feedback about hosts that supported open Web proxy ports. This would have been a more directed and perhaps more informative scan if the IP numbers that were scanned had been live hosts.

The Ubiquitous RingZero Trojan

The observed RingZero attack in a monitored network involved many different source IPs scanning mostly inactive TCP ports: 3128 (squid proxy server), 80 (normal HTTP port), and 8080 (an alternative HTTP port). About half a dozen of these scans were detected on a Class B subnet every hour. Many other sites all over the world that were capable of detecting this activity reported seeing it, too.

An initial theory was that all this activity was coming from spoofed source IPs with an unknown intent. However, Ron Marcum, a system administrator at Vanderbilt University, discovered a Windows host in his network that was doing this kind of scanning and captured the software called RingZero. At the *System Administration, Networking, and Security* (SANS) conference in October 1999, the RingZero software was dissected.

When activated in a test network, the host on which it was installed began to scan random hosts for the Web proxy ports. If open Web proxy server ports were discovered, they were sent back to an ftp site that aggregated this information for the collector. It is assumed that the collector then planned to use this knowledge for some future plundering. To date, we still see RingZero scanning activity and it is still unknown what the infection method is and how an infected host selects the IP numbers to scan for proxy ports.

One of the most common methods of mapping is to issue ICMP echo requests. A host (or hosts) responds to an ICMP echo request with an ICMP echo reply to signal it is a live host. This is what the ping command does; it issues an ICMP echo request and waits for an ICMP echo reply. Many security and network administrators have responded to this invasive ICMP scrutiny with the knee-jerk reaction of blocking ICMP echo requests. This is a good and necessary reaction, but this is only a partial solution because it is only a minor impediment to the insistent pursuer. Blocking ICMP echo requests has motivated hackers to invent other scanning methods using other protocols.

In Chapter 2, the section, "An ACK Scan," showed how TCP scans can use the ACK flag to attempt to identify live hosts. This can be used as an alternative network scanning method that blocks ICMP echo requests. The next sections look at some of the conventional and esoteric mapping techniques used.

Tireless Mapper

The following scan shows the classic mapping technique of sending individual ICMP echo requests to all hosts in a given subnet. In this case, the 192.168.117 Class C subnet is scanned for all live hosts. As you can see, this is a very noisy scan:

```
00:05:58.560000 scanner.net > 192.168.117.233: icmp: echo request
00:06:01.880000 scanner.net > 192.168.117.139: icmp: echo request
00:12:45.830000 scanner.net > 192.168.117.63: icmp: echo request
00:15:36.210000 scanner.net > 192.168.117.242: icmp: echo request
00:15:58.600000 scanner.net > 192.168.117.129: icmp: echo request
00:18:51.650000 scanner.net > 192.168.117.98: icmp: echo request
00:20:42.750000 scanner.net > 192.168.117.177: icmp: echo request
00:26:36.680000 scanner.net > 192.168.117.218: icmp: echo request
00:27:30.620000 scanner.net > 192.168.117.168: icmp: echo request
```

If a site doesn't specifically look for ICMP activity, however, this might go unnoticed. So, the age-old philosophical question becomes, if a hacker maps your entire network and no one is listening, does it make any noise? Alarming on individual ICMP echo requests likely would generate a lot of alerts from an IDS, so IDSs usually do not issue alerts for individual ICMP echo requests. Yet, an IDS that examines more generic scan activity that exhibits a one-to-many source-to-destination IP relationship would correctly trigger on such a scan. In other words, if the IDS looks for one source IP connecting to many different destination IPs in a given time period—for instance, seven connections per hour—it would discover the preceding scan.

Efficient Mapper

Most likely, the preceding scan was automated so that it wasn't a labor-intensive effort for the not-so-wily scanner. But why bother with all the volume if
ICMP is a protocol that can be sent to a broadcast address and can ping many
hosts with a couple of commands? That is what the following scanner
attempts:

```
13:51:16.210000 scanner.net > 192.168.65.255: icmp: echo request
13:51:17.300000 scanner.net > 192.168.65.0: icmp: echo request
13:51:18.200000 scanner.net > 192.168.66.255: icmp: echo request
13:51:18.310000 scanner.net > 192.168.66.0: icmp: echo request
13:51:19.210000 scanner.net > 192.168.67.255: icmp: echo request
13:53:09.110000 scanner.net > 192.168.67.0: icmp: echo request
13:53:09.940000 scanner.net > 192.168.68.255: icmp: echo request
13:53:10.110000 scanner.net > 192.168.68.0: icmp: echo request
13:53:10.960000 scanner.net > 192.168.69.255: icmp: echo request
13:53:10.980000 scanner.net > 192.168.69.0: icmp: echo request
```

It appears that the scanner is attempting to map the 192.168 subnet. The third
octet in the IP number changes from 65 to 69 in this excerpt from a larger
scan. You can see the final octet fluctuate between 0 and 255. The 255 in the
final octet is the classic broadcast address. The 0 in the final octet is a broadcast
address for hosts that have a TCP/IP stack based on the UNIX *Berkeley
Software Distribution* (BSD) operating system. Using both these broadcast
addresses, all live hosts in an accessible network should respond.

This should convince you to deny into your network any activity destined
for these broadcast addresses. I don't know of any legitimate activity for traffic
destined for broadcast addresses except for diagnostic activity. The section,
"Smurf Attack," shows that disallowing this activity prevents Smurf amplification by your network.

Clever Mapper

In examining the next scan, you can see a new variation on an old mapping
scheme:

```
06:34:31.150000 scanner.net > 192.168.21.0: icmp: echo request
06:34:31.150000 scanner.net > 192.168.21.63: icmp: echo request
06:34:31.150000 scanner.net > 192.168.21.64: icmp: echo request
06:34:31.150000 scanner.net > 192.168.21.127: icmp: echo request
06:34:31.160000 scanner.net > 192.168.21.128: icmp: echo request
06:34:31.160000 scanner.net > 192.168.21.191: icmp: echo request
06:34:31.160000 scanner.net > 192.168.21.192: icmp: echo request
06:34:31.160000 scanner.net > 192.168.21.255: icmp: echo request
```

Look at the scanning pattern. You can see that ICMP echo requests are being sent to the Class C subnet of 192.168.21. Now look at the final octet of the IP address. You can see that the first request is sent to the 0 broadcast address, and the last one is sent to the 255 broadcast address. This isn't new; you saw this in the preceding scan.

Notice in the final octet of the other IP numbers, however, that they seem to span 64 IP numbers. For instance, the first IP number has a final octet of 0, and the following one has a final octet of 63. That is 64 total IP addresses. What is the significance of 64? Well, a typical Class C subnet has 256 addresses between the 0 and 255 range.

It is possible to subdivide a Class C network so that you have multiple smaller networks by assigning an appropriate subnet mask. One way to do this is to have four individually addressable subnets with 64 hosts each. In this scheme, the network and broadcast addresses change accordingly. The network and broadcast addresses for those four subnets are the IP numbers that you see in the scan. So, it turns out that the scanner believes that this scanned network might have a different addressing scheme than the Class C "natural" division. If this were truly the addressing scheme for the 192.168.21 subnet, all live hosts might respond. Even if the subnet is a standard Class C and the activity is not blocked, this will still ping all hosts on the network because it uses the .0 and .255 broadcast addresses. If you need a refresher about address classes, reference the "Logical Addresses, IP Addresses" section in Chapter 1.

Cerebral Mapper

One final scan shows a different mapping technique using another ICMP request type. The ICMP address mask request queries a host for the subnet mask of the network on which it resides. Remember all the trouble that the preceding scanner went through to try to determine the addressing scheme? That could have been avoided entirely by using the following ICMP address mask request:

```
20:39:38.120000 scanner.edu > router.com: icmp: address mask request (DF)
20:39:38:170000 router.com > scanner.edu: icmp: address mask is 0xffffff00
(DF)
20:39:39.090000 scanner.edu > router2.com: icmp: address mask request (DF)
20:39:39:230000 router2.com > scanner.edu: icmp: address mask is 0xffffff00
(DF)
20:39:40.090000 scanner.edu > routerx.com: icmp: address mask request (DF)
20:39:40:510000 routerx.com > scanner.edu: icmp: address mask is 0xffffff00
(DF)
```

This is not a classic mapping technique per se, but it can provide some initial reconnaissance. The quest here is to examine the subnet mask of different routers. Typically, only routers respond to address mask requests so the scanner might discover additional reconnaissance of the repliers. As discussed in Chapter 1, the subnet mask assigned to a computer system tells it how many bits in its IP address designate the network and how many designate the host.

If a scanner can determine a subnet mask of a network, he knows exactly how many hosts need to be scanned. Although the subnet mask of a host usually can be determined from looking at the first octet of the IP number, this request might discover the networks that don't have a "natural" subnet mask. That type of knowledge cannot be obtained from looking at the IP number alone. In this example, the scanned routers respond with subnet masks of a hexadecimal ffffff00. This translates to a decimal 255.255.255.0 subnet mask of the network on which they reside. This means that these hosts all belong to a Class C network. Querying for address masks is another type of ICMP activity that should be disallowed into the network, for obvious reasons.

Summary of Mapping

Let's briefly recap the discussion about mapping. Mapping can be done using the following methods:

- Sending individual ICMP echo requests to hosts in a network
- Sending ICMP echo requests to the broadcast addresses of a network
- Sending ICMP echo requests to network and broadcast addresses of subdivided networks
- Sending an ICMP address mask request to a host on the network to determine the subnet mask to better understand how to map efficiently

Normal ICMP Activity

This section examines some of the expected uses of ICMP—specifically, several different error messages that ICMP sends to inform a host of some kind of problem situation. Looking at mutant ICMP activity is more intriguing, but you've got to be able to understand what's normal before you can recognize abnormal ICMP activity.

Host Unreachable

In the following ICMP output, you can see an error message to `sending.host`, which is attempting to send traffic to a target host:

```
router > sending.host: icmp: host target.host unreachable
```

For some reason, the `target.host` is unreachable—perhaps no host resides at the requested IP address, perhaps the host is temporarily unavailable, or perhaps the host is suffering from some kind of misconfiguration that prevents it from responding.

In a situation such as this, the host obviously cannot send an error message, so the router that oversees the target host's network intervenes to deliver the message. In this case, the router informs the sending host that the target host is unreachable. As you can probably guess, this gives a scanner valuable information that he can use to help him map the network. If a scanner is collecting information about live hosts in a network to later scan, those that have been identified as unreachable would likely not be scanned again. This makes any subsequent scans more focused.

The valuable reconnaissance information that can be gleaned from many of the ICMP unreachable commands can be detrimental to the security of a given network. Cisco router access control lists have a statement `no ip unreachables` that can silence the router interface from issuing the ICMP unreachable messages.

Port Unreachable

The ICMP output that follows demonstrates how a target host informs a sending host that a requested UDP port is not listening. In this example, the sending host attempts to send traffic to the target host on the UDP *network time protocol* (ntp) port:

```
target.host > sending.host: icmp: target.host udp port ntp unreachable (DF)
```

Therefore, the protocol used to deliver the error message is ICMP. Remember that when you examined TCP, that protocol had a different way of informing a sending host that a port was not active. It returned a packet with the TCP RESET flag set to indicate that the port was not listening. UDP has no built-in mechanism to report about this error, so it enlists ICMP to assist.

Again, you can see that valuable reconnaissance can be gained from this ICMP error message—namely that scanned UDP ports that do not respond with this message could be listening ports. But, it is also possible that scanned UDP ports that do not respond might never have received that scan due to packet loss. It is also possible that outbound port unreachable messages are blocked from leaving the network. So, you can see that the absence of a port unreachable message from a scanned UDP port is not a definitive confirmation that the port is listening.

Admin Prohibited

Take a look at another possible problem situation with the following output:

```
router > sending.host: icmp: host target.host unreachable - admin prohibited
```

In this scenario, a sending host is attempting to deliver traffic to a target host. A router is at the gateway of the target host network.

The router has an access control list that prohibits certain types of traffic from entering the network. This could be a port that is blocked, a protocol that is blocked, or possibly the source IP or subnet that is denied access, or the destination IP or subnet that is protected. A router might respond to this condition with an ICMP "unreachable - admin prohibited" message. Although this ICMP message does not indicate what is being blocked (a destination port, a source IP, or an IP protocol, for instance), an astute scanner can attempt different combinations of connections and figure out what is being disallowed into the network and possibly find other avenues into the network that are not blocked.

Need to Frag

Another ICMP message warns that a desired host is unreachable because of a problem with fragmenting a datagram:

```
router > sending.host.net: icmp: target.host unreachable - need to frag (mtu
1500)
```

The DF output in TCPdump means that the Don't Fragment flag is set. As the name implies, if this flag is set, fragmentation will not be done on the datagram. If this flag is set and the datagram crosses a network in which fragmentation is required, the router discovers this, discards the datagram, and sends an ICMP error message back to the sending host.

The ICMP error message contains the *maximum transmission unit* (MTU) of the network that required fragmentation. Some hosts conversing in TCP intentionally send an initial datagram across the network with the DF flag set as a way to discover the smallest MTU for a particular source-to-destination path. If the ICMP error message is returned with the smallest MTU, the host then packages all datagrams bound for that destination in small enough chunks to avoid fragmentation. The intent is to eliminate the overhead and inefficiencies in packet loss associated with fragmentation.

Time Exceeded In-Transit

This ICMP message informs a sending host that a datagram has overstayed its welcome on the Internet:

```
routerx > sending host: icmp: time exceeded in-transit
```

IP needs a way to flush a lost datagram from the Internet, perhaps one that is in some kind of routing loop in which it is bouncing aimlessly between routers. The means used to prevent wayward datagram activity involves a field in the IP header known as the *time-to-live* (TTL) value.

Different operating systems set different initial TTL values. To examine default initial TTL values set by operating systems, go to http://project. honeynet.org/papers/finger/traces.txt.

When a datagram traverses a router on its travel from the source to destination, each router decrements the TTL value by 1. If the value ever becomes 0, the router discards the datagram and sends an ICMP "time exceeded in-transit" message back to the sending host. Chapter 5, "Stimulus and Response," shows how traceroute uses this ICMP "time exceeded in-transit" message along with incrementing TTL values to discover and record interim routers along the path from a given source to destination.

Embedded Information in ICMP Error Messages

It is helpful to understand that when an ICMP error message is returned, there is some additional information that is supplied in the datagram. Specifically, after the actual ICMP message, you will find the IP header followed by eight bytes of protocol header and data of the original datagram that caused the error, as seen in Figure 4.2. This information allows the receiving host to associate this error with the sending process and react appropriately. An external response to an ICMP error message is not expected because RFC 1122 describes this as one of the conditions for which no ICMP reply should be generated.

It is also useful to be aware that not all TCP/IP stacks will precisely copy the IP header and following eight bytes. It would seem logical that the embedded information following the ICMP error message, reflecting the first 28 bytes of the offending packet, would exactly match the first 28 bytes of the offending packet. In fact, nmap can be used to discover a remote host's operating system by sending normal and aberrant traffic to a target host. It looks for responses and behavior of the target host that will distinguish it from standard expected behavior to assist in operating system classification. One test in a series of traffic to the target host attempts to send a datagram to a closed UDP port. The desired response to this is an ICMP "port unreachable" message. But, nmap examines several of the fields in the ICMP error message containing the IP header and following eight bytes of the initial probe of the UDP port. It examines these fields to see if they match the fields in the datagram that elicited the error. This information is used to determine the operating system.

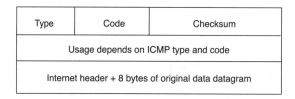

Type	Code	Checksum
Usage depends on ICMP type and code		
Internet header + 8 bytes of original data datagram		

Figure 4.2   ICMP error message format.

Summary of Normal ICMP

In the previous sections, you examined some of the many ICMP messages that you might see while monitoring your network. You also saw many of the different informative ICMP error messages. As you noticed, these can be sent by either hosts or routers that discover a problem.

These sections also discussed the notion that some of the ICMP unreachable errors are best prevented from leaving your network if you are concerned about the reconnaissance information that could be gathered from them.

Malicious ICMP Activity

Not unexpectedly, it was just a matter of time until ICMP became tainted in purpose. Today, ICMP has been corrupted for use in many different types of denial-of-service attacks, and it has been used in a most stealthy attack as a covert channel. This section examines some of these malicious uses of ICMP.

Black Ice

As I was driving to work one wintry morning after a night of precipitation, it occurred to me that the day's commute was much like the philosophy of my job as a security analyst. I cautiously navigated the long, winding, snow-covered driveway; slowed my pace; shifted to a lower gear descending the steep hill out of the neighborhood; and safely drove around the abandoned car in my lane going uphill. I treated the identified hazards with due caution and respect, but it was the unseen dangers such as black ice that worried me.

> Each day, as I analyze traffic to our sites, I have this omnipresent uneasy feeling about what it is I am not seeing—the black ice of our networks. I have seen firsthand the persistence, guile, and cleverness that the Internet pirates use to try to find and exploit what they want. As a security analyst, this "What am I missing?" semi-paranoid attitude is one you must adopt. If you become too complacent about the security of your site, your site could spin out of control from the unidentified perils.

Smurf Attack

The infamous Smurf attack, shown in Figure 4.3, preys on ICMP's capability to send traffic to the broadcast address. Many hosts can listen and respond to a single ICMP echo request sent to a broadcast address. This capability is used to execute a denial-of-service attack against a hapless target host or network.

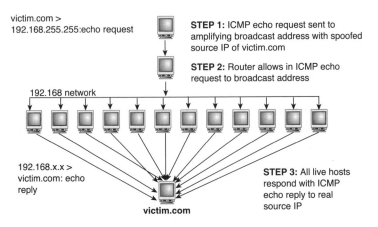

Figure 4.3   Anatomy of a Smurf attack.

First, a malicious host must craft an ICMP echo request with a spoofed source IP to a broadcast address of an intermediate network. The spoofed source IP chosen is that of the victim target host/network. Next, the intermediate site must allow broadcast activity into the network. If it does, the ICMP echo request is sent to all hosts on the given subnet to which the broadcast was sent. Finally, all the live hosts in the intermediate network that respond send an ICMP echo reply to what they believe to be the sender, or the victim host. The victim host or network on which it resides can become choked with all the activity and can suffer a degradation or denial-of-service attack if the following conditions exist:

- The malicious user sends many ICMP requests to the broadcast address.
- The intermediate site allows inbound broadcast traffic.
- The intermediate site is large and has many responding hosts. On the other hand, many smaller intermediate sites might be used to achieve the same result.
- The target site has a slow Internet connection. To be more precise, the Internet connection must be susceptible of being overwhelmed by too many packets for the supported bandwidth. Although it is possible to inundate and clog *any* Internet connection given enough traffic, slower connections are more vulnerable.

Therefore, this is another reason that you want to deny broadcast traffic from entering into your network. Your site cannot be used as a Smurf amplification network if broadcast traffic is not allowed.

Tribe Flood Network

The *Tribe Flood Network* (TFN) attack is another denial-of-service attack that uses ICMP for communication. Figure 4.4 depicts the attack. Unlike the Smurf attack, which originates from one source and uses one intermediate network as an amplification point, the TFN attack enlists the help of many distributed hosts, known as daemon or zombie hosts. Hence, the *term distributed denial of service* (DDoS) is a more accurate description of the use of dispersed hosts to participate in an attack.

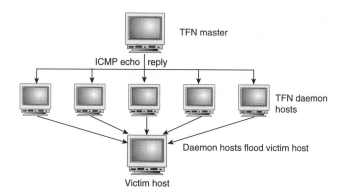

Figure 4.4   Tribe Flood Network attack.

This attack requires a TFN master host and daemon hosts to be established. These are typically compromised hosts on which TFN was installed. The master TFN host then instructs the daemon hosts to attack a victim host, perhaps simultaneously. The communication between the master and daemon host is done using the ICMP echo reply. The daemons can send the target host a UDP flood, a TCP SYN flood, an ICMP echo request flood, or a Smurf attack. The master instructs the daemon what to do by sending commands in the ICMP echo reply. The ICMP identification number field in the ICMP header of the ICMP echo reply is used to direct the daemons of the action to take. The data portion of the ICMP echo reply is used to send arguments.

You might be wondering why this attack uses ICMP echo replies instead of ICMP echo requests. The reason is that more sites block ICMP echo requests because they are aware of the hazards of allowing them in the network. However, they may allow ICMP echo replies in to get responses from pings to hosts outside the network and because they don't realize the threats posed by rogue ICMP echo requests.

As you have probably concluded, by using several distributed intermediate hosts simultaneously to flood the target host, a denial-of-service attack against the target network or target host is the anticipated outcome. If you want to read more about TFN, go to www.cert.org and search for incident IN-99-07.

Self-Inflicted Denial of Service?

It was December 29, 1999. As I prepared to begin my stint at a Y2K center for the Office of the Secretary of Defense, I mulled over the rumors of impending cyberspace doom. The widespread consensus was that there would be massive denial-of-service attacks directed against infrastructure services such as power and transportation. Despite the hackers' promised plans of drunken celebration with the masses, the prevailing sentiment was that the release of distributed denial-of-service tools such as TFN coincided with the arrival of the new millennium.

In response to the perceived threat, many sites all but shut down or greatly restricted access to their networks. The irony of this was noted by a coworker who said, "It seems rather funny to avoid a denial-of-service attack by turning off the services yourself."

WinFreeze

The WinFreeze attack essentially causes a susceptible host to attack itself—an ugly kind of self-mutilation:

```
router > victim.com: icmp: redirect 243.148.16.61 to host victim.com
router > victim.com: icmp: redirect 110.161.152.156 to host victim.com
router > victim.com: icmp: redirect 245.211.87.115 to host victim.com
router > victim.com: icmp: redirect 49.130.233.15 to host victim.com
```

```
router > victim.com: icmp: redirect 149.161.236.104 to host victim.com
router > victim.com: icmp: redirect 48.35.126.189 to host victim.com
router > victim.com: icmp: redirect 207.172.122.197 to host victim.com
router > victim.com: icmp: redirect 113.27.175.38 to host victim.com
router > victim.com: icmp: redirect 114.102.175.168 to host victim.com
```

The ICMP redirect message informs a sending host that it has tried to use a nonoptimal router and tells the sending host to add a more optimal router to its routing table. The WinFreeze attack can cause a vulnerable Windows NT host to suffer a denial of service by flooding it with ICMP redirect messages. This is executed on a network on which the victim host resides and purports to send ICMP redirect messages from the router. When the Windows host receives a flood of these messages, it attempts to add these changes to its own routing table and could suffer from degraded performance.

In the preceding output, the router is informing victim.com to redirect its traffic to many different random IP numbers to itself. The host victim.com might be overwhelmed when trying to apply all those changes to its own routing table.

Loki

Probably the most subversive and destructive use of ICMP to date is known as Loki. In Norse mythology, Loki was the god of trickery and mischief. So too is the Loki exploit the master of trickery. As you have seen, ICMP is intended to be used to inform of error conditions and to make simple requests. As such, intrusion analysts prior to the release of Loki regarded ICMP as a fairly harmless protocol, except for the denial-of-service attacks generated using it and for the network mapping information it could provide if not blocked.

Loki uses ICMP as a tunneling protocol for a covert channel. A covert channel is one that uses a transport method or data field in a secret or unexpected manner. In other words, the transport vehicle is ICMP; but operationally, Loki acts much like a client/server application. If a host is compromised and a Loki server is installed, it can respond to traffic sent to it by a Loki client. For instance, the Loki client could send a request to the Loki server to cat/etc/passwd to display the password file. The Loki client user then would see the output from the display, capture it, and possibly crack the password file. You can find more information on Loki at www.phrack.com issue 49, article 6.

The danger in this whole scheme is that a seemingly innocuous protocol is being used to do some very sophisticated and potentially damaging exchanges. Again, ICMP was never intended to support applications such as this. My advice to the intrusion analyst is to regard ICMP traffic with heightened suspicion and to stop just shy of outright paranoia.

Unsolicited ICMP Echo Replies

Now, try your hand at some analysis and put into practice some of the theory you just learned about ICMP exploits by examining the output that follows:

```
reply.com >192.168.127.41: icmp: echo reply
reply.com >192.168.127.41: icmp: echo reply
reply.com >192.168.127.41: icmp: echo reply
reply.com >192.168.127.41: icmp: echo reply
reply.com >192.168.127.41: icmp: echo reply
reply.com >192.168.127.41: icmp: echo reply
```

What you observe here is a host, reply.com, sending the 192.168.127.41 host ICMP echo reply traffic. This would not be unusual if the 192.168.127.41 host had sent an ICMP echo request eliciting these responses. However, this is not the case; no outbound ICMP echo requests were sent from 192.168.127.41. Why might someone initiate such activity? You learn possible reasons in the next three sections.

One thing to keep in mind is that for this kind of activity to be detected, you must have some kind of IDS or supporting software capable of maintaining state. This means that you must be able to determine whether any prior traffic had issued ICMP echo requests. Many IDSs do not maintain state information and cannot detect such anomalous activity. Let's examine some of the possible theories that might explain this anomalous activity.

Theory 1: Spoofing

The first theory poses the possibility that you see this traffic because someone has borrowed the source IP 192.168.127.41 and has issued ICMP echo requests to reply.com using the spoofed source IP; reply.com then replies to the real 192.168.127.41 IP address. If you saw ICMP echo replies from many other hosts on the same network as reply.com, you could be a Smurf target.

A dramatic increase in spoofing activity has arisen, so this is the most common explanation for this type of activity. Typically, when you have witnessed unsolicited ICMP echo replies that appear to be using your spoofed source IPs (in this example, 192.168.127.41), you might see other unsolicited activity from the same intermediate host (in this example, reply.com). You usually don't see this activity in isolation—you might see these replies going to many different 192.168.127 hosts, not just a single reply multiple times.

Theory 2: TFN

A second theory involves the TFN attack. You learned that the TFN master communicates with its TFN daemons using ICMP echo replies.

Therefore, another possibility is that the host receiving the unsolicited ICMP echo replies, 192.168.127.41, has become a victim TFN daemon. Although the ICMP identification value field is used to direct the daemon host to attack the victim, the exact value found in this field might not be predictable if the attacker changes the default source code. The more obvious way to determine whether the 192.168.127.41 has become an unwitting TFN daemon is to examine the outbound activity from 192.168.127.41 after receiving the ICMP echo requests. If it sends a flood of unexplained traffic outbound, it is possibly participating in a TFN attack.

Theory 3: Loki

The final theory is that this could be an exchange between a Loki client and a Loki server. When Loki traffic is exchanged, it might not have a pattern of each ICMP echo request generating a reply. It is possible for the Loki server to respond with multiple ICMP echo replies to a single ICMP echo request.

Original releases of Loki had a signature of a static value in the sixth and seventh bytes (starting with byte 0) of the ICMP message. This could be determined by dumping the traffic using TCPdump with hexadecimal output and observing the lack of change in this field that is the ICMP sequence number. This field is usually unique for each ICMP echo request sent out and, much like the IP header identification number, increments by 1 or 256 for each subsequent ICMP echo request. Later incarnations of Loki might use encryption and might not be decipherable in this manner.

As you have witnessed, ICMP echo traffic, whether request or reply, can facilitate some noxious activity. So, this is an excellent candidate for blocking by a packet-filtering device.

Summary of Malicious ICMP Traffic

To wrap up this section, you learned that ICMP has been manipulated in use for other purposes than the intended ones. ICMP can be used in a denial-of-service attack, as you observed in the Smurf and WinFreeze attacks. ICMP was used more as a conduit for communication in the TFN attack. It might not be used directly as a denial-of-service attack, but it enables a denial-of-service attack to occur by providing the communication vehicle between the TFN master and daemons. Finally, you saw that Loki has completely altered the original purpose of ICMP by using it as a tunneling mechanism for malicious activity.

To Block or Not to Block

After reading about all the havoc that ICMP now can wreak, it appears that ICMP left Kansas along with Dorothy and Toto. From a reconnaissance aspect, if you can elicit any of the following ICMP messages from a host, you know you have reached a live host:

- "protocol unreachable"
- "port unreachable"
- "IP reassembly time exceeded"
- "parameter problem"
- "echo reply"
- "timestamp reply"
- "address mask reply"

Also, if you can get a router to report ICMP host unreachable errors, it is possible to inversely map a network assuming that those hosts which do not have this error reported are indeed live hosts.

As if this isn't enough information, the following common ICMP messages are sent by routers only so if you can elicit any of the following, you can identify a site's routers:

- "fragmentation needed but don't-fragment bit set"
- "admin prohibited"
- "time exceeded in transit"
- "network unreachable"
- "host unreachable"

And, finally, we can discover more reconnaissance by the following ICMP messages:

- "admin prohibited: can assist in examining what type of traffic the site blocks"
- "address mask reply: gives the subnet mask of the network on which the responding host resides"
- "time exceeded in transit: used in traceroute to discover routers and network topology"
- "protocol unreachable: can be used to inversely map a host's listening protocols"

- "port unreachable: can be used to inversely map a live host's listening UDP ports"
- "fragmentation needed but don't fragment bit set: can be used to determine the MTU of links for use in attacks that use fragments"

Given all the reconnaissance that ICMP can supply, why not just unconditionally block all incoming and outgoing ICMP traffic? Some sites do just this, but let's examine some of the repercussions of blocking all inbound ICMP.

Unrequited ICMP Echo Requests

Obviously, your ability to do diagnostic activity using ping is broken when you block both inbound ICMP echo requests and echo replies. The good news is that ICMP echo requests and replies cannot be used as a front for stolen goods if blocked. The inconvenience suffered by this loss might be justified by the improvement of your security posture, eliminating a possible stealthy avenue into your network.

You might face a temptation to block only inbound ICMP echo requests, which would enable you to do diagnostics from your network and receive a response by virtue of the ICMP echo response gaining inbound access. The hackers know this, however, and as you have witnessed with Tribe Flood Network and Loki, they are relying more on the use of ICMP echo reply as a delivery mechanism.

Kiss traceroute Goodbye

Whether you use the UNIX **traceroute** command or the Windows **tracert** command to discover the routers through which a datagram travels on its path from source to destination, blocking inbound ICMP prevents you from executing these commands from your network to other networks. These commands require inbound ICMP "time exceeded in-transit" messages to operate correctly. By preventing all ICMP into the network, you break your use of traceroute outbound.

The Windows **tracert** command uses the ICMP echo request, so blocking inbound ICMP precludes a user from doing a tracert to a machine in your network. The UNIX **traceroute** uses UDP as the protocol, however, so blocking inbound ICMP does not prevent someone from executing a UNIX **traceroute** to a host in your network.

Silence of the LANs

As you learned in this chapter, ICMP can inform about unreachable conditions to a particular host or port. When you block all inbound ICMP messages, hosts or routers on your network cannot receive these informative messages. This does not produce catastrophic results, but it does cause some inefficiencies. As an example, a host on your network might attempt a TCP connection to another host that might be down. This could elicit a "host unreachable" message from a remote router, but the host attempting this connection doesn't receive the ICMP unreachable message because it is blocked. The sending host retries until it times out, thereby sending unnecessary traffic.

Broken Path MTU Discovery

As discussed previously, when possible, a host sending TCP traffic tries to avoid fragmentation of datagrams. This is done using path MTU discovery. As covered in this chapter, a sending host uses the Don't Fragment flag in a discovery packet. The intent is for the discovery packet to reach the destination host without being fragmented, or for the sending host to receive an ICMP "need to frag" message with the value of the smaller MTU found in the message.

Therefore, blocking all inbound ICMP breaks this mechanism and causes some significant problems. A host sending the discovery packet expects to receive an ICMP "need to frag" message if fragmentation is required. Because it receives no such message due to the inbound ICMP block, it continues to send oversized datagrams with the Don't Fragment flag set. These are dropped, but the sending host is never informed of this. Packets sent that are smaller than the smallest MTU along the path arrive at the destination, but larger ones do not.

So, if you choose to block ICMP, make sure that you make an exclusion to allow "host unreachable - need to frag" ICMP messages into your network.

Summary

ICMP is a protocol that is supposed to be used to alert hosts of problem conditions or to exchange simple messages. It can be transmitted between two hosts exclusively, or it can be transmitted to multiple hosts using the broadcast address.

Regard ICMP as a potential threat. This chapter has identified some of the current known malicious uses of ICMP. No doubt, many more will come, with many new flavors of unknown subversions.

Block inbound ICMP, but do so wisely and selectively. Although you will prevent potentially malicious traffic from entering your network, make sure that you understand the adverse consequences to your own network of blocking inbound ICMP traffic.

5

Stimulus and Response

U P UNTIL THIS CHAPTER, YOU HAVE BEEN exposed to mostly stimulus activity.
Not much time or discussion has been invested presenting the unique
responses from different stimuli. This served you well when new theories and
concepts were introduced so as not to add layers of complexity to new
material. Hopefully, now that you understand the basic theory, you are ready
to diversify your exposure.

Most current network intrusion detection systems have very high rates of
false positives. In other words, they cannot yet make wise decisions on
whether traffic coming across a given network is harmful or innocuous. So,
the network intrusion-detection system (NIDS) often errs on the side of caution, and alarms when there is no problem. There are many reasons for this,
but the short explanation is that most times the signatures or rule set that the
NIDS uses to determine suspicious traffic are too generic. If these signatures
cannot be or are not more precisely customized, the NIDS will often alert
when no problem exists.

Therefore, the analyst must make the distinction between false positive and
valid alarms. You examine the traffic associated with the alarm and determine
whether it is a false alarm. To make such a determination, you need to have a

foundation in what seemingly normal or abnormal traffic looks like. Common sense dictates that all aspects of standard stimuli and responses cannot be covered in this chapter. The intention is to impart some general knowledge, however, so that you can make a more intelligent determination of the kind of traffic you observe on different networks.

This chapter first exposes you to the expected behavior of typical applications and protocols. Next, you learn about a category of activity that manifests expected, yet uncommon behavior. Finally, you descend from the sublime to the ridiculously abnormal activity.

This is much like the evolution of a budding courtship. Both partners are on their best behavior at first because good manners are expected. The comfort zone seeps in after awhile, and the expected fine etiquette deteriorates from furled pinkies while drinking tea to random slurps. Familiarity certainly breeds bad manners as time passes and the first hardy belch rumbles.

The Personal Hazards of Working with False Positives

Several months ago, I was driving to work when I saw a simultaneous red flash of both the battery and brake indicator lights appear on the dashboard of my car. They disappeared immediately, but it concerned me. This happened several more times on the remainder of the commute.

I am the first to admit that I am a mechanical moron and should never question anything my car professes to tell me because it is far smarter than I am about its health. Yet, it seemed strange to me that these seemingly unrelated lights flashed together. After all, unless I had battery-powered brakes (and I was almost certain I didn't), there was no logical correlation in my mechanically challenged mind of the two different lights. I tried to explain it away as a false positive convincing myself that perhaps a loose wire of some sort was the culprit instead of real mechanical problems.

Some time passed and the problem got worse, so I gave in and called the service shop. I told the service manager about the problem and her response told me she was doing her very best not to yell, "You moron! " into the phone. Despite her training in customer relations, she could barely contain her rage at my stupidity. She told me that it was my car's alternator and I could be stranded— or some other catastrophic things could happen like the car could blow up, or I could put an eye out, yadayadayada. Needless to say after hearing the "sky-is-falling" prognosis of my car and my life, I brought the car in to be repaired right away, and the problem went away.

I got to thinking about the incident and began to reflect that I had been a relatively conservative and cautious person most of my life who, years ago, would have taken the car into the shop at the first sign of trouble. What had changed in all these years? My only guess is that I'm so used to looking at NIDS outputs of false positives that I try to explain everything away in that same light. In other words, I believe nothing any more because everyone and everything is a liar!

The Expected

What the heck is normal traffic anyway? It would be an exercise in futility—and undoubted head-bobbing boredom—to try to demonstrate all aspects of normal behavior. To make this a more manageable and interesting task, this section reviews situations and traffic patterns that are likely to be the bulk of what you will see on your network. Specifically, the response behaviors of hosts and routers are examined when different traffic is sent and received under different conditions with different protocols.

A very hard challenge in developing this material was trying to elucidate what is "normal." Because expected behavior entails so many facets and dimensions, it is impossible to discuss them all here. Ironically, normal might best be described as not abnormal. For this reason, this book discusses many examples of deviant behavior.

Request for Comments

Is there some kind of standard baseline for what is expected? Request for Comments (RFCs) contain the foundation documentation for the Internet. They elaborate the expected standards for individual protocols. The Internet is best viewed as a series of different protocols, each documented by one or more RFCs. RFCs do not change after they are issued; protocol enhancements are documented by issuing new RFCs. Some of the most pertinent RFCs for this section include the following:

- **RFC 793**. This RFC discusses the Transmission Control Protocol (TCP), describing the functions to be performed by TCP, the program that implements it, and its interface to programs or users requiring its services.

- **RFC 768**. This RFC discusses the functioning of the User Datagram Protocol (UDP), which is an unreliable connectionless protocol.

- **RFC 791**. This RFC discusses the Internet Protocol (IP), the protocol that provides for transmitting blocks of data called datagrams from sources to destinations.

- **RFC 792**. This RFC discusses the Internet Control Message Protocol (ICMP), the protocol that deals with errors in datagram processing.

You can find more information about RFCs at www.rfc-editor.org.

TCP Stimulus–Response

This section examines responses to an attempted telnet connection made under various conditions such as a host that doesn't listen on the telnet port or a router blocking the connection. Telnet is used as a representative TCP application. You will see some of the varied responses to the identical stimulus. Obviously, this is not an exhaustive list of all conditions that might be encountered with an attempted telnet connection. The particular set of conditions has been selected for illustration because it represents some of the most common.

Destination Host Listens on Requested Port

A host, tel_client.com, attempts to telnet to myhost.com, which listens on port telnet (TCP port 23).

Stimulus:

```
tel_client.com.38060 > myhost.com.telnet: S 3774957990:3774957990(0) win 8760
<mss 1460> (DF)
```

myhost.com offers telnet and connection is permitted.

Response:

```
myhost.com.telnet > tel_client.com.38060: S 2009600000:2009600000(0) ack
3774957991 win 1024 <mss 1460>
```

The previous TCPdump output examines the expected response when client host tel_client.com attempts to connect to the telnet port on destination host myhost.com. You have already been exposed to the concept of the three-way handshake for TCP session establishment. If you remember, the first part of the process is for the client to initiate a TCP connection with the SYN flag set to the server to signal the desire to connect. tel_client.com issues such a SYN connection request to myhost.com to connect to the telnet port.

Now, if myhost.com offers telnet, access is permitted, and no other impediments arise; you see the expected response of myhost.com replying to the request with a SYN/ACK. This says that myhost.com is listening at the telnet port and can establish this telnet connection. The final part of the three-way handshake not shown would be tel_client.com responding to myhost.com with a TCP connection with only the ACK flag set.

Destination Host Not Listening on Requested Port

Look at the following TCPdump output to see the response from the same attempted telnet connection. This time, the scenario changes and myhost.com does not listen for telnet connections. The expected response is a RESET/ACK that is an abrupt termination to the connection.

Stimulus:
```
tel_client.com.38060 > myhost.com.telnet: S 3774957990:3774957990(0) win 8760
<mss 1460> (DF)
```

myhost.com does not offer telnet.

Response:
```
myhost.com.telnet > tel_client.com.38060: R 0:0(0) ack 3774957991 win 0
```

In the response, you see that the ACK number 3774957991 from myhost.com is one more than the tel_client.com's SYN of 3774957990. This means that myhost.com received the telnet attempt, and this would be the expected sequence number of the next data byte. Yet, the R in the response indicates a connection RESET or termination because myhost.com does not listen on port telnet. After the RESET/ACK is issued by myhost.com, there should be no reply from tel_client.com.

Destination Host Doesn't Exist

What happens if tel_client.com attempts a telnet connection to myhost.com, but myhost.com doesn't exist? Looking at the following TCPdump output, you see an example of such an exchange. Often a router responds to a situation such as this in which a host cannot respond. In this case, router.com, the default router for the subnet on which myhost.com was formerly found, informs tel_client.com using ICMP that myhost.com is unreachable.

Stimulus:
```
tel_client.com.38060 > myhost.com.telnet: S 3774957990:3774957990(0) win 8760
<mss 1460> (DF)
```

myhost.com doesn't exist.

Response:
```
router.com > tel_client.com: icmp: host myhost.com unreachable
```

This implies that myhost.com is a host with a registered domain name system (DNS) IP address, but the IP number is no longer active or the host is currently down or suffering from some kind of misconfiguration preventing it from responding. The response from router.com informs of this unreachable error condition using ICMP as the protocol to deliver the message to tel_client.com.

Destination Port Blocked

The next TCPdump output shows another possible condition. What if a filtering router blocks the telnet port? What kind of response will you see? Again, the router for myhost.com, router.com, informs tel_client.com that myhost.com is unreachable and qualifies that this is because of an `admin pro-hibited filter`, meaning that the access was blocked. router.com was just trying to be helpful and informative in this and the previous situations examined, but it is giving out some valuable reconnaissance information if someone is probing your network. It is possible to silence Cisco routers by putting a `no ip unreachables` statement in the access control list of the appropriate interface as you learned in Chapter 4, "ICMP." This prevents the router from being as verbose and limits the information that it divulges.

Stimulus:
```
tel_client.com.38060 > myhost.com.telnet: S 3774957990:3774957990(0) win 8760
<mss 1460> (DF)
```

Router responds to blocked telnet request.

Response:
```
router.com > tel_client.com: icmp: myhost.com unreachable - admin prohibited
filter
```

Destination Port Blocked, Router Doesn't Respond

This TCPdump output illustrates what happens when a router blocks traffic, but the router has been muzzled from issuing unreachable messages. Because no ICMP error message informs tel_client.com that something is amiss, it stubbornly continues to send retries to connect. The number of retries and the time intervals in which they are sent are based on the TCP/IP stack of the operating system of the host sending the retries. Finally, the host tel_client.com gives up on the connection after it has exhausted the maximum number of retries.

Stimulus:
```
17:14:18.726864 tel_client.com.38060 > myhost.com.telnet: S
3774957990:3774957990(0) win 8760 <mss 1460> (DF)
```

Router does not respond to blocked telnet request.

Response:
```
17:14:21.781140 tel_client.com.38060 > myhost.com.telnet: S
3774957990:3774957990(0) win 8760 <mss 1460> (DF)
17:14:27.776662 tel_client.com.38060 > myhost.com.telnet: S
3774957990:3774957990(0) win 8760 <mss 1460> (DF)
17:14:39.775929 tel_client.com.38060 > myhost.com.telnet: S
3774957990:3774957990(0) win 8760 <mss 1460> (DF)
```

The topic of retries or retransmissions will be examined in greater detail in Chapter 9, "Examining Embedded Protocol Header Fields."

UDP Stimulus-Response

A DNS query is used in this section to examine how UDP responds to different stimuli. Specifically, a listening domain port and a nonlistening port are inspected. Because the other stimuli examined in the previous section for TCP (such as a host that doesn't exist or the domain port blocked at the router) elicit very similar responses for the UDP DNS query, they don't merit repetition.

Destination Host Listening on Requested Port

Looking at the following example, you see nslookup.com does a DNS query to myhost.com on a port domain from the preceding TCPdump output. Chapter 6, "DNS," explains the TCPdump DNS output more thoroughly. You see a DNS identification number, 51007, which is used to pair up responses with requests. myhost.com receives the query and responds. myhost.com communicates on port domain (53) to nslookup.com, responding to DNS identification number 51007. The 1/0/0 is TCPdump DNS jargon for returning one answer resource record, no authority records, and no other records. As with TCP, you see that the UDP exchange was done using an ephemeral port, 45070, on the client and the well-known domain server port. The response from myhost.com uses these established ports.

Stimulus:

```
nslookup.com.45070 > myhost.com.domain: 51007+ (31) (DF)
```

myhost.com runs the domain service and responds.

Response:

```
myhost.com.domain > nslookup.com.45070 51007 1/0/0 (193) (DF)
```

Destination Host Not Listening on Requested Port

Observe the following TCPdump output. In this case, myhost.com responds with an ICMP message that UDP port domain is unreachable. Again, this produces some good reconnaissance about what services a target host does or does not offer. This time it is a loose-lipped host, not a router that offers more detail than necessary.

Stimulus:

```
nslookup.com.45070 > myhost.com.domain: 51007+ (31) (DF)
```

myhost.com doesn't run the domain service and responds.

Response:

```
myhost.com > nslookup.com: icmp:myhost.com udp port domain unreachable
```

In Chapter 9, you will learn that nmap can scan for listening UDP ports. It attempts to do this by assuming that scanned target host UDP ports for which no ICMP "port unreachable" messages are returned are listening ports. This is sometimes referred to as inverse mapping because there is no direct indication that the ports are listening.

Unlike listening TCP ports that respond at the TCP protocol level with a SYN/ACK, most UDP ports will not respond at the UDP protocol level with a simple connection request. For instance, the previous DNS query to UDP port 53 received a response because it was communicating at the levels above the protocol level such as the application level. If you were to examine the embedded payload, you would find a properly configured DNS query. The nmap UDP port scanning sends 0 bytes of payload and therefore cannot communicate above the protocol level.

ICMP Stimulus–Response

ICMP, as you have learned, differs from TCP and UDP. Naturally, the expected set of responses differs as well. This very brief summary explains ICMP's uniqueness:

- ICMP doesn't use protocol ports to converse.
- ICMP can be a one-way transmission to inform of an error condition with no observed response.
- ICMP can be a request with an expected reply.

The error responses that might be encountered using ICMP are typically availability issues, such as if the host exists or whether access is allowed to the host. These are similar to those observed with the TCP examples. Rather than rehash more of the same, the Windows **tracert** command is introduced to demonstrate normal ICMP response used to discover a route from a source to destination host.

Windows tracert

The **tracert** command uses the ICMP echo request and ICMP echo reply pair, also known as ping, to discover the routers through which a datagram passes on its path from source to destination host. The command output looks like this:

```
tracert target.my.com
Tracing route to target.my.com [1.2.3.4]
over a maximum of 30 hops:
  1   129 ms   126 ms   130 ms  router.my.com [1.2.3.1]
  2   229 ms   124 ms   118 ms  target.my.com [1.2.3.4]
Trace complete.
```

When you execute the **tracert** command, you see the intermediate routers through which the ICMP echo request passes. This example shows only one, router.my.com, before reaching the destination host target.my.com.

Each router and the destination host receive three separate ICMP echo requests, and **tracert** output displays the round-trip time for each of those datagrams to reach the router or destination host. For instance, the first three ICMP echo requests sent to router.my.com took 129, 126, and 130 milliseconds to complete the round-trip with an ICMP echo response. The multiple iterations to one router or host are done in case one or more ICMP echo requests or replies is dropped or lost because of network problems. Next, target.my.com receives three ICMP echo requests and replies with three ICMP echo replies.

TCPdump of tracert

This following TCPdump output is the result of executing the previous **tracert** command:

```
tracer.net > target.my.com: icmp: echo request [ttl 1]
router.my.com > tracer.net: icmp: time exceeded in-transit
tracer.net > target.my.com: icmp: echo request [ttl 1]
router.my.com > tracer.net: icmp: time exceeded in-transit
tracer.net > target.my.com: icmp: echo request [ttl 1]
router.my.com > tracer.net: icmp: time exceeded in-transit
tracer.net > target.my.com: icmp: echo request
target.my.com > tracer.net: icmp: echo reply (DF)
tracer.net > target.my.com: icmp: echo request
target.my.com > tracer.net: icmp: echo reply (DF)
tracer.net > target.my.com: icmp: echo request
target.my.com > tracer.net: icmp: echo reply (DF)
```

tracert sends the first ICMP echo request in an IP datagram with a time-to-live (TTL) value of 1. The TTL is a value set by a sending host and decremented by each network device through which the packet traverses. TTL provides a means of discarding packets that have overstayed their welcome on the Internet and might be bouncing aimlessly. If a router decrements the TTL and the value becomes 0, the packet must be discarded and an ICMP "time exceeded in-transit" error message is returned.

In the previous output, after a TTL with a value of 1 is observed, the router router.my.com sends an ICMP "time-exceeded in-transit" message. This is because it decremented the TTL and discovered a value of 0. It must then discard the packet and inform the sending host.

When used for **tracert**, however, the original source host receiving this ICMP error message records the router from which it came. If necessary, **tracert** then sends another ICMP echo request in an IP datagram, but increments the TTL value by 1. This process repeats until the ICMP echo request finally makes its way to the destination host and receives an ICMP echo reply.

By default, three different ICMP requests are sent to each new hop for redundancy in case a packet is dropped. Notice that tracer.net sends an ICMP echo request to target.my.com. Immediately, you see the reply from router.my.com complaining via the ICMP "time exceeded in-transit" message that the TTL value has been decremented to 0. This is seen for all three different ICMP echo requests. The host tracer.net then increments the TTL to 2, which is enough to allow it to get to the actual destination host, target.my.com. The reason that you do not see TCPdump display the TTL value of 2 is because the default behavior of TCPdump is to print the TTL only when it has a value of 1 to warn of an impending problem. target.my.com responds to all the ICMP echo requests with echo replies. If you want to examine the TTL regardless of value using TCPdump, use the command line option **–vv**.

Protocol Benders

Between the expected and abnormal falls a netherland of applications that exhibit normal, yet unconventional, behavior. These applications deviate from the expected behavior because they were designed differently. These patterns are presented so that if you encounter them, you will understand that this is normal traffic.

Specifically, FTP and UNIX Traceroute will be discussed. FTP is considered to be a protocol bender because it defies the convention of using one ephemeral and one server port for the duration of the FTP connection. The UNIX Traceroute is an unusual application because it combines ICMP and UDP to navigate from source to destination and record all routers on the way.

FTP

The expected behavior of TCP that you have witnessed so far is to establish the two ports used by the client and server during the three-way handshake. The client usually selects an ephemeral port greater than 1023, and the server listens on a well-known port. Throughout the remainder of the established TCP session, the client and server talk only on these established ports. FTP differs from most other TCP services, because it communicates using two different server ports. The first port is port 21, which is known as the standard FTP command port. The second port is used for data passed between the client and the server. The actual port used is different for active and passive FTP, as you will soon see.

Active FTP

Active FTP is so named because the FTP server opens up the data connection to the client. Both active and passive FTP use port 21 to issue FTP commands, such as those to retrieve or store a file. But, in active FTP, the second is port 20 for FTP data passed between the client and the server. The FTP data port is used to exchange a file between the two hosts or to send a listing of file directories from the server to the client.

Look at the following TCPdump output for an active FTP session to see an unusual, but normal, change of TCP ports:

Session negotiation:

```
ftp.client.com.35955 > ftp.server.com. 21: S 1884312222:1884312222(0)
ftp.server.com.21 > ftp.client.com.35955: S 3113925437:3113925437(0) ack
1884312223
ftp.client.com.35955 > ftp.server.com.21: . ack 1
ftp.server.com.21 > ftp.client.com.35955: P 1:24(23) ack 1
ftp.client.com.35955 > ftp.server.com.21: . ack 24
```

dir command issued by the user:

```
ftp.server.com.20 > ftp.client.com.35956: S 3558632705:3558632705(0)
ftp.client.com.35956 > ftp.server.com.20: S 1901007864:1901007864(0) ack
3558632706
ftp.server.com.20 > ftp.client.com.35956: . ack 1
```

In the preceding example, the FTP connection is established between ftp.client.com using ephemeral port 35955 and server port 21. The three-way handshake is completed and some data (usually a welcoming message) is passed between the two. This is similar to what you have witnessed with other TCP protocols.

Next, the user issues the FTP **dir** command from the client requesting a listing of the directories on the server. A new connection is established from source port 20 of the server to the ephemeral port 35956 on the client. Although you do not see it in the output, the client informed the server that it would be listening on ephemeral port 35956 via the FTP **port** command. After this new three-way handshake is completed, ftp.server.com can send the directories to ftp.client.com on this established connection. Additional exchanges of data cause the establishment of new connections and the selection of new ephemeral ports. This is called active FTP because the FTP server initiates the data connection to the client. As you might guess, this presents some problems for packet-filtering devices that would have to indiscriminately allow traffic into the network coming from source port 20. Passive FTP avoids these problems by having the internal FTP client make the data connection.

Passive FTP

Passive FTP differs from active FTP in the manner in which the data connection is established. It uses the identical method of connecting to FTP port 21 to establish the command port. But, as you observed with active FTP, the problem arises when a packet-filtering device must allow initial SYNs in from source port 20 to a high-numbered port inside the packet-filtering device. What is to keep a hacker from using this hole as a way into the network? After all, the packet-filtering device might not be examining the content of the packet using this hole and cannot be sure it is indeed FTP traffic.

Passive FTP avoids this problem altogether by having the client initiate the connection to the server. Remember that active FTP required that the server initiate the connection to the client. Look at the following output of a passive FTP session establishment:

Session negotiation:

```
ftp.client.com.44890 > ftp.server2.com.21: S 4276284026:4276284026(0) win
8760 <mss 1380> (DF)
ftp.server2.com.21 > ftp.client.com.44890: S 1669630260:1669630260(0) ack
4276284027 win 8280 <mss 1460> (DF)
ftp.client.com.44890 > ftp.server2.com.21: . ack 1 win 9660 (DF)
```

dir command issued by the user:

```
ftp.client.com.44891 > ftp.server2.com.3967: S 4282611109:4282611109(0) win
8760 <mss 1380> (DF)
ftp.server2.com.3967 > ftp.client.com.44891: S 1669768808:1669768808(0) ack
4282611110 win 8280 <mss 1460> (DF)
ftp.client.com.44891 > ftp.server2.com.3967: . ack 1 win 9660 (DF)
```

When ftp.client.com issues the **dir** command on the current command connection, it causes a data connection to be established. You don't see this in the TCPdump output, but ftp.server2.com informs the client via the FTP port command that it will be listening on port 3967. The client issues the SYN connection to that port and the server responds with a SYN/ACK. The directory listing is done via this connection. Because the client is making an outbound connection to the server, the subsequent responses from the server can be allowed back in the packet-filtering device with relatively strong confidence that this is a "safe" connection. This involves less risk than allowing active FTP connections by permitting all inbound source port 20 through the packet-filtering device.

UNIX Traceroute

The UNIX Traceroute program discussed next shows a combination of UDP and ICMP to discover the path that a datagram takes from source to destination. This traceroute program is similar in function to the Windows Tracert; instead of using ICMP to discover the routers and destination host, however, it uses UDP.

The intermediate routers that are discovered respond as you saw in the Windows Tracert with ICMP "time-exceeded in-transit" messages when an IP datagram has a TTL value decremented to 0. Again, this process is repeated until the UDP datagram makes its way to the destination host by incrementing the starting TTL value by 1 for each new hop to be forged beyond the previous one. The UDP destination port chosen is one typically in the 33000–33999 range—one that almost surely does not listen. The intention is to elicit an ICMP "UDP port unreachable" message that signals to traceroute that the destination host has been found. Like tracert, the default behavior for traceroute is to send three different connections to each router or host. This example alters the behavior to send only one for simplicity:

```
tracer.com.62615 > target.com.33456: udp 12 (DF) [ttl 1]
router.com > tracer.com: icmp: time exceeded in-transit
[tos 0xc0]
tracer.com.62615 > target.com.33457: udp 12 (DF)
target.com > tracer.com: icmp: target.com udp port 33457 unreachable (DF)
```

In the preceding output, you see tracer.com send a UDP datagram to destination port 33456 of target.com. The initial TTL value is set to 1. As soon as this packet hits router.com, it decrements the TTL value to 0 and returns an ICMP "time exceeded in transit" message to tracer.com. When tracer.com receives this, it sends another UDP datagram to target.com. This is different from the first one because it increments the destination port to 33457 and, while you cannot tell from the standard TCPdump output, it increments the initial TTL to 2. This allows the datagram to traverse the first router, router.com, and take one more hop. That additional hop takes it to the destination host target.com that does not listen on port 33457 and returns an ICMP "port unreachable" message.

You should be aware that both the UNIX traceroute and the Windows tracert only work if specific ICMP messages are allowed into the network of the host executing the commands. Both versions require that ICMP "time exceeded in-transit" messages be allowed into the network. The UNIX traceroute requires that ICMP "port unreachable" messages be allowed, and Windows tracert requires that ICMP echo requests be allowed.

You are probably asking whether these types of ICMP messages should be permitted inbound to your network. This really depends on the security posture you adopt. At the most protected and restricted sites, this is not necessarily recommended. The risks might far outweigh the benefits because it is possible to use these ICMP messages for purposes other than the ones for which they were designed, as was witnessed with the discussion of Loki in Chapter 4.

However, if your site is a more open one and you are willing to accept the risks, allowing these ICMP messages can provide some obvious benefits of route discovery along with informative feedback to internal hosts in your network.

Summary of Expected Behavior and Protocol Benders

Here is a brief synopsis of what has been covered so far in this chapter. The RFCs are the standards documents upon which TCP/IP and the Internet were built. They describe how things are supposed to work when everyone conforms to the same rules. Unfortunately, hackers have discovered that different implementations of TCP/IP react differently to deliberate violations of the RFC standards. That's one of the foundations of hacking: deliberately exploiting exceptional conditions that the implementers of the TCP/IP code believed would never happen. Hackers often attempt to identify operating systems by sending strange stimuli and observing the host's responses. The final part of this chapter looks at some of the reactions of systems to these deliberate deviations.

As previously discussed, there are unique responses for the same stimulus depending on the circumstances and availability of the requested service. Responses also depend on a host or router's capability to respond to a particular connection. Each of the different protocols has different expected responses. Finally, you see in protocol benders some unusual, but not abnormal, behavior exhibited by some applications.

Abnormal Stimuli

This section examines some of the blatantly anomalous behaviors that hackers might throw your way. These behaviors have many purposes, and each is examined for the different categories discussed. These categories and anomalies are not all-inclusive; you might find many more.

Evasion Stimulus, Lack of Response

You see a port scan of victim.org from stealthy.com with the FIN flag alone set in the TCPdump output that follows. This is a sneaky way of determining whether a given port is active. The expected behavior per RFC 793 is that a listening port that is scanned should not respond; a port that is not listening should respond with a RESET/ACK. This maps the services that a target host offers. Take a look:

```
stealthy.com.50141 > victim.org.5: F 0:0(0) win 4096 (DF)
stealthy.com.50141 > victim.org.3: F 0:0(0) win 4096 (DF)
```

```
stealthy.com.50141 > victim.org.26: F 0:0(0) win 4096 (DF)
stealthy.com.50141 > victim.org.45: F 0:0(0) win 4096 (DF)
stealthy.com.50141 > victim.org.17: F 0:0(0) win 4096 (DF)
stealthy.com.50141 > victim.org.7: F 0:0(0) win 4096 (DF)
stealthy.com.50141 > victim.org.51: F 0:0(0) win 4096 (DF)
stealthy.com.50141 > victim.org.52: F 0:0(0) win 4096 (DF)
stealthy.com.50141 > victim.org.30: F 0:0(0) win 4096 (DF)
stealthy.com.50141 > victim.org.53: F 0:0(0) win 4096 (DF)
stealthy.com.50141 > victim.org.20: F 0:0(0) win 4096 (DF)
```

The reason that this scan is considered more stealthy than a scan that probes
ports with an attempted SYN connection is that some intrusion detection systems might not pick up a FIN scan. Historically, probes of open ports were
done using SYN scans, and earlier intrusion detection systems were developed
using this signature. When the hackers realized that their scans were being
detected, however, they tried to elude notice by launching FIN scans that
would map the active ports but might not be noticed. This scan can be
launched using **nmap −sF victim.org** to inform nmap to do a stealthy
FIN scan.

Evil Stimulus, Fatal Response

Denial-of-service (DoS) attacks might attempt to starve a host of resources
needed to function correctly. There are many different varieties of DoS attacks.
Jolt2 is an attack that consumes so much of the target host's memory resources
that it cannot function. Here is some sample output from Jolt2:

```
10:48:56.848099 verbo.com > win98.com: (frag 1109:9@65520)
10:48:56.848099 verbo.com > win98.com: (frag 1109:9@65520)
10:48:56.848295 verbo.com > win98.com: (frag 1109:9@65520)
10:48:56.848295 verbo.com > win98.com: (frag 1109:9@65520)
10:48:56.848351 verbo.com > win98.com: (frag 1109:9@65520)
10:48:56.848351 verbo.com > win98.com: (frag 1109:9@65520)
10:48:56.848420 verbo.com > win98.com: (frag 1109:9@65520)
10:48:56.848420 verbo.com > win98.com: (frag 1109:9@65520)
10:48:56.848584 verbo.com > win98.com: (frag 1109:9@65520)
```

Jolt2 sends an endless stream of ICMP echo requests (by default, although
other protocols can be used) to a target Windows host. These are sent as fragments with the same fragment ID but also with duplicate non-zero fragment
offsets.

Because all fragments but the first in the fragment train carry only data, not
protocol headers, the receiving host only knows the embedded protocol is
ICMP. A problem exists for certain Windows 98, Windows NT, and Windows
2000 hosts when they do not receive the initial 0 offset fragment. The target
host becomes consumed with packet reassembly, and memory usage shoots
way up leading to a DoS.

When looking at the TCPdump output of the Jolt2 activity, all you know is that host verbo.com is sending some kind of packets to the win98.com host. You see a repeated fragment ID of 1109, a fragment length of 9, and a fragment offset of 65520. The Jolt2 source code assigns the fragment offset a static value of 65520. This brings the total close to the 65535 maximum. Initially, you might think this worked because of the fragment offset number. However, when this value was changed in the source code to something quite a bit lower and the code was recompiled, the DoS still occurred.

To test the response of the target host, a ping process was executed on the malicious host verbo.com to win98.com before and during the time the Jolt2 code was run. The DoS was almost immediate after the Jolt2 code was executed. The win98.com host neither responded to pings nor keyboard input. It recovered after the attack was stopped and did not require rebooting.

The Motivation Behind Scanning

One of the first phases in any attempt to break into a host on a network is to do some kind of reconnaissance on the network or a particular host. An attacker might have a new piece of code that was just released that enables him to get root access if he can find a vulnerable host. Or, an attacker might just be interested in getting into a host or multiple hosts in any way possible. Different hackers have different goals for hacking. Perhaps the host or network is being sought to participate in a distributed denial-of-service attack. Or, perhaps the interest is in compromising a host from which to launch other attacks and hide the true identity of the hacker.

The attacker must scan the network in some fashion to discover live hosts, and later discover hosts susceptible to exploits by scanning service ports. For instance, the attacker might have acquired some software that could gain root access on hosts offering vulnerable DNS servers. Chances are good that he would scan the network for any host listening on the DNS port. After discovering those, the attacker might try to execute the DNS exploit code on hosts running DNS.

The scanning phase is one that might be done blatantly at night when it is less likely that a network is being watched. It might be done from a compromised host so that when it is discovered, the attacker's identity will not be known. Or, the hacker might try to launch the scans using methods that might go undetected, known as stealth scans. These scans are considered more furtive because they use unconventional techniques that NIDS are not likely to pick up. Some of the scanning techniques also attempt to fingerprint the operating system. Many times a given exploit might plague a subset of operating systems. For the hacker to have a better chance of success, reconnaissance must be done to find hosts running a particular operating system.

No Stimulus, All Response

This is really just a fancy name for IP spoofing. Appendix A, "Exploits and Scans to Apply Exploits," discusses this in more detail. In the following

TCPdump output, it appears that many 1.2 hosts are receiving ICMP "time exceeded in-transit" messages. They are being informed that traffic, which they sent to a host, had a TTL expire in a datagram. Naturally enough, this implies that all the 1.2 hosts sent some kind of traffic that elicited these responses. That is not the case, however; no outbound traffic is found from these hosts. Here is the output:

```
router.com > 1.2.10.72: icmp: time exceeded in-transit
router.com > 1.2.18.13: icmp: time exceeded in-transit
router.com > 1.2.11.67: icmp: time exceeded in-transit
router.com > 1.2.16.13: icmp: time exceeded in-transit
router.com > 1.2.19.1: icmp: time exceeded in-transit
router.com > 1.2.1.252: icmp: time exceeded in-transit
router.com > 1.2.13.56: icmp: time exceeded in-transit
router.com > 1.2.143.6: icmp: time exceeded in-transit
router.com > 1.2.13.15: icmp: time exceeded in-transit
```

Can you guess the explanation for this traffic? Given the title of the section, it should be a no-brainer. The 1.2 hosts were spoofed, and traffic was sent to a foreign network using them as a source IP. The reason for this is sheer speculation because you see only one side of the action; however, the most likely explanation is that some kind of flood of activity or harassment against the foreign network was undertaken.

How do you know that source IP router.com is not doing some kind of reconnaissance of the destination 1.2 hosts? Couldn't this type of traffic elicit some kind of response from a router, if not a host? The problem is that this is an ICMP error message, and RFC 1122 dictates that an ICMP error message cannot elicit another ICMP error message because that might lead to some kind of endless loop when an error condition was encountered. Because no other protocol would respond to this activity, the spoofing theory is the most logical.

Backscatter

A very interesting study was conducted and a paper was written about attacks such as the one discussed in the section, "No Stimulus, All Response." The authors nicknamed the attacks *backscatter*. The authors studied activity on their class A network on the Internet over an extended time. They were able to infer backscatter attacks on the Internet by examining different protocol responses for which there were no requests. This indicated that IP addresses from their network were being spoofed. Using this information, they were able to deduce the number and types of attacks that occurred on the Internet during that time. The frequency and types of activity occurring on the Internet are pretty amazing. The study, "Inferring Internet Denial-of-Service Activity," can be found at www.cs.ucsd.edu/~savage/papers/UsenixSec01.pdf.

Unconventional Stimulus, Operating System Identifying Response

This section discusses some examples of attempts to fingerprint the operating system of a target host by sending unconventional stimuli and then evaluating the target host's responses. The nmap program is one scanning tool that can remotely attempt to identify a target host's operating system.

The reason that malicious hackers attempt to identify a host's operating system is because they can then pair appropriate exploits with vulnerable operating systems. It is potentially damaging reconnaissance information if someone can determine the operating system of a remote host. Sure, some sites are open enough that the operating system type and version can be harvested from banners associated with telnet or FTP connections. These might not be readily available for all sites, however; and even if they are, they might not be accurate. Every operating system has a TCP/IP stack implementation that differs slightly. If a hacker or software can send specific packets, knowing how a particular operating system should respond, the hacker can tell Linux from Solaris, (sometimes) without requiring any other information.

nmap sends some unexpected stimuli, including the following, to identify a host's operating system based on the replies:

- **An unsolicited FIN to an open port**. There should be no response according to RFC 793, but some hosts do respond with a RESET. The output was examined in the previous section, "Evasion Stimulus, Lack of Response," to show how this traffic can be used to map listening ports with more stealth than conventional SYN scans.

- **Bogus "reserved" TCP flag values**. nmap sends these to see whether the target host resets the bits to 0 for those nonexistent flags. Many operating systems think these bits are bogus; however, those that are ECN-aware might not, as discussed in the following section.

- **Anomalous TCP flag combinations**. Mutant flag combinations are sent with the expectation that most target hosts will not respond, but a handful might respond, uniquely identifying their operating system.

- **No TCP flag values**. nmap sends these to see how the target host handles this anomalous situation.

Bogus "Reserved" TCP Flags

One fingerprinting method is to send bogus TCP flag settings. Figure 5.1 shows the configuration of the TCP flag byte. The TCP flag byte contains all the possible TCP flag settings. Remember from Chapter 2, "Introduction to

TCPdump and TCP" that the TCP flag settings tell much about the purpose of a given TCP segment. Because there are only six TCP flags, there are 2 extra bits in the TCP flag byte. Before the invention of something known as Explicit Congestion Notification (ECN), these high-order reserved bits were expected to have a value of 0. ECN is discussed more thoroughly in Chapter 9.

To examine all the bits set in the TCP flag byte, you need to execute the standard version of TCPdump with the -x option that dumps the collected datagram in hexadecimal. You cannot check the value of the 2 high-order bits with standard TCPdump output.

A byte is represented as two hexadecimal characters, or nibbles. The low-order nibble contains the bit settings for the PUSH, RESET, SYN, and FIN flags. Turn your attention to the high-order nibble to examine the value of the reserved bits. The bogus TCP flag settings that nmap tests attempt to give these bits a value. If the high-order nibble has a value greater than 3, this indicates that one or both of the reserved bits are set. You can arrive at this value because the ACK bit when set has a value of 1 times 2^0 (or 1) and the URG bit when set has a value of 1 times 2^1 (or 2). These two values combined equal 3. Any value greater than 3 in the high-order nibble is anomalous unless ECN is being used.

The following TCPdump output shows an nmap scan that attempts to discover more about the behavior of the TCP/IP stack of target.com to help identify the operating system. This particular attempted connection set one of the reserved TCP flag bytes—specifically, the bit to the left of the URG bit. First, you see the regular TCPdump output, but it gives no clue to the underlying bogus TCP flag bit settings. The following hexadecimal output shows all fields, including the TCP flag byte field:

```
scanner.com.44388 > target.com.domain: S 403915838:403915838(0) win 4096
<wscale 10,nop,mss 265,timestamp 1061109567 0,eol> (DF)

[4500 003c 7542 4000 3b06 15bd 0102 0304
0102 0305] ad64 0035 1813 443e 0000 0000
a042 1000 fa4c 0000 0303 0a01 0204 0109
080a 3f3f 3f3f 0000 0000 0000
```

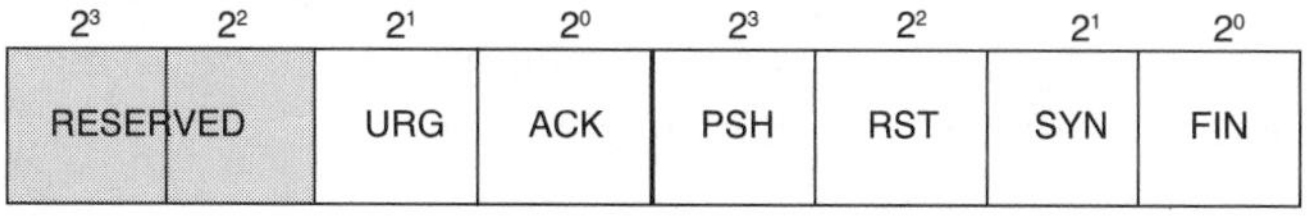

2^3	2^2	2^1	2^0	2^3	2^2	2^1	2^0
RESERVED		URG	ACK	PSH	RST	SYN	FIN

Figure 5.1   TCP flag byte.

Looking at the hexadecimal output, the first 20 bytes of the IP header are in brackets. The TCP header and any data follow this; the 13th byte into the TCP header (marked in bold) is the TCP flag byte. You see that the value is a hexadecimal 42. Looking at the high-order nibble (or the value of 4), it is greater than 3, meaning that the low-order reserved bit has been set. The scanner's hope is that the response to this bogus flag setting indicates something unique about the operating system.

Now, take a look at the response of target.com to scanner.com. Our interest and nmap's interest is the response to the bogus TCP flag bit set. Again, the normal TCPdump output display does not show the reserved bits of the TCP flag byte. The hexadecimal dump that does show the TCP flag byte follows this:

```
target.com.domain > scanner.com.44388: S 4154976859:4154976859(0) ack
403915839 win 8855 <nop,nop,timestamp 16912287 1061109567,nop,wscale 0,mss
265> (DF)

[4500 003c e04e 4000 ff06 e6af 83da d684
83da d683] 0035 ad64 f7a7 ea5b 1813 443f
a012 2297 fd3f 0000 0101 080a 0102 0f9f
3f3f 3f3f 0103 0300 0204 0109
```

Look at the response to the bogus TCP flag bits in the preceding TCPdump output. target.com responds with a SYN/ACK—nothing rancid here. It appears that target.com did not react to the abnormal TCP flag bit set. How do you know? The hexadecimal output of the transaction shows that the response has the SYN and ACK bit set in the TCP flag byte with a hexadecimal value of 12 (in bold). The ACK bit is in the low-order bit of the high-order nibble, so it represents the value 1. The SYN bit is in the low-order nibble, second bit from the left, and represents the 2 value. Therefore, the response discarded the bogus TCP flag bit. Another operating system might have preserved that bit, and it would have been reflected in the TCP flag byte.

Anomalous TCP Flag Combinations

RFC 793 elaborates normal TCP flag state settings and transitions in extensive detail. It seems likely that most operating system TCP/IP stacks would conform to the specifications. For the most part, they do, but there are the rare exceptions that do not conform and are therefore identifiable by their lack of conformity. Look at the following TCPdump output from an excerpt of traffic produced by running nmap in operating system fingerprinting mode (**-O** command line option) for a host named win98:

```
nmap -O win98

20:33:16.409759 verbo.47322 > win98.netbios-ssn: SFP 861966446:861966446(0)
win 3072 urg 0 <wscale 10,nop,mss 265,timestamp 1061109567[|tcp]>

20:33:16.410387 win98.netbios-ssn > verbo.47322: S 49904150:49904150(0) ack
861966447 win 8215 <mss 1460> (DF)
```

The scanning host sends a packet with the TCP flags of SYN, FIN, and PUSH simultaneously set. Logically, it appears that this is an anomalous flag trio because a SYN flag starts a connection, a FIN flag closes a connection, and a PUSH flag sends data after a connection is opened or before a connection is closed. It would seem a natural reaction that a host receiving this connection would ignore it or perhaps RESET it because it makes no sense. Yet, the Windows 98 target host appears to interpret this as session establishment and responds with a SYN and an ACK. This unique reaction helps identify the responding host as having a Windows TCP/IP stack.

No TCP Flags

As another example of nmap fingerprinting, look at the following TCPdump output. It shows a TCP segment with no TCP flag bits set. This is another instance of sending a mutant TCP flag byte setting. In this case, no flag bits have been turned on; this is also known as a null session:

```
scanner.com.44389 > target.com.domain: . win 4096 <wscale 10,nop,mss 265,
timestamp 1061109567 0,eol> (DF)

[4500 003c 7543 4000 3b06 15bc 0102 0304
0102 0305] ad65 0035 1813 443e 0000 0000
a000 1000 fa8d 0000 0303 0a01 0204 0109
080a 3f3f 3f3f 0000 0000 0000
```

Look at the previous hexadecimal output. The TCP flag byte field, which is in bold, has a value of 00. This means that no TCP flags have been set. Most hosts will not respond to a null session, yet some must, otherwise nmap would have no reason to send this kind of traffic.

A normal TCP flag byte has at least one flag bit set. The host target.com did not respond at all to this null session TCP segment. The lack of response provides some clue about the operating system. Another operating system might distinguish itself by responding differently, perhaps by replying with a RESET.

Using TCP Options for OS Identification

Look at the following TCPdump output from an nmap scan with the focus on the bolded TCP options:

```
scanner.com.44388 > target.com.domain: S 403915838:403915838(0) win 4096
<wscale 10,nop,mss 265,timestamp 1061109567 0,eol> (DF)
target.com.domain > scanner.com.44388: S 4154976859:4154976859(0) ack
403915839 win 8855 <nop,nop,timestamp 16912287 1061109567,nop,wscale 0,mss
265> (DF)
```

One of the other methods that nmap uses to identify a particular operating system is to send many different TCP options. Some operating systems do not support all these options, and the response discards some. Also, some operating systems set different values for some of the TCP options, further differentiating the fingerprint. Unlike the other examples discussed so far, these are not unconventional stimuli, but are mentioned because they help identify the remote operating system.

Finally, different operating systems will store these options in a different order in the TCP header, which is indicated by the order in which TCPdump lists them. All this information can contain a bounty of identifying clues. As you see in the response to the preceding options, the order has been changed and some of the values have been altered (such as the wscale changing from 10 to 0 in the response). Also notice that the nop and eol options are rearranged or disappear in the response. These fields are used to pad TCP options to 4-byte boundaries and might not be needed in the response.

For an in-depth discussion of TCP options, take a look at RFC 1323. Some of the TCP options seen in the TCPdump output are as follows:

- **–wscale.** This option allows the TCP window size to increase to a value greater than 65535 bytes. This is typically used to increase throughput of TCP over high-bandwidth, long-delay networks.

- **–timestamp.** This option records round-trip time measurements. These measurements are often necessary to optimize throughput based on changes in network conditions.

- **–nop.** This option is used to add a 1-byte pad to TCP options. TCP options must fall on 4-byte boundaries; and if they are less than 4 bytes, the nop is used to pad.

- **–eol.** This is the end-of-list option used to pad a final byte to a 4-byte boundary.

Summary of Abnormal Stimuli

You see that there are many variations of abnormal activity. Different types of abnormal activity have different purposes. Some try to evade the vigilant eye of NIDS or circumvent filtering. Others are blatantly hostile because they attempt a denial of service against a target host.

You must also be aware that sometimes what you might perceive to be hostile activity is actually a response from a host responding to your spoofed addresses. Finally, programs, such as nmap, use unique stimuli to elicit responses with identifying characteristics of the target operating system

Summary

As far as expected responses are concerned, remember there are no absolutes. Not every operating system's TCP/IP stack is from the same mold shaped by a set of identical defining RFCs. Some operating systems do not follow the RFCs' expected behavior. This does not necessarily indicate some kind of mutant response. This is more a reflection of a lack of standardization.

There is a very important point to learn from stimulus-response theory. A common knee-jerk reaction from observing traffic that appears to be some kind of scan or repeated activity directed against your network is to jump to the immediate conclusion that you are under attack from the source IP. You are likely to label the source IP as the aggressor. Take a moment and think before you automatically make such an assessment. Granted, many times you will be correct. But, think about the possibility that this was an elicited response. (There might have even been some kind of catalyst to which the alleged aggressor is responding.) For instance, your source IPs might have been spoofed. This concept is easy to assimilate in theory, but hard to remember in practice.

Conversely, when you get some kind of response activity, such as an unsolicited ICMP echo reply, it is very possible that the source host is indeed the aggressor. As discussed in Chapter 4, the Tribe Flood Network (TFN) attack uses an ICMP echo reply as the communication vehicle between the master and daemons to launch or control a distributed denial of service (DDoS) attack. If you have any doubt about observed activity, the best advice is to examine the entire captured datagram and scrutinize the header fields and payload for anomalies. You have to adopt the attitude that nothing is predictable all the time when you examine network traffic.

6

DNS

WHY DEVOTE AN ENTIRE CHAPTER TO DNS? Isn't DNS used to translate a host name to an IP address and that's about it? Sure, that is a big and important part of DNS, but DNS is much more.

DNS servers are probably one of the most common targets of reconnaissance and exploit efforts. Your DNS server is a cherished prize for a hacker to compromise, so hackers are going to see how vulnerable it is by pounding on it for weaknesses. DNS servers are targeted for the following reasons:

- DNS servers can provide a lot of reconnaissance information about hosts in preparation for launching an attack of a targeted network.

- DNS is used to resolve host names and IP addresses; so if a hacker can dupe a DNS server or actually seize control of a DNS server, she can manipulate name or address translations for malicious purposes. Often, weak methods of authentication rely on a host having a particular host name or IP address. If normal translations can be subverted, authentications can be corrupted.

- DNS servers are accessible and information sharing entities. The port commonly associated with DNS traffic, UDP port 53, is often left open on packet-filtering devices so that internal name servers can function.

This chapter covers these topics along with DNS theory and practical applications. You learn how DNS queries are answered, how DNS servers interact with other DNS servers, how DNS can be used to discover information about a site, and ways that DNS can be used for exploit purposes. In short, this information will aid you in applying network security and analyzing the nature of DNS traffic seen on the network.

Back to Basics: DNS Theory

Again, TCPdump is enlisted to help explain and visualize what occurs with different types of DNS transactions. Specifically, this section examines how a DNS query is issued and answered. DNS differs from a normal client/server application, such as telnet, where the client requests a connection to a desired server and the interaction is between those two hosts. For DNS, however, when a client issues a DNS query, a DNS server accepts the query, perhaps interacts with one or more additional DNS servers, and then returns the response to the client.

This section looks at the structure of DNS as a distributed system, and it examines host name to IP address resolution. It also discusses the role of master (formerly known as primary) and slave (formerly known as secondary) name servers and discusses the interaction between them. You learn that unlike other services, DNS can switch between UDP and TCP protocols, depending on the kind of DNS activity.

The Structure of DNS

DNS is a globally distributed system that depends on the cooperative interaction of many DNS servers to store records about "domains" and to communicate with each other. A domain is a subset of DNS records associated with a logical grouping. For instance, sans.org is a collection of records containing IP addresses, host names, name servers, and more associated with the sans.org domain. Figure 6.1 depicts the hierarchical nature of DNS.

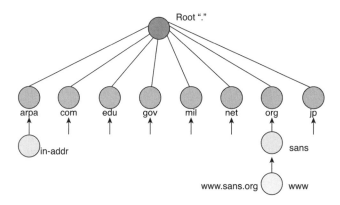

Figure 6.1   DNS, the pyramid scheme.

Logically, the top node of the DNS tree is known as root—designated by the period (.). Functionally, this is represented by root servers that can act as the starting point for DNS resolutions. These servers just point to other DNS servers that might have dominion over the DNS records being sought. You are probably familiar with the top-level domains, those falling directly under the root servers (the long-established .edu, .org, .com, .net, .mil, and .gov; and the recently established .aero, .biz, .coop, .info, .museum, .name, and .pro, to name the domestic domains). There are additional top-level domains for foreign countries, such as .jp for Japan.

Steppin' Out on the Internet

Suppose that you want to visit www.sans.org, which is the home page for the System Administration, Networking, and Security (SANS) Institute. You enter http://www.sans.org in your browser, and seconds later you see the www.sans.org page.

Now, remember that IP datagrams use IP addresses for all source and destination addresses. IP knows nothing about host names. The human mind is more likely to remember that the capital of Florida is Tallahassee, than it is to remember the value of pi to 10 fractional digits is 3.1415926536, even though both take 11 characters (excluding the decimal) to represent. Names have more order and less randomness than numbers, so you tend to remember them better. This is why you speak in host names rather than IP addresses. It is apparent that some kind of translation mechanism is required between the way you reference hosts (via host names) and the way TCP/IP must reference hosts (via IP addresses).

So, how did this translation from www.sans.org to an IP address mysteri-
ously occur behind the scenes? Before you could even send out a request to
www.sans.org, your host had to know an IP address. Your host needs this IP
address to insert into the datagram when it sends the connection request to
www.sans.org out on the network. The following section unveils this somewhat
transparent process.

Recursive Versus Iterative Queries

DNS queries come in two different varieties: recursive and iterative. A recursive query requires a
name server to find the answer to the query itself. In other words, it might query name servers,
such as root name servers that do not know the answer to the query but know references of name
servers that possibly have the answer to the query. The name server must follow all the references
until it finds a name server that has the answer. The bottom line is that a recursive query asks the
queried DNS server to be the workhorse and finds an answer while the querying DNS server waits
for the answer or performs unrelated queries.

An iterative query asks a name server to fetch the answer to a query. If the name server doesn't
have the answer, it returns to the querying name server a reference of another name server that
possibly has the answer to the query. The queried name server does not pursue finding the answer;
the querying name server must pursue finding the answer to the query itself.

DNS Resolution Process

Figure 6.2 shows the beginning of the process of resolution from host name
www.sans.org to IP address.

You see your browser is on host.my.com and it attempts resolution of
www.sans.org. Assuming that your host is not a name server, it is mostly passive throughout the resolution process. It just fires off the request for the
translation and resumes the process of connecting to the www.sans.org page
after it receives a resolution of the IP address. The workhorse behind the
resolution process is the DNS server that is queried (in this case, dns.my.com).
Generally, a default name server is chosen at the time the operating system is
installed on a given client machine. On UNIX machines, the information is
stored in the file /etc/resolv.conf. The DNS server is set as a TCP/IP property
in the Network portion of the Control Panel for Windows hosts. This default
DNS server typically is managed locally and is located somewhere on your
organization's intranet. dns.my.com is this site's DNS server.

On the client host, the TCP/IP applications, such as telnet, FTP, Netscape,
or Internet Explorer, call "resolver" library routines to obtain DNS resolution.
When you requested www.sans.org, application software issued a call to resolve
the host name to an IP address. In this case, a gethostbyname call is sent from

host.my.com to the DNS server. This requests host name translation of
www.sans.org to an IP address. The DNS server receives this request, processes
it, and returns it to host.my.com.

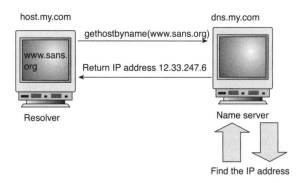

Figure 6.2 Client resolver, the handoff.

Figure 6.3 shows the second part of the resolution journey after leaving
host.my.com. You see dns.my.com assumes the actual task of finding the
answer of the IP of www.sans.org. For simplicity of theory (although this
might be perceived as adding complexity to the actual resolution process),
assume that dns.my.com knows nothing about www.sans.org or any other host
in the .org domain. dns.my.com begins its search with a DNS root server to
find the resolution.

If a DNS server has to resolve an unknown external host name and it has
no knowledge of the host's associated domains, it must contact a root name
server. Root name servers are more than just a starting point—they maintain a
mapping between domain names (sans.org) and the authoritative name
servers—DNS servers that maintain DNS records for those domains. When
the local name server, dns.my.com, asks a root name server for the IP address
of www.sans.org, it gets back a referral to the name servers for sans.org.

You might ask how dns.my.com knows the names and IP addresses of
the root servers to contact. Obviously, the local name server must be
preconfigured with a list of known root name servers. This information
is maintained by the InterNIC and may be downloaded from
ftp://ftp.rs.internic.net/domain/named.ca.

Continuing the resolution adventure, the root server lets dns.my.com know
where to continue its search. The root server has returned a referral to the
name server server1.sans.org as an authoritative name server for www.sans.org.
Figure 6.4 depicts dns.my.com querying server1.sans.org and receiving an
authoritative answer, the IP address of 12.33.247.6.

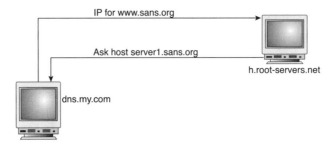

Figure 6.3   DNS server resolution, the cry for help.

Figure 6.4   DNS server resolution, from the horse's mouth

TCPdump Output of Resolution

You can examine the traffic that this DNS request generated by observing the TCPdump output that follows:

```
host.my.com.1716 > dns.my.com.53: 1+ (35)
dns.my.com.53 > h.root-servers.net.53: 12420 (30) (DF)
h.root-servers.net.53 > dns.my.com.53: 12420- 0/3/3 (153) (DF)
dns.my.com.53 > server1.sans.org.53: 12421+ (30) (DF)
server1.sans.org.53 > dns.my.com.53: 12421* 1/3/3 (172)
dns.my.com.53 > host.my.com.1716: 1* 1/3/3
(197) (DF)
```

First, host.my.com (the client exchanges from host.my.com are in bold) issues the request to resolve www.sans.org to dns.my.com. TCPdump analyzes DNS at the application level, which is why you don't see the word udp embedded in the output even though this is UDP. UDP is the protocol selected for the transmission of the majority of DNS traffic because the queries and responses are often short and the application itself can tolerate lost data. When anticipated data is not received, the DNS query is reissued.

Next, dns.my.com attempts a connection to h.root–servers.net on port 53.
Notice that both source and destination ports are 53. h.root-servers.net
responds back to dns.my.com using source and destination ports 53 as well. A
discussion of the numbers and notations found at the end of each TCPdump
record is found in the next section, "Strange TCPdump Notation." h.root-
servers.net does not have the answer to the query. It has a reference of another
DNS server that either has the answer or has a reference of who might have
the answer. Querying name servers for the IP of www.sans.org is an iterative
process that yields a reference of another DNS server that might have the
answer. This process repeats until contacting a name server that has the IP
address answer.

Because h.root-servers referred dns.my.com to another DNS server, in the
third line of the preceding output, you see dns.my.com query this server,
server1.sans.org, for the IP for www.sans.org. server1.sans.org happens to
"own" the DNS record for www.sans.org and can return the IP address associated with www.sans.org to dns.my.com. At long last, dns.my.com delivers the
response to host.my.com.

TCPdump has a unique format that contains necessary insight into what is
happening between DNS connections. Look at the next section to help you
decipher the TCPdump output.

Strange TCPdump Notation

Look at the exchange between dns.my.com and h.root-servers.net that follows:

```
dns.my.com.53 > h.root-servers.net.53: 12420 (30) (DF)
h.root-servers.net.53 > dns.my.com.53: 12420- 0/3/3 (153) (DF)
```

The first line of TCPdump output is the query from dns.my.com to the root
server. The first field that you have not seen before in conventional TCPdump
output is the number 12420, following the colon after destination port 53.
This is the DNS identification number. It is a unique identifying number that
a DNS server or client uses to match a query and response. dns.my.com issues
the request to the root server with the number 12420, and when it receives a
response, it can pair it to the request. You have to be aware that a busy
dns.my.com is probably doing a lot of other queries while it is doing yours, so
it has to be able to match multiple queries with responses. The length of the
UDP payload (not including the IP or UDP headers) is 30 bytes. And, the
Don't Fragment (DF) flag is set so that this datagram won't be fragmented.

The response to query 12420 follows. A dash after 12420 signifies that
recursion was not desired. This means that dns.my.com told the root server
that it wanted a response that referenced where the next DNS server is—it did
not want the root server to pursue finding the response itself.

Root servers are very busy computers, processing many initial DNS requests, and they cannot process queries in a recursive fashion like dns.my.com can. Root servers are only expected to give whatever knowledge they have about a good reference in pursuit of the answer. If you were hopelessly lost in a city somewhere and came across a policeman directing traffic at a busy intersection, you would know better than to ask him directions to Aunt Sadie's place. If you had the poor sense to ask, the best you could hope for is a general hasty reference to a gas station that could give you better directions.

In the response from the root server, you see some strange output in the format of 0/3/3. This says that there were zero answer records, meaning no IP address was found, but three authority records were found and three additional records were found. An authoritative server is one that "owns" and maintains records for a given domain. You don't see this in the TCPdump output, but the three authoritative servers (server1.sans.org, ns.BSDI.COM, and ns.DELOS.com) and the three additional records are shown with the pairing of the authoritative DNS servers with their IP addresses.

ARTHORITY RECORDS
sans.org	nameserver = server1.sans.org
sans.org	nameserver = ns.BSDI.COM
sans.org	nameserver = ns.DELOS.COM

ADDITIONAL RECORDS
server1.sans.org	Internet address = 167.216.198.40
ns.BSDI.COM	Internet address = 206.196.44.241
ns.DELOS.COM	Internet address = 65.102.83.117

The section, "Using DNS for Reconnaissance," shows you how to use the **nslookup** command to discover this information. By sending the IP addresses in additional records, when using the returned authoritative name servers, subsequent resolutions are unnecessary to translate those returned host names to IP addresses. Any one of those DNS servers has authority for the sans.org domain and can answer the query. As you saw, dns.my.com selects the first one, server1.sans.org, to use for the final resolution.

Finally, examine the remainder of the TCPdump output from the resolution process:

```
dns.my.com.53 > server1.sans.org.53: 12421+ (30) (DF)
server1.sans.org.53 > dns.my.com.53: 12421* 1/3/3 (172)
dns.my.com.53 > host.my.com.1716: 1* 1/3/3
(197) (DF)
```

dns.my.com has been informed that there are several authoritative servers, and it selects the first one, server1.sans.org, for resolution. It issues a new query 12421 and asks for recursion, noted by the plus sign. Essentially, dns.my.com has tasked server1.sans.org to find the IP address. In this case, server1.sans.org is an authoritative name server for www.sans.org, so it can answer the query itself. If it were not the authoritative name server, however, it would be asked to find the IP address by recursively issuing queries to other name servers until an IP address was found. Not all DNS servers are configured to perform recursive queries; so even though recursion might be desired, it is not necessarily done.

server1.sans.org responds to the query. The asterisk means that this is an authoritative response. This says that the record for www.sans.org is in the DNS database that server1.sans.org maintains. One answer is returned—in this case, the IP address of www.sans.org, 12.33.247.6. You do not see the IP in the TCPdump output, but that is what is in the payload of the UDP datagram. The three authority records and three additional records that were previously discussed are returned here too. Lastly, after dns.my.com has the IP address, it returns it to host.my.com, the original querier.

Caching: Been There, Done That

This section briefly explains what happens to received responses. DNS servers cache or save responses that they receive. This makes the resolution process more efficient if the same DNS queries do not have to be repeated over and over again. This also potentially reduces the number of hits that other DNS servers take responding to queries. Chances are pretty good that the same host name to IP resolution that was requested once may be requested again soon thereafter. But, as you will soon see in the section, "Cache Poisoning," these savings, gained by caching responses, will open up some security risks if cached responses are not authentic and valid.

If you were to ask for the www.sans.org web page again soon after the first request, the resolution process would differ a little. Your host still issues a gethostbyname call to resolve the IP address for www.sans.org. When dns.my.com receives this request, however, it checks its cache as usual before trying to resolve it. If everything is working correctly, dns.my.com finds the record residing in cache and returns the IP address to host.my.com.

How long do cached records stay around on the DNS server? Well, it depends. Each cached record might have a different life span. It turns out that each response of a DNS resource record has a DNS time-to-live (TTL) value. Don't confuse this TTL value with the IP header TTL. They represent two very different and distinct functions. The DNS TTL value is set by the responding DNS server and cached by the receiving name server for the TTL time value. DNS servers that update records often are more likely to have lower TTL values than relatively static servers have.

Berkeley Internet Name Daemon

Berkeley Internet Name Daemon (BIND) is the *de facto* standard DNS implementation in use on the Internet today. Older versions of BIND are 4.x.x, whereas the more current versions are 8.x.x and 9.x.x. When you observe DNS servers that communicate with both source and destination ports of 53, it is usually indicative of the default behavior of BIND 4.x.x. By default, BIND versions 8 and later assign an ephemeral source port greater than 1023 in a querying DNS server datagram, similar to the behavior that you witnessed with other client applications, such as telnet.

However, BIND versions 8 and later can be configured to mimic version 4 behavior by using a default source port of 53. This is done using the **query-source address * port 53** configuration file substatement. Some sites find that this configuration better suits existing firewall/router access rules.

Reverse Lookups

Occasionally, you will be given an IP address and want to see whether it resolves to a host name. This is done via a gethostbyaddr call by the client resolver.

Remember, DNS is a distributed hierarchy of responsibility, and resolution begins at the root node and continues down in the DNS tree. You saw top-level domain nodes, such as .org, .mil, .edu, and so forth. A special domain has been reserved for resolution of IP addresses to host names. At the top-level domain, this is the arpa suffix. A second-level domain follows, known as in-addr. The tree expands outward beneath this for the legal first octets in the IP address, as you see in Figure 6.5. In the case of the IP for www.sans.org, for instance, the first octet is 12. Beneath this follows a subtree with the next node of 33, the second octet of the www.sans.org IP address. Continuing with this logic, the 247 and 6 nodes for the final two octets fall below. Only this subtree is examined in this example, but this subtree spans all the possible IP addresses just as the other top-level domains begin the expansion of all the host names.

Resolutions of IP to host name are known as reverse lookups. When DNS attempts a reverse lookup for 12.33.247.6, the application software reformats this as a query to 6.247.33.12.in-addr.arpa. The order of the octets is reversed to conform to the host name notation. For name www.sans.org, the name is formulated by starting at the bottom of the DNS tree with node www, moving up to node sans, and topping out at node org. Similarly, with the IP address, you must move from the most specific to the most general.

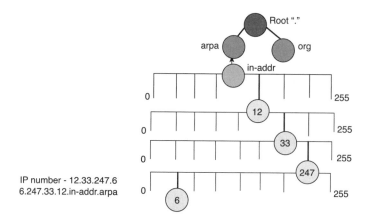

Figure 6.5 Reverse lookups, IP address to host name.

Master and Slave Name Servers

Each domain must have a master server, upon which database records of names and IP addresses are maintained. Then, for redundancy sake, one or more slave servers are often created in case the master server ever goes down. If there is no redundancy built in and the only DNS server for a particular domain were to go down, no queries could be answered for hosts in that domain. Unless entries were cached at other DNS sites, resolution of hosts in the domain whose DNS server was down could not be accomplished. Slave servers can share the load of responding to queries with a fully functioning master name server.

DNS information is maintained on the master server in flat text files. The slave name servers periodically contact the master name server to see whether any updates have been made for a particular domain. If so, the slave servers with older versions of BIND download all information for that domain, even if only one record has been modified. Newer versions of BIND will allow incremental updates that will download only changed records.

Zone Transfers

This section examines how changes are propagated from the master to the slave name server. When the slave server restarts, or when it periodically queries the master server and finds updated records, a zone transfer is performed between the master and slave servers.

This is just a transfer of the zone maps or DNS records from the master server to the slave server. Unlike most DNS transactions, this is done using

TCP because there is potentially a lot of data and reliable delivery is important. The zone transfer seems like an innocuous process. It usually is between
the same domain master and slave servers. Yet, what if a hacker could do a
zone transfer of your domain data for your internal hosts? This would give
him all the IP addresses and hosts in your domain. This is very valuable data
that should not be readily available to anyone.

Obviously, you would like to try to prevent this kind of misuse. You can do
this in a couple of ways. In versions of BIND 4.9.3 and later, configuration
parameters enable the DNS administrator to specify IP addresses or subnets
authorized to do zone transfers. BIND 4.9.x has an xfernets directive, and
BIND 8 and 9 have an allow-transfer substatement to control zone transfers.

If your version of BIND does not support this feature, another option is to
block inbound traffic to TCP port 53. This block prevents transfers, but might
block other legitimate data as well (as discussed in the very next section). If
this is your only option, however, it is preferable to prevent the zone transfer,
even at the expense of blocking other legitimate data.

UDP or TCP

As discussed earlier, typically, DNS traffic is sent using UDP because answers
are often succinct, and a best-delivery effort can be tolerated because responses
to DNS queries not received can be reissued. Because there is more data for
zone transfers, and reliable exchange is required, they are an exception to the
UDP protocol and are done using TCP.

The maximum allowable size for a UDP DNS payload response is 512
bytes. What happens if the data contained in the DNS message exceeds 512
bytes? First, the response is returned with the truncated bit turned on. This bit
is found in the flags field spanning offset bytes 2 and 3 of the DNS message:

```
dns.my.com.53 > dns.verbose.com.53: 18033 (43) (DF)
dns.verbose.com.53 > dns.my.com.53: 18033¦ 7/0/0 (494)
dns.my.com.37404 > dns.verbose.com.53: S 518696698:518696698(0) win 8760 <mss
1460> (DF)
dns.verbose.com.53 > dns.my.com.37404: S 199578733:199578733(0) ack 518696699
win 8760 <mss 1460> (DF)
```

In the preceding output, look carefully at the second line of TCPdump output. The response is from dns.verbose.com to dns.my.com. After the DNS
identification number, 18033, you see a vertical line, or UNIX pipe symbol.
This is the notation that TCPdump uses to alert you that the DNS record has
been truncated. The response of seven resource records would have exceeded
the 512-byte payload limit. You see that 494 bytes of payload are returned,
consisting of complete answers that do not exceed the limit.

Therefore, dns.my. com reissues the DNS query using TCP. You see the attempted SYN connection from dns.my.com to dns.verbose.com. dns. verbose.com responds with a SYN/ACK, indicating that it is listening on port 53. The information is then transferred using TCP as the protocol.

Some sites will block all inbound TCP traffic with either a source or destination port of 53 to prevent unauthorized zone transfers. But, this will also block any queried external DNS server from resolving large responses. That is what happens in the preceding output. The fourth line in the previous output shows the packet with the SYN/ACK from dns.verbose.com that got blocked. Our packet-filtering device in front of dns.my.com blocks a TCP connection from dns.verbose.com source port domain (53). That is why the three-way handshake is never completed and the large DNS response is never delivered. To avoid this problem, block traffic to TCP destination port 53 only and allow traffic from TCP source port 53 that has an already established connection.

Summary of DNS Theory

DNS relies on a complex interweaving of many DNS servers. You must be able to examine traffic to and from your DNS server to understand the nature of the activity. TCPdump is an adequate tool to use; but at times, you have to use other tools to examine the content of the datagrams to see whether problems exist. Typical DNS servers on active networks receive a lot of traffic, and hackers can use the volume of normal activity as a smoke screen for malicious activity.

Using DNS for Reconnaissance

Given the notion that DNS is a global database, it is an excellent source for reconnaissance. DNS information is intended to be freely shared and freely available in the spirit of cooperation. At one time in the evolution of the Internet, this was a relatively innocuous philosophy. In today's climate of hungry pirates, however, it seems quite naive. Here are some ways in which reconnaissance can be done using DNS.

The nslookup Command

nslookup acts much like a DNS client would, but displays the information so that you can see it. In fact, that is how the authoritative name server host names and IP addresses for the sans.org domain were obtained. This is a very helpful interactive tool that can be used on a UNIX or Windows NT (and beyond) host. Some UNIX operating systems are beginning to replace the **nslookup** command with the **dig** (Domain Internet Groper) command.

You can ask many more questions of a DNS server than just the host name. Using nslookup, you can formulate queries and see the kinds of responses you get. There is also a debug setting that enables you to see more of the data in the DNS message that is sent and returned than just the query and response values.

Look at the following output to get an idea of the capabilities of the nslookup tool. You see host.my.com issue the **nslookup** command. You then enter into the nslookup interactive process and receive notification of the default DNS server, dns.my.com and its associated IP address (192.168.4.4) used to resolve your queries. The output follows:

```
host.my.com% nslookup
Default Server:  dns.my.com
Address:  192.168.4.4

> www.sans.org
Server:  dns.my.com
Address:  192.168.4.4

Name:    www.sans.org
Address:  12.33.247.6
```

At the greater than (>) prompt, www.sans.org is entered to find its IP address. Again, you get confirmation of the DNS server and IP address being used to resolve the query. You see the answer below that of 12.33.247.6.

Name That Name Server

How does someone discover what your DNS server is? Given the number of reconnaissance attempts targeting DNS servers only, there must be a way to find out. Actually, it is rather easy to find this out using nslookup:

```
> set type=ns
> sans.org
Server:  dns.my.com
Address: 192.168.4.4

NON-AUTHORITATIVE ANSWER
sans.org        nameserver = NS.DELOS.COM
sans.org        nameserver = server1.sans.org
sans.org        nameserver = NS.BSDI.COM
```

```
AUTHORITATIVE ANSWERS CAN BE FOUND FROM
NS.DELOS.COM      Internet address = 65.102.83.117
server1.sans.org  Internet address = 167.216.198.40
NS.BSDI.COM       Internet address = 206.196.44.241
```

Assuming that you are at a subcommand prompt of the **nslookup** command, enter the subcommand **set type=ns**. You have just set the option to return an answer of a name server(s) to subsequent queries issued. Bump up one node on the DNS tree and query for sans.org to see the name servers for this domain. You discover all the name servers for sans.org, both host names and IP addresses. This appears to be a pretty good place to start the reconnaissance effort for a site. After discovering the name servers, one might scan those name servers for potential security deficiencies or to see what kind of Internet services or daemons are being run on the DNS server.

HINFO: Snooping for Details

HINFO records are yet another record type stored by DNS. These are information records and another potential source for reconnaissance. A DNS server administrator has the option of entering host information, specifically the CPU type and operating system, when creating a new or maintaining an existing DNS record. If trusted intranet hosts use the DNS server, this is a way to maintain an inventory of the hosts without too much risk.

Because this provides too much information to unknown Internet users, many administrators do not enter these parameters. Obviously, if this type of information can be harvested from a DNS server, a hacker can get some serious intelligence about the site.

```
> set type=hinfo
> host49
Server:  dns.my.com
Address:  192.68.4.4

host49.my.com CPU = SunSparc          OS = Solaris
my.com nameserver =dns.my.com
dns.my.com     Internet address = 192.68.4.4
```

Set the type to **hinfo** as a subcommand in nslookup. Information is queried for host49, which is a fictional renaming of a real host. host49.my.com is a Sun SPARC running a version of the Solaris operating system. It is possible that a hacker's efforts might be foiled by outdated data kept in the HINFO records. This is probably one of the few times that less-than diligent maintenance is a desirable thing.

List Zone Map Information

One of the easiest ways to discover a lot of information about a domain is to try to list all the zone map information. Assume that there is a domain with the lackluster name of fakeplace.com. You can attempt to dump the records associated with the domain using the following subcommand in the nslookup utility:

```
> ls -d fakeplace.com
```

If the site has not disabled the dissemination or transfer of the data, the DNS server lists all records for the domain fakeplace.com. As a bonus to the information collector, this site also maintains HINFO records.

```
whish      1D IN HINFO       "SGI" "Irix"
1D IN A               192.168.1.239
susie      1D IN HINFO       "IBM-RS/560F" "unix"
1D IN A               172.16.16.13
pixie      1D IN HINFO       "IBM-RS/560F" "unix"
1D IN A               172.12.16.14
bandit     1D IN HINFO       "PC" "Win98"
1D IN A               192.168.3.107
adder      1D IN HINFO       "IBM-RS/530" "unix"
1D IN A               172.16.133.4
hub21      1D IN HINFO       "Cabletron-MMAC3" "SNMP"
1D IN A               192.168.26.80
switch3    1D IN HINFO       "Switch" "3COM"
1D IN A               192.168.7.130
```

This information harvesting can occur only if the site allows indiscrimate access to TCP destination port 53, because TCP is the transport protocol used to deliver this information.

Dig

Another information gathering technique is to query a DNS server for its BIND version number:

```
dns.my.com% dig @MYDNS.COM version.bind txt chaos

; <<>> dig 8.1 <<>> @MYDNS.COM version.bind txt chaos
; (1 server found)
;; res options: init recurs defnam dnsrch
;; got answer:
;; ->>HEADER<<- opcode: QUERY, status: NOERROR, id: 10
;; flags: qr aa rd ra; QUERY: 1, ANSWER: 1, AUTHORITY: 0, ADDITIONAL: 0
;; QUERY SECTION:
;;      version.bind, type = TXT, class = CHAOS

;; ANSWER SECTION:
VERSION.BIND            0S CHAOS TXT    "4.9.7-REL"
```

A tool called **dig** (which stands for Domain Internet Groper) comes with many implementations of BIND. It has many of the same capabilities as nslookup. You have an option to display the version number of BIND running on a DNS server. The format of the command is as follows: **dig** followed by the at sign (**@**), followed by the name of the DNS server you want to examine, followed by the option **version.bind**, followed by the word **TXT** and the word **CHAOS**. The word **TXT** tells DNS that the type of entry you are searching for is a TXT record found in the DNS database. This is just a different record type, much as HINFO records and NS records are different types. Finally, you see the word **CHAOS**, which is a query class that is mostly obsolete.

This **dig** command has queried for the version number of MYDNS.com. You see that it is running an older version 4.9.7 of BIND. For someone conducting reconnaissance, this is valuable information. If a hacker can pair a BIND vulnerability with the version discovered, she is better able to target the name server for attack. BIND versions 8.2 and later have an options statement in the configuration file /etc/named.conf that will return a message instead of the version number. You select the contents of the message, perhaps something like "unknown version of BIND." But, if you feel mischievous, your message can return the wrong version of BIND just to confuse the information gatherer.

Tainting DNS Responses

As discussed earlier, DNS requires the cooperation of many unknown or untrusted hosts to function properly. You have to blindly trust that the response received to a DNS query is genuine. Unfortunately, this is not always the case. This section presents a sampling of DNS problems and perversions related to DNS record authentication.

A Weak Link

One of the weaknesses in using host names to allow or deny access to a given service is that if a host can assume a bogus identity of a trusted host, all authentication can be subverted. Think of the types of access allowed based on host name or perhaps on an entire domain name. Do you allow access to an intranet web server for all internal hosts because they are part of your domain? Or, do you use UNIX hosts that allow access without user ID and password authentication based on a trusted host name? That can be very risky behavior if true identities are altered to masquerade as trusted hosts. A host name can be changed on a host itself, on a DNS server that has been compromised and altered until discovered, or on a DNS server temporarily by corrupting a cached DNS record.

Versions of BIND, beginning with BIND 8.3, include DNS Security Extensions (DNSSEC) to provide better authentication mechanisms based on cryptographic signatures to validate the integrity and origin of DNS data. To authenticate a set of responses, a responding DNS server will "sign" them by encrypting a hashed incarnation of the set of responses with the DNS zone's private key. This signature will be returned to the resolver via a new resource record known as SIG. The resolver needs to get the DNS server's public key for the appropriate zone, which is done using another new resource record known as KEY. After it is obtained, the recipient decrypts the signature using the public key to obtain the original hash of the data. The recipient then computes its own hash of the received set of responses, using the same algorithm the DNS server used. It compares the response it receives, and if it matches the decrypted one from the server, it means that the data has not been altered and it is from the professed source.

Cache Poisoning

A Computer Emergency Response Team (CERT) advisory (CA-97.22, issued in August 1997) warns of a vulnerability in versions of BIND. Versions before release 8.1.1 were vulnerable to caching malicious or misleading data from a remote server. A hostile user could use a remote DNS server to put incorrect DNS records in the cache of a victim DNS server.

For this to happen, first, an evil user must force your vulnerable local name server to query the evil user's hacked DNS server. The query is for some innocent piece of information, but the response contains corrupted resource records that your vulnerable DNS server caches.

This "poisoned" data is then returned in any responses for the poisoned record asked of the tainted DNS server. The cache-poisoning techniques are used to corrupt the mapping between host names and IP addresses.

Another of the cache-poisoning exploits is successful because it sends answers with a query record. When any type of DNS traffic is sent, a DNS message is contained in the datagram. The same DNS message format is used for both queries and responses. It appears that some errant versions of BIND cache whatever they find in the response section of the DNS message. They don't check to make sure that the record is a response and not a query. The evil user sends a query to your vulnerable DNS server with poisoned answers in the query, and the DNS server caches these tainted responses.

Figure 6.6 shows an example of how cache poisoning can work. Suppose there is a wicked user who crafts a DNS message with a response in the request. This same user can then send a query using the source host evil.dns.net and the destination DNS server of ns04.baweb.com, the authoritative name server for www.hillary2000.org.

This crafted packet has a query for the IP address of www.hillary2000.org, but it includes an IP address in the response part of the DNS message, which gives the IP address of 206.245.150.74. This is not the real IP address associated with www.hillary2000.org, as you will soon see.

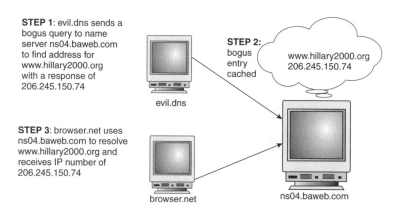

Figure 6.6 DNS cache poisoning.

ns04.baweb.com suffers from the inability to tell query from response, and therefore caches the answer it received in the query. Its cache has just been poisoned with a bogus host name and IP pairing. Now, to complete the ruse, there must be a DNS server on behalf of a user or process that consults ns04.baweb.com for the IP address for www.hillary2000.org. In response, the cached answer of 206.245.150.74 is returned.

This is a real-world example in alleged political cyber-warfare. In July 1999, Hillary Clinton launched a web site, www.hillary2000.org, which promoted her to-be-declared run for the U.S. Senate from New York.

When some users attempted to contact this site, however, they were redirected to a rival site, www.hillaryno.com (IP address 206.245.150.74). The supporters of then New York City mayor Rudolph Giuliani maintained this site. (Mayor Giuliani, at the time of these mysterious occurrences, was an undecided contender for the same seat; he subsequently decided not to run.)

The speculation is that this might have been a cache-poisoning hack that successfully diverted Hillary supporters to the Giuliani page. In other words, www.hillary2000.org was paired with the IP address for www.hillaryno.com. Of course the people who maintained the www.hillaryno.com site, disavowed all knowledge of any wrongdoing.

So, you see that the arsenal of political dirty tricks has now entered the realm of cyberspace. This would be a very hard kind of hack to trace or prove if the cache were poisoned to reroute users.

Summary

DNS is a distributed hierarchy of name servers that provides different types of resolutions, such as IP addresses and host names. Unlike typical client/server interactions, the resolution of a DNS query might involve multiple DNS servers and multiple connections. And, unlike other client/server interactions, DNS might use UDP, or TCP, or both as the transport protocol to do resolutions.

DNS servers can provide a wealth of reconnaissance information because historically, DNS servers have been the purveyors of host name to IP address pairing information. Sadly, as the Internet has become less safe and less trusted, it is best to silence DNS servers by offering only limited information.

BIND software has a notorious history of security problems. Several exploits have been discovered in recent years that have allowed root level access from buffer overflow attacks. But, it is pretty much impossible to use the Internet today without some kind of interaction with DNS. This doesn't mean that you should innocently trust answers received from other DNS servers, but you should certainly safeguard your own DNS server as much as possible. Upgrade your DNS server to the newest versions, take advantage of the latest security features, and configure your site's DNS servers to restrict the information shared.

II

Traffic Analysis

7

Packet Dissection Using TCPdump

T HE NEXT FOUR CHAPTERS EXPLORE USING TCPDUMP to analyze network traffic. TCPdump provides some wonderful benefits when used with a signature-based NIDS in a network. Most often, when signature-based NIDS detect some kind of anomalous activity, it is due to a pre-defined signature discovering a malicious packet. Typically, the NIDS will alert on the activity and perhaps capture the single packet that it perceives to contain an event of interest.

There are several problems with this method. First, as anyone who has ever used a NIDS knows, these systems are prone to generating alerts when there really is no problem. This is known as a false positive. The reason that many NIDS generate false positives is because signatures are not specific enough and the packet is not examined in context with those that precede it or those that follow.

It really is helpful to have a tool such as TCPdump running in the background capturing traffic into and out of the network—kind of like a traffic audit trail. Although TCPdump, by default, doesn't capture the entire packet, you still have much of the pertinent information captured in the headers—where the traffic came from, where it is going, and what the purpose of the packet is. The signature-based NIDS can inspect the packet on its own for payload anomalies.

The captured TCPdump traffic can be used to distinguish real alerts from false positives. Assuming that your NIDS affords you access to the signature and access to the packet that caused the alert to fire, you can examine the given packet for problems. Additionally, you can use the TCPdump traffic collected before and after the alert to assist in the assessment. There have been many times when examining collected TCPdump records has provided the extra detail to allow more accurate assessments of alerts generated by a NIDS.

The quest is to become proficient at doing analysis of traffic apart from a NIDS, which is what the next four chapters will teach you.

We start off with the most basic analysis possible—looking at the packet at the bit level. Chapter 8, "Examining IP Header Fields," will show you how to dissect a packet for the rare occasion when a packet-sniffing tool is not adequate for packet interpretation. Next, Chapters 9, "Examining Embedded Protocol Header Fields," and 10, "Real-World Analysis," discuss another level of interpretation—examining fields in the packet. As we discovered when looking at TCP/IP, it is impossible to tell what is abnormal unless we are familiar with what is normal. The same goes for understanding the fields in a packet. Next, in Chapter 11, "Mystery Traffic," we will move one layer higher in the analysis process by looking at the packet as a whole. In other words, discovering the intent of the packet. After we have completed this topic, we will look at some real-world events from monitored traffic using TCPdump. Here, we will study a synthesis of packets to understand some incidents. Finally, Chapter 12, "Writing TCPdump Filters," looks at beginning forensics in an attempt to further explain a specific real-world event. We will delve into passive fingerprinting and try to determine if activity has been spoofed or is from many different real sources.

Background Activity Isn't Always Noise

As mentioned many times in the book, a NIDS is required for detecting pre-defined anomalous behavior, whether it is some suspicious payload in a packet or some violation of protocol. Although there are NIDS that can be configured to dynamically capture packets after the suspicious one, NIDS do not save packets that are of no current interest. That is why the use of TCPdump or any other tool that can capture background traffic is advocated. There will be events of interest that might not have pre-defined signatures.

Years ago, I was a member of a military CERT team when we received an email from an administrator of another site who informed us that he believed that a computer from our network had been used to break into a computer on his network. He supplied us with the alleged date, time, source, and destination IPs. He gave us one other valuable piece of information: he believed a user account with the name of Darren had been added to the password file. Immediately, we researched the complaint and discovered that the source IP from our network alleged to be involved was a static IP associated with our dial-in pool of addresses. This was many years ago, before DHCP was in vogue. The owner of the IP address was a well-respected manager who seemed the antithesis of the stereotypical hacker. We asked around and discovered the man had a teenage son named Darren. With no sense of culpability or shame, the employee readily admitted to the security officer that he'd given his military dial-in account number, username, and password to his son. Yet, he vehemently denied that his son would be involved in hacking.

At that point, it was up to the security team to prove any guilt. We began our efforts by searching the TCPdump records from the day and time of the incident, and several days before and after to amass a profile of the use of the IP. We discovered that the source IP had connected to the destination IP reported by the system administrator and that the user of the source IP had visited literally hundreds of pornography sites as well. But the activity of the user of the IP had set off no alerts on the NIDS. Only the audit trail of TCPdump records allowed us to resolve the complaint.

Think about the use of alarms in department stores. Most are equipped with some kind of burglar alarm to sound if there is a break-in or intrusion after hours. And, most have a device that alarms on your way out of the store if you haven't deactivated some kind of indicator by paying for a piece of merchandise. So, the department store alarms are equipped to alert on some pre-defined conditions.

Yet, department stores also have video cameras at doors or other locations in the store. These cameras record an audit trail of activity that might be entirely unrelated to break-ins and thefts. I remember a news report about a sought-after kidnapper who had used his credit card number at a Wal-Mart. This same Wal-Mart had cameras that captured his and the kidnapped child's images on video. His activity didn't set off any alarms, yet having the background tape of store activity assisted law enforcement in identifying and capturing the kidnapper.

Why Learn to Do Packet Dissection?

With all the tools, both free and commercial, available to do packet interpretation for you, why is it necessary to re-invent the wheel by performing your own packet dissection? If programs such as Ethereal can perform every layer of interpretation from the frame header to protocol decodes appropriate for the packet's particular payload, why would you even need to know how to interpret hex or bit output of the packet? Well, these are excellent and accurate dissection tools when you have a packet with expected values and predictable pedestrian behavior. When someone crafts a packet with unusual or unexpected values, these tools might fall far short of being accurate.

As an example, early in 2001, a program known as sidestep was released by Robert Graham, a Chief Technical Officer (CTO) of an NIDS company. The assertion of the author that was demonstrated by sidestep was that NIDS must be protocol-aware so that they will not be susceptible to techniques used to elude detection. There is a derogatory term *network grep*, or *packet grep*, that is used to describe a NIDS that simply looks for a string of characters in a packet as a signature for discovering malicious activity. The UNIX **grep** command searches for a string of characters in text or files, hence the term network grep. If a NIDS is not protocol-aware, it might be duped by simple manipulations of payload.

Sidestep can be run in evasive mode for different protocols such as DNS, RPC, and several others to prove the author's point. In the DNS evasive mode, sidestep queries a DNS server for the version of BIND it is running. A DNS server readily responds to this if it has not been silenced from giving out this potentially valuable information. If a normally formatted version of BIND query is issued, most NIDS detect this by looking for the string "07version04bind". The numeric prefixes, also known as labels, seen before "version" and "bind" simply tell how many characters are found in the following node.

RFC 1035 explains the use of pointers in DNS payloads. The legitimate use of pointers is found in a DNS response when there are multiple records returned with repeated information. For instance, what if you issued a query that returned several hosts with a node of veryveryverylongname? If you have host1.veryveryverylongname.com returned as a first response, a second response that needs to reference host2.veryveryverylongname.com can include the node host2 and point to the position of the occurrence of veryveryverylongname.com in the first response. This obviously shortens the response quite a bit, especially if you have several responses with veryveryverylongname.com in them. If you want more details on the concept of using pointers in a DNS query, look at the section, "Sidestep DNS Queries."

Pointers can be used in queries as well for evasion purposes, as demonstrated by running sidestep. It is no longer necessary to have the node "version" precede the node "bind" in the string of characters in the DNS query. Pointers can direct the decoding of the query so that the node "bind" could precede the node "version" in order, but not in the order in which they are decoded by the DNS server. The DNS server happily responds to a query with pointers, yet a NIDS that does a network grep for "07version04bind" is blind to the query.

Before all of this was discovered, I tried to understand the evasive machinations employed by sidestep. I ran the code in evasive mode and used Ethereal. Ethereal was great at doing packet capture and decoding all the normal behaviors and values, but it was as clueless as I was when it came to discovering the evasive techniques used. At that point, I was decoding bits and reading RFCs. Indeed, most times, you will not be involved in this type of sleuth work, and your packet sniffers/decoders will be excellent and reliable tools. Yet, for the rare times when they fail, you will be left to your own wiles to understand the packets, which is why we are about to discuss packet dissection. And, if you aren't convinced that learning packet dissection is worthwhile, another benefit is that it helps you become infinitely more familiar with the protocol that you are analyzing.

Sidestep DNS Queries

To get a better understanding of the need for a NIDS to be protocol savvy, we'll examine DNS queries that are formed by running sidestep. First, most NIDS, whether protocol aware or not, should catch a normal query. The evasive query will be discussed next to contrast it with the normal query and demonstrate that a NIDS that looks for strings in a packet would probably miss the clever manipulations employed.

Normal Query

Let's examine the output that was generated by TCPdump from the sidestep program using a normal query. This is displayed in standard TCPdump output followed by a hexadecimal dump of the packet to understand the context of the activity:

```
12:39:30.027400 10.100.100.201.1128 > DNS.SERVER.domain:  10+ TXT CHAOS)?
version.bind. (30)

4500 003a 052c 0000 8011 c056 0a64 64c9     E..:.,.....V.dd.
0a64 6402 0468 0035 0026 6325 <000a 0100     .....h.5.&c%....
0001 0000 0000 0000 0776 6572 7369 6f6e     .........version
0462 696e 6400 0010 0003>                    .bind.....
```

First you see the standard TCPdump display output of host 10.100.100.201 querying DNS.SERVER on UDP port 53 (domain) with a DNS identification number of 10 and with recursion desired (+) for a TXT type record and a CHAOS class record of version.bind.

Let's examine the hexadecimal output of the actual DNS query. The DNS portion of this packet has been delimited with the < > to easily identify the part of the record we will scrutinize.

DNS questions have a prescribed format. A DNS question has a series of nodes that end in a 00 to form the question. We typically see nodes that are separated by periods when we express a hostname or IP address. For instance, if an IP address resolution were desired for www.yahoo.com, the DNS question that would be generated would treat the name as a series of nodes—www, yahoo, and com. Preceding each node is a byte count that tells how many bytes are in the following node.

The version.bind question that was generated using sidestep's normal option is as follows:

```
0776 6572 7369 6f6e 0462 696e 6400
```

The bolded bytes represent labels. The first label is 07, which means that there should be 7 bytes in the first node of the query. In this instance, the hex characters that follow are the ASCII representation of the node "version". Next, you see a label of 04 meaning that there are 4 bytes in the following node, which is the hex representation of the ASCII "bind". A 00 label ends the query, which is the final label that is seen.

Each question requires a DNS type and class, each of which is a 2-byte field. The various different types and classes can be found in RFC 1035, but for the purposes of the BIND version query, these must be a type of TXT represented by a 16 (or hex 0010) and a class of CHAOS represented as a 3 (or hex 0003). An accessible DNS server that does not prevent version.bind queries will respond to the above query with the version of BIND that is running.

Evasive Query

Let's examine the output that was generated by TCPdump displayed in hexadecimal to understand the evasive activity:

```
12:39:56.674320 10.100.100.201.1129 > DNS.SERVER.domain:  42 (32)

4500 003c 0577 0000 8011 c009 0a64 64c9    E..<.w.......dd.
0a64 6402 0469 0035 0028 e445 <002a 0000    .....i.5.(.E.*..
0001 0000 0000 0000 0756 6572 7369 6f6e    .........Version
c01a 0010 0003 0442 494e 4400>             .......BIND.
        ¦                      ¦
        ¦                      ¦
        ¦                      ¦
        V                      V
   Pointer 26            26 Bytes
   bytes into DNS
   Payload
```

Look at the hex output. You will see the query name (in bold) of evasive mode. The name starts, as before, with a label of 07 followed by the first node of the query. What had previously been all lowercase letters in "version" now is "Version". This would successfully elude any string matching software that does not do uppercase/lowercase conversions.

That is not the entirety of the ruse used here. Look at the next byte: c0. A label has a maximum value of 63 and a hexadecimal c0 is 192 when converted to decimal. Any time that a label has the two high–order bits of the byte set to 1 (a hex c), it is considered a pointer. A pointer is the number of bytes into the

DNS message where the next label (or pointer) is to be found. In this case, we see that the pointer is a hexadecimal 1a or a decimal 26. Therefore, we have to count 26 bytes from the beginning of the DNS message to find the next node. The DNS message is delimited between the < > on the left side of the output.

Moving 26 bytes into the DNS message directs us to the string beginning with 0442 494e 4400. The 04 is the label 26 bytes into the DNS message, and as expected, it is followed by 4 bytes that represent the string "BIND". The query then ends when a label of 00 is encountered. It appears that resolution of the query resumes at the next byte after the first pointer in the query name. This brings us back to the string "0010 0003" that represents the query type of TXT and a query class of CHAOS. This query elicits the version of BIND running on the queried DNS server if the DNS server does not prevent queries for the version of BIND.

Sidestep can be found at www.robertgraham.com/tmp/sidestep.html.

Introduction to Packet Dissection Using TCPdump

When you run TCPdump in standard mode, it will dump the most pertinent fields in the packet. More fields will be collected than displayed in the default 68 bytes of capture (14 bytes for Ethernet frame header and the remainder for the IP packet). Yet, all of the fields will not be displayed unless you ask for TCPdump to display the output in hexadecimal mode using the **–x** command line option. The first thing that you have to do before attempting any kind of packet dissection is arm yourself with the standard layouts of the various kinds of TCP/IP headers such as IP, TCP, UDP, and ICMP. There are many sources of these including the RFCs.

Look at the following output to see a sample of hexadecimal output from TCPdump using the **–x** command line option:

```
11:55:52.069484 192.168.143.5 > 192.168.143.101: icmp: echo request

4500 0054 064b 0000 4001 bc12 c0a8 8f05
c0a8 8f65 0800 620a 850a 0000 889f 4b39
510f 0100 0809 0a0b 0c0d 0e0f 1011 1213
1415 1617 1819
```

It looks like a big jumble of garbage at first glance. Let's begin methodically to describe the output. First, each character you see is a hexadecimal character, as you might have astutely intuited from the fact that we are doing hex output. (Okay, enough sarcasm.) Each hex character can have a value of 0 to 0xf, which corresponds to 0 to 15 decimal. Again, the 0x notation means hexadecimal. And, each hex character is 4 bits, also known as a nibble. That means two hex characters are 8 bits or one byte. Finally, each row of hex dumped by TCPdump has 16 bytes or 32 hex characters.

The trick is "superimposing" this hex output over a standard layout of the fields. In this case, we are looking at an IP header followed by some embedded protocol that we will discover as we progress. Take a look at Figure 7.1. It shows the standard IP header layout that we've examined several times before in the book. Let's just make sure we can look at a field or two before we move on. For instance, the first field you see in the IP header layout is the IP version number, which is 4 bits long. If we look at the previous hex dump, we see that the first hex character is a 4. This is the IP version number or IP version 4.

That was fairly simple. Let's try something a little more advanced. Another very important field is the protocol field found in the IP header. This tells us the embedded protocol that follows the IP header. If you look at Figure 7.1, you'll see that the 8-bit protocol field is found in the third row of the IP header. This layout is different from the hex dump because each row contains 32 bits of output or 4 bytes. No matter, we can still find the displacement of the protocol field from the beginning of the IP header (again, another annoying reminder that we start counting at offset 0). So, each row contains 4 bytes, and we find the protocol is located in the 9th byte offset of the IP header. The 9th byte offset found in the hex dump is 01. A value of 01 in this field means that the ICMP protocol follows the IP header. Other common values that we will examine are a value of 06 means TCP follows, and a hex 11 or decimal 17 means that UDP follows the IP header.

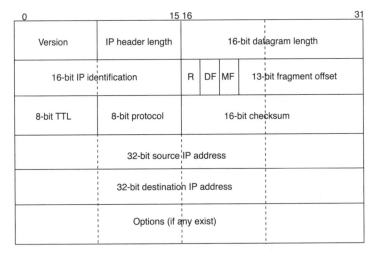

Figure 7.1 IP header layout.

Where Does the IP Stop and the Embedded Protocol Begin?

We just learned how to determine what embedded protocol follows the IP header—a very significant step in doing packet dissection. The next problem we encounter is knowing where headers stop and other parts of the packet begin. A normal IP header with no IP options such as source routing has a length of 20 bytes. An IP header greater than 20 bytes long should contain IP options. The IP header length is found in the 0 byte offset of the IP header in the low-order nibble. This is the hex character that follows the IP version number. But, we find a value of 5 there. How does that relate to a normal 20-byte header? The IP header length is expressed in 32-bit words, meaning that any value found in this field must be multiplied by 4.

Although it would be nice and a whole lot less complicated if all the many lengths fields found in the packet were expressed in bytes, this just isn't the case. You might be thinking (or cursing to yourself), why couldn't the wise creators of TCP/IP have been more merciful and standardized on bytes? The most likely reason is that when TCP/IP was created years ago, hardware and software were much slower and it took longer to send more data, even a couple of bits. The thought was that if bits could be compressed, they could be processed or sent more quickly. So there is some rhyme and reason to what you might perceive as random mayhem.

Now that we know that we have a 20-byte IP header, we count 20 bytes into the hex data that we find in previous hex output. When we deal with length bytes, we have a total of 20 bytes. We aren't concerned about offsets, so we don't need to start counting at 0. We simply count off a number of total bytes, in this case 20. We have 16 bytes in the first row of hex output and need only to count off 4 more in the second row to take us to where the IP header stops and the ICMP header begins in this packet. The ICMP header begins with the first two bytes of 0800.

Other Length Fields

Let's look at some other length fields in the IP packet. Ultimately, we need to know how to interpret these values to be able to decode the packet.

The IP Datagram Length

Another very important field is the IP packet total length. Fortunately, this is expressed in bytes so we don't have to manipulate it in any way. This field is found in the second and third bytes offset of the IP header. The only tricky part is computing this from hex to decimal.

Converting Hex to Decimal

Taking hex output and converting it to decimal might not be intuitive, so we need a review. Any time you need to convert hex to decimal for a field, do the following:

1. Figure out how many hex characters are in the field by examining the protocol layout.

2. Start at the rightmost hex character.

3. Represent each hex character in the field as an increasing power of 16 beginning with an exponent of 0.

4. Multiply each base by exponent and add all individual products.

For instance, in the previous example, we find the value of 0054 in the IP datagram total length. Going step by step to translate it to decimal:

1. The IP datagram length is 16 bits.

2. This is 4 hex characters of output.

3. Start at the rightmost hex character (4).

4. Represent each hex character as an increasing power of 16 (16^0 through 16^3).

5. Multiply each base by exponent and add all individual products.

16^3	16^2	16^1	16^0
0	0	5	4

$5*16^1 + 4*16^0 = 84$

In the previous example, we are looking at the length field. We have 4 hex characters because the length is a 16-bit field. We really only need to label the two rightmost hex characters because they are non-zero. After we do this, we find we have a 4 in the 16^0 position; this is really the 1's position meaning we have 4*1 or 4. The next character of 5 is in the 16^1 position. So, we multiply 5*16 for a product of 80. We add these two products together to get the final result of 84.

TCP Header Length

Like the IP header, the TCP header can also have options. Also, like the IP header length, the TCP header length is found in a nibble that is a representation of 32-bit words. This value, like the IP header length value, must be multiplied by 4 to get the TCP header length. A TCP header with no options is 20 bytes long. The TCP header length is found in the high-order nibble of the 12th byte offset of the TCP header. This is an important value because it determines where the TCP header stops and where the TCP payload begins.

Here is standard output followed by the hex output from a TCP header with no TCP options:

```
15:43:40.705372 1.2.3.4.63220 > 4.3.2.1.139: S 776342897:776342897(0) win
3072

4500 0028 e34f 0000 3a06 e534 0102 0304
0403 0201 <f6f4 008b 2e46 0d71 0000 0000

5002 0c00 b85f 0000>
```

The TCP segment is delimited by the less than and greater than signs. The highlighted value is the TCP header length, and as expected, we find a 5. After we multiply that by 4, we get a standard TCP header of 20 bytes.

Now, look at the hex output for a TCP header with TCP options:

```
15:48:24.620314 1.2.3.4.3088 > 4.3.2.1:139 S 1212214992:1212214992(0) win
32120 <mss 1460,sackOK,timestamp 7748460 0,nop,wscale 0> (DF)

4500 003c 11a8 4000 4006 70c8 0102 0304
0102 0304 <0c10 008b 4840 eed0 0000 0000
a002 7d78 92b4 0000 0204 05b4 0402 080a
0076 3b6c 0000 0000 0103 0300>
```

You see that it has a TCP header length of 0xa, which is a decimal 10. This value multiplied by 4 indicates a TCP header length of 40 bytes. If you look at the standard TCPdump output before the hex dump, you see that this TCP header includes such options as maximum segment size of 1460, selective acknowledgement (sackOK), timestamp, a nop (no operation) to pad to a 4-byte boundary, and a window scale (wscale). These options need to be stored in the TCP header.

Increasing the Snaplen

Here's a question: Why do you only see 54 bytes of output in the following hex output displayed even though the default number of bytes capture is 68? Check it out:

```
4500 0054 064b 0000 4001 bc12 c0a8 8f05
c0a8 8f65 0800 620a 850a 0000 889f 4b39
510f 0100 0809 0a0b 0c0d 0e0f 1011 1213
1415 1617 1819
```

The answer is that TCPdump captures 14 bytes of the Ethernet frame header, yet it does not display them unless explicitly directed. To display the captured frame header use the command **tcpdump −e**:

```
20:55:48.520619 0:10:b5:39:c6:93 0:10:b5:39:c6:9a ip 102
192.168.143.5 > 192.168.143.101: icmp: echo request
```

There will be times that you will be interested in examining the frame header. One of the reasons for this would be to identify the source MAC address to try to determine where the packet came from—a host or perhaps a router.

In the previous output, which uses Ethernet encapsulation defined by RFC 894, the bolded text is a result of the **-e** option. First, you see the source and destination MAC addresses (source MAC of 0:10:b5:39:c6:93 and destination MAC address of 0:10:b5:39:c6:9a). You might be thinking that these are bogus MAC addresses because they are so close together, but they are genuine MAC addresses. These are two Compaq PCs ordered at the same time. The MAC addresses are followed by the type of packet that follows the frame header. Some of the types of traffic you are likely to see are IP, ARP, and RARP (reverse ARP). These fields are all stored in the frame header. The final displayed field is the length, in bytes, of the entire frame including the frame header and the data in the encapsulated frame header. In this case, it is a frame header of 14 bytes and a following IP datagram of 88 bytes to give 102. A value of 0x0800 in the type field indicates an IP datagram follows the frame header. The IP packet must be at least 46 bytes in length and the frame length information is *not* contained anywhere in the Ethernet RFC 894 frame header. The snapshot length, or snaplen for short, is the number of bytes that TCPdump collects. The default snaplen of 68 bytes is usually enough to capture the IP header, embedded protocol header, and some data. But, if there are many options, either IP header options or TCP options, all of the headers might not be captured.

If you want to increase the default snaplen, use the **-s** TCPdump command line option. As a test case, let's say we want to capture the entire datagram for each record we read or process on an Ethernet network. In this case, we need to increase the snaplen to the maximum size of the datagram plus the frame header. Ethernet has a maximum transmission unit of 1500. If you add 14 bytes for the frame header, the snaplen must be 1514 bytes—**tcpdump -s 1514**. Now, to check if we've collected the entire datagram, we run TCPdump with a snaplen of 1514:

```
4500 0054 064b 0000 4001 bc12 c0a8 8f05

c0a8 8f65 0800 620a 850a 0000 889f 4b39
510f 0100 0809 0a0b 0c0d 0e0f 1011 1213

1415 1617 1819 1a1b 1c1d 1e1f 2021 2223
2425 2627 2829 2a2b 2c2d 2e2f 3031 3233
3435 3637
```

If we dump the collected record in hexadecimal, we find we've collected more than the default 54 bytes. The actual datagram length is found in the 2nd and 3rd bytes offset of the IP header. We discover a hex 54 in this field, which we recently computed is a decimal 84 bytes. And, we see that we've collected all 84 bytes.

Dissecting the Whole Packet

We have covered all the fundamentals required to dissect a packet. Okay, get the scalpel out and let's see if we can attempt a couple of IP packet dissections. Here's a short review of what we need to do to accomplish our dissection:

- Identify the embedded protocol in the packet. This is found in the 9th byte offset of the IP header.
- Determine what the embedded protocol is based on the value found.
- Identify where the header(s) stop(s), and examine the IP header length.
    - Tells where the IP header stops and the embedded protocol begins.
- Examine the embedded protocol header length
    - Tells where the embedded protocol payload begins.

One of the first steps in discovering what type of activity is embedded in the datagram is to discern the embedded protocol. Remember, you have an IP header and you will find the embedded protocol in the 9th byte offset into the IP header. Remember that the most common values you will see here are 01 for an embedded ICMP message, 06 for an embedded TCP segment, and a hex 11 or decimal 17 for an embedded UDP datagram.

After you've discovered this, you need to know how many bytes are in the IP header. Usually, this is 20 bytes, but it can be more if there are IP options. The IP header length field is found in the low-order nibble of the 0 byte offset of the IP header. Remember that this is expressed as a 32-bit word, so this value has to be multiplied by 4 to translate to bytes. If you count off this number of bytes into the IP header, you will discover where the IP header stops and the embedded protocol begins.

Next, you need to examine the embedded protocol. You'll have to get the proper header configuration for the protocol and translate the values that you find in the hexadecimal output. For UDP, the header length remains static at 8 and the payload follows. But, a header has a different format depending if the protocol is ICMP, TCP, or UDP.

TCP header lengths can vary, so you'll have to find the TCP header length field. This is 12 bytes offset into the TCP header, specifically, the high-order nibble. Again, like the IP header length, this is expressed as a 32-bit word and the value will have to be multiplied by 4 to convert it to bytes. This informs you where the TCP header stops and the payload starts.

Here is the hex dump of our specimen for dissection:

```
4500 0054 f23b 4000 ff01 d121 0102 0304

0403 0201 0000 9f00 d646 0000 b4cb 863a
```

```
56af 0e00 0809 0a0b 0c0d 0e0f 1011 1213

1415 1617 1819 1a1b 1c1d 1e1f 2021 2223

2425 2627 2829 2a2b 2c2d 2e2f 3031 3233
3435 3637 0000 4e00
```

Let's approach this in two different parts. In the first part, we'll attempt to discover the embedded protocol and the length of the IP header. We see that the embedded protocol is ICMP because we have a 0x01 value (bolded) in the protocol field 9 bytes offset into the IP header. That indicates that an ICMP echo reply message follows the IP header (last 2 bytes of 0201).

Because the IP header is 20 bytes, we discover where the IP header stops and the ICMP header and data begin. The ICMP header begins at the 2 bytes 0000 following the final 2 bytes of the IP header.

In our second step of dissection, we need to examine the ICMP message header. Remember that each individual character you see in the hex output represents a nibble or 4 bits. So, two hex characters are one byte. Use Figure 7.2 to assist in decoding the ICMP message.

When examining ICMP, the ICMP header format can vary depending on the ICMP message type and code. The first two bytes of the ICMP header are really pertinent when trying to assess what type of ICMP message you have. These are the message type and message code fields.

There are many possible different values for these fields that can be found at `www.iana.org/assignments/icmp-protocols`; however, we see a very common one in the above record. An ICMP message with a type of 00 and a code of 00 is an ICMP echo reply. The standard TCPdump output for this output is as follows:

```
1.2.3.4 > 4.3.2.1: icmp: echo reply (DF)
```

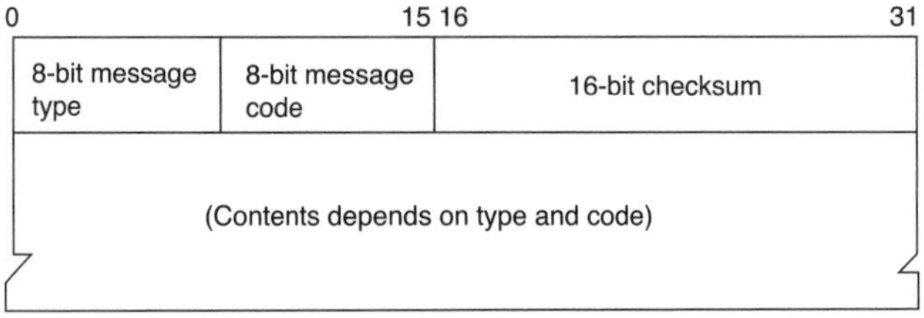

Type	Code	Message
0	0	Echo reply
8	0	Echo request

Figure 7.2 ICMP header layout.

Let's try one more exercise in packet dissection:

```
4500 0030 df3c 4000 8006 633f 0102 0304
0403 0201 0b64 0015 48f3 05b1 0000 0000
7002 2000 50b6 0000 0204 05b4 0101 0402
```

This is a different protocol than ICMP. What is of most interest is the embedded protocol destination port. This tells you the purpose of this particular packet. Although the TCP and UDP headers are different, they share a similar characteristic of having the source port in bytes 0 and 1 offset of the embedded header and the destination port in bytes 2 and 3 offset of the embedded header.

Once again, we find an IP datagram with a 20-byte IP header. But, this time we find that we have TCP as the embedded protocol as ascertained by looking at the bolded protocol field in the previous hex dump.

The significant piece of information that helps us assess the function of the TCP segment is the destination port. This is found in the bolded value of 0015 positioned in offset bytes 2 and 3 of the TCP header.

We determine that the decimal translation is port 21, which is ftp. The destination port field has a hexadecimal value of 0015. To translate this to decimal, we find a 1 in the 16^1 position and a 5 in the 16^0 position. When these 2 values are added, we have 16 + 5, which gives us destination port 21.

So, we have some kind of ftp exchange. This is the beginning of the 3-way handshake so we have no payload. Yet, it helps to look at the TCP header length found in the high-order nibble of the 12th byte offset of the TCP header. A value of 7 is found here and this must be multiplied by 4 to figure out that there is a 28-byte TCP header. This means that there are TCP options; and examining the following standard output of TCPdump for the datagram, we see that there are options of maximum segment size (mss), two nops to pad 4-byte boundaries, and a selective acknowledgement (sackOK):

```
18:26:48.888088 1.2.3.4.2916 > 4.3.2.1.21: S 1223886257:1223886257(0) win
8192 <mss 1460,nop,nop,sackOK> (DF)
```

Freeware Tools for Packet Dissection

Now that you've manually labored your way through packet dissection, here are some excellent tools to help you out. Just to remind you of why we struggled with our own packet dissections at all, you will sometimes find packets that have been crafted and that are not analyzed accurately by tools whose interpretations rely on properly configured packets.

Ethereal

Ethereal is free, available for both Windows and UNIX, and is particularly user-friendly because it has a GUI to assist in navigating the capture and analysis. Ethereal can read TCPdump binary output captured using the **−w** option. It can also use TCPdump filters to selectively capture or display records. Ethereal is an especially useful tool because it allows you to analyze a captured record from many different perspectives.

Figure 7.3 shows a snapshot of Ethereal output. In the top screen, you see a highlighted record. If you move to the middle screen, you can view the frame header, the IP header, and the TCP header, including more information about many of the fields. Also, Ethereal is protocol-aware for many protocols and attempts to interpret the payload according to RFC and protocol specs.

Figure 7.3   Ethereal output.

tcpshow

Tcpshow is good at translating the header field values relieving you of having to know what field is where, computing exact lengths, and figuring out hex values. It also attempts to interpret the payload. If the payload is ASCII, it can be translated. But, there are also services such as NetBIOS that have additional layers of translation that are not done by tcpshow and the output is incoherent. Remember that unless you increase the default snapshot length of 68

bytes, most of the time you will not capture the entire datagram. This means
that not all of the payload will be available for interpretation by tcpshow.

Tcpshow can be run by using the following command:

```
tcpdump  -enx | tcpshow -nolink
```

This command reads TCPdump records from the network and feeds them to
tcpshow. We use the TCPdump options of **-enx** to read the frame header for
interpretation purposes (the **-e** option), not resolve hostnames (the **-n** option),
and dump the output in hex (the **-x** option). The **-nolink** option in tcpshow
says not to display the frame header information like MAC addresses. Here is
some output from an ICMP record that was captured:

```
Packet 1
IP Header
        Version:                    4
        Header Length:              20 bytes
        Service Type:               0x00
        Datagram Length:            40 bytes
        Identification:             0xB5CB
        Flags:                      MF=off, DF=on
        Fragment Offset:            0
        TTL:                        254
        Encapsulated Protocol:      ICMP
        Header Checksum:            0xB229
        Source IP Address:          1.2.3.4
        Destination IP Address:     4.3.2.1

ICMP Header
        Type:                       echo-reply
        Checksum:                   0xBC9C

ICMP Data
        .<Q..........c.
```

As you can see, tcpshow provides a lot of assistance in interpreting a packet. It
decodes the IP header, liberating you from figuring out field displacements,
converting lengths to bytes, and converting hexadecimal to decimal—to name
a few of the functions that it performs. And, it attempts to decode the embedded protocol header and data. In this case, the ICMP data is not ASCII-based
so tcpshow's interpretation is not intelligible. Ethereal is a much better tool to
use to interpret the payload because it is protocol-aware.

TCPdump –X Option

One final tool for payload interpretation is TCPdump itself. Versions of
TCPdump later than 3.4 have a new **-X** option. This simply attempts to interpret payload from hex to ASCII characters. It actually does this for the entire
packet, which is not appropriate for numeric-based fields. But, if your goal is

to interpret ASCII-based payloads, this works well without the use of additional tools such as Ethereal or tcpshow. Here is an example of the output from running TCPdump with the **–X** option:

```
17:21:53.457019 1.2.3.4.ftp > 4.3.2.1.1607: P 1:81(80) ack 1 win 32120 (DF)
[tos 0x10]

0x0000      4510 0078 1691 4000 4006 6b93 0102 0304    E..x..@.@.k.....
0x0010      0403 0201 0015 0647 a940 1471 309a 93ee     ...e...G.@.q0...
0x0020      5018 7d78 14fa 0000 3232 3020 7665 7262    P.}x....220.verb
0x0030      6f20 4654 5020 7365 7276 6572 2028 5665    o.FTP.server.(Ve
0x0040      7273 696f 6e20 7775 2d32 2e35 2e30 2831    rsion.wu-2.5.0(1
0x0050      2920 5475 6520 5365 7020 3231 2031 363a    ).Tue.Sep.21.16:
0x0060      3438 3a31 3220 4544 5420 3139 3939 2920    48:12.EDT.1999).
0x0070      7265 6164 792e 0d0a                        ready...
```

If you look at the rightmost column, you can see the interpretation of the data that has been passed using ftp. You can also see from the first two lines of this column that the header interpretations are incorrect because these are numeric, not ASCII-based values.

Summary

Most of the time, you will find that relying on tools such as Ethereal to decode packets is accurate and pain-free. Ethereal comes with a great GUI interface that allows you to drill down to fields and interpreted values. But, a very rare occasion will arise when more conventional tools are either not available or do not accurately interpret the packet. When you encounter such a situation, you do not want to be intimidated by looking at a nasty hex dump.

Just remember to approach it methodically. You need to get a standard layout for the protocol or header or fields that you want to examine. Then, make sure that you discover the embedded protocol that follows the IP header. Calculate the length of the IP header remembering that the value you find in the IP header field must be multiplied by 4. Then, look at the embedded header and determine the pertinent values in it. Using this approach, you should be able to decipher any hex dump you are given.

8

Examining IP Header Fields

THIS IS THE FIRST OF TWO CHAPTERS that examines fields in the IP packet. This chapter focuses on fields in the IP header, whereas the following chapter looks at fields in the embedded protocol (TCP, UDP, and ICMP) headers. As we continue our journey of looking at traffic from many different perspectives, another view we can assume is to look at the functions of fields in the headers and normal and abnormal values found in those fields. If we are familiar with the purpose of the fields and acquainted with normal values, we should be able to detect mutant or malicious values. When you begin to look at NIDS output or even TCPdump output on a regular basis, this knowledge will come in very handy for detecting problem packets or identifying the nature of malicious traffic.

Insertion and Evasion Attacks

Before we look at individual fields in the IP header, we'll make a digression about types of attacks that might thwart a NIDS' capability to detect malicious activity. As we examine fields in the datagram, we will reference possible insertion or evasion attacks that may be done by manipulating certain field values.

There is a landmark paper written in 1998 called "Insertion, Evasion, and Denial of Service: Eluding Network Intrusion Detection." The authors Thomas Ptacek and Timothy Newsham discuss attacks that can elude detection by the NIDS by using methods of sending traffic that will cause the NIDS and the destination host to interpret packets differently. The paper is an excellent treatise of different conditions that can cause a NIDS to improperly analyze potentially malicious traffic. The authors conducted several different tests against NIDS to prove their theory.

Along with the denial of service of a NIDS, the paper basically discusses the idea of individual attacks to confuse the NIDS. The first is known as insertion. This is where the attacker sends traffic to a target destination host. One or more of the packets sent is accepted or seen by the NIDS, yet it never reaches the destination host; or if it does, the destination rejects it as faulty. The point that the authors make is that the NIDS and the destination host evaluate traffic differently or perhaps even see different traffic.

A second attack is known as evasion. This involves the same idea of sending traffic to a target destination host. Although the destination host sees the same traffic that the NIDS does, it scrutinizes the packets differently than the NIDS. Perhaps the NIDS rejected one or more packets, but the destination host accepted them. Again, the NIDS and the destination host see the traffic differently. Although the term *reject* brings up some semantic issues especially when compared with actions of packet-filtering devices, it is the terminology used in the paper itself. An evasion attack is successful because the NIDS fails to analyze the packet or data in the packet as the destination host does, allowing the destination host to see a packet or data that the NIDS does not.

Insertion Attacks

Examining how an insertion attack might work, let's say we have a NIDS that is on a different network, such as the DMZ, from many of the hosts that it is guarding. Further, let's also say that the NIDS is looking for signatures that might indicate some kind of problem or notable traffic. One of those signatures might be to look for traffic to telnet, TCP port 23, with a content of REWT as a sign of some backdoor account to telnet.

Now, we have an attacker who has remained undetected in planting a Trojan telnet on a target host and now wishes to log in to that host using the REWT account. The attacker has done some reconnaissance on our network and knows more about the network topology and behavior than we care for him to know. It is possible for the attacker to elude notice of the NIDS if he can make the NIDS accept a packet that the end host will not accept or will never see.

In Figure 8.1, the attacker sends three different packets destined for TCP port 23 of the target host, each with one or more characters in the payload. The first contains the letter R, which both the NIDS and the end host receive, examine, and accept. A second character of O is sent that has a bad TCP checksum. Checksums validate the integrity of the packet and if they are not correct, the packet should be discarded. Let's say that the NIDS sees this packet, is not programmed to validate the TCP checksum, and blindly accepts the packet as a valid part of the stream of characters being sent to the destination host. The destination host receives the packet, validates that the TCP checksum is incorrect, and discards the packet. The attacker has managed to insert a character that causes the NIDS to fail to recognize a real attack or action against the end host. Finally, a third packet is sent with a payload of EWT that both the NIDS and the destination host receive and accept.

The NIDS has assembled the TCP stream and concludes it is not a threat because the NIDS does not have a signature for TCP port 23 with a content of ROEWT. Yet, the destination host reassembles this stream as REWT and happily starts a telnet session with a user of REWT that is undetected by the NIDS. Note: This is an oversimplified discussion of this attack; TCP sequence numbers need to be synchronized correctly for this to work properly.

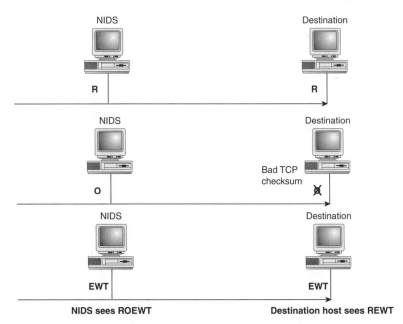

Figure 8.1 A sample insertion attack.

Evasion Attacks

In the case of evasion depicted in Figure 8.2, the destination host sees or accepts a packet that the NIDS rejects. In this case, we are still looking for a telnet session with user REWT to the target destination host. If the attacker can send the traffic in such a manner that the NIDS rejects a packet that the end host accepts, this eludes detection.

A possible scenario for this attack is sending data on the SYN connection. Although not typical of normal connections, sending data on SYN is valid per RFC 793. The data on a SYN connection should later be considered part of the stream after the three-way handshake has been completed. Let's say we have a first packet that arrives on the network with a SYN packet destined for TCP port 23 of our target host. It has a payload of R in the SYN packet. The NIDS only looks for payload after the three-way handshake has been completed, so it totally misses that data. The destination host receives the same packet and knows to store the R for the stream after the three-way handshake is completed. We then have the packets that complete the three-way handshake, each with no data in them, as expected. Finally, we have a normal packet with the letters EWT as the payload destined for the target host TCP port 23.

The result is that the NIDS reassembles the TCP stream for destination host port 23 with a complete payload of EWT. This doesn't match any signature it knows. The destination host, on the other hand, reassembles the stream as REWT and happily starts the Trojaned telnet session.

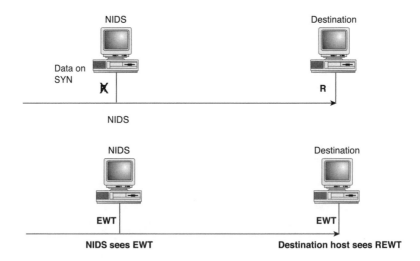

Figure 8.2   A sample evasion attack.

To summarize the paper mentioned earlier, there are many techniques that can be used for insertion and evasion attacks against a NIDS. Although the paper doesn't cover application layer attacks such as HTTP obfuscations, we find that application attacks are a growing trend in evasion. Many of the various attacks are successful just because the NIDS cannot predict the reaction of every possible destination host's TCP/IP stack to various attacks. There are many facets of the TCP/IP stacks that differ among operating systems.

Although keeping track of a lot of this information is feasible for the NIDS, understand that as you require the NIDS to perform more functions and duties, the NIDS will become slower in processing all traffic to the point where it might begin to drop packets. Ultimately, it is a tradeoff of functionality and speed, and speed is the current winner. One way to deal with the possibility of evasion or insertion attacks is to install a host-based IDS on resources that require more protection or scrutiny. The host-based IDS sees the same packets that the host sees, but this is as far as its resistance to evasion goes. The host would still need the application-level savvy to handle application-based evasion attacks.

This paper can be found at: `www.robertgraham.com/mirror/Ptacek-Newsham-Evasion-98.html`.

IP Header Fields

Let's begin our examination of the fields in the IP header. Each field will be discussed in terms of its function, any pertinent information about normal and abnormal values, reconnaissance that may be obtained from examining the field, and evasion or insertion attacks possible using the field.

IP Version Number

The only valid IP version numbers currently in use are 4 and 6, for IPv4 and IPv6, respectively. IPv4 is the most common and pervasive version number thus far. IPv6 is not yet in wide use in user networks in North America, although it is slowly being deployed in the Internet backbone. It is also being used in Europe and Asia.

The IP version field must be validated by a receiving host and if not valid, the datagram is discarded and no error message is sent to the sending host. RFC 1121 states that the datagram must be silently discarded if an invalid value is discovered. So, crafting a datagram with an invalid IP version would serve no purpose other than to test if the receiving host complies with the RFC.

Also, if a packet arrives at a router with an invalid IP version, it should be discarded silently. Using this as a means of an insertion attack is rather difficult unless the attacker is on the same network as the NIDS. If this is the case and a series of packets is sent to the end host with an invalid IP version and a NIDS does not discard them, this is an insertion attack—something the NIDS accepts that the destination host or intermediate router after the NIDS should surely reject.

Protocol Number

You have already learned that the IP protocol number indicates the type of service that follows the IP header. A list of all the supported protocol numbers and names can be found at `www.iana.org/assignments/protocol-numbers`. Conveniently, later versions of nmap have the capability to scan a host for listening protocols. This is done using the **-sO** option. The target host is scanned for all 256 possibilities of protocols. Protocols are deemed listening when no ICMP "protocol unreachable" message is returned. The following text shows an nmap scan for live protocols and the returned nmap assessment:

```
nmap -sO target

Starting nmap V. 2.54BETA1 by fyodor@insecure.org ( www.insecure.org/nmap/ )
Interesting protocols on myhost.net (192.168.5.5):
(The 250 protocols scanned but not shown below are in state: closed)

Protocol    State     Name
1           open      icmp
2           open      icmp
6           open      tcp
17          open      udp
```

Here is a sample of the traffic that the protocol scan generated:

```
07:30:31.405513 scanner.net > target.com: ip-proto-124 0 (DF)
07:30:31.405581 scanner.net > target.com: ip-proto-100 0 (DF)
07:30:31.405647 scanner.net > target.com: ip-proto-166 0 (DF)
07:30:31.405899 target.com > scanner.net: icmp: target.com protocol 124
unreachable (DF)
07:30:31.788701 scanner.net > target.com: ip-proto-132 0 (DF)
07:30:32.119538 target.com > scanner.net: icmp: target.com protocol 166
unreachable (DF)
07:30:34.098715 scanner.net > target.com: ip-proto-236 0 (DF)
07:30:34.098782 scanner.net > target.com: ip-proto-129 0 (DF)
07:30:34.098849 scanner.net > target.com: ip-proto-229 0 (DF)
07:30:32.779583 target.com > scanner.net: icmp: target.com protocol 236
unreachable (DF)
07:30:34.099557 target.com > scanner.net: icmp: target.com protocol 109
unreachable (DF)
```

The nmap scan examines all 256 different protocol types. A host that receives this type of scan should respond with an ICMP "protocol unreachable" message to any protocols that it doesn't support.

Although the supported protocols of a host are interesting, another possible piece of reconnaissance from this type of scan is that the host is alive. This is a more stealthy type of scan that might not cause an intrusion-detection system to alarm. However, if the site has a "no ip unreachables" statement on the outbound interfaces of the gateway router or if it blocks all outbound ICMP, this information is not leaked to the scanner. In that instance, the scan is useless.

There is a flaw in the logic used by nmap to discern listening protocols. Nmap assumes that the absence of an ICMP "protocol unreachable" message means that the protocol is listening. Yet, conditions such as the scanned site blocking outbound ICMP messages prevent the nmap scanner from getting these messages. There are other conditions, such as dropped packets, that might also cause the loss of packets and falsely influence nmap. However, the author of nmap tried to consider such situations. Nmap sends duplicate packets for each protocol to deal with the problem of packet loss. Also, if nmap gets no ICMP protocol unreachable messages back, it doesn't assume all protocols are listening. Instead, it wisely assumes that the traffic is being "filtered" and reports this.

A Bloody Simple Analogy

Nmap uses the philosophy of the absence of communication is the confirmation of a condition to determine listening protocols. In other words, the absence of an "ICMP protocol unreachable" message is the confirmation that the protocol is listening. As we've seen, there are some flaws associated with this method.

This philosophy reminds me of the real-world situation of going to the doctor's office for some blood work. Because the doctor and staff are very busy people, they usually tell you on your way out that they will not call you unless they discover something wrong. They are basically telling you that the absence of communication, the lack of a phone call, is a confirmation of a condition, that you are healthy as a horse.

Yet, if you are even a bit cynical, you understand the possible problems with this situation. All kinds of things can go wrong such as losing your blood in the doctor's office before it gets sent to a lab, losing your blood on the way to or from the lab, or even losing your blood at the lab. Just because you don't hear from the good doctor doesn't necessarily mean that everything is copasetic.

Similar problems can beset a packet. A packet can get lost in transit or it can be dropped or blocked at many points in its journey. Nmap attempts to deal with some of these problems, yet the absence of communication might not always be a confirmation of a condition.

Differentiated Services Byte (Formerly Known as Type of Service—The Prince of Fields)

It seems that the former Type of Service byte has undergone several rounds of alterations since its incipient creation. One of these alterations in RFC 2481 and more currently RFC 3168 calls for the two low-order bits of the differentiated services byte to be used for Explicit Congestion Notification (ECN). The purpose here is that some routers are equipped to do Random Early Detection (RED) or active queue management of the possibility of packet loss.

When congestion is severe, it is possible that a router can drop packets. RED attempts to mitigate this condition by calculating the possibility of congestion in the queue to a router interface and marking packets that might otherwise have been dropped as experiencing congestion.

There are two possible values of the ECN bits to inform that the sending host is ECN-capable. The ECN-capable Transport (ECT) bit settings can either be 01 or 10 in these two low-order bits of the differentiated services byte in Figure 8.3. These settings indicate that the sender is ECN-aware. If the sender is ECN-aware, a router that uses RED attempts not to drop the packet, but instead sends it with the Congestion Experienced (CE) bits enabled, and the receiver reacts to this. The bit setting for Congestion Experienced is 1s in both of the ECN bits. We'll discuss the receiver's response in more detail when we cover the TCP fields in the next chapter.

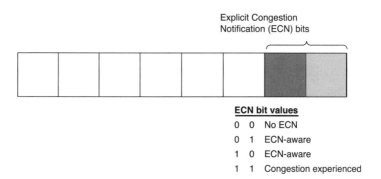

Figure 8.3   The Differentiated Services byte and ECN.

The Don't Fragment (DF) Flag

The Don't Fragment (DF) flag is a field in the IP header that is set when fragmentation is not to occur. If a router discovers that a packet needs to be fragmented, but the DF flag is set, the packet is dropped and an ICMP message "unreachable - need to frag (MTU size)" is delivered to the sending host. Most current routers include the maximum transmission unit (MTU) size of the smaller link that required the fragmentation.

Fragmentation comes with some overhead, so you should avoid it altogether. If one fragment of the fragment train is not delivered, all fragments must be re-sent. Because of this, when some TCP/IP stacks send data, they first send a discovery packet with the DF flag set. If the packet goes from source to destination without any ICMP errors, the selected datagram size of the discovery packet is used for subsequent packets. If an ICMP message is returned with an "unreachable error – need to frag" message and the MTU is included, the packet is resized so that fragmentation does not occur. This assumes the site allows these ICMP messages inbound.

Some operating system TCP/IP stacks set the DF flag on certain types of packets, and nmap uses this as one of the tests to try to fingerprint the operating system. Also, an attacker can use the DF flag as a means of an insertion attack. This means the NIDS would have to be on a network with a larger MTU than the final destination host. In this case, one or more packets among a series of others have the DF flag set. The NIDS receives the packet(s) and accepts it, but the end host never receives the packet(s) because fragmentation is required, yet the DF flag was set.

The More Fragments (MF) Flag

The More Fragments (MF) flag tells you that one or more fragments follow the current one. All fragments except the final one should have the MF flag set. The way that a receiving host detects fragmentation is that this flag is set or the fragment offset field in the IP header is set to a non-zero value.

Mapping Using Incomplete Fragments

Another mapping technique is to try to elicit an ICMP IP "reassembly time exceeded" message from hosts on a scanned network. This can be done by sending an incomplete set of fragments to hosts that are being mapped. For this to work properly, the destination host has to be listening on the port that is scanned if the traffic is TCP or UDP. When the scanned host receives the first fragment, it sets a timer. If the timer expires and the receiving host has not received all the fragments, it sends the ICMP "IP reassembly time exceeded" error back to the sending host.

It is important to note (according to RFC 792) that for the ICMP "IP reassembly time exceeded" error to be generated, the first fragment must not be the missing one. If no first fragment is received, the host receiving the fragments never sets the timer. RFC 1122 recommends that the timer expire between 60 seconds and 2 minutes, though we'll see that is not always the case.

```
hping2 -S -p 139 -x win98
```

```
06:49:36.986218 verbo.2509 > win98.netbios-ssn: S 1980004944:1980004944(0)
win 512 (frag 38912:20@0+)
06:50:41.636506 win98 > verbo: icmp: ip reassembly time exceeded
```

```
hping2 -S -p 21 -x  linux
```

```
11:56:04.064978 verbo.2450 > linux.ftp: S 1198423806:1198423806(0) win 512
(frag 39067:20@0+)
```

```
11:56:34.056813  linux > verbo: icmp: ip reassembly time exceeded [tos 0xc0]
```

Hping2 is freeware that is used to generate different types of traffic. Hping2 is first executed with the **–S** option to send a packet with a SYN, a destination port of 139, **-p 139**, and the **–x** option to set the More Fragment flag. One packet is sent to the destination host win98, which as you might guess is a Windows 98 host listening on TCP port 139.

The fragment sent is actually the entire SYN packet—20 header bytes and a 20-byte TCP header. There is no data to send, but the receiving host has no way of knowing this because the MF flag is set. You can see that the MF flag is set by looking at the + in the previous output of TCPdump. The Windows host took approximately one minute and five seconds to time out the fragment reassembly clock. That is when you see the ICMP "IP reassembly time exceeded" message returned.

The next hping2 test is tried on a Linux (2.2 kernel) host on a listening ftp port. The Linux host took about thirty seconds to time out on incomplete fragments sent to destination port 21.

IP Numbers

IP numbers are 32-bit fields. The source IP number is located in the 12th through 15th bytes offset of the IP header; the destination IP number is located in the 16th through 19th bytes offset of the IP header.

What are some unnatural values for source IPs entering your network? If you see an IP number entering your network that purports to be from your network, there is a problem. Most likely, someone has crafted this packet and is spoofing an IP address in your range. A packet-filtering device should shun this traffic. Additionally, you should never see source IPs coming from the loopback address 127.0.0.1, nor should you see any source IPs that fall in the

Internet Assigned Numbers Authority (IANA) reserved private network numbers defined in RFC 1918. These address ranges can be found at `www.iana.org/assignments/ipv4-address-space`. Their intended use is for local internal networks only.

As far as traffic leaving your network, it should have a source IP number that reflects your network's address space. If you see an IP number coming from inside your network that has an IP number of a different address space, it is either being spoofed or there is a misconfiguration problem with a host inside your network. In either case, this traffic should not be allowed to leave your network. This prevents hosts in your network from participating in distributed denial of service attacks because participant or zombie hosts usually use spoofed source IP numbers so that they cannot be located. Other types of scans use decoy or spoofed source IP's as a smokescreen. By disallowing outbound traffic that is not part of your address space, these scans will be ineffective as well.

You should also never see a source IP with the loopback 127.0.0.1 address leaving your network because that identifies the local host. And, you should never allow source IP's in the reserved address ranges to leave your network.

Finally, you shouldn't allow traffic with a broadcast destination IP address into or out of your network. Such destination addresses are typically used to quickly map other networks or use them as Smurf amplification sites.

IP Identification Number

The IP identification value is found in bytes 4 and 5 offset of the IP header. For each new datagram that a host sends, it must generate a unique IP ID number. This value is normally incremented by 1, although some use an increment of 256, for each new datagram sent by the host.

This unique value is required in case the datagram becomes fragmented. All fragments from the datagram share this same IP ID number. This is also referred to as the fragment ID number. It is the number that is used by the receiving host to reassemble all fragments associated with a common datagram.

The range for IP ID values is 1 through 65,535 because this is a 16-bit field. Usually, you don't see IP ID numbers with a value of 0. When the maximum value of 65,535 for the IP ID value is reached, it should wrap around and start again. Different source IPs directing traffic to your network should manifest a different chronology of IP ID values. So, if you see different "alleged" source IPs sending traffic to your network and they appear to have a chronology of incrementing IP ID numbers, it is possible that the source IPs are being spoofed.

As with just about any other field or value in the IP datagram, this value can be "crafted" so as to render it meaningless for interpretation. For instance, if an attacker used a tool that sent all packets with the identical IP ID, they would offer no meaningful forensic value about the attacker's host. The **−vv** option of TCPdump can be used to display the IP ID number along with the time-to-live (TTL) value.

Time to Live (TTL)

The TTL is an 8-bit value that is set by the host sending the datagram. Initial TTL values are different depending on the TCP/IP stack used, as you can see in Table 8.1 that was obtained at `project.honeynet.org/papers/finger/traces`. As we have discussed, each router that the packet travels on its way to the destination host must decrement the TTL value by 1. If a router ever discovers a value of 0 in the TTL, it must discard the packet and return an ICMP "time exceeded in-transit" message back to the sender. This banishes lost packets such as those stuck in a routing loop. This can be used as a possible insertion attack if the NIDS sees the packet, yet the TTL is low enough to be expired by a router before it reaches a target host.

Table 8.1 **Initial TTL Values by Operating System**

OS	Version	Platform	TTL
Windows	9x/NT	Intel	32
AIX	4.3.x	IBM/RS6000	60
AIX	4.2.x	IBM/RS6000	60
Cisco	11.2	7507	60
IRIX	6.x	SGI	60
Linux	2.2.x	Intel	64
OpenBSD	2.x	Intel	64
Solaris	8	Intel/Sparc	64
Windows	9x/NT	Intel	128
Windows	2000	Intel	128
Cisco	12.0	2514	255
Solaris	2.x	Intel/Sparc	255

What if you want to test to see if a packet is from the source IP it says it is from? You can look at the arriving TTL, estimate the initial TTL by using Table 8.1, and subtract the arriving TTL from the initial TTL to give you the hop count for the packet to arrive on your network. Then, a traceroute could be executed to see if the number of hops taken back to the alleged source IP approximates the number of hops originally taken into your network. It is possible that the route back to the alleged source IP might be different than the route taken to your network because of the dynamics of routing, but they often do have close hop counts, assuming that there are no major router or traffic problems along the way.

Chances are, if you have different source IPs concurrently entering your network, they have different arriving TTL values. If you see different source IPs entering your network at the same time, doing the same type of activity, with identical arriving TTLs, it is possible that this might be source IP spoofing.

Be aware that some scanning programs purposely randomize the initial TTL value just to eliminate this vestige of the true origin of the datagram.

Looking at the IP ID and TTL Values Together to Discover Spoofing

Examine the following output:

```
07:31:57.250000 somewhere.de > 192.168.104.255: icmp: echo request
(ttl 246, id 5134)
07:34:18.090000 somewhere.jp > 192.168.104.255: icmp: echo request
(ttl 246, id 5137)
07:35:19.450000 somewhere.ca > 192.168.104.255: icmp: echo request
(ttl 246, id 5141)
```

This output shows traffic from three purportedly different source IPs to the same infrequently referenced destination IP. The timestamps are within minutes of each other, and the chronology of the IP identification values is worth examining. What is strange about the IP identification values, and why might someone send traffic such as this?

What are the odds that the IP identification values are coincidentally incremental from three alleged different sources to the same destination IP—192.168.104.255? The particular subnet 192.168.104 does not have active hosts, so this makes the traffic even more suspicious. Although this could be a huge coincidence, it is more likely that someone on one host was sending ICMP echo requests (ping) to the infrequently referenced internal 192.168.104.255 address.

Recall that the IP identification value is a 16-bit field with a range of values from 1 to 65,535. The clustering of values between 5134 and 5141 is highly unlikely for three unique sources. It also appears to be a particularly inactive host (perhaps a single user PC) sending the packets, judging by the small increments in the IP identification values over several minutes. This assumes that the IP identification numbers have not been crafted.

As with much unusual traffic seen on the network, the *what* is far easier to figure out than the *why*. Maybe this was a mapping attempt with one real source and two spoofed sources. This emits a smokescreen effect; even if we noticed this, chances are we wouldn't be able to identify the real source IP anyway.

Let's examine this same traffic, but now let's look at it in terms of the TTL values. Oddly, all the arriving TTL values are identical. This tends to confirm the speculation that all three packets originated from the same host. What are the chances that three different source IPs sending traffic to our network had a probable (uncrafted) initial TTL of 255 *and* each was 9 hop counts away *and* they all had an interest in the same IP address at approximately the same time?

Using the **–vv** option of TCPdump can give us two additional fields of display that can assist in determining if suspicious traffic has been spoofed.

When this traffic was detected on the network, traceroutes were executed back to the alleged source IPs in an attempt to determine if they were real or spoofed source IPs. Here are the results of the traceroutes:

```
traceroute somewhere.de
    arriving TTL:              246
    probable initial TTL:      255
    expected hop count back:   9
    actual hop count back:     13

traceroute somewhere.jp
    arriving TTL:              246
    probable initial TTL:      255
    expected hop count back:   9
    actual hop count back:     13

traceroute somewhere.ca
    arriving TTL:              246
    probable initial TTL:      255
    expected hop count back:   9
    actual hop count back:     12
```

This example of using traceroutes isn't very conclusive. Each of the three different source IPs had approximately 12 or 13 hops back from the network upon which the sensor sniffed the packets. However, it does offer an example of the mechanics used to attempt to validate the authenticity of the source IP.

The hop count back from the traceroute is believably close to the expected hop count. Yet, using the IP identification values in conjunction with these results, these source IPs probably were spoofed. A hop count back to the source IP that varies widely from the expected hop count is a better indication that the source IP was spoofed. Also, if the actual hop counts back to the three different source IPs differed more substantially from each other, this too would be a better indicator of spoofing.

There are a couple of caveats associated with using traceroute for forensics. First, you might be unable to do traceroutes to/from your network because of router/firewall blocks of ICMP traffic, specifically "time exceeded in-transit" and "port unreachable" messages. Second, note that traceroute to a real IP might not be desirable because it can potentially illuminate your interest in a site.

IP Checksums

Checksums are used to ensure that data has not gotten corrupted from source to destination. The algorithm used for TCP/IP is to divide the data that is being checksummed into 16-bit fields. Each 16-bit field has a 1's complement operation done on it and all of these 1's complement values are added. The final value is considered to be the checksum.

The IP checksum is found in the 10th and 11th bytes offset of the IP header. The IP checksum covers all fields in the IP header only. This checksum is different than the checksums that are computed for the embedded protocol fields because it is validated along the path from source to destination. Embedded protocol checksums such as TCP, UDP, and ICMP are validated by the destination host only. The IP checksum is validated by each router through which it passes from source to destination and finally is validated by the destination host as well.

If the computed checksum does not agree with the one found in the datagram, the datagram is discarded silently. No attempt is made to inform the source host of a problem. The idea is that higher-level protocols or applications will detect this and deal with it.

The formula for the IP header checksum is used for all other embedded checksums as well. First, we divide the IP header into 16-bit fields. Because the IP header length is always a multiple of 4 bytes, we do not have to worry about extra fields that do not fall on 16-bit boundaries.

After all of the fields are separated, we take the 1's complement of each. This operation simply flips the bit. All of these individual 1's complement values are added to form the checksum. For example:

4	5	0	0	Hex Representation
0100	0101	0000	0000	Binary Representation
1011	1010	1111	1111	1's Complement

In the previous output, you see the first 16 bits of a very common beginning to an IP header. Each hex value is represented in four binary bits and each of these bits is flipped. This becomes the 1's complement value. This operation is commutative so you can add the hex values of the 16-bit fields and then take the 1's complement and the resulting checksum should be the same.

The IP checksum is examined and recomputed for each hop on the way from source to destination. Intermediate routers validate the IP checksum, and if it is correct, the TTL value is decremented by 1. The IP header checksum must be recomputed to reflect this change in the IP header. Remember that this checksum validates the fields in the IP header only, not the rest of the datagram that consists of the embedded protocol header and data.

The rationale for checking the IP checksum for each hop makes sense when you think about it. The worst-case scenario is that the destination IP becomes corrupted. It makes no sense to forward a packet that has been corrupted because the corruption might alter the intent of the packet.

Although the IP checksum and all other checksums found in the datagram find most packet corruption, there is a problem. It is possible for entire 16-bit fields to be swapped and yet the checksum will remain the same.

```
4500   003c

4500 = 0100 0101 0000 0000          1011 1010 1111 1111
003c = 0000 0000 0011 1100          1111 1111 1100 0011
                                    1011 1010 1100 0010


003c   4500

003c = 0000 0000 0011 1100          1111 1111 1100 0011
4500 = 0100 0101 0000 0000          1011 1010 1111 1111
                                    1011 1010 1100 0010
```

Look at the previous output. We swap the first two 16-bit fields (4500 003c) in the IP header. The computed checksum for the correct sequence of these 16-bit fields is 1011 1010 1100 0010 (this doesn't include the high-order bit carryover). But, if we reverse the fields and compute the checksum, it is exactly the same. A datagram with 16-bit fields swapped is a vastly different datagram in meaning and resolution when fields are swapped. So, this is obviously a drawback of using this computation.

Why not use a more complicated and reliable algorithm for the checksum? This computation is done for each packet that a router receives. The simpler the algorithm, the quicker the computation time. The checksum algorithm is a fast and mostly reliable algorithm, and the clean swap of 16-bit fields is a rare occurrence. To read more about IP checksums, look at RFC 1071.

Summary

Let's summarize some of the ideas conveyed in this chapter. First, although your NIDS is a necessary tool for risk mitigation, it is not a panacea for detecting all malicious traffic. One reason for this is that insertion and evasion attacks can cause the NIDS to incorrectly scrutinize network traffic. There are many different attacks that can be used and it is simply impossible for a NIDS to know how every different target host on a network will react to a packet. A NIDS cannot know the nuances of each individual host's implementation of the TCP/IP stack. As well, the NIDS is not aware of network topology differences that can be used in some of the attacks such as packets with low TTL numbers that will never reach the target host. The use of host-based IDS can be used to fortify the security provided by the NIDS.

A savvy analyst should be aware of the types of fields and possible values that are found in the IP header. This is valuable knowledge when examining packets for anomalous values. Recognizing mutant values might not explain the intended purpose of the packet, but it should draw your attention to the packet. From there, it might be possible to determine the nature of the traffic.

9

Examining Embedded Protocol Header Fields

THIS SECOND CHAPTER ON EXAMINING HEADER FIELDS discusses the fields in the headers found after the IP header, namely the TCP, UDP, and ICMP headers. As we discovered in the previous chapter, it is imperative that anyone performing traffic analysis be familiar with the purpose of the fields and expected values. This is the only way to unearth values that are not normal and might be a reflection of some kind of malicious activity.

Because this is a fairly extensive topic, the chapter addresses fields in each of the protocols individually. Hopefully, this will partition the protocols into more manageable chunks of learning.

TCP

Back in Chapter 2, "Introduction to TCPdump and TCP," we discussed that TCP is a reliable protocol. This means that TCP oversees the exchange of data and knows when there is a possible problem by using fields such as sequence and acknowledgement numbers to order and keep track of the exchanged data. There are many more fields in the TCP header than UDP and ICMP have because TCP needs to maintain state and provide optimal flow control between sender and receiver. We'll examine these fields and others in the context of normal and abnormal use.

Ports

The port fields are two separate 16-bit fields in the TCP header, one for source (bytes 0 and 1 offset from the TCP header) and another for destination (bytes 2 and 3 offset from the TCP header) port. The valid range of values is between 1 and 65535. The use of port 0 is anomalous and considered to be a unique "signature" of an improper port setting.

When a source host wishes to connect to a destination host, an ephemeral source port is typically selected in the range of ports greater than 1023. For each new connection that the host attempts that is not a retry, a different ephemeral port should be selected. The concept of TCP retries or retransmission will be covered later in this chapter in the section, "Retransmissions." In a scan scenario, you will likely see the source port value incrementing by 1 for each new connection.

One of the telltale signs of an nmap SYN scan to find open TCP ports is a static source port retained over multiple new TCP connections. For example:

```
nmap -sS sparky

09:40:43.964215 verbo.47247 > sparky.1548: S 2401927088:2401927088(0) win
2048
09:40:43.964412 verbo.47247 > sparky.24: S 2401927088:2401927088(0) win 2048
09:40:43.964465 verbo.47247 > sparky.1547: S 2401927088:2401927088(0) win
2048
09:40:43.964553 verbo.47247 > sparky.2564: S 2401927088:2401927088(0) win
2048
09:40:43.964604 verbo.47247 > sparky.1484: S 2401927088:2401927088(0) win
2048
09:40:43.964642 verbo.47247 > sparky.1460: S 2401927088:2401927088(0) win
2048
09:40:43.964695 verbo.47247 > sparky.628: S 2401927088:2401927088(0) win 2048
09:40:43.964748 verbo.47247 > sparky.1112: S 2401927088:2401927088(0) win
2048
```

Although we would expect the source port of scanner verbo to change for each new SYN connection to new ports of target host sparky, the source port number remains constant as 47247.

In contrast, look at the default behavior exhibited by another scanning tool known as hping2. The **–S** option of hping2 performs a different kind of SYN scan. It increments the source port as expected, yet it attempts to open destination port 0 of its target. The intent of this type of scan obviously is not to find a listening port. This type of scan is used to elicit a RESET response to see if a host is alive, because there should be no hosts listening at port 0. Here's the output from hping2:

```
hping2 -S sparky

09:44:13.882207 verbo.1788 > sparky.0: S 1553132317:1553132317(0) win 512
09:44:14.876837 verbo.1789 > sparky.0: S 1894028093:1894028093(0) win 512
09:44:15.876836 verbo.1790 > sparky.0: S 2032501562:2032501562(0) win 512
09:44:16.876832 verbo.1791 > sparky.0: S 851202745:851202745(0) win 512
```

TCP Checksums

As mentioned previously, the embedded protocols have checksums as well. These cover the embedded header and respective data for TCP, UDP, and ICMP. Unlike the IP checksum, these are end-to-end checksums calculated by the source and validated by the destination host-only. The TCP checksum has been chosen to represent the embedded protocol checksums. UDP does not require a checksum to be computed, unlike IP, TCP, and ICMP. However, it is highly recommended.

The embedded protocol checksums for TCP and UDP are computed using a pseudo-header in addition to the embedded protocol header and data. A pseudo-header consists of 12 bytes of data depicted in Figure 9.1: the source and destination IPs, the 8-bit protocol found in the IP header, and a repetition of the embedded protocol length (this is the protocol header length plus the number of data bytes). The zero-pad field found in the 8th byte offset is used to pad the 8-bit protocol field to 16 bits because checksums are performed on 16-bit blocks of data.

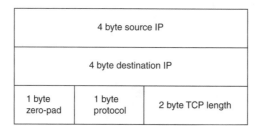

Figure 9.1   TCP checksum pseudo-header fields.

Why is the pseudo-header necessary? This is a double check that is used by the receiving host to validate that the IP layer has not accidentally accepted a datagram destined for another host or that IP has not accidentally tried to give TCP a datagram that is for another protocol. If there is some errant corruption that occurs in transit, the validation of the IP checksum may or may not discover this, but some fields from the IP header are included in the pseudo-header checksum computation to help protect against this.

Let's examine a very specific example of how the pseudo-header protects against delivering the packet to the wrong host. Figure 9.2 is offered to assist in visualizing the process. Assume that we have a host that sends a packet to destination IP 1.2.3.4. We will use TCP as the embedded protocol, but it really doesn't matter if the transport layer is TCP or UDP because both use the pseudo-header. The transport layer checksum includes the pseudo-header fields in the checksum computation. Therefore, for the destination IP, a value of 1.2.3.4 is used in the TCP checksum computation.

On its way from the sending host, the packet travels through a router that, as you remember, must validate the IP checksum before forwarding it. Suppose the router validates the IP checksum, decrements the TTL, and then needs to recompute the new IP checksum. For some unforeseen reason, the IP layer of the router somehow corrupts the destination IP to be 1.2.3.5. The IP checksum is recomputed using the corrupted destination IP. The IP checksum is valid so the packet continues on towards the wrong destination, IP 1.2.3.5.

Assume that the IP 1.2.3.5 exists. The corrupted packet arrives at the wrong destination IP. The IP layer validates the checksum and it is correct because destination IP 1.2.3.5 was used in the IP checksum computation by the corrupting router. The packet is pushed up to the transport layer where TCP uses the pseudo-header fields in the checksum validation. But, the TCP checksum validation uses destination IP 1.2.3.5 in the corrupted packet IP header for validation comparison against the packet's actual TCP checksum. However, this does not match the TCP pseudo-header checksum from the sending host that used 1.2.3.4 as the destination IP in the pseudo-header checksum. Host 1.2.3.5 then discards the packet because the embedded protocol checksum does not match the computed checksum done by the destination host.

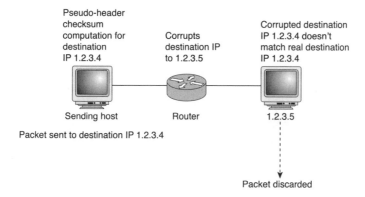

Figure 9.2 Pseudo-header checksum protection.

A Cry for Help

While reading literature on the purpose of the pseudo-header, it made perfect sense to me that it is used as an additional check to make sure that the packet isn't sent to the wrong host or protocol. Yet, for the life of me, I couldn't envision how this was done. I asked several colleagues, but they too shared my confusion when it came to giving an example. I ended up writing noted author and TCP/IP expert, Doug Comer, who shared the example of a router corrupting the destination IP number. I would like to extend many thanks to Mr. Comer for clearing up the confusion.

TCP Sequence Numbers

The TCP sequence numbers are used to uniquely identify the beginning byte of each TCP segment that is sent. This is a way to keep track of all the TCP data that is sent and received in a TCP stream. Most times, there is more TCP data than can be sent in one TCP segment. Or, some services such as rlogin might send a character at a time over a TCP stream requiring multiple streams per session. Because TCP is a reliable protocol, we must have a mechanism to account for data being sent and received. In part, that is done using TCP sequence numbers.

These sequence numbers should not be repeated unless there is a retry of the same connection if an initial attempt fails and the sender receives no error from either the intended receiver or some kind of packet-filtering device. The initial sequence number (ISN) is the first sequence number that is used in the TCP exchange between the sending and receiving hosts. Each host in the exchange selects a unique initial sequence number when sending the initial SYN connection to the other host.

The formula that TCP/IP stacks use to select their initial sequence number is examined by nmap to help fingerprint the operating system. There is a file that comes with nmap, nmap-os-fingerprints, that has a list of many different operating systems and versions. Nmap performs a given set of tests against a target host. Nmap can categorize a particular operating system by matching the values in responses to different normal and abnormal stimuli sent by the scanning host with the expected values for a given operating system.

The first test executed by an operating system fingerprinting nmap scan is one that examines the initial sequence numbers generated by a receiving host from sent connections to a listening port. Different TCP/IP stacks use different formulas to generate the ISN. Some of the older operating systems used a predictable increment for the ISN for each new connection. But someone watching and sniffing could possibly predict and hijack a connection using this information, as was done in the infamous Mitnick attack. Other operating systems have a time-dependent formula that predictably increases the ISN based on a given time change. This, too, is not considered very secure. The most secure formula for ISN generation is a random, unpredictable one. As a tidbit of information, the SYN that we refer to as the flag to start a TCP connection is actually an abbreviation for synchronize sequence numbers. The following execution of nmap using the operating system fingerprint scan option (-O) shows open ports, TCP sequence number prediction difficulty, and guessed operating system.

```
nmap -O sparky

(The 1495 ports scanned but not shown below are in state: closed)
Port            State       Service
23/tcp          open        telnet
25/tcp          open        smtp
111/tcp         open        sunrpc
513/tcp         open        login
32771/tcp       open        sometimes-rpc5
32772/tcp       open        sometimes-rpc7

TCP Sequence Prediction: Class=random positive increments
                         Difficulty=46112 (Worthy challenge)
Remote OS guesses: Solaris 2.6 - 2.7, Solaris 7
```

Using **nmap –O** to scan the Solaris host sparky and identify the operating system discovers that the generation of initial sequence numbers is based on a formula using "random positive increments." And, it reports that predicting a new TCP sequence number would be a "worthy challenge." Sparky is a Solaris 2.7 host, and it appears to be fairly impervious to someone guessing a new TCP sequence number based on a previous one or based on time.

Acknowledgement Numbers

The method that TCP uses to ensure that data is received is via an acknowledgement. The receiving host sets the acknowledgement flag and the acknowledgement number, which are validation that the receiving host did indeed get the data. The acknowledgement number sent by the receiving host actually represents the next expected TCP sequence number it should receive.

Because a SYN connection consumes one sequence number, and because the acknowledgement value is one more than this sequence number, a valid acknowledgement number must be greater than 0. There is one rare qualification of this. It is possible to use all 2 billion plus TCP sequence numbers available with the 32-bit field in which they are stored. If, by chance, the last TCP sequence number sent is the largest 32-bit number allowed, the receiving host wraps around and acknowledges that the next expected sequence number is 0. This is an infrequent occurrence.

Nmap can attempt to identify live hosts by sending a remote host a TCP connection with an unsolicited ACK flag set. This method of host identification is often more successful than pinging the host because many sites now block inbound ICMP echo requests. Yet, a router that doesn't maintain state may allow in "established" traffic in which the ACK flag is set. The desired response to the unsolicited ACK is a RESET from the remote host, which indeed indicates that the remote host is alive regardless of whether the scanned port is listening. Current versions of nmap have a telltale signature because the ACK flag is set, yet the acknowledgement number is 0 as shown in the following output.

```
verbo.52776 > win98.netbios-ssn: . ack 0 win 4096 <wscale 10,nop,mss
265,timestamp 1061109567[|tcp]>
```

TCP Flags

TCP flags are used to indicate the function of a given TCP connection or session. The SYN flag starts a session and the FIN flag terminates a session gracefully. A RESET is used to abort a session. The ACK flag is set to indicate an acknowledgement of data by the receiver. The ACK flag is set on all packets after the initial SYN. The PUSH flag is typically used to tell the sending host to write all of its buffered data to send to the destination host and for the destination host to PUSH it up to the TCP layer. It is actually possible to send data without the PUSH flag set when all of the data in the sending buffer is not completely emptied. Finally, the URGENT flag is used to indicate that data has the highest priority.

The TCP flags have many different valid combinations. And, there are many different invalid combinations that are used for different purposes. Early in the evolution of NIDS, many would examine traffic for initial SYN attempts only. Scanners realized this and would send a SYN/FIN combination that might elicit a response from a host. Different operating system TCP/IP stacks respond differently to mutant flag settings, so this is used to attempt to finger-print the operating system. We will examine some of the situations in which valid and invalid flag combinations can occur over the next several sections.

TCP Corruption

Just because you see mutant TCP flag combinations, it is not necessarily an indication of malicious behavior. Packets can and do get corrupted, and it is possible for TCP flags to be unnaturally set after some kind of corruption in the TCP portion of the packet.

Look at the following packet received on a Shadow NIDS. This was an attempted Napster connection back in the days when Napster was a free and legal method of exchanging MP3s:

```
host.home.com.1310 > napster.com.6699: SRP [bad hdr length] (DF)
```

There are two anomalies that stand out looking at the record. The first is the mutant flag settings of SRP, meaning that all three of the SYN, RESET, and PUSH flags are set simultaneously. The next sign is TCPdump's notation of bad hdr length.

A bad hdr length is an error generated by TCPdump when the specified TCP header length is greater than the actual TCP segment (header and data) length. Because there is no field in the IP datagram that holds the value of the TCP segment length (header and data), TCPdump computes this value by using fields it does have. It subtracts the IP header length from the IP datagram total length. For properly formatted packets, this reflects the true TCP segment length. One of the validity checks performed by TCPdump is to test if the packet's specified TCP header length in bytes is greater than the computed TCP segment length. If this comparison is true, there is something definitely wrong with a length field, and that is when the bad hdr length error is displayed.

It will be become apparent why TCPdump believes this by examining the following hex dump output. First, the IP header is contained between the brackets and the TCP header between the less than and greater than signs:

```
[4500 0028 8974 4000 7406 a9c5 1804 ee22
80f4 4c7b] <051e 1a2b 0000 029d 9efe a721
a7ae 5010 2058 ac31 0047 0050>
```

Now let's turn our attention to the length fields in the packet. First, look at the IP total datagram length in the bolded 2nd and 3rd bytes offset of the IP header. You should see a 0x28 or 40-byte IP datagram length. The IP header length is found in the bolded low-order nibble of the 0 byte offset of the IP header. As we know, this value of 5 represents a 20-byte IP header.

The protocol field in the 9th byte offset of the IP header has been bolded to highlight the embedded protocol. Because we discover a 06 in that field, we know that a TCP header follows. The computed TCP segment length is then 40–20, giving us 20 bytes for TCP header and data. This is room enough for a TCP header with no options and no data such as might be found on a plain SYN attempt.

Yet, in the TCP header length, we find a length of 0xa in the bolded high-order nibble of the 12th byte offset, which indicates a 40-byte TCP header after we multiply it by 4 to translate from 32-bit words to bytes.

Using these fields, do you know why TCPdump generates the bad hdr length error? This is a datagram with a total length of 40, including a 20-byte IP header length, yet a TCP header that professes to be 40 bytes. We need a minimum IP datagram length of 60 to house this data if indeed there has been no corruption.

Is it possible that this packet has been corrupted and the checksum is invalid? Remember, if this involved packet corruption in the TCP header or data, the only host that will detect this is the destination host. The NIDS sensor typically does not validate a TCP checksum.

Here is what we can deduce about this packet. Chances are that the IP header is fine because the previous router did not drop it. Routers are supposed to validate the IP checksums and silently drop packets with inaccurate ones. Now, before reaching the destination host and having the TCP checksum validated, it passes by the sensor where TCPdump finds a problem with it. It is possible that the router corrupted the IP header after the checksum was computed, but the header otherwise appears to be normal.

At this point, we don't know if the packet has been accidentally corrupted or intentionally corrupted for whatever reason. The only other ways to verify packet corruption is to manually compute the checksum of the received packet on the sensor or examine how the receiving host (napster.com) reacts. The problem with looking at how napster.com reacts is that if the checksum is invalid, we will see no response. Yet, if the checksum is valid, this weird combination of flags might not elicit a response either. If we do observe an unlikely response from napster.com (most likely a RESET), this means that the checksum is valid and the packet wasn't corrupted on route from source to destination. This means that the packet was most likely crafted with mutant values at the source. Too, there is always the possibility of cleanly swapped 16-bit fields that would corrupt the packet, but there would be no manifestation of it in the checksum.

Vern Paxson, creator of an IDS named Bro, talks of traffic he has labeled "crud" in his paper "Bro: A System for Detecting Network Intruders in Real-Time." His definition of crud is "innocuous implementation errors" that create traffic pattern pathologies that look similar to genuine attacks. He cites examples of an errant TCP/IP stack that routinely sets the URG flag on a SYN attempt and another that sets the DF flag on traffic fragments. Although this is different than packet corruption, the important point to keep in mind is that not all-anomalous traffic you witness is malicious. It is remotely possible that a very small amount is due to corruption, or crud.

ECN Flag Bits

Until very recently, the two high-order bits of the TCP byte were known as the reserved bits. They had no purpose, and the value found in the bits should have been 0. However, when tools such as nmap came along, it was discovered that these bits could be used to try to help fingerprint a remote operating system. Different operating system TCP/IP stacks would respond uniquely when these bits were set.

Some would reset the bits to 0, and others would simply leave them with the current value. Hence, some insight could be made of the remote host's operating system TCP/IP stack. This alone might not be enough to inform the scanner of the operating system, but used in conjunction with several other tests, the operating system could be conjectured with a high probability.

Remember back when we were discussing the differentiated services byte in Chapter 8, "Examining IP Header Fields," we introduced a new purpose for the two low-order bits known as Explicit Congestion Notification (ECN)? The intent was for a router to be able to notify a sender that there was congestion in the network and to reduce its sending rate.

How exactly does that occur? Currently, as discussed in the ECN RFC 3168, the only transport capable of reacting to that congestion notification is TCP. So, TCP must be prepared to deal with this. The RFC offers using the two high-order bits of the TCP flag byte (see Figure 9.3) as fields for ECN. The bit to the right of the high-order bit is known as the ECN-echo bit. This bit is turned on when TCP receives a packet that has the Congestion Experienced bits set in the differentiated services byte of the IP header. This means that both end-points of the TCP conversation are ECN-capable, which is determined during the three-way handshake.

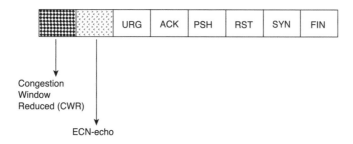

Figure 9.3 The ECN bits of the TCP flag byte.

If TCP sets the ECN-echo bit, the purpose is to inform the sender to reduce the rate at which it is sending data because there is congestion between the sender and receiver. Upon receipt of a TCP segment with the ECN-echo bit set, the sender reduces its congestion window, the size of the sending buffer, by half. After it reacts in this manner, it turns on the Congestion Window Reduced (CWR) bit to inform the other side of the conversation that remedial action to reduce congestion has occurred. This bit is found in the high-order bit of the TCP byte flag.

Although this mechanism helps reduce the number of packets dropped, it is anticipated that many existing NIDS will begin to alarm on these new TCP flag bytes being used. Right now, most uses of these bits are for scanning purposes only. Also, some packet-filtering devices will not allow inbound TCP segments with these bits set. So, much customization will have to be done to smoothly introduce ECN and distinguish it from the rogue scans.

Operating System Fingerprinting

When nmap is placed in operating system fingerprinting mode with the **–O** option, it sends some mutant flag combinations when an open port is discovered. Look at the following output from nmap remote operating system scans:

```
nmap -O win98

20:33:16.409759 verbo.47322 > win98.netbios-ssn: SFP 861966446:861966446(0)
win 3072 urg 0 <wscale 10,nop,mss 265,timestamp 1061109567[|tcp]>

20:33:16.410387 win98.netbios-ssn > verbo.47322: S 49904150:49904150(0) ack
861966447 win 8215 <mss 1460> (DF)

nmap -O sparky
```

```
20:37:00.738412 verbo.50107 > sparky.echo: SFP 2326441544:2326441544(0) win
2048 urg 0 <wscale 10,nop,mss 265,timestamp 1061109567[|tcp]>

nmap -O linux

20:44:50.370158 verbo.42318 > linux.ftp: SFP 1749165064:1749165064(0) win
1024 urg 0 <wscale 10,nop,mss 265,timestamp 1061109567 0,eol>
```

In the first scan of a Windows 98 host, the mutant flag combination of
SYN/FIN/PUSH/URG is sent to the Windows port 139. This is a NetBIOS
session service port, and the Windows host listens on this port. Yet, amazingly
enough, it responds with an acknowledgement! This behavior is not what we
expect.

In the second nmap scan, the same technique of sending the mutant combination of SYN/FIN/PUSH/URG flags to a listening Solaris port (echo) is
attempted, and no response is elicited. This same combination of flags is sent to
a listening Linux ftp port in the third scan, and no response is received. This is
the expected behavior, which conforms to RFC specifications. Yet, you can see
how this test can be used to distinguish Windows hosts from all others.

As a new analyst, it is often difficult to distinguish between what appears to
be malicious behavior and TCP/IP stacks that don't conform to the RFC
specifications. It is hard to understand the intent when a response isn't as you
expect. Many times, even an experienced analyst does not know if abnormal
TCP flag settings are an indication of some wayward TCP/IP stack or someone up to no good.

Retransmissions

What if an initial TCP connection is attempted, yet the host attempting the
connection doesn't receive a response from the destination host? A destination
host might not respond because it might not be up or might not exist. A
router might attempt to deliver an ICMP message about the destination host
being unreachable, but if the router has been silenced from delivering unreachable messages, the sending host will never know that there is a problem. A
destination host might be sitting behind some kind of packet-filtering device
that blocks the connection inbound, yet silently drops the connection without
informing the sending host.

It is also possible that the destination host responds positively (SYN/ACK)
or negatively (RESET/ACK), yet for some reason the sending host doesn't
receive these replies.

Additional attempts or retransmissions are made to contact the host in situations like this. The number of retransmissions and the time intervals in which

they are attempted varies by TCP/IP stack. Eventually, the sending host ceases the connection attempts.

How can you distinguish retransmissions or retries from separate new TCP connections to a destination host? The source ports remain the same, and the TCP sequence numbers don't change for retransmissions. This is not a fail-safe detection method. It is also possible that the sender is crafting packets that use the same source ports and TCP sequence numbers.

Examine the following set of retries—specifically, look at the time and the IP identification number changes. The IP identification numbers should change on a retry as well as a set of unique connections. The sending host generates an entirely new packet for the retry so the IP identification number should increment or wrap:

```
17:14:18.726864 1.1.1.1.62555 > 192.168.44.63.3128: S 20583734:20583734(0)
win 8192 <mss 1380>(DF) (ttl 17, id 15697)
17:14:21.781140 1.1.1.1.62555 > 192.168.44.63.3128: S 20583734:20583734(0)
win 8192 <mss 1380> (DF) (ttl 17, id 33873)
17:14:27.776662 1.1.1.1.62555 > 192.168.44.63.3128: S 20583734:20583734(0)
win 8192 <mss 1380> (DF) (ttl 17, id 46113)
17:14:39.775929 1.1.1.1.62555 > 192.168.44.63.3128: S 20583734:20583734(0)
win 8192 <mss 1380> (DF) (ttl 17, id 54353)
```

Now, look at the time changes between attempted retries. Between the first and second connection attempts, the wait is approximately 3 seconds. This doubles to 6 seconds between the second and third connections. And, finally, this doubles again to 12 seconds between the third and fourth attempts. This doubling of the backoff time might not always be witnessed—different TCP/IP stacks use different retry-time algorithms for the subsequent retries.

Often, analysts not familiar with the concept of retries misread what is happening here. They erroneously believe that an attacker is attempting multiple connections to the destination host. Instead, the retries are automatically generated by TCP.

Using Retransmissions Against a Hostile Host—LaBrea Tarpit Version 1

A very clever defender against the Code Red worm scans of web servers, Tom Liston, wrote a program that "tarpits" scanners looking for unassigned IP numbers. Typically, when you see activity to an unassigned IP address, it might mean someone is scanning hosts on your network. He named his code LaBrea after the La Brea Tar Pit.

Here is how LaBrea works. It is installed on a local host and first listens for ARP requests to unassigned IP numbers. Usually, a router generates this ARP request for the unknown IP number. When no ARP reply is generated by a real host after three seconds, the LaBrea host fakes a response to an ARP reply.

If a SYN follows from the scanning host (in this case, usually an infected Code Red host), the LaBrea host fakes a SYN/ACK response. LaBrea does not examine the destination port, so this program could be used against any TCP scan or attempted TCP connection to an unassigned IP number. The scanning host then completes the three-way handshake and attempts to send some data. The LaBrea host now deliberately fails to respond by never ACKing the data sent by the scanning host. Thus, the scanning host is tarpitted in retransmissions until it times out. This consumes resources on the scanning host and slows its capability to scan, especially if it waits for a response to proceed with further scanning.

Let's examine what happens step by step in the LaBrea tarpit:

```
ARP request for unassigned IP 192.168.143.236

18:34:32.757821 arp who-has 192.168.143.236 tell 192.168.143.1
18:34:35.743528 arp who-has 192.168.143.236 tell 192.168.143.1

After 3 seconds and no ARP reply, LaBrea host fakes reply

18:34:35.743591 arp reply 192.168.143.236 (0:0:f:ff:ff:ff) is-at
0:0:f:ff:ff:ff
```

First, LaBrea looks for ARP requests on the local network. These usually come from the local routing device. If it sees no ARP reply after three seconds (this is the default wait time, however it can be changed by a command line option), it fakes an ARP reply. In this case, we see an ARP request for host 192.168.143.236 from the local router 192.168.143.1. This is an unassigned IP number. No ARP reply is seen and another ARP request is generated three seconds after the initial one.

After three seconds, the LaBrea host fakes an ARP reply and tells 192.168.143.1 that the MAC address for 192.168.143.236 is a bogus 0:0:f:ff:ff:ff. Neither the 192.168.143.236 address nor the MAC address is real. This is a way to allow the routing device to respond to the scanner without generating an ICMP unreachable error. Now, the LaBrea host will look for any traffic destined for the bogus MAC address going across the network.

After the bogus MAC address is generated by LaBrea, the scanning host's SYN attempt is answered by the LaBrea host simulating a listening host and port as shown.

```
Infected Code Red host requests SYN

18:34:35.743817 codered.victim.com.1113 > 192.168.143.236.www: S
301190748:301190748(0) win 8192 <mss 1460,nop,nop,sackOK> (DF)
```

LaBrea host spoofs ACK

```
18:34:35.743940 192.168.143.236.www > codered.victim.com.1113: S
2516582400:2516582400(0) ack 301190749 win 10
```

Infected Code Red host completes three-way handshake

```
18:34:35.744190 codered.victim.com.1113 > 192.168.143.236.www: . ack 1 win
8576 (DF)
```

In the previous output, you see the codered.victim.com host attempt a SYN connection to the unassigned destination IP address 192.168.143.236 destination port 80 (www). LaBrea then generates a response to this connection with a SYN/ACK from the non-existent IP address 192.168.143.236. And, as expected, the codered.victim.com host completes the three-way handshake. The connection is now "established."

Next, the codered.victim.com host attempts to send 10 bytes of data to fill the receive buffer of the bogus web server 192.168.143.236 as can be seen in the following output:

```
Code Red host sends 10 bytes of data
18:34:35.745555 codered.victim.com.1113 > 192.168.143.236.www: . 1:11(10) ack
1 win 8576 (DF)
Retransmission at +6 seconds
18:34:41.746643 codered.victim.com.1113 > 192.168.143.236.www: . 1:11(10) ack
1 win 8576 (DF)
Retransmission at +12 seconds
18:34:53.743027 codered.victim.com.1113 > 192.168.143.236.www: . 1:11(10) ack
1 win 8576 (DF)
Retransmission at +24 seconds
18:35:17.735734 codered.victim.com.1113 > 192.168.143.236.www: . 1:11(10) ack
1 win 8576 (DF)
Retransmission at +48 seconds
18:36:05.741181 codered.victim.com.1113 > 192.168.143.236.www: . 1:11(10) ack
1 win 8576 (DF)
Retransmission at +96 seconds
18:37:41.911995 codered.victim.com.1113 > 192.168.143.236.www: . 1:11(10) ack
1 win 8576 (DF)
3 minutes 6 seconds later retransmissions stop
```

There is no PUSH flag set as you are used to seeing because the PUSH flag is only set when the sending host empties its sending buffer. But, because codered.victim.com's send buffer is greater than 10 bytes, the only flag you see is the ACK flag acknowledging receipt of the bogus initial SYN connection from 192.168.143.236.

Now, here comes the tarpit. There is no acknowledgement of the data sent by codered.victim.com. So, it must retransmit the data. The retransmission timer for this particular host has an exponential backoff where it doubles the time between retries. Of the several runs of LaBrea attempted, the first retry varied in wait time from three to twelve seconds after the initial try. Several attempts used the six-second wait as manifested in the previous output.

Five retries and three minutes and six seconds after the initial attempt to send data, the codered.victim.com host gives up. But it has expended resources and been delayed in its scanning for this duration. If the scanning host waits for the response from the LaBrea host before continuing the scan, it has been slowed down in its efforts. This is more effective if the scanning host is tarpitted over and over again for all unassigned IPs on this network.

Although it appears very tempting to use LaBrea, make sure that you understand the implications of doing so. First, as currently written, the tarpit is performed for any TCP connection for which there is no real destination IP, regardless of destination port number. If a real host in the network temporarily experiences problems and is unable to respond to an ARP request, legitimate connections might be erroneously tarpitted. Also, it appears that firewalls that maintain state tables of connections can become encumbered by the tarpitted connections. LaBrea code can be found at `www.hackbusters.net`.

La Brea Tar Pit

La Brea Tar Pit is located in Los Angeles's Hancock Park. It was the site of a natural accumulation of tar that formed over oil. During the Early Pleistocene time (about 2.5 million years ago), animals became tarpitted and died when attempting to drink at the site or cross the tar formation.

TCP Window Size

The TCP window size is the method employed by a receiving host to inform the sending host of the current buffer size for data sent for that connection. This is a flow control mechanism because it is dynamic. The window size becomes smaller for all data that has been received, but not yet processed by the receiving host. If the receiving buffer ever becomes full, the window size becomes 0 informing the sending host to temporarily halt transmission of any more data. After the receiving host has processed some of the data in the buffer, it sends a window size update to the sending host to inform it to resume sending data.

As you can see, flow of control for TCP sessions is mostly done by the receiving host by use of the window size. We have a tendency to assume that the sender is really the one controlling the flow of data across the network. But, for the most part, the receiver is the director of the data flow.

Initial window sizes are used by nmap to determine the operating system. Different TCP/IP stacks select different initial window sizes, which is used to help fingerprint the operating system.

LaBrea Version 2

If you recall, the original version of LaBrea was able to slow down a scanning or attacking host for the amount of time it took the attacker's TCP connection to time out from lack of a response after the three-way handshake. Depending on the attacker's TCP/IP stack implementation of the number of retries and the backoff time between timeouts, the attacker could be delayed several minutes.

LaBrea's author, Tom Liston, improved on his own concept using another technique known as the TCP persist timer. As we just learned, if a receiving host's TCP window is filled and it cannot accept any more data from the sender, it notifies the sender to cease sending data by setting the window size to 0. Ordinarily, when the receive buffer frees up space by sending the data to TCP, a TCP segment follows with a window size greater than 0. What if this new window advertisement is lost? Both sender and receiver would be frozen waiting for the other to act.

There is a mechanism to deal with this known as a window probe. After a timer expires and the sender has not received any new window advertisement from the receiver, the sender transmits a TCP window probe that carries 1 byte of payload with the exclusive purpose of soliciting a response from the receiver to discover if the window size has been increased. The sender persists in sending window probes until the window size increases or until either of the end-host applications terminates.

The new version of LaBrea uses the persist timer to tarpit the attacker for an indefinite amount of time, as you can see from the following TCPdump output. It works exactly like the previous version of LaBrea up through the three-way handshake. Instead of not responding, LaBrea reacts to the sender's data with an acknowledgement, but with a window size of 0. It doesn't increase the window size via a window update forcing the scanner to send a window probe. The LaBrea host responds to the window probe, but again advertises the window size as 0. This pattern of window probe and a response of a window size of 0 continues indefinitely. This tarpits the attacker into a persistent connection with the LaBrea host if there is no intervention. Take a look at the output:

```
19:28:07.577541 codered.victim.com.2045 > 10.10.10.155.www: S
882335286:882335286(0) win 8192 <mss 1460,nop,nop,sackOK> (DF)
19:28:07.577618 10.10.10.155.www > codered.victim.com.2045: S
998514038:998514038(0) ack 882335287 win 5
19:28:07.577879 codered.victim.com.2045 > 10.10.10.155.www: . ack 1 win 8576
(DF)

19:28:07.581366 codered.victim.com.2045 > 10.10.10.155.www: . 1:6(5) ack 1
win 8576 (DF)
19:28:07.581437 10.10.10.155.www > codered.victim.com.2045: . ack 6 win 0
19:28:09.820965 codered.victim.com.2045 > 10.10.10.155.www: . 6:7(1) ack 1
win 8576 (DF)
19:28:09.821041 10.10.10.155.www > codered.victim.com.2045: . ack 6 win 0
19:28:14.424567 codered.victim.com.2045 > 10.10.10.155.www: . 6:7(1) ack 1
win 8576(DF)
19:28:14.424646 10.10.10.155.www > codered.victim.com.2045: . ack 6 win 0
19:28:23.621770 codered.victim.com.2045 > 10.10.10.155.www: . 6:7(1) ack 1
win 8576 (DF)
19:28:23.621845 10.10.10.155.www > codered.victim.com.2045: . ack 6 win 0
19:28:42.016162 codered.victim.com.2045 > 10.10.10.155.www: . 6:7(1) ack 1
win 8576 (DF)
19:28:42.016237 10.10.10.155.www > codered.victim.com.2045: . ack 6 win 0
19:29:18.804962 codered.victim.com.2045 > 10.10.10.155.www: . 6:7(1) ack 1
win 8576 (DF)
19:29:18.805038 10.10.10.155.www > codered.victim.com.2045: . ack 6 win 0
```

We join our session after the faked ARP reply by the LaBrea host. For orientation purposes, we see the three-way handshake completed by the Code Red victim host, codered.victim.com, and the LaBrea host pretending to be host 10.10.10.155. The codered.victim.com host then sends 5 bytes of data (in bold output) because that was the advertised window size of the bogus 10.10.10.155 host. The 10.10.10.155 LaBrea host responds with an acknowledgement of receipt of data, but a window size of 0. The codered.victim.com host waits a couple of seconds when it doesn't get any notification of a window size increase and sends a 1-byte window probe to 10.10.10.155. The LaBrea host lazily responds to the window probe essentially telling the inquirer to chill out; it is still alive and running, but is not ready for any data just yet. As you witness, this cycle is repeated with the probing host increasing its wait time for future probes and becoming tarpitted indefinitely.

UDP

UDP is a much less complicated protocol to discuss than TCP because it doesn't have any of the fields that ensure reliable delivery. UDP does not make any guarantees that data will be delivered and leaves this function to applications to handle. This section will examine the fields found in the UDP header and how UDP port scanning is accomplished.

Ports

Just as with TCP ports, UDP port fields are two separate 16-bit fields in the TCP header—one for source and another for destination. The valid range of values is between 1 and 65535; the use of port 0 is typically a signature of unusual activity.

When a source host wishes to connect to a destination host, an ephemeral port is typically selected in the range of ports greater than 1023. For each new sending connection, a different ephemeral port should be selected.

UDP Port Scanning

Unlike TCP that responds with either a positive response (SYN/ACK) to a listening port or a negative response (RESET/ACK) to a non-listening port, UDP doesn't respond to an initial connection with any positive feedback. But, a live host responds with a negative response of ICMP "port unreachable" to a non-listening UDP port. This is how scanners determine if the UDP port is listening or not. This is another more stealthy way to scan for live hosts, assuming the site does not block outbound ICMP error messages.

So, the absence of an ICMP "port unreachable" error is construed as an open port. What if the scanning packet got dropped on its way to the target host? Or what if the target host responds with an ICMP "port unreachable" message, but the site blocks outbound ICMP messages? Or what if the site blocks inbound UDP and blocks all outbound ICMP or ICMP unreachable messages so that the scanner cannot receive an ICMP "admin prohibited" message to know this? This can be misconstrued as a listening port. Nmap scans the same UDP ports many times to try to deal with the case of dropped packets. If one packet is dropped and the network is not under duress or having problems, chances are one of the repeated packets will not be dropped. And once again, nmap is intelligent enough to know that the lack of any response is more likely an indication of filtering of some sort by the destination site than it is of all UDP ports listening.

This is a UDP port scan in the 32771 to 34000 range to look for open Remote Procedure Call (RPC) ports on a Solaris host. Nmap found many of these ports open. It assumes that a port is open if no ICMP "port unreachable" message was returned. As we have discussed, this is not always true.

```
nmap -sU sparky -p 32771-34000

WARNING:  -sU is now UDP scan -- for TCP FIN scan use -sF
Starting nmap V. 2.12 by Fyodor (fyodor@dhp.com, www.insecure.org/nmap/)
Interesting ports on sparky (1.1.1.100):
```

```
Port     State      Protocol    Service

32771    open       udp         unknown
32772    open       udp         unknown
32773    open       udp         unknown
32774    open       udp         unknown
32782    open       udp         unknown
32783    open       udp         unknown
32784    open       udp         unknown
32785    open       udp         unknown
32786    open       udp         unknown
32797    open       udp         unknown
```

The following TCPdump output shows a sample from UDP port scanning. Any port in the scanned range that sparky does not generate an ICMP "port unreachable" message for is assumed to be listening:

```
07:09:08.286810 verbo.62865 > sparky.32787: udp
07:09:08.286847 verbo.62865 > sparky.32775: udp
07:09:08.286878 verbo.62865 > sparky.32788: udp
07:09:08.286924 verbo.62865 > sparky.32789: udp
07:09:08.286969 verbo.62865 > sparky.32791: udp
07:09:08.287046 verbo.62865 > sparky.32774: udp
07:09:08.287094 verbo.62865 > sparky.32781: udp
07:09:08.287162 verbo.62865 > sparky.32772: udp
07:09:08.287229 verbo.62865 > sparky.32789: udp

07:09:08.287793 sparky > verbo: icmp: sparky udp port 32788 unreachable (DF)
07:09:08.977544 sparky > verbo: icmp: sparky udp port 32791 unreachable (DF)
07:09:09.657361 sparky > verbo: icmp: sparky udp port 32781 unreachable (DF)
07:09:10.157301 sparky > verbo: icmp: sparky udp port 32787 unreachable (DF)
07:09:10.817315 sparky > verbo: icmp: sparky udp port 32789 unreachable (DF)
```

UDP Length Field

The UDP length is the number of bytes found in the UDP header plus the number of bytes found in the UDP payload. The UDP header is 8 bytes so the minimum length for the UDP length is 8 bytes. The maximum theoretical byte length of an IP datagram is 65535. Given this, and that the IP header is a minimum of 20 bytes long, the theoretical maximum UDP length value is 65515.

Many UDP applications limit the length of the UDP datagram to 8192 bytes, although we saw where DNS limited the DNS payload to 512 bytes. Also, the TCP/IP stack of a given operating system as implemented in the kernel might limit the length of the UDP datagram.

ICMP

ICMP is another protocol that is fairly simple as far as the fields found in the header. Like UDP, ICMP does not guarantee delivery of the message, so its structure and fields are straightforward. ICMP fields will be examined in terms of normal and malicious use.

Type and Code

Remember that ICMP has no ports. There must be a method indicating what type of ICMP message is being sent or received. The first two bytes of the ICMP message are the ICMP message type and code, respectively. The message code is a subcategory under the message type.

For instance, there are two possible message codes for a message type of 11, which represents the time exceeded category. If the message code is 0, it is a "time exceeded in-transit" message. If the message code is 1, it is an IP "reassembly time exceeded" message. Valid values of ICMP message types and codes are found at www.iana.org/assignments/icmp-parameters.

Identification and Sequence Numbers

If you examine some ICMP requests such as the echo request, you'll find some additional fields in the ICMP header. These are the ICMP identifier found in bytes 4 and 5 offset of the ICMP header and the ICMP sequence number found in bytes 6 and 7 offset of the ICMP header.

These fields are used in an echo request/echo reply pair to uniquely identify requests and match them with responses. For UNIX hosts, the ICMP ID is typically the process ID of the ping that generated the traffic. There can be several simultaneous ping commands so the identifier in both the echo request and echo reply informs the pinging host what reply is connected with what request. Each ping can generate several echo requests and the sequence number is the manner in which they are tracked in order to see if there are missing packets. Here is the output from a ping request that demonstrates the change in ICMP sequence numbers.

```
PING sparky (1.1.1.100) from 1.1.1.5 : 56(84) bytes of data.

64 bytes from 1.1.1.100: icmp_seq=0 ttl=255 time=0.8 ms
64 bytes from 1.1.1.100: icmp_seq=1 ttl=255 time=0.9 ms
64 bytes from 1.1.1.100: icmp_seq=2 ttl=255 time=7.3 ms

16:33:07.400700 verbo > sparky: icmp: echo request

4500 0054 038d 0000 4001 bed1 0101 0105
0101 0164 0800 9e12 c402 0000 0391 8439
1d1d 0600 0809 0a0b 0c0d 0e0f 1011 1213

1415 1617 181916:33:07.401479 sparky > verbo: icmp: echo reply (DF)

4500 0054 7146 4000 ff01 5217 010018f64
010018f05 0000 a612 c402 0000 0391 8439
1d1d 0600 0809 0a0b 0c0d 0e0f 1011 1213
1415 1617 1819
```

Let's examine the ICMP identifier and sequence numbers in the context of the previous output's ping. We ping host sparky from verbo and see from the output that the sequence number begins at 0 and increments for each new echo request sent out. In this case, the ping process was aborted after the third echo request.

If you examine the hex dump, you'll see that the identifier is a hex c402 or decimal 50178. Because the pinging host is a Linux host, we assume this is the process ID of the ping. This value will remain static for all echo requests and replies associated with this ping. The sequence number, on the other hand, will increase by 1 for each new echo request sent and will be cloned in the associated echo reply. Had all the echo requests and replies associated with this ping process been displayed, we'd see four additional records, two echo requests, and two echo replies. The identifier would be the same for all, but the sequence number would be 1 for the second set of echo requests and replies, and it would be 2 for the third set.

Misuse of ICMP Identification and Sequence Numbers

Because the ICMP identifier and sequence number fields were not likely to receive careful scrutiny in the past, they were chosen to signal exploit traffic to the receiving host. In the case of the a DDoS known as Stacheldraht, the ICMP identifier value of 667 was used to initiate connections between handler and agent hosts in an ICMP echo reply. The ICMP identifier value of 666 was used to respond from agent to handler with another ICMP echo reply. In Tribe Flood Network, an ICMP identifier value of 456 was used to initiate a connection between client and daemon and a value of 123 was used to respond—both using ICMP echo replies too. Finally, Loki of many years ago had a static hex value of 0xf001 or 0x01f0 in the ICMP sequence number.

These are all valid values for those fields so tuning a NIDS to look solely for those values in those fields might generate some false positives. It is best to examine these packets statefully in the context in which they occurred.

Summary

As we wind up our two-chapter scrutiny of header fields in the IP datagram, we finish our examination of the embedded protocol fields. By far, TCP is the busiest of the protocol headers because of all of the fields required to maintain reliability, state, order, and data flow control. As you would imagine, the initial values selected for some of these fields provide a wealth of information for nmap operating system fingerprinting scans. As well, some of the fields can be used for invasion or insertion attacks as we saw demonstrated with the TCP checksum example in the previous chapter.

UDP and ICMP header fields are uncomplicated in purpose. Still, UDP ports can be scanned using nmap by searching for ports for which no ICMP "port unreachable" message is returned. ICMP messages can provide reconnaissance when allowed to leave the network, and nmap makes use of examining the embedded messages after the ICMP header to identify remote operating systems. Finally, the ICMP identification and sequence numbers have been used for stealthy purposes in DDoS attacks or covert protocol exchanges.

10

Real-World Analysis

No DOUBT YOU'VE HAD YOUR FILL of healthy, low-fat theory on packet dissection and header fields. How about bringing on some of the more interesting, tasty, real-world traffic? That is what we are about to embark on in this chapter. For you to understand the analysis that will be shown here, it was necessary to lay the groundwork in previous chapters first.

To refresh your memory of the intent of this section, we want to analyze traffic from many different viewpoints. We've evolved from bits and fields in previous chapters to inspecting one or more packets for their intent and explaining some actual events of interest that were captured by Shadow from sites.

The transition from understanding theory to actually explaining some traffic that you see is not necessarily an easy or intuitive one. It takes time and exposure to some interesting traffic before you gain the confidence and experience to make this transition. The examples shown in this chapter should help you get started.

You've Been Hacked!

The simplicity of this first real-world event belies its poignancy. In a former lifetime, I worked for a local military Computer Emergency Response Team (CERT). I worked an early shift beginning about 5:30 A.M. to avoid the brunt of the rush hour traffic from the suburbs of one of the nation's most awful commuting cities, Washington, DC. I walked into the office one morning, and the phone was already ringing—not a good sign unless it is Ed McMahon calling to tell me I'd won the Publisher's Clearinghouse Sweepstakes. Instead, the call was from one of our parent military CERTs informing us that we'd had a break-in over night.

As a bit of background, the parent CERT used a different set of tools to monitor our site than we did, and would sometimes call when it had an inquiry about traffic or to report something noteworthy, as in this case. The CERT supplied the date, approximate time, and source and destination IPs associated with the break-in, but could supply no more information than this when queried.

The destination IP of the alleged victim host was a DNS server at the site. This was probably one of the best maintained hosts on the site; it had the most recent patches of BIND, it had all ports closed except for secure shell (SSH) from specific source addresses and DNS queries, and it had been stripped of all unnecessary user accounts. It was not as if this was some legacy system sitting openly on a DMZ with no recent attention, superfluous ports open, and unrestricted access. Still, although my first reaction was skepticism, I wasn't naive enough to think that any host connected to the Internet was impervious to attack. After all, this was a DNS server, and the venerable BIND software has been plagued with a history of problems, including buffer overflow attacks that allowed remote root access.

A rational way to approach this early morning report was to use TCPdump records from Shadow to examine all traffic to and from our DNS server from the alleged attacker's IP address. Before showing you an excerpt of the results of that, let's just re-examine what an established TCP session looks like in terms of TCPdump.

Three-Way Handshake:

```
boulder.myplace.com.38060 > aspen.myplace.com.telnet: S 3774957990:
3774957990(0) win 8760 <mss 1460> (DF)
aspen.myplace.com.telnet > boulder.myplace.com.38060: S 2009600000:
2009600000(0) ack 3774957991 win 1024 <mss 1460>
boulder.myplace.com.38060 > aspen.myplace.com.telnet:. ack 1 win 8760 (DF)
```

Data Exchange:

```
boulder.myplace.com.38060 > aspen.myplace.com.telnet: P 1:28(27) ack 1 win
8760 (DF)
aspen.myplace.com.telnet > boulder.myplace.com.38060: P 1:14(13) ack 1 win
1024
aspen.myplace.com.telnet > boulder.myplace.com.38060: P 14:23(9) ack 28 win
1024
```

Session Termination:

```
aspen.myplace.com.telnet > boulder.myplace.com.38060: F 4289:4289(0) ack 92
win 1024
boulder.myplace.com.38060 > aspen.myplace.com.telnet: .ack 4290 win 8760 (DF)
boulder.myplace.com.38060 > aspen.myplace.com.telnet: F 92:92(0) ack 4290
win 8760(DF)
aspen.myplace.com.telnet > boulder.myplace.com.38060: .ack 93 win 1024
```

First, for two hosts to exchange some kind of data, they have to complete the three-way handshake. In this case, we have host `boulder.myplace.com` requesting to connect to host `aspen.myplace.com` on port telnet. Host `aspen.myplace.com` offers telnet service; and the two hosts synchronize sequence numbers and the connection is established.

Next, typically a client connects to a host for the purpose of exchanging some data. And in this case, we witness the exchange between both hosts as we see 27, 13, and 9 bytes of data sent respectively in the three PUSH packets displayed. More data was exchanged before the session was terminated, but that is not shown because it really adds no new insight into this discussion.

Finally, the two hosts gracefully sever the connection by exchanging and acknowledging FIN packets. That is what normal TCP sessions look like.

Now, examine some of the traffic from the alleged break-in:

```
whatsup.net.24997 > dns.myplace.com.sunrpc: S 2368718861:2368718861(0) win
512 <mss 1460>
whatsup.net.25002 > dns.myplace.com.139: S 4067302570:4067302570(0) win 512
<mss 1460>
whatsup.net.25075 > dns.myplace.com.ftp: S 1368714289:1368714289(0) win 512
<mss 1460>
dns.myplace.com.ftp > whatsup.net.25075: R 0:0(0) ack 1368714290 win 0 (DF)
whatsup.net.25177 > dns.myplace.com.1114: S 3231175487:3231175487(0) win 512
<mss 1460>
whatsup.net.25189 > dns.myplace.com.tcpmux: S 368146356:368146356(0) win 512
<mss 1460>
whatsup.net.25118 > dns.myplace.com.22: S 2035824356:2035824356(0)          win
512 <mss 1460>
```

The malicious host is `whatsup.net` and our DNS server is `dns.myplace.com`. We see a bunch of attempted SYN connections to various different ports staring with port 111, also known as sunrpc or portmapper, port 139, NetBIOS session manager, ftp, and so on. We see no response from the DNS server except to return a RESET on the ftp query. We can surmise that the packet-filtering device blocked the other ports we see, yet not ftp. When the DNS server received the ftp SYN attempt, it responded with a RESET because it didn't listen at that port.

This is just an excerpt of the traffic seen, yet it all was similar except for the different destination ports attempted. The point is that there were no successful three-way handshakes, data exchange, or session terminations witnessed. Unless there was some kind of unknown backdoor into our network that was not monitored, it appears that this was a simple scan of the DNS server and not a break-in.

After analyzing this traffic, I called the person who had reported the break-in. I shared my results and asked what kind of evidence they had that there was a break-in. The person replied that one of their parent CERT organizations had reported this and was just passing the information on to our site. I got the contact information for the original person who reported the incident and called to inquire why he believed we had suffered an intrusion. The response was that he had reported it as a scan, and it had been mistakenly communicated to me as a break-in.

My mission had not been to determine culpability; it was to determine what kind of solid evidence anyone had to refute my belief that we had only had a scan. But, as it turned out, there really was no break-in after all. This incident brought home the necessity for having an audit trail of activity into and out of the network. Had we not had the TCPdump records of the scan, we would have had no evidence to refute the intrusion claim. We would have had to trust the caller and believe that we had an intrusion that none of our NIDS had detected.

We could have logged on to the DNS server. Yet, there would be an absence of any evidence, if we were lucky. There would be no changes in any of the Tripwire logs that maintained integrity audits of important files, there would be no rootkits, and there would be no changes to password files or inetd startup files. It would be impossible to know for certain that there had been no intrusion; there would be lingering doubt that we just were not seeing the manifestations of the break-in, perhaps because of installed rootkits and Trojaned software. In such a case where you are still uncertain about the health of the host, there are not a lot of options. You have to rebuild the system from the ground up—not a desirable task.

Prior to this event, I had been a proponent of Shadow and had been collecting TCPdump activity at monitored sites. This converted me to a die-hard Shadow user, and I now use Shadow for all sites that I monitor. Truthfully, it doesn't matter if you use TCPdump or any other collection mechanism. What matters is that you have this historical capture of the traffic entering and leaving your network. And, you don't need to capture payload, just the header portions of the records, to understand the nature of the activity as was demonstrated in this incident. Indeed, it also can be helpful to capture payload if you have enough space, even if only to keep it a couple of days before archiving it.

Netbus Scan

In the next incident, we examine a scan to destination port 12345, which is typically associated with the netbus Trojan that affects Windows hosts. This particular scan was launched against a Class B subnet so that it set off all kinds of alarms. The network that was scanned had some high-numbered port access open through the packet-filtering devices.

The following records provide a very brief excerpt of the detected traffic. This scan attempted connections to more than 65,000 IPs in the target network. It is important to note that this traffic was collected on a sensor located behind (inside) the packet-filtering device. This is the traffic that actually got inside the network. Scans happen! In fact, they happen all the time on this particular network. It's not that this network is any more inviting than others; it is just a fact of life that scanning is inevitable and frequent. Knowing this, you cannot get too worked up when you see scans. However, this is inside the packet-filtering device making it more than a curiosity, as we will later see. Here are the records:

```
bigscan.net.1737 > 192.168.7.0.12345: S 2299794832:2299794832(0) win 32120
<mss 1380,sackOK,timestamp 120377100[|tcp]> (DF)

bigscan.net.1739 > 192.168.7.2.12345: S 2299202490:2299202490(0) win 32120
<mss 1380,sackOK,timestamp 120377100[|tcp]> (DF)

bigscan.net.1741 > 192.168.7.4.12345: S 2293163750:2293163750(0) win 32120
<mss 1380,sackOK,timestamp 120377100[|tcp]> (DF)

bigscan.net.1743 > 192.168.7.6.12345: S 2298524651:2298524651(0) win 32120
<mss 1380,sackOK,timestamp 120377100[|tcp]> (DF)

bigscan.net.1745 > 192.168.7.8.12345: S 2297131917:2297131917(0) win 32120
<mss 1380,sackOK,timestamp 120377100[|tcp]> (DF)

bigscan.net.1747 > 192.168.7.10.12345: S 2291750743:2291750743(0) win 32120
<mss 1380,sackOK,timestamp 120377100[|tcp]> (DF)

bigscan.net.1749 > 192.168.7.12.12345: S 2287868521:2287868521(0) win 32120
<mss 1380,sackOK,timestamp 120377100[|tcp]> (DF
```

We see the scanning host bigscan.net methodically moving through the 192.168.7 subnet with a unique scan search pattern of looking at the .0 address and even final octets thereafter.

Netbus Hijinks

Netbus is a tool that allows remote access and control of a Windows host. After a host is compromised, it behooves the attacker to have a means of future access to the host. Netbus is one of many backdoor Trojans that can be run to provide stealthy access. It predates another, more familiar backdoor Trojan, Back Orifice. Both Netbus and Back Orifice have user-friendly GUI interfaces to easily control the remote compromised host.

Not All That Runs on Port 12345 Is Malicious

The OfficeScan virus eradication package for the corporate enterprise listens on TCP port 12345 on the desktop host. The enterprise software accommodates central virus reporting, automatic update (apparently via port 12345 on the updated host), and remote management for ease of use to assist in monitoring and configuration.

If you ever see a host that listens on TCP port 12345, it is possible that it might be a helpful rather than harmful process. Given the range of possible listening ports 1 through 65535, I'd much prefer to see the white hats (good guys) select listening ports that don't share commonly used hacker ports.

Let's go for the jugular and see if there is any need to further investigate this scan. We want to examine the hosts in the internal network and see if they responded to the scan. The TCPdump filter to examine this would look for traffic from the internal network of 192.168 with a source port of 12345 and a TCP flag pair of SYN and ACK. This means that we have a listening host, which can be potentially very dangerous. Our filter could have used the IP number of the scanning host instead of or in conjunction with the internal subnet address.

The TCPdump command used to extract response records associated with the scan reads from the binary file of collected records for the site, and identifies this scan as one that involved the internal 192.168 subnet and port 12345. The TCPdump command is further refined by using a filter that looks at the 13th byte offset of the TCP header, where the TCP flag byte is located, and looks for the ACK flag and the SYN flag set simultaneously. Here is the TCPdump command and the output generated from it:

```
tcpdump -r tcpdumpfile 'net 192.168 and port 12345 and tcp[13] = 0x12'

mynet.edu.12345 > bigscan.net.3698: S 2633608519:2633608519(0) ack 2346088305
win 49152 <mss 1380,nop,nop,timestamp 2662730[|tcp]> (DF)
```

The good news is that only one host responded. The bad news is that one host responded! When it was discovered that there was a responding host, this incident was escalated to the highest priority because we believed we had a host offering the netbus Trojan, a natural conclusion. The scan and subsequent discovery that there was a responding host occurred by 7:00 A.M., meaning that most of the staff had not yet arrived at work. In the interim, the network group was contacted and told to disallow any inbound or outbound traffic to or from the responding host by blocking it at the packet-filtering device. Also, the local computer incident response team was mobilized to scan the host for vulnerabilities and track down the owner.

After some superficial probing, the incident response team discovered that the host was a Silicon Graphics, Inc. (SGI) running an older version of Irix (SGI's version of UNIX). As a veteran of incident response teams, I remembered that older versions of Irix used to come configured with an account of lp (line printer) with no password. Tragically, a telnet connection to the host allowed me access to the host, using the lp account and no password. This discovery pretty much ruled out that this was a netbus problem because the responding host ran a version of UNIX, but we did have a rogue port answering and a host that had little, if any, security.

Concurrently, the search for the host's system administrators continued. Ownership records were dated and the host had been tossed from administrator to administrator as people moved in and out of the organization and assignments changed. This particular host had a rich history of neglect because the user-administrators were scientists or engineers who were never really trained in administration, let alone security. This is a common paradigm of neglect because many research departments do not have the budget to hire trained administrators. The users are usually overburdened workers who just need to keep the host running.

The system administrators of the SGI hosts finally arrived at work. As suspected, they had no idea what was listening on port 12345. It was also quite apparent that they and their users had little concern or appreciation for security. We told them it was necessary to disconnect the host from the network and begin backups for forensic purposes. An argument ensued when one of the users became indignant about needing to have the host up and accessible on the network. The leader of the incident response team politely told him that he had two options: first, to cooperate and willingly cede control, or second, to have the network connection unceremoniously severed by wire cutters. It seems the light bulb went on at that point, and they agreed to cooperate.

When we finally got access to the system, we wanted to make sure that the host was listening on port 12345. The process of making backups on this host was long and cumbersome, so we didn't want to make them do anything unnecessary. At the same time, we didn't want to ruin any forensic evidence by poking around too much. Only one command was attempted—the **netstat –a** command to make sure that port 12345 was running.

Can you see the flaw of executing the **netstat** command? In hindsight, it seems this was really not such a wise move. Had the **netstat** command reported that port 12345 was not listening, this would have been extremely suspicious and more indicative of a Trojaned or rootkit netstat program running on the host that was altered to not report that port 12345 was listening. But, this was not the case; port 12345 was listening.

System backups were started to preserve any forensic evidence in case some kind of prosecution ever had to be done. Finally, when the backups were completed, we had an opportunity to examine the system. We didn't want to disturb it in any way prior to the backups.

A very handy command in this situation is the **fuser** command. This is not available for all UNIX operating systems, but it is available on Irix and Linux:

```
[root@irix]#   fuser 12345/tcp
12345/tcp:            490
```

The command was issued to find the process number associated with port 12345 on TCP. By looking at the netstat output, you don't know the process that is running the service on port 12345. The **fuser** command returns the process number of the software running on that port.

Next, you have to find what that particular process number is running. That can be done using the **ps** command and then examining the output for the process number, in this case 490:

```
[root@irix]#   ps -ef | grep 490
root        490   483   0 Sep19 ? 00:02:17 /usr/local/bin/license_manager
```

You see that there is a license manager running. When this appeared on the console with the system administrator watching, he remarked that he had recently installed a license manager. He had no idea what port it listened on. The mystery was solved! This was the best possible resolution considering the alternatives. But, give me a break—what reputable license manager software maker would use a default listening port of 12345?

Before this host was allowed back on the network, it was cleaned up with the assistance of a savvy UNIX administrator. An initial vulnerability scan of the host produced about twenty pages of high- and medium-range security problems. It was scanned again after the changes and upgrades to make sure that no known vulnerabilities existed.

Other Commands to Display Programs Associated with Ports

The UNIX command lsof can be used, as well, to list information about files opened by processes. This comes with many UNIX operating systems, but can be downloaded and added if it is not available. To find the process ID associated with the service listening on port 901 using lsof, execute the following:

```
lsof -i TCP:901
```

```
COMMAND PID USER   FD   TYPE DEVICE SIZE NODE NAME
inetd   387 root    9u  IPv4 369     TCP *:swat (LISTEN)
```

You see that port 901 is associated with the inetd process. This is the Internet daemon that starts most of the listening services. Some additional information is displayed in the last column; port 901 is associated with Samba Web Administration Tool (swat). You should find this started in the file /etc/inetd.conf:

```
grep swat /etc/inetd.conf
swat        stream  tcp    nowait.400     root /usr/sbin/swat swat
```

A Windows tool known as fport (available with a tool search on www.securityfocus.com) can be used to associate processes with ports on which they run. Here is a sample output from running fport on a Windows 2000 host:

```
FPort v1.31 - TCP/IP Process to Port Mapper
Copyright 2000 by Foundstone, Inc.
http://www.foundstone.com
Securing the dot com world

Pid    Process         Port  Proto Path
384    svchost    -> 135    TCP   C:\WINNT\system32\svchost.exe
8      System     -> 445    TCP
496    MSTask     -> 1025   TCP   C:\WINNT\system32\MSTask.exe
8      System     -> 1027   TCP
1692   SshClient  -> 3705   TCP   C:\Program Files\SSH Communications
Security\SSH Secure Shell\SshClient.exe
1892   OUTLOOK    -> 4040   TCP   C:\Program Files\Microsoft
Office\Office\OUTLOOK.EXE


384    svchost    -> 135    UDP   C:\WINNT\system32\svchost.exe
8      System     -> 445    UDP
220    services   -> 1026   UDP   C:\WINNT\system32\services.exe
916    iexplore   -> 1341   UDP   C:\Program Files\Internet
Explorer\iexplore.exe
1892   OUTLOOK    -> 4024   UDP   C:\Program Files\Microsoft
Office\Office\OUTLOOK.EXE
```

Although this turned out to be a non-incident in terms of intrusions, it does illustrate a very noteworthy point. It is extremely helpful to be able to do a quick assessment of potential reconnaissance or potential damage from scan activity of your network. Most NIDS report about scans, notifying you that they have occurred. But, the more relevant knowledge is this: did any host respond to the scans? That is where TCPdump recorded activity is once again invaluable.

How Slow Can you Go?

This event concerns a remotely monitored site that had poor response time on a good day. One day while attempting to examine activity, the response time became painfully slow. It was so slow, you could type in one character and it would take about 30 seconds to see it echoed back on the screen. This was pretty annoying, but signaled that the site had some issues other than normal poor response time.

Although this was occurring, we were collecting a copy of their Shadow sensor data at our site. In an attempt to explain the poor response time, the site's Shadow events of interest were examined. It showed that they were getting a lot of fragmented activity directed at their network address of 192.168.133.0 (this is a translated address for anonymity purposes). Upon further examination, it was discovered that this had been going on for many hours. Here is a sample of the records that they were getting:

```
12:01:12.150572 dos.com > 192.168.133.0: (frag 54050:1480@4440+)
12:01:17.560572 dos.com > 192.168.133.0: (frag 54050:1480@2960+)
12:01:17.570572 dos.com > 192.168.133.0: (frag 54050:1480@4440+)
12:01:22.200572 dos.com > 192.168.133.0: (frag 54050:1480@1480+)
12:01:22.210572 dos.com > 192.168.133.0: (frag 54050:1480@2960+)
12:01:22.220572 dos.com > 192.168.133.0: (frag 54050:1480@4440+)
12:01:22.230572 dos.com > 192.168.133.0: (frag 54050:1480@5920+)
12:01:27.240572 dos.com > 192.168.133.0: (frag 54050:1480@2960+)
12:01:27.250572 dos.com > 192.168.133.0: (frag 54050:1480@5920+)
12:01:37.230572 dos.com > 192.168.133.0: (frag 54050:1480@1480+)
12:01:37.240572 dos.com > 192.168.133.0: (frag 54050:1480@2960+)
12:01:37.240572 dos.com > 192.168.133.0: (frag 54050:1480@4440+)
12:01:37.250572 dos.com > 192.168.133.0: (frag 54050:1480@5920+)
12:01:42.300572 dos.com > 192.168.133.0: (frag 54050:1480@1480+)
```

You see dos.com sending fragmented packets to the network address. As mentioned, this activity had been happening for several hours. There are a couple of problems with the traffic that need to be examined. See if you can find the three problems associated with fragmentation in the previous TCPdump output.

First, a normal fragmented packet train usually has two or more parts:

- There is an initial fragment that has an offset of 0 and the More Fragments flag set (+):

```
frag 54050:1480@0+
```

Recall that the fragment format is as follows:

```
frag FRAG-ID:BYTES-IN-CURRENT-FRAGMENT@OFFSET-INTO-FRAGMENT-DATA [+]
```

- There might be intermediate fragments that are neither the first nor last fragments. An intermediate fragment has a non-zero offset and the More Fragments flag set. The + flag indicates that the more fragments bit is set or there is another fragment following the one being sent. The More Fragments flag is set in the first and intermediate fragments.

- There is a final fragment, one in which the more fragments bit is not set: no + flag.

This activity appeared on Shadow's hourly wrap-up from the default because both the fragmentation and the destination address having a final octet of 0 (the network address 192.168.133.0).

The fragmentation that is seen in this log has some definite problems:

1. There is no first fragment—one that has an offset of 0.

2. You see repeated offsets for fragments that are in the same fragment train with the fragment ID of 54050. For instance, the fragment offset 4440 is repeated several times.

3. There is no final fragment—one that doesn't have the More Fragments flag (+) set.

It is possible that the offset values are not chronological because the fragments don't necessarily arrive in the order in which they were sent.

After doing some research about the topology of the remote site, we discovered that our sensor was located behind (inside) a packet-filtering device that blocked inbound ICMP echo requests. That is the reason we believe that the initial fragment was never seen. Keep in mind that only the first fragment in the fragment train carries the embedded protocol header, such as the information to say that these packets were associated with ICMP echo requests. We can only surmise that the fragmented activity was associated with the dropped ICMP echo requests.

The packet-filtering device that blocked this activity was a router that did not keep track of state. Therefore, it blocked the first fragment of the fragment train because it was the one that contained the information that this was an ICMP echo request. The router had no means of associating the first fragment with subsequent ones. It appears obvious to us that the subsequent packets all share the same fragment ID and are assumed to be associated with the blocked one. Yet, this router did not maintain that information and allowed the subsequent fragments into the network.

However, this doesn't explain why no final fragment was observed. This should have nothing to do with a router that is incapable of keeping track of state. The only explanation for not receiving a final fragment is that is was intentionally omitted.

Normally, fragments are reassembled by the destination host only and not by intermediate routers through which they travel. However, in this case, the router attempts to reassemble the fragmented packets because they are sent to the network address 192.168.133.0 on which the router resides. This particular router has an old Berkeley Software Distribution (BSD) TCP/IP style stack that responds to this "broadcast" so that it attempts to reassemble the fragments.

The router has limited cache for reassembly. The combination of the repetition of the same fragment ID, the more fragments bit set in every fragment, and the missing first and last fragments severely encumbered the router so that it couldn't do routing work. The router would never time out on reassembly of these packets because it kept seeing evidence that more fragments were coming. This was a successful denial of service (DoS) against the router. When the hostile IP was blocked on an external router, the response time returned to normal.

Why didn't this router expire the incomplete set of fragments with an ICMP "IP reassembly time exceeded" message? After all, isn't this a prime candidate for resource exhaustion, waiting for a fragment or fragments that are never sent? The problem is that for the "IP reassembly time exceeded" message to be delivered and for the receiving host to expire the fragments, the first fragment must be received. Because the outermost router blocked these, the first fragment never arrived, and others could not be expired.

Although some routers block incoming ICMP echo requests, denial of service attacks against the router should not occur for "normal" traffic. The DoS attack succeeded against this particular router because of the broadcast address, the repeated fragment ID, and the missing fragments. After the problem was discovered, the activity was blocked from the hostile source IP address. This blocked all inbound traffic including fragments because the IP address is repeated in each of the IP headers of every fragment.

This was successful, and the response time returned to its normal slow (but not painful) state. The attackers must have sensed this; chances are that the monitored site must have foolishly sent ICMP errors that indicated that their activity was blocked. The attackers responded by attempting the same attack with a different source IP address on the same subnet.

Explanation Acknowledgement and Additional Reference
Many thanks and much credit to Vicki Irwin of the SANS Institute for her assistance in figuring out
the router DoS. She referenced the following for a discussion of this and similar exploits:

www.cisco.com/warp/public/770/nifrag.shtml

RingZero Worm

Let's wrap up our foray into real-world analysis by examining the RingZero
Worm. This worm would probably be considered ancient in Internet time
because it was discovered in the latter part of 1999. Plenty has transpired concerning malicious code since that time, yet some of the concepts that can be
learned from examination of the worm activity are timeless. This presents a
good transition into the next and final chapter of this section that delves more
deeply into forensics.

The first indication that the monitored site had some new and unusual
activity was that Shadow reported many different attempts to connect to TCP
port 3128, the squid web proxy server. These attempted connections occurred
many times an hour and were from source hosts from all over the world.
Although it has become rather commonplace today with malicious code such
as Code Red and nimda to see many different source IPs scanning many different destination IPs, in late 1999, it was a rarity. Here is an excerpt of the
kind of activity seen for one hour at the monitored site:

```
12:29:48.230000 4.3.2.1.1049 > 172.16.54.171.3128: S 9779697:9779697(0) win
8192 <mss 1460> (DF)
12:29:58.070000 4.3.2.1.1049 > 172.16.54.171.3128: S 9779697:9779697(0) win
8192 <mss 1460> (DF)
12:30:10.960000 4.3.2.1.1049 > 172.16.54.171.3128: S 9779697:9779697(0) win
8192 <mss 1460> (DF)

12:44:54.960000 1.2.3.4.3243 > 172.16.187.212.3128: S 356330349:356330349(0)
win 8192 <mss 1460> (DF)
12:44:57.930000 1.2.3.4.3243 > 172.16.187.212.3128: S 356330349:356330349(0)
win 8192 <mss 1460> (DF)
12:45:03.930000 1.2.3.4.3243 > 172.16.187.212.3128: S 356330349:356330349(0)
win 8192 <mss 1460> (DF)
12:45:15.930000 1.2.3.4.3243 > 172.16.187.212.3128: S 356330349:356330349(0)
win 8192 <mss 1460> (DF)

12:46:13.070000 1.1.1.1.2262 > 172.16.99.110.3128: S 20315949:20315949(0) win
8192 <mss 1460,nop,nop,sackOK> (DF)
12:46:16.080000 1.1.1.1.2262 > 172.16.99.110.3128: S 20315949:20315949(0) win
8192 <mss 1460,nop,nop,sackOK> (DF)
12:46:22.070000 1.1.1.1.2262 > 172.16.99.110.3128: S 20315949:20315949(0) win
8192 <mss 1460,nop,nop,sackOK> (DF)
```

Three different source IPs—4.3.2.1, 1.2.3.4, and 1.1.1.1—are attempting connections to three different internal destination IP addresses. Because many of the scanned destination IPs in our network were not active, there appeared to be no prior reconnaissance that would target live hosts only. Each source host retries (source ports and TCP sequence numbers do not change) the connection several times because the destination hosts do not respond, and no ICMP error message is returned to indicate that the destination hosts are unreachable. Looking at the timestamps, you can see that these connection attempts occurred at different times during the 12:00 hour.

Our site was not the only one that witnessed this activity; the Naval Surface Warfare Center was also seeing these scans as well as ones to destination port 80 and 8080. Other sites witnessed this activity, and soon, it became apparent that this activity was very widespread.

The initial assessment of the activity was someone attempting to find open web proxy servers. Open proxy servers sometimes offer a "tunnel" through which a hacker can gain access and assume the source IP of the proxy to hide his tracks. At this point, because the traffic was coming from all over the world, one theory was that the source IPs had been spoofed and it was just a handful of hosts involved. Again, this attack pre-dates the notion of distributed denial of service (DDoS) attacks, so we were unaccustomed to dealing with many source hosts to many destination host attacks.

The verbose option (**-vv**) of TCPdump might provide some assistance in determining whether or not the source IPs were spoofed. The same TCPdump records are examined again, but this time using the verbose option:

```
12:29:48.230000 4.3.2.1.1049 > 172.16.54.171.3128: S 9779697:9779697(0) win
8192 <mss 1460> (DF) (ttl 19, id 9072)
12:29:58.070000 4.3.2.1.1049 > 172.16.54.171.3128: S 9779697:9779697(0) win
8192 <mss 1460> (DF) (ttl 19, id 29552)
12:30:10.960000 4.3.2.1.1049 > 172.16.54.171.3128: S 9779697:9779697(0) win
8192 <mss 1460> (DF) (ttl 19, id 39792)

12:44:54.960000 1.2.3.4.3243 > 172.16.187.212.3128: S 356330349:356330349(0)
win 8192 <mss 1460> (DF) (ttl 19, id 962)
12:44:57.930000 1.2.3.4.3243 > 172.16.187.212.3128: S 356330349:356330349(0)
win 8192 <mss 1460> (DF) (ttl 19, id 11714)
12:45:03.930000 1.2.3.4.3243 > 172.16.187.212.3128: S 356330349:356330349(0)
win 8192 <mss 1460> (DF) (ttl 19, id 22466)
12:45:15.930000 1.2.3.4.3243 > 172.16.187.212.3128: S 356330349:356330349(0)
win 8192 <mss 1460> (DF) (ttl 19, id 33218)

12:46:13.070000 1.1.1.1.2262 > 172.16.99.110.3128: S 20315949:20315949(0) win
8192 <mss 1460,nop,nop,sackOK> (DF) (ttl 116, id 35676)
12:46:16.080000 1.1.1.1.2262 > 172.16.99.110.3128: S 20315949:20315949(0) win
8192 <mss 1460,nop,nop,sackOK> (DF) (ttl 116, id 46428)
```

```
12:46:22.070000 1.1.1.1.2262 > 172.16.99.110.3128: S 20315949:20315949(0) win
8192 <mss 1460,nop,nop,sackOK> (DF) (ttl 116, id 57180)
12:46:34.080000 1.1.1.1.2262 > 172.16.99.110.3128: S 20315949:20315949(0) win
8192 <mss 1460,nop,nop,sackOK> (DF) (ttl 116, id 2397)
```

Let's scrutinize these records, but this time in terms of source IP spoofing. The salient advice to remember when looking for spoofed source IPs is to look for similarities in the fields or characteristics of packets. More likely than not, an attacker will not take time to "craft" in differences in the packets, and there will be some traces of unlikely similarities. Conversely, when distinct source IPs truly represent different source hosts, differences in packet characteristics should be apparent. Given this knowledge, what differences can you find among the three different source IPs of the previously shown traffic?

For starters, you pretty much have to do fourth-down-and-punt with the IP identification numbers. The time gaps between when each set of initial connections received is too great to see real trends in IP identification numbers. Ten minutes pass between the first and second set of connections, which is enough time for the IP identification numbers of a busy host to go through all 65,535 numbers and wrap. You would ordinarily look for a chronology of very close IP identification numbers, which would indicate source IP spoofing. But, this can only be done if the time changes are insignificant.

What about the arriving TTL values? They look promising for spoofing because both the first two sets of connections involving source IPs of 1.2.3.4 and 4.3.2.1 have an arriving TTL value of 19. However, the third set from 1.1.1.1 has an arriving TTL value of 116.

Are there any other differences? Look at the TCP options for the connections. The first two source IPs share the same TCP options, a maximum segment size (mss) of 1460. Yet, the third source IP also has a selective acknowledgement (sackOK) that must be padded with two noop's to fall on a 4-byte boundary.

Finally, look at the number of retries per attempted connection and the backoff time between initial tries and retries and between subsequent retries. The first source IP 4.3.2.1 has an initial try and two retries. The backoff time between retries is approximately 10 seconds. Next, IP 1.2.3.4 has one initial try and three retries with the retry attempts doubling in the amount of time before subsequent ones. Finally, the source IP 1.1.1.1 behaves much like 1.2.3.4 as far as retries in that it has three retries with a doubling of the backoff time. From all the forensics from the preceding dump, we can pretty much conclude that these are actual separate source IPs.

When the traffic was observed, we took the TTL values, estimated the initial TTL values, and subtracted the arriving from the initial values. This gave us the number of hop counts that the datagram took to arrive on the sensor net-work. Then, we executed a traceroute back to the source IP to see if the expected hop count was close to the actual hop count.

About a dozen traceroutes were attempted; most had a hop count credibly close to the actual hop count. Also, all the targeted IPs were alive, which might not be the case had random IPs been chosen for spoofing. It would be rare if someone were doing mass amounts of spoofing using hand picked live IP numbers only. Usually, it is a far more random selection of spoofed source IP numbers.

This kind of widespread scan was difficult to explain examining one site. Before the days of www.incidents.org, Stephen Northcutt asked SANS mem-bers to look at traffic at their individual sites and see if they could provide any explanations about the activity. Hundreds of sites reported similar activity.

A couple of sites were able to see the HTTP request that was executed, and it appeared to implicate a host www.rusftpsearch.net. The site was available for a few days and it appeared to be collecting IPs of any open proxy servers found.

Ron Marcum of Vanderbilt University discovered a PC on his network that was scanning hosts on other networks looking for ports 80, 8080, and 3128. He discovered a Trojan called RingZero that appeared to be the culprit. At a SANS conference in 1999, conference members and instructors installed the program that was discovered on the Vanderbilt host and examined what it did. They were able to recreate that this Trojan would scan other hosts on web ports.

The suspected infection means is via email or mp3 sharing. But, this semi-nal malicious code is one of the first that infected hosts and gathered some valuable information from the hosts, and then used the infected hosts to scan other hosts. This is the same model used for scans and attacks today, albeit quite a bit more sophisticated.

Summary

Without unnecessarily belaboring the point, the events described in this chapter have demonstrated the added value of having TCPdump or Shadow running at a site to capture the background traffic. The first incident of a non-intrusion showed how TCPdump can be invaluable because its purpose is not exclusively to show alerts of events of interest, but to capture all traffic. It can provide an audit trail of activity that occurred, or more descriptively in this case, of activity that did not occur.

In addition, TCPdump was used in the scan incident to assess the reaction of hosts on the monitored network to the scan. Scans can be harmless distractions when there is no response by the scanned hosts, or in this case, they can be a reason for concern. Although most NIDS will inform you of scans, none will automatically alert you of responding hosts.

In the third and final events, TCPdump was used to get very specific information about the fragments or packets in order to make more accurate evaluations of the nature of the attack. You can even begin to do forensic investigation about the type of hosts that are conducting the hostile activity. You will see a more thorough discussion of passive analysis of hostile traffic in the next chapter.

11

Mystery Traffic

Many times as a security analyst, you see some kind of interesting traffic and wish that you had the time or resources to investigate it or understand it better. You have a much better chance of being able to do this if you are in a research position rather than a busy operational environment where your exclusive purpose is to make sure that no unauthorized access occurs.

One such opportunity to do analysis of an event of interest arose at a site where Shadow was used to capture traffic. The site was the target of some extensive unexplained activity directed at TCP destination port 27374, which is often used by SubSeven.

The explanation and findings of the traffic are discussed in this chapter. When we witnessed this activity, we had a gut feeling that we were seeing something unique just because of the sheer volume of it. We used Shadow's collected TCPdump records to analyze different fields and aspects of the packet to come to our conclusions. This was a team effort conducted with the help of co-workers Vern Stark and David Heinbuch.

My suspicion is that many people who gravitate to the position of security analyst enjoy working puzzles or mysteries. The mystery of this traffic was unraveled simply using TCPdump record capture, Perl programming to examine and summarize different aspects of the traffic, and Excel to plot the findings. Working on this puzzle was not only a great learning experience of doing traffic evaluation, and recovery after making errant assumptions, but it provided a lot of entertainment to some true bit-heads.

The Event in a Nutshell

Examination of an hour's traffic on June 29, 2001 at 12:00 captured by a Shadow sensor positioned outside a monitored site's perimeter firewall revealed a large number of source hosts scanning what appeared to be the site's Class B address space for TCP destination port 27374. Shadow retrospectively analyzes each hour's traffic for anomalies. Anomalies, or more accurately, events of interest, are culled by running the previous hour's collected TCPdump traffic through a series of TCPdump filters. One of the filters looks for attempted TCP SYN connections from outside the network to a host in the network.

TCP destination port 27374 is associated with a Trojan known as SubSeven that can allow full access to the victim's machine. We have seen plenty of large scans to the SubSeven port; however, we had never seen a scan that generated such a large volume of traffic—nor had we seen one that had come from multiple concurrent sources.

> **Correlation of Similar Activity**
>
> About this same time, the System Administration, Networking, and Security (SANS) Internet Storm Center released a report on June 26, 2001 about a Microsoft Windows worm named W32.leave.worm. The speculation was that this worm was used to make the infected host a participant host, also known as a zombie, in distributed denial of service (DDoS) attacks. According to the report, the worm spread via connections to hosts listening on TCP port 27374. The report noted that the worm scanned predetermined network blocks associated with @Home and Earthlink for destination port 27374. However, it made no mention of synchronized scanning, nor did it mention scanning of networks other than those previously mentioned. Although the described worm activity appeared to be different than the activity that was witnessed at the monitored site, it was possible that the worm activity had mutated since the initial report.

The Traffic

The following output represents a handful of TCPdump records to provide the general "flavor" of the activity. The source and destination hosts are bold. These are the first ten records associated with the activity on June 29; there are four different source hosts involved in scanning ten different destination hosts.

The timestamps associated with the records should be regarded with caution. The sensor that captured these records is running Redhat Linux 7.1 with a packet-capturing mechanism known as turbopacket compiled into the kernel. It is supposed to contain a method for more efficient buffering, but it also appears that the timestamp precision has been lost. Timestamps should have microsecond fidelity, but these timestamps appear to have 10-ms resolution:

```
12:16:31.150575 ool-18bd69bb.dyn.optonline.net.4333 > 192.168.112.44.27374: S
542724472:542724472(0) win 16384 <mss 1460,nop,nop,sackOK> (DF) (ttl 117, id
13444)
12:16:31.160575 ool-18bd69bb.dyn.optonline.net.4334 > 192.168.112.45.27374: S
542768141:542768141(0) win 16384 <mss 1460,nop,nop,sackOK> (DF) (ttl 117, id
13445)
12:16:31.170575 24.3.50.252.1757 > 192.168.19.178.27374: S
681372183:681372183(0) win 16384 <mss 1460,nop,nop,sackOK> (DF) (ttl 117,id
54912)
12:16:31.170575 24-240-136-48.hsacorp.net.4939 >192.168.11.19.27374: S
3019773591:3019773591(0) win 16384 <mss 1460,nop,nop,sackOK> (DF) (ttl 117,
id 39621)
12:16:31.170575 ool-18bd69bb.dyn.optonline.net.4335 > 192.168.112.46.27374: S
542804226:542804226(0) win 16384 <mss 1460,nop,nop,sackOK> (DF) (ttl 117, id
13446)
12:16:31.170575 cc18270-a.essx1.md.home.com.4658 > 192.168.5.88.27374: S
55455482:55455482(0) win 8192 <mss 1460,nop,nop,sackOK> (DF) (ttl 117, id
8953)
12:16:31.170575 24.3.50.252.1759 > 192.168.19.180.27374: S
681485650:681485650(0) win 16384 <mss 1460,nop,nop,sackOK> (DF) (ttl 117, id
54914)
12:16:31.170575 cc18270-a.essx1.md.home.com.4659 > 192.168.5.89.27374: S
55455483:55455483(0) win 8192 <mss 1460,nop,nop,sackOK> (DF) (ttl 117, id
9209)
12:16:31.170575 24.3.50.252.1760 > 192.168.19.181.27374: S
681550782:681550782(0) win 16384 <mss 1460,nop,nop,sackOK> (DF) (ttl 117, id
54915)
12:16:31.170575 cc18270-a.essx1.md.home.com.4660 > 192.168.5.90.27374: S
55455484:55455484(0) win 8192 <mss 1460,nop,nop,sackOK> (DF) (ttl 117, id
9465)
```

DDoS or Scan

At first, it was not apparent if this was some kind of attempted DDoS or an actual coordinated scan of some sort. During the examination of the activity, we were fortunate (from the analysis perspective) to receive additional activity on July 2, 2001 at 16:00 that was remarkably similar. After we received the second scan, we began in earnest to look at individual fields found in the received packets of both sets of activity to interpret the nature and intent of the activity.

Source Hosts

In the first scan, 132,706 total packets were received and there were 314 unique source hosts involved. Of those hosts, only 17 (approximately 5.4 percent) did not have DNS registered host names. In the second scan, 157,842 total packets were received. There were 295 unique source hosts with only 24 (approximately 8.1 percent) with unresolved host names. This alone is quite telling. Two choices for categorizing the source hosts are that they either do or do not reflect the genuine source host that is sending the traffic. If the source host reflects the actual sender, no subterfuge is used in sending the packet. If the source host is not the actual sender, a spoofed source IP number is placed in the packet.

Typically, when source IP numbers are spoofed, it is a random generation of different IP numbers in the instance of a flood. Other attacks might use a selection of one or more source IP numbers that might be either a decoy or an eventual target of some kind. When the source host reflects the true sender, the intent is more likely than not to be able to receive a response to the sent traffic.

Therefore, it appears that the activity that was seen is using genuine source IP numbers. If this were a flood and the source IPs were spoofed using randomly generated IP numbers, it is statistically unlikely that these IP numbers would resolve to host names 91.9 to 94.6 percent of the time. It would be unusual that IP numbers would be spoofed using a predetermined set of IP numbers that resolved to host names, because this takes a lot of effort for little or no gain.

It can be speculated that, because of the sheer number of source hosts involved, they most likely represent zombie hosts that have somehow been exploited and owned. Many of these source networks are associated with cable modem or DSL providers such as @Home and AOL. This corroborates the speculation of zombie hosts because home users are more likely to be unaware of security threats and less protected than most commercial or larger networks with some kind of perimeter protection.

Destination Hosts

Next, the analysis moved to examination of the destination hosts to provide more evidence of a scan. The scanned network is Class B with the possibility of 65,535 IP numbers to scan. The first scan targeted 32,367 unique destination hosts and the second scan targeted 36,638 unique destination hosts. An initial unsubstantiated reaction to missed subnets was that there was some prior reconnaissance performed to directly target live hosts. After more thorough examination of the destination hosts, it was evident that many of the destination IP numbers that were scanned had no associated live hosts.

The more plausible explanation for the missing destination subnets and destination hosts is that perhaps the zombie or zombies that were assigned the mission of scanning those subnets were somehow not active or responsive during the scan and did not participate. A single missing destination host in an otherwise scanned subnet might be interpreted as a dropped initial packet rather than an omitted destination IP number.

Although one unique source host scanned most destination hosts, multiple source hosts scanned some destination hosts. The scanner appears to have some redundancy of scanned hosts to ensure a response.

Scanning Rates

Another indication of a scan versus a flood was the scanning rate of the source hosts. Both scans sustained some kind of activity for five or six minutes; however, the ramp-up time was fast, and there was a burst of activity for the first two minutes.

The measure of bandwidth consumption was as follows. Each packet was a SYN packet with TCP options and no payload. Most packets had a length of 48 bytes, a few had more, and a few had 4 bytes less, depending on the number and types of TCP options used. Packets had a standard 20-byte IP header with no IP options. Because the majority of packets had a length of 48 bytes, this was used as the packet length for the computation of bandwidth consumption. Because throughput or bandwidth is measured in bits per second, the packet length was 384 (48 ∗ 8) bits.

The scan on June 29 reached a maximum rate of 1.7Mbps at peak. The second scan on July 2 reached a maximum rate of 2.4Mbps at peak. This did not adversely affect the monitored site, but a site with a smaller ingress pipe such as a T-1 with 1.554Mbps capacity might have suffered a temporary denial of service as a side effect of the scan. Figure 11.1 shows the bits per second during peak scan minutes.

Looking at the plots in Figure 11.1 together, it is apparent from the general contours that the scanning rates for both scans were very similar. In fact, both scans reached peak scanning rates at exactly 21 seconds after the scan began. As discovered later, after examining the traffic using different representations, this peak activity indicated some kind of coordination by the "commander" who allocated scanning assignments and rates for the zombies.

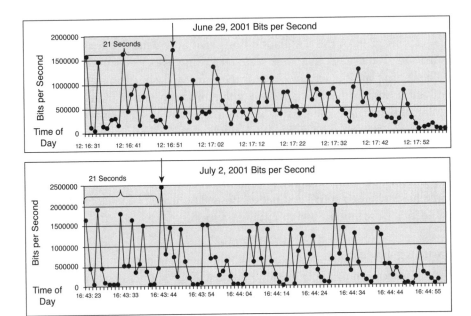

Figure 11.1   Bits per second.

Peak rates could have occurred because there were more scanning hosts during that second or because the number of packets sent by hosts increased. Further scrutiny of the data revealed that the peaks and valleys correlated with an increased number of scanning hosts.

The 21-second peak rate that was observed yet again on a third scan on November 1 was indeed a mystery. However, it was observed that the scanning hosts sent retries of initial SYN connections that received no response. This is typical TCP behavior, and many TCP/IP stacks will attempt 3 retries after the initial SYN, with a formula of waiting 3 seconds before the first retry, doubling the wait time to 6 seconds for the second retry and doubling the wait time yet again to 12 seconds for the third and final retry. Hence, the aggregate time that passes between the initial SYN and the final retry is 21 seconds. And so, when initial SYN attempts only were plotted by time as in Figure 11.2, the 21-second peak disappears.

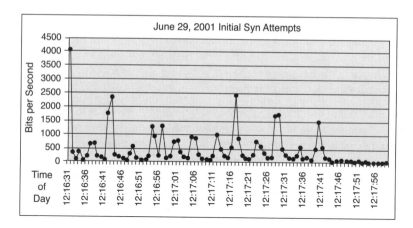

Figure 11.2   June 29, 2001 initial SYN attempts.

This only partially explains the 21-second peak. If this peak were due strictly to retries alone of the same hosts, similar peak activity should be observed at 3 and 9 seconds as well. Figure 11.3 shows two separate types of connection attempts by time for the June 29 scan—the solid line shows initial SYN attempts and the dashed line shows retries of those initial SYN attempts. This more completely explains the 21-second peak.

Peak activity occurs at 12:16:52. As expected, this corresponds to the 3rd retry of the spate of attempted SYN connections sent at 12:16:31. Furthermore, it corresponds to the second retry of the deluge of another set of initial SYN attempts sent 9 seconds before peak activity at 12:16:42. More so, in both scans, it appears, at least at first, that the wave of initial SYN connections comes in 12-second intervals. The overlap of retries from this particular timing pattern is why the 21-second peak activity was witnessed.

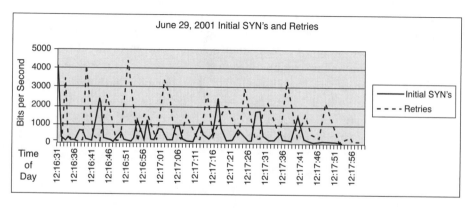

Figure 11.3   June 29, 2001 initial SYNs and retries.

The 21-Second Mystery

One of the most intriguing revelations of the examination of this SubSeven traffic was the 21-second time preceding the peak activity for the initial two scans, and later a third, that were observed. It was clear that there was some meaning and explanation associated with this; this couldn't be a mere coincidence because it occurred three times.

I have an annoying habit: When I'm stumped and frustrated by my inability to figure something out, I start plaguing colleagues. Most have learned to dismiss me with some plausible excuse like, "There are free donuts in the cafeteria. See you later." But, I cornered my co-worker and longtime bicycling buddy, Vern, and asked him to ponder this mystery. Within seconds, and still a good chance to get those cafeteria donuts, he said, "Oh, that's easy; it's the combined backoff times for retries." This insight made us rethink our approach, and we eventually plotted the traffic separately for initial SYNs and retries, allowing us to discover that the 21-second peak rate was an overlap of retries from different initial waves of SYN activity.

Fingerprinting Participant Hosts

The assumption now is that the zombie hosts have been "infected" with some malware that is generating the scanning activity. The question then becomes this: Is there a specific operating system that has been exploited, transforming the host into a zombie for this scan? An examination of passive fingerprints can assist in identification of zombies' operating systems. This assumes that the packets coming from these hosts are not crafted to change default values, such as TCP window size, initial TTL, and TCP options.

Passive fingerprinting categorizes operating systems by looking at unique field values in the packets that have been sent. As we have discussed, different operating system TCP/IP stacks choose unique values for certain fields, such as Time to Live (TTL), TCP window size, and TCP options. There are also other fields that can be examined, such as the Type of Service (TOS) value and the don't fragment (DF) flag. But, because most operating systems use a default TOS value of 0 and set the DF flag, this might only determine the small percentage of unusual values sent from other operating systems. And, these two fields are best examined in conjunction with other fields and not alone.

Table 11.1, provided by the Honeynet Project, was used in determining some of the scanning hosts' operating systems. The lines that are highlighted represent the operating system and associated fingerprints of the majority of the scanning hosts that were observed for this activity.

Table 11.1 **Passive Fingerprinting Values by Operating System**

# OS	VERSION	PLATFORM	TTL	WINDOW	DF	TOS
#---	-------	--------	---	-----------	--	---
DC-OSx	1.1-95	Pyramid/NILE	30	8192	n	0
Windows	**9x/NT**	**Intel**	**32**	**5000-9000**	**y**	**0**
NetApp	OnTap	5.1.2-5.2.2	54	8760	y	0
HPJetDirect	HP_Printer		59	2100-2150	n	0
AIX	4.3.x	IBM/RS6000	60	16000-16100	y	0
Cisco	11.2	7507	60	65535	y	0
DigitalUnix	4.0	Alpha	60	33580	y	16
IRIX	6.x	SGI	60	61320	y	16
OS390	2.6	IBM/S390	60	32756	n	0
Reliant	5.43	Pyramid/ RM1000	60	65534	n	0
FreeBSD	3.x	Intel	64	17520	y	16
JetDirect	G.07.x	J3113A	64	5804-5840	n	0
Linux	2.2.x	Intel	64	32120	y	0
OpenBSD	2.x	Intel	64	17520	n	16
OS/400	R4.4	AS/400	64	8192	y	0
SCO	R5	Compaq	64	24820	n	0
Solaris	8	Intel/Sparc	64	24820	y	0
FTX(UNIX)	3.3	STRATUS	64	32768	n	0
Unisys	x	Mainframe	64	32768	n	0
NetWare	4.11	Intel	128	32000-32768	y	0
Windows	**9x/NT**	**Intel**	**128**	**5000-9000**	**y**	**0**
Windows	**2000**	**Intel**	**128**	**17000- 18000**	**y**	**0**
Cisco	12.0	2514	255	3800-5000	n	192
Solaris	2.x	Intel/Sparc	255	8760	y	0

This table of information was obtained at `http://project.honeynet.org/ papers/finger/traces.txt`.

Arriving TTL Values

If you recall, the arriving TTL values can be used to help identify the scanning host's operating system. Different operating systems use different initial TTL values when sending a packet. Each router through which the packet travels on its journey from source to destination host examines the TTL value and decrements it by 1. This becomes an indication of the number of "hops" that the packet has traveled. If a router ever discovers a TTL of 0, it discards the packet and sends back an ICMP error message of "time exceeded in-transit" to the sending host. This informs the sending host that the packet has exceeded its welcome on the Internet. This is a mechanism that is used to discard lost packets, such as ones that have become caught in a routing loop.

Initial TTLs of many operating systems have typical values of 32, 64, 128, and 255. These might be different per protocol—TCP, UDP, or ICMP. For instance, Windows NT 4.0 Service Pack 6 has an initial TTL value of 128 for TCP and an initial TTL value of 32 for ICMP packets sent. Fortunately, this examination is limited to TCP so there is no need to account for protocol differences. The arriving TTL values are examined and are helpful in estimating the initial TTL values. The caveat here is that although most operating systems will be configured to use the default initial TTL values, these can be changed. All that can be determined with absolute certainty from the arriving TTL is that it is less than the initial TTL. Of course, this assumes that the source host and destination host are not directly connected to the same local network, in which case the packet could pass from source to destination without the TTL being decremented.

Examination of Figure 11.4 for June 29, 2001 shows that there are three clusters of arriving TTL values for the scans. More specifically, the closest scanning host appears to be 8 hops away, and the most distant appears to be 25 hops away from the capturing sensor interface. The assumption is that the scanning hosts had initial TTL values of 128, 64, and 32, and the arriving TTL values are associated with an initial TTL value that is greater than the initial TTL value by the least amount. For instance, if an arriving TTL is 50, it is assumed to have an initial TTL value of 64 and not 128, although either initial TTL value would be valid.

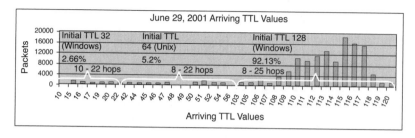

Figure 11.4   June 29, 2001 arriving TTL values.

In the June 29 scan, the largest percentage of scanning hosts, 92.13, had an estimated initial TTL of 128. More than 37 percent of the hosts with an initial TTL of 128 were approximately 11 to 13 hops away from the sensor. According to Table 11.1, an initial TTL value of 128 is indicative of Windows 9x/NT/2000. An initial TTL value of 32 is Windows 9.x/NT, which comprised 2.66 percent of the scanning hosts. The initial TTL value of 64 is associated with many of the UNIX platforms, including the Linux 2.2.x kernel. The percentage of hosts with an initial TTL of 64 was 5.2.

Examination of Figure 11.5 for July 2, 2001 shows the same clustering. More specifically, the closest scanning host appeared to be 8 hops away, and the most distant appeared to be 27 hops away from the capturing sensor interface.

Looking at the July 2 scan, the largest percentage of scanning hosts, 92.29, had an initial TTL of 128. More than 37 percent of the hosts with an initial TTL of 128 were approximately 11 to 13 hops away from the sensor. 2.36 percent of the scanning hosts had an initial TTL of 32. Finally, 5.35 percent of the scanning hosts had an initial TTL of 64.

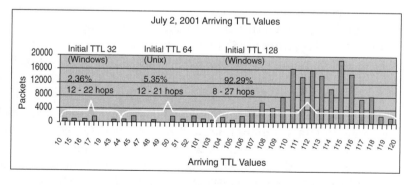

Figure 11.5   July 2, 2001 arriving TTL values.

The determination from this is that the scanning hosts are not exclusively Windows hosts, but it appears that Windows hosts are the majority of the scanners. This means that whatever malware is exploiting the scanning hosts, it is not exclusive to Windows.

Although the x-axis scaling for plots in Figures 11.4 and 11.5 doesn't readily show this, there was a very distinct clustering around the estimated initial TTL values. For instance, in the June 29 scan, there is a noticeable gap or absence of packets with arriving TTL values between 22 and 42 and between 56 and 103. Similar behavior is observed for the July 2 scan.

TCP Window Size

A host advertises the TCP window size when it attempts to make an initial connection. The window size is a dynamic value that changes as information is exchanged between hosts and represents the current TCP buffer size for the incoming data. This buffer allows multiple packets to be sent and queued before passing them to TCP and the application. More simply, a given operating system has a default value for the TCP window size, and the window size can change dynamically as data is received and processed.

But, the initial window size can be used to fingerprint the operating system. The user or administrator can customize this, but commonly the default is used.

As you can see in Figure 11.6, the bulk of the connections had an initial window size of 8192. This is associated with Windows 9x/NT connections according to Table 11.1. Although the table doesn't have a window-size entry for 16384, research has discovered it is associated with Windows 2000. Table 11.1 alludes that a window size of 65535 is associated with Cisco. However, it appears that the high percentages associated with this window size would include other operating systems.

Search engines on the Internet failed to find any operating system associations with a window size of 65535. Attempts were made to examine a week's collection of TCPdump data for the monitored site to find hosts that had a window size of 65535. Only a dozen of approximately 5,500 hosts were found with a window size of 65535. A scan by nmap could not determine the operating systems. Some of the hosts had ports open, such as 135 and 139, which would indicate Windows versions prior to Windows 2000. Others had port 445 listening, which was introduced in Windows 2000 to support Server Message Block (SMB) talking directly over TCP/IP without the need for the intermediate layer of NetBIOS over TCP/IP (NBT). Yet, other hosts with a window size of 65535 listened at ports 111 (portmapper), 515 (line printer daemon), and 6000 (X11), which are all associated with UNIX hosts. No conclusions could be reached about the operating system associated with a window size of 65,535 based on these findings.

Other unique window sizes that were seen were 32120, associated with Linux, which was found in the June 29 scan only and comprised .19 percent of the total scanning hosts. A window size of 8760 was seen in both scans and reflects a Solaris host. The first scan had 5.21 percent hosts with this window size, and the second scan had 6.60 percent hosts with this window size.

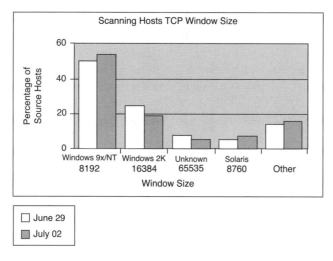

Figure 11.6   Scanning host TCP window size.

The conclusion that can be drawn examining the TCP window size is the same as examining the arriving TTL values. Looking at Figure 11.6, most of the scanning hosts appear to have a window size associated with Windows, yet it also appears that operating systems other than Windows are involved in the scanning too.

TCP Options

Another interesting field for examination is the Maximum Segment Size (MSS), which is found in the TCP options. This represents the maximum amount of payload that a TCP segment can carry. This does not include the TCP header and the IP header. Generally speaking, the MSS is 40 bytes less than the Maximum Transmission Unit (MTU), assuming a 20-byte IP header with no IP options and a 20-byte TCP header with no TCP options. The MTU can then be used to determine the media on which the sending host resides.

In some instances, although not this one, the MTU, and hence the MSS, might reflect the path MTU. The sender might send a "discovery" packet that looks for the smallest MTU from source to destination by setting the DF flag on the packet. If no ICMP error messages are returned, it is assumed that using the size of the local MTU for packaging packets will not cause fragmentation. If an ICMP error message "unreachable – need to frag (mtu ###)" is returned, it contains the MTU size (###) of the link that is smaller than the size of the local MTU. The sender can decrease the size of the packets to avoid fragmentation. The point is that it is possible that the MSS might not reflect the local MTU. However, because there is no indication of discovery packets or that path MTU was used, the assumption is that the MSS does reflect the local MTU.

Figure 11.7 reveals that the greatest percentage of scanning hosts resided on a link with an MTU of 1500. This is indicative of Ethernet, found in LAN connections or DSL. The MTU of 576 is associated with PPP or ISDN. Finally, the MTU of 1454 is associated with PPP over Ethernet that is also found on DSL connections.

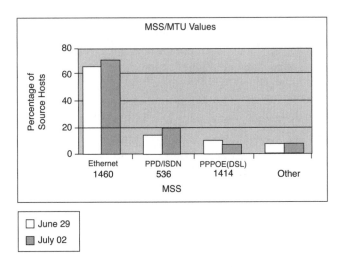

Figure 11.7 MSS/MTU values.

Although the MSS of 536 is associated with PPP and dial-up modems, it is supposed that most of the hosts reside on ISDN, which uses the same MSS. The scenario is that these are all zombie hosts that are directed to do some type of activity at a given time. Either they respond to a catalyst or they all have some kind of time synchronization and are directed to respond at a given time.

The idea of participants from dial-up modems is worth some reflection. First, if a zombie is associated with a dial-up connection, this might not be a sustained connection unless there is some kind of dedicated phone line for the traffic. Additionally, many dial-up connections are at the mercy of Dynamic

Host Configuration Protocol (DHCP) with a leased IP number for a certain period of time. How would the "commander" direct a zombie with a changing IP number to launch the activity? One guess is that the zombies report home to the commander periodically. Therefore, only ones that are active and online just before the attack are directed to participate in the attack.

Another question arises from this discussion. It has already been determined that zombies have assignments of mostly unique address ranges to scan. Is there some kind of formula used to assign the address ranges to scan so that the maximum numbers of hosts get scanned?

The suspicion is that most of the participating zombies have a sustained and dedicated Internet connection, but this doesn't adequately explain the missing destination hosts and subnets.

TCP Retries

As mentioned, when a source host attempts a TCP connection to a destination host and is unsuccessful, yet gets no indication of the failure, it attempts one or more retries. A source host is not notified of a failure if the connection packet never gets to the destination or the destination host's response doesn't get back to the source. In the case of our scanned network, the activity to port 27374 was blocked. Yet, the firewall that blocks the activity "silently" drops the packet with no notification in the form of an ICMP error message to the original source host that there is a problem. The purpose of the silent drop is so that no additional reconnaissance is disseminated about our network perimeter and defense.

For the purposes of this investigation, a TCP retry is defined as one that has the same source and destination hosts, ports, and TCP sequence numbers as the initial attempt. The number of successive retries and the backoff time between retries is TCP/IP stack dependent.

Retries are associated with source code that uses socket connections. In other words, the source code is written so that the socket calls go through the proper layers of the TCP/IP stack. In this case, the socket uses the TCP and IP layers to form the appropriate headers and values for those headers.

The alternative is known as a raw socket, which does not use the TCP/IP stack to form the packet. Instead, the programmer is responsible for supplying the appropriate headers and data. This packet is written directly to the network interface card. Many scanners such as nmap and hping2 use raw sockets.

This scan manifested multiple retries when the destination host was unresponsive. What does this mean? That regular and not raw sockets were used? First, the scanning host really wanted to maximize the opportunity to elicit a response from the destination host—more indicative of scan behavior than flood behavior. Flood behavior would likely send packets using raw sockets as fast as possible. Second, raw sockets require an additional level of complexity because they require the installation of an application programming interface for packet capture on the scanning host—either winpcap for Windows or libpcap for UNIX. The use of standard sockets simplifies the setup required to scan.

Summary

The determination is that this was a very efficient scan looking for hosts listening on TCP port 27374. The scan was conducted by zombie hosts, which were mostly Windows hosts. It appears that hosts with other operating systems were involved, yet they played only a small part in the percentage of scanning hosts. The significance of this is that the means of infection of the zombie hosts does not appear to be Windows-specific. It is unknown whether the percentage of Windows-based scanning hosts and the percentage of scanning hosts that have other operating systems actually mirror the percentage of Windows versus all other operating systems that are found on the Internet. The implication here would be that the operating systems of the zombie hosts might be consistent with a normal distribution found on the Internet. Another implication is that the percentage of zombie hosts having a particular operating system might represent the ease of compromise for that operating system.

Is the sole purpose of this scan to efficiently identify hosts listening on port 27374? It can be surmised that not all of the zombie hosts were exploited by the SubSeven Trojan. SubSeven is a Windows-based Trojan, and it appeared that not all the zombie hosts were Windows. Perhaps there are SubSeven Trojans that have been developed for other operating systems as well. Whatever the exploit used to "own" the zombies, the "commander" knew about the owned zombie hosts and had no need to scan to find them. Is it possible that this scan search was to find other candidate zombies owned by another commander? This assumes that these new zombie hosts would be Windows-based because they would be listening at the SubSeven port. The new zombies may be used for activity other than the scanning that was witnessed at our site.

Whatever the purpose of this scan, it looks like a pretty sophisticated way to maximize a scan. In a couple of minutes, over 30,000 destination hosts were scanned. This activity demonstrates the evolving sophistication in zombie activity and malicious code in general, as we have witnessed with Code Red and nimda worms. It also shows the burgeoning number of exploited hosts that can be marshaled into active duty because of the innocence or disbelief of home users, paired with always-on connectivity, and operating systems and applications that come ready-assembled for looting and pillaging.

Filters/Rules for Network Monitoring

12

Writing TCPdump Filters

THIS IS THE FIRST OF THREE CHAPTERS that discusses writing filters or signatures to detect anomalous behavior. The authors have chosen to discuss these particular filters and signatures for a couple of reasons. The first is because these signatures are available with freeware and available to the masses—even the impoverished. The second reason is that there are so many IDS packages today, it is almost impossible to cover them and yet not be accused of bias or favoritism because of omissions. As a fair compromise, we have chosen this chapter to discuss TCPdump and the following two chapters to discuss Snort signatures.

This chapter discusses how to select records from TCPdump using filters to detail the specifics of records of interest. The following chapter will introduce the reader to Snort (a free NIDS) and Snort signatures. The final of the three chapters will provide additional information on composing Snort signatures.

The time-honored TCPdump program comes with an extensive filter language that you can use to look at any field, combination of fields, or bits found in an IP datagram. If you like puzzles and don't mind a bit of tinkering, you can use TCPdump filters to extract different anomalous traffic. Mind you, this is not the tool for the feint of heart or for those of you who are shy of getting your brain a bit frazzled. Those who prefer a packaged solution might be better off using the commercial products and their GUIs or filters.

This chapter introduces the concept of using TCPdump and TCPdump filters to detect events of interest. TCPdump and TCPdump filters are the backbone of a freeware IDS Shadow, and so the recommended suggestion is to download the current version of Shadow at `www.nswc.navy.mil/ISSEC/CID` to examine and enhance its native filters. This takes care of automating the collection and processing of traffic, freeing you to concentrate on customizing the TCPdump filters for better detects.

Specifically, this chapter discusses the mechanics of creating TCPdump filters. You learn different techniques for excavating bytes and bits within the IP datagram using these filters. Different TCPdump filters are developed to show you how to extract events of interest. This chapter tries to build on these foundations and leads up to developing more complex and advanced filters.

The Mechanics of Writing TCPdump Filters

By default, TCPdump examines or collects all of the records read from either the network or from a file. But often you will want to examine or collect only records with specific values set in identified fields in the IP datagram to look for signs of malicious activity directed at your network. TCPdump filters can be used to specify an item of interest, such as a field in the IP datagram for record selection. Such items might be part of the IP header (the IP header length, for example), the TCP header (TCP flags, for example), the UDP header (the destination port, for example), or the ICMP message (message type, for example).

TCPdump provides some macros for commonly used fields, such as "port" to indicate a source or destination port, or "host" to indicate an IP number or name of a source or destination host. We won't use these in the examples—not for the sake of proud academics, but because the fields we are interested in do not have macros, and so we must use the format of referencing a field by the protocol and displacement in terms of bytes into that protocol.

TCPdump assigns a designated name for each type of header associated with a protocol. Much as you would expect, "ip" is used to denote a field in the IP header or data portion of the IP datagram, "tcp" for a field in the TCP header or data of the TCP segment, "udp" for a field in the UDP header or data of the UDP datagram, and "icmp" for a field in the ICMP header or data of the ICMP message.

Now, we have to reference a field in a given protocol by its displacement in bytes from the beginning of the protocol header. For instance, ip[0] indicates the 0 byte offset of the IP datagram, which happens to be part of the IP header (remember, counting starts at 0). tcp[13] is byte 13 offset into the TCP segment, which is also part of the TCP header, and icmp[0] is the 0 byte of the ICMP message, which is the ICMP message type.

For this discussion, we use the following format to create a TCPdump filter:

```
<protocol header>[offset:length] <relation> <value>
```

All the initial filters this chapter covers reference Figure 12.1, which is the standard layout of the IP header. Notice that each of the rows has 32 bits, ranging in value from 0 through 31. Essentially, each row is composed of 4 bytes—and don't forget that counting starts with 0. That is one of the hardest things to commit to memory.

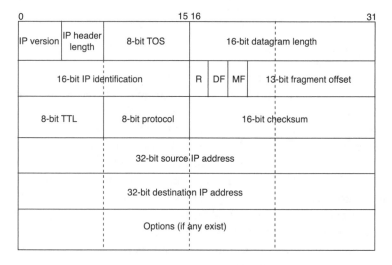

Figure 12.1 The IP header.

Suppose that you want to use TCPdump to select any datagram that has an embedded protocol of ICMP. Refer to Figure 12.1 and notice this particular protocol field is located 9 bytes offset (last reminder: start counting at 0) into the IP header. Therefore, we denote this field as ip[9]. Notice also that the TCPdump filter format called for an offset:length; the implied length is 1 byte, and the length is typically used if you want to span more than a single byte. Now that you have located the 1-byte field that stores the embedded protocol, you need to know that a value of 1 in this field represents ICMP. To compose the entire filter to find ICMP records, use the filter ip[9] = 1. If this were used to collect records off the network, you would run TCPdump as follows:

```
tcpdump 'ip[9] = 1'
```

This reads from the default network interface and collects only ICMP records. You embed the filter in single quotation marks to keep the UNIX shell from trying to interpret the filter. Another TCPdump option used for more complicated filters is the –F option of TCPdump, which points TCPdump to a file where the filter is located. You could create a file, /tmp/filter, containing the text "ip[9] = 1" which could then be used in the following command:

```
tcpdump -F /tmp/filter
```

This would have yielded the same results as the TCPdump command that included the filter in the command line itself. This option is usually used for long filters or automated TCPdump processes to avoid command-line entry of the filter.

Bit Masking

We need to introduce a couple more concepts while we're at it. The TCPdump filter language is not a robust language compared to the constructs and operations available in other languages such as C or Perl, for instance. Often, we have to go back to the ancient roots of assembler language—like manipulations to extract fields that don't fall on byte boundaries.

TCPdump is fairly straightforward and coherent when you are dealing with a field that falls on a byte boundary and you are looking at all 8 bits. Although you have discovered how to span bytes by specifying the length after the offset, what happens if you want to look at only certain bits or a range of bits in a byte? In other words, you don't want to look at the entire byte. This is where things get a little hairy, and this discussion assumes that you have mastered the rudiments of binary and hexadecimal.

Preserving and Discarding Individual Bits

Take a look at the structure of the IP header again. Now look at the first byte in the IP header and notice that it is actually two 4-bit fields. Each of these 4-bit fields is known as a *nibble*. What if you wanted to examine the 4-bit header length only, and didn't care about the value in the 4-bit version field? You really just want to look at the low-order nibble. How do you discard the high-order nibble so that you can concentrate on the value of the 4-bit IP header length alone? In essence, you want to turn the high-order 4 bits into 0s. Doing so enables you to reference the first byte and look at the low-order nibble alone. If the question "how the heck do I do that?" is rolling around the tip of your tongue, you are following this discussion in hot pursuit.

Remember back to Boolean arithmetic? A well-deserved groan or two is merited or even expected. Personally, I don't remember anyone who enjoyed a good truth table, but unfortunately, you have to delve back into the far recesses of your brain to resurrect the Boolean AND operator. Does Table 12.1 bring back any nightmares?

Table 12.1 **AND Truth Table**

BIT A	AND	BIT B	RESULT
0		0	0
1		0	0
0		1	0
1		1	1

This table shows all the possible binary bit values and the results of ANDing the bits. The only time that 2 bits have a resulting value of 1 is when both ANDed bits are 1. What does this mean to this discussion of TCPdump filters? You might have forgotten the original challenge: You need to zero out the high-order nibble of the first byte in the IP header so that you can focus on the low-order nibble. Well, what if you can AND the value found in the first byte of the IP header with all 0s in the high-order nibble, which has the effect of discarding them? Then, you can preserve the original value in the low-order nibble by ANDing all those bits with 1s.

Consider how this is done. Take a look at Figure 12.2. In the rectangles, you see the first byte of an actual IP header divided into two 4-bit chunks. Examine the value in the datagram; the high-order nibble has a value of 0100 with a 1 in the 2^2 position, which yields 4. This is the version of IP—IP version 4, in this case. Now look at the low-order nibble. It has a value of a 1 in the 2^2 position and a 1 in the 2^0 position, so we have a 4 + 1 (or 5). This is the IP header length. Very unfortunately, the metric for this is not bytes as you might expect. It would be a lot easier that way, but to save on space required to store this value, this represents not a byte, but a word. A word is 32 bits, or 4 bytes. To convert a value that you find in this length field to bytes, you must multiply by 4. This means that this is a 20-byte header length, which is typical for a header that has no options.

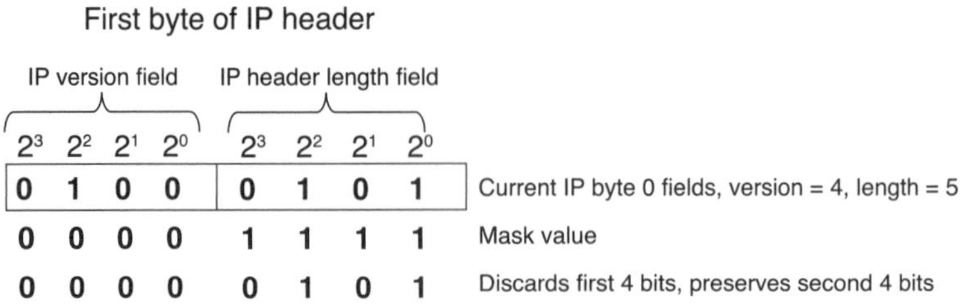

First byte of IP header

IP version field				IP header length field				
2^3	2^2	2^1	2^0	2^3	2^2	2^1	2^0	
0	1	0	0	0	1	0	1	Current IP byte 0 fields, version = 4, length = 5
0	0	0	0	1	1	1	1	Mask value
0	0	0	0	0	1	0	1	Discards first 4 bits, preserves second 4 bits

Figure 12.2   Bit masking.

Creating the Mask

Let's get on with the task of discarding the four high-order bits. Look at Figure 12.2 again, but this time at the line under the actual value found in the first byte of the IP datagram. This is what we have designated the "mask," or the byte that will be ANDed with the original value, bit by bit to discard the high-order bits and preserve the low-order bits. If you were to start the process at the high-order (leftmost) bit, you would find a 0 in the value bit and a 0 in the mask bit. On the line below it, you see the resulting bit is 0. Logically, we have a 0 in the value bit that we AND with a 0 in the mask bit and the result is a 0. Remember, if we AND any value bit with a 0, the result is a 0. Using this line of thought, our other mask bits for the high-order nibble are also 0s. As you see, the resulting value for the high-order nibble is 0000, which is exactly what we wanted—to zero-out this field to focus on the lower-order nibble.

Because we are dealing with an entire byte, we also need to mask the low-order nibble—we cannot ignore that. Staring with the leftmost bit of the low-order nibble, we find a 0 in the value bit and a 1 in the mask bit. These two values ANDed yield a 0, thereby preserving the original value bit. Next, we see that a 1 in a value bit ANDed with a 1 in the mask bit also preserves the value bit. You can see the pattern; all 1s in the mask for the low-order nibble preserves the low-order nibble. And, looking at the resulting value, we see that we have accomplished what we set out to do—to look exclusively at the value of the IP header length. Yes, we have to go through all of this because we cannot look at just part of a byte! *Whew!* We need to cover just one more step about the mechanics of writing filters and then we can turn to the actual filters themselves. How do we tell TCPdump to perform the AND operation and with what value?

First, we want to represent the mask bytes as two hexadecimal characters. 0000 1111 can be translated to 0x0f. The 0x informs TCPdump that this value is in hexadecimal; its default base is decimal. Here is how to construct the partial filter:

```
ip[0] & 0x0f
```

This says to take the value found in the 0 byte offset of the IP header and AND it with a hexadecimal value of 0f.

Putting It All Together

We are dealing with the 0 byte offset of the IP header. We AND that byte with a hexadecimal 0x0f and we have just managed to focus on the IP header length. Why might you want to isolate this field? One very good reason is to test for the presence of IP options. The normal IP header is 20 bytes, or five 32-bit words. That means that an IP header that might contain a dangerous IP option such as source routing would have a length of greater than 5 found in this field. IP options are almost never used any more for anything other than evil intent, so we want to know whether IP options exist. Recall from the TCPdump filter syntax that you need a relation and a value. The entire filter to find a signature of an IP datagram that has IP options is as follows:

```
ip[0] & 0x0f > 5
```

That is it. The end of a very long story. I know this seems like a lot of work and a lot of theory, but it truly does get easier as you get more practice. I warned you about the tinkering part; if you followed this and think you understand, however, you're well on your way to examining any field including bits of the IP datagram. Not many intrusion-detection systems offer this capability. With TCPdump, you lose no fidelity in your ability to capture and analyze data. Again, not many intrusion-detection systems can make this claim. That is why it might be worth your while to become familiar with TCPdump and TCPdump filters.

TCPdump IP Filters

Some of the telltale indications in the IP header that you might be a target of reconnaissance include traffic sent to your broadcast addresses, fragmentation, and the presence of IP options. You should never see legitimate traffic sent to your broadcast addresses from outside your network, and you should block this traffic as previously mentioned to prevent the likes of mapping and Smurf attacks. As you learned, fragmentation is a natural enough byproduct of a data-gram traveling to a network that originated on a network with a larger MTU. But, you also saw how fragmentation can be used for denial-of-service attacks or to try to bypass notice by an IDS or routers that cannot keep track of state.

Detecting Traffic to the Broadcast Addresses

Let's define the broadcast address as one with a final octet of 255 or 0. This includes most broadcast addresses subdivided on classic byte boundaries. Take a look again at Figure 12.1. The destination address is found in bytes 16 through 19 (32 bits) of the IP header. We are only concerned with the final octet, or byte 19. We can describe the broadcast addresses as follows:

```
ip[19] = 0xff
ip[19] = 0x00
```

or as a combined filter as follows:

```
ip[19] = 0xff or ip[19] = 0x00
```

We tend to express ourselves in hexadecimal and not decimal, but you could have as easily written this filter:

```
ip[19] = 255 or ip[19] = 0
```

Depending on where the sensor host is that runs the TCPdump filter, you might pick up broadcast traffic inside your network. Assume, for example, that your inside network is 192.168.x.x. To further qualify this filter to examine only traffic directed toward your network from a foreign source, you tweak the filter as follows:

```
not src net 192.168 and (ip[19] = 0xff or ip[19] = 0x00)
```

The preceding introduced a new operator, the not, to negate; and a couple of new macros: src, to indicate the traffic originated from this source, and net to indicate a subnet. This filter says you want to look at any traffic that originates from a source network other than your own that is destined for the broadcast addresses. If you start TCPdump with this filter or collect TCPdump data and later read it back with this filter, it picks up attempted mapping efforts of your network.

Detecting Fragmentation

In this section, you exercise some of your new knowledge of the mechanics of writing TCPdump filters to look for fragmentation. All fragments in a normal fragment train except the last one have the more fragments bit set. If you can discover how to locate this field and see whether it is set, you can find most of the fragmented traffic directed your way. Look again at Figure 12.1. You see that the more fragments bit is in the second row of the IP header. Can you figure out what byte it is in?

Specifically, if you count into the IP header, you will find it in the 6th byte offset. It is the third bit from the left of the high order-bit. Look at Figure 12.3 to see how you might mask all surrounding bits except this one. Your mask needs to be 0010 0000, which is a hexadecimal 0x20. Your filter becomes ip[6] & 0x20 != 0. You use a generic relation and value of != 0. This means that the more fragments bit is set. Why not just say ip[6] & 0x02 = 1? After all, aren't you testing that the exact bit is set? Not really. The problem with this is that you are not testing the bit value, but the resulting value of masking the original byte and the mask byte. Therefore, you need to examine the resulting value in context of where it falls in the whole byte. If the more fragments bit is set, it falls in the byte in the 2^5 position of the byte, which is 32. A generic != 0 is a little easier to express the result. Alternatively, you can write the filter as ip[6] & 0x02 = 32. Keep in mind that because fragmentation is not always malicious, you are likely to generate false positives with this filter.

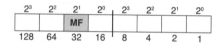

Figure 12.3 Identifying the more fragments bit.

You have now seen how to express three TCPdump filters for potentially anomalous settings in the IP header. Now, turn your attention to some of the other protocols and how you can use TCPdump filters to discover other sorts of events of interest.

TCPdump UDP Filters

Many backdoors and Trojans use UDP ports, such as port 31337 used by Back Orifice. To detect UDP connections, you must decide on which UDP ports you want to examine directed activity. Take a look at www.snort.org/ports.html for an idea of some of the types of ports you might want to watch. Configure your filters to watch for activity to these ports. If you want to look for traffic to Back Orifice, for example, your filter is as follows:

```
udp and dst port 31337
```

The labor is not in figuring how to express this as a TCPdump filter; as you see, it is trivial. The labor is involved in deciding which ports you want to include, adding them to the filter, and keeping the filter current with the real world of ever-expanding UDP exploits.

Consider a popular UDP application, traceroute. The UNIX traceroute works by attempting to send UDP datagrams to high-numbered ports of the destination host. If a host on your network is that destination host, you want to be alerted of the attempted or successful traceroute. If you begin by looking at UDP activity to ports in the 33000–33999 range, you will find most of the traceroute activity. Be warned that Windows traceroutes use ICMP echo requests and replies, so this signature does not detect that activity. And, be forewarned that some versions of the UNIX traceroute enable the user to provide command-line options, one of which is a destination port. Therefore, this filter might not capture all traceroute activity, but it will find most of the conventional activity.

Figure 12.4 shows the layout of the UDP header. Notice that the UDP destination port number is found in bytes 2 and 3 of the UDP header.

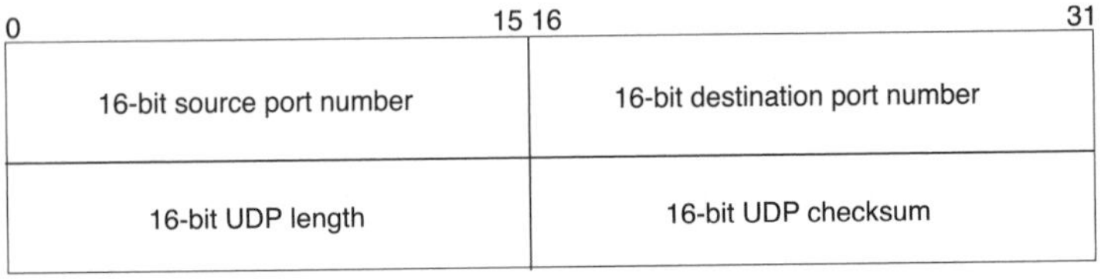

0	15 16	31
16-bit source port number		16-bit destination port number
16-bit UDP length		16-bit UDP checksum

Figure 12.4 The UDP header.

A very insightful question to ask is this: "Why don't we use the port macro rather than byte displacements?" For instance, why can't we use this filter:

```
dst port >= 33000 and dst port < 34000
```

The problem is that when TCPdump uses a range such as this and not one exact value, you have to express that field in terms of the primitive protocol and displacement and forgo the use of macros. The correct syntax to discover traceroutes then becomes this:

```
udp[2:2] >= 33000 and udp[2:2] < 34000
```

Notice the first use of the length option [2:2] to span bytes. You need to examine two consecutive bytes starting at byte 2 offset. You can further limit the amount of traffic that this filter extracts by examining the TTL value along with the destination port. Traceroute operates by manipulating the TTL value found in the IP header. Traceroute records the routers that it traverses and does so using an incrementing TTL value. More often than not, you will see a TTL of 1 on the sensor host running TCPdump before it crosses a router that will expire it. This is a signature of traceroute. Therefore, let's embellish the traceroute filter to include the TTL value to eliminate some of the noise associated with discovering traceroutes. The TTL field is found in the IP header; it has no macro to reference it and if you look once again at Figure 12.1, you find it in the 8th byte offset. Here is what the new filter would look like:

```
udp[2:2] >= 33000 and udp[2:2] < 34000 and ip[8] = 1
```

This gives you an idea of some of the UDP filters. TCPdump filters can also be used for ICMP traffic. Specifically, some of the good candidates for detection of anomalous ICMP traffic are address mask requests, someone trying to discover the MTU of your network sending datagrams with the don't fragment bit set and receiving back messages from your router with the MTU, and Loki. All these filters are so simple to write. We will leave these for you to try. Here are the signatures of TCPdump filters for you to write on your own:

- The address mask request has a value of 17 in the 0 byte offset of the ICMP message.

- The fragmentation required, but DF flag set message has a 3 in the 0 byte offset of the ICMP message and a 4 in the 1st byte offset of the message.

- A signature for Loki was an echo request (an 8 in the 0 byte offset of the ICMP message) or an echo reply (a 0 in the 0 byte offset of the ICMP message and in the 6th and 7th bytes offset of the ICMP message). You would have a hexadecimal value of 0xf001 or 0x01f0.

Answers to ICMP filters:

```
- icmp[0] = 17

- ((icmp[0] = 3) and (icmp[1] = 4))

- (((icmp[0] = 0) or (icmp[0] = 8)) and
  ((icmp[6:2] = 0xf001) or (icmp[6:2] = 0x01f0)))
```

TCPdump TCP Filters

TCPdump filters for TCP traffic are mostly concerned with initial SYN connections and other types of anomalous flag combinations that might indicate some kind of reconnaissance or mapping efforts. We want to look for initial SYN connections because they inform us of attempted connections to a TCP port. This doesn't necessarily mean that they were successful. If your TCPdump sensor is located outside a packet-filtering device that blocks access to the TCP destination port, it will never reach the host. And, if the traffic is allowed through the packet-filtering device, it is possible that the host doesn't offer the attempted service. You can glean a lot of intelligence by detecting this activity, the least of which is discovering rogue TCP ports that hosts on your network might be offering.

Filters for Examining TCP Flags

Figure 12.5 relates to most of the remaining filters in this chapter.

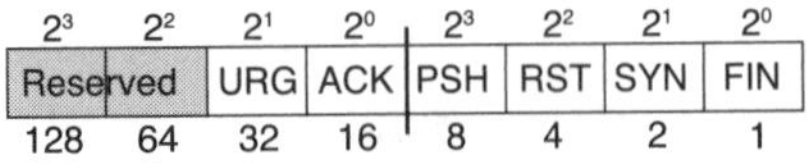

2^3	2^2	2^1	2^0	2^3	2^2	2^1	2^0
Reserved		URG	ACK	PSH	RST	SYN	FIN
128	64	32	16	8	4	2	1

Figure 12.5   The TCP flag byte.

The TCP flag bits are located in the 13th byte offset of the TCP header. Because you are looking for individual bits in the bytes, you need to perform some bit masking to select the flag or flags you want to examine. Begin by writing a filter to extract records with the SYN flag alone set:

```
tcp[13] & 0xff = 2
```

Why this filter? We see that our mask consists of all 1s. Why didn't we use a mask of 0s in all fields except the SYN flag (tcp[13] & 0x02 = 2)? By masking a bit with a 0, the resulting value is necessarily 0. The value bit could be 1, however, and the 0 mask would discard it. If this is confusing, try an example.

Suppose that you want to look at TCP segments with the SYN flag alone set. Okay, now suppose that you have a TCP flag byte with both the SYN and ACK flags set. The binary value that you would see for the TCP flag byte would be 0001 0010. If that were masked with 0000 0010, you would end up with a result of 0000 0010, which is 2. Therefore, masking with 0s in fields other than the SYN flag selects TCP segments with other flags set along with the SYN flag. To prevent this from occurring, you use the original filter and preserve all the value bits; the resulting value will not be 2 if any other value bit is set. If the ACK bit were set, you would have a resulting value of 18 from the new mask. This filter does not select records with other flags set along with the SYN flag.

Because you are looking for the SYN flag alone set, to be perfectly simple about this particular filter, you can specify it by:

```
tcp[13] = 2
```

This will assure that only the SYN flag is set because if any other flag is set, the resulting value when adding up all the bits set in the byte will not be 2. For instance, let's say that you have a byte with an errant SYN and URG flag set together. The URG flag is found in the position of the byte that has a value of 32 and the SYN flag is found in a position with a value of 2. Therefore, the resulting combined value of these two bits set would be 34 and would not match the filter.

Take a look at some other TCP flag combinations you might want to know about:

- **tcp[13] & 0xff = 0** alternatively **tcp[13] = 0**   This shows null scans with no flags set. This condition should never occur.

- **tcp[13] & 0xff = 3** alternatively **tcp[13] = 3**   This shows activity where both the SYN and FIN flags are set simultaneously; this is definitely an anomalous condition. You might want to alter the filter to tcp[13] & 0x03 = 3, because this gets any activity with both the SYN and FIN flags set, as well as any other flags set. In this case, you don't necessarily want to exclude this to SYN and FIN alone.

- **tcp[13] & 0xff = 0x10 and tcp[8:4] = 0**   This shows activity with the ACK flag set, but with an acknowledgement value of 0. This is usually an anomalous condition because the three-way handshake necessarily consumes a sequence number. Logically, an acknowledgement value would have to be 1 greater than the initial sequence number meaning it will be non-zero. This filter is offered because it often captures nmap operating system fingerprinting scans that send TCP traffic to various destination ports with the ACK flag alone set, but a 0 value in the acknowledgement field.

  It is rarely possible that a 0 acknowledgement can be legitimate if the sender has sent a sequence number where all the bits in the sequence number are 1 − in other words $2^{32} - 1$. The next expected sequence number would then wrap around and be 0.

- **tcp[13] >= 64**   Figure 12.5 shows two high-order bits in the TCP flag byte that are labeled reserved bits. These two bits should be 0s; if they are not, something might be amiss. The first reserved bit is found in the 2^6 (64) position, and the second is found in the 2^7 (128) position. If either or both bits are set, the value for the TCP flag byte is greater than or equal to 64. Our old friend nmap sometimes sets the bit that is in the 64 position to perform operating system fingerprinting. Most hosts reset these values to 0s, but some leave the set value. This is used by nmap to help classify the operating system behavior.

  More recently, these erstwhile-reserved high-order TCP flag bits are now associated with something known as Explicit Congestion Notification (ECN). This is a technique for reducing congestion in a network. How can you distinguish legitimate ECN traffic from nmap operating system scans? ECN traffic should have a non-zero value in the differentiated services byte (formerly known as the type of service byte), whereas nmap will have a 0 in this field. If you care to read more about ECN, reference RFC 3168.

These are just some of the different combinations of TCP flags that you can examine. This is not an exhaustive list and I encourage you to play with these filters and develop different combinations.

Detecting Data on SYN Connections

Before letting you loose to develop some TCPdump filters of your own, let's take a look at one advanced filter that will summon up all the various bits and pieces you have learned in the chapter about developing filters and then some. In Chapter 2, "Introduction to TCPdump and TCP," you learned that data should not be sent before the three-way TCP handshake has been completed. You saw this activity with the 3DNS product, which is a nuisance but ostensibly not malicious. You also read about the example of a scan that a site received in which there was data included on the SYN. It was feared that this type of activity might be an attempt to elude an IDS that started stream or data assembly for data received after the three-way handshake only.

It seems prudent then to try to develop a TCPdump filter that would detect this activity. You could later put in exclusions for annoying false alarms from 3DNS activity. The problem is that no field in the TCP header has the number of bytes in the TCP payload. You do have a bevy of other fields that have length values in them, however. Specifically, in the IP datagram, you have two length fields in the IP header. One is the length of the entire IP datagram, and the other is the length of the IP header alone. In the TCP segment, you have the length of the TCP header. Figure 12.6 shows that the length of the IP datagram minus the length of the IP header minus the length of the TCP header should leave the TCP payload length.

"Piece of cake," you say? You will encounter some complications, or challenges (your choice). Notice the different metrics in different fields; the IP datagram length is in bytes, whereas the IP header and TCP header are in 32-bit words. You must standardize to bytes and convert the header lengths to bytes by multiplying them by a factor of 4. This is quite manageable. You have already dealt with the IP header length, and so you have pretty much conquered that.

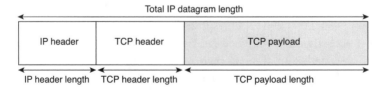

Figure 12.6   Calculating the TCP payload length.

One final bit of nastiness that you need to address is the TCP header length seen in Figure 12.7. Look carefully at where this is located; it is in the high-order nibble of the 12th byte. You already know that you have to zero-out the low-order nibble to deal with the high-order nibble exclusively, but you aren't quite ready to tackle the formula just yet. Because this is in the high-order nibble, it is really multiplied by a factor of 16, so it has to be normalized.

Suppose, for example, that you have a TCP header length of 24 bytes that includes a 20-byte header and some TCP options. Remember that you have to convert to 32-bit words, so you need to divide by 4 to compute the value that would be found in the TCP header length field. You would find a value of 6 in this field. Assume you have also masked the low-order nibble so that the hexadecimal value remaining in this byte is 60. The binary representation of this byte is 0110 0000. A 1 is in the 2^6 position (64) and a 1 is in the 2^5 position (32), which really means you have 96. Because this field is in the high-order nibble, it is really 16 times a value found in a low-order nibble. To normalize this back to 6, you need to divide by 16. Summing up all the manipulations to this field, you want to normalize by dividing by 16 and then convert to bytes by multiplying by 4. Now you are ready to tackle this filter.

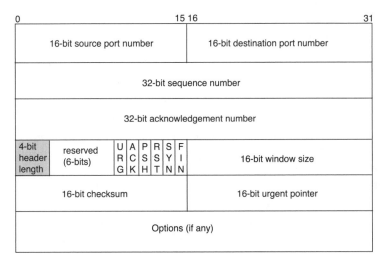

Figure 12.7 The TCP header.

Let's revisit the conditions and formula we want in pseudo-code before attempting the TCPdump filter.

If the SYN flag alone is set, subtract from the IP datagram total length, the IP header length converted to bytes, and the TCP header length normalized and converted to bytes, and check to see whether the resulting value is non-0.

SYN flag alone is set:

```
tcp[13] & 0xff = 2  or alternatively tcp[13] = 2
```

Total length of the IP datagram:

```
ip[2:2]
```

IP header length converted to bytes:

```
((ip[0] & 0x0f)*4)
```

TCP header length normalized and converted to bytes:

```
((tcp[12] & 0xf0)/16*4)
```

which is the same as:

```
((tcp[12] & 0xf0)/4)
```

Now put it all together to see the final filter:

```
tcp[13] & 0xff = 2
and
    (    ip[2:2] -
        ((ip[0] & 0x0f)*4) -
        ((tcp[12] & 0xf0)/4)
    ) != 0
```

This discovers any traffic that attempts to include data on the initial SYN. Pretty awesome!

Summary

This chapter has shown that although TCPdump filters might not win most-likely-to-succeed in a beauty pageant of IDS filters, they can do some amazing things. Yes indeed, you need to get your hands soiled and you need to think pretty darn hard many times when attempting to debug a filter that does not work. But, these filters give you full access to your data. I cannot emphasize enough that when you smell something foul with your data, you want the ability to analyze at the bit level. TCPdump filters afford you this power. Literally, you want to leave no bit unturned when you are conducting in-depth analysis.

Most of the filters that you write using TCPdump will probably use macros and probably won't require any bit masking. When you need to examine individual bits or disjoint bits in a byte, however, you must isolate the bits of interest using bit masking. The other gotcha with TCPdump discussed in this chapter is standardizing on metrics with different length fields—make sure you convert to bytes. Finally, remember that the location where bits fall in the byte is significant. It might be necessary to normalize if you are dealing with bits in the high-order nibble. If you are up to the challenge of all of this, I think you will get a true sense of satisfaction after you have mastered the deciphering of data and the creation of potentially revealing filters.

Introduction to Snort and Snort Rules

SNORT IS AN OPEN SOURCE FREE NIDS that was developed by Marty Roesch. It was initially written so that Marty could do traffic sniffing at his job and has grown to a full-featured NIDS. Along the way, Marty has attracted a vast following of admirers and coders who work collectively to enhance the code and issue new releases. In early 2002, Snort was downloaded from its home at www.snort.org over 10,000 times a week to protect government, corporate, home, and educational sites.

Snort is a signature-based NIDS that uses a combination of rules and pre-processors to analyze traffic. The rules offer a simple and flexible means of cre-ating signatures to examine a single packet. The preprocessor code allows more extensive examination and manipulation of data that cannot be done via rules alone. Preprocessors can perform a variety of tasks such as IP defragmentation, portscan detection, web traffic normalization, and TCP stream reassembly, to name a few. Preprocessors give Snort the capability to look at and manipulate streams, as opposed to the single-packet-at-a-time view rules use.

The current version of Snort in March 2002 is 1.8.3 and is a compact 1.8 megabytes of source code. It is extremely portable and currently runs on approximately 23 different platforms including Linux, Solaris, BSD, IRIX, HP-UX, Mac OS X, and Win32. Snort is also easily configurable and flexible, allowing users to create their own signatures and alter the base functionality through the use of plug-ins. Plug-ins are code that can optionally be compiled into Snort at installation time and offer features such as active response to malicious traffic.

The focus of this section of the book is writing filters and signatures, so many aspects of Snort will not be discussed, such as installation, configuration, and output. If you would like more information on these topics about Snort, please visit www.snort.org. This chapter will cover an introduction to Snort, the anatomy of a Snort rule, and explore fields and possible values found in the first part of a Snort rule known as the rule header. The next chapter will continue rule writing by discussing the second part of the rule known as the rule options. It will also cover writing more advanced rules.

An Overview of Running Snort

Snort can be run in various modes from simply dumping sniffed traffic to the screen, to NIDS mode where Snort is able to compare the network traffic with a preconfigured set of signatures known as rules that are housed in one or more files. The latter is the most common mode in which to run Snort.

Snort is typically run from the command line, whether it is run on a UNIX or Windows host. There is software offered known as IDScenter, which provides a Windows GUI interface, as well as Demarc/Puresecure, which provides a Windows and UNIX GUI interface. There are many command-line options that can be used, but the most practical one (-c snort.conf) allows the user to place Snort in NIDS mode by informing it of the configuration file to be used. As the name implies, this is where Snort configuration occurs, including assigning variables used in the rules values, informing Snort which preprocessor options to use, and telling Snort which rules to include in traffic analysis. A skeleton configuration file named snort.conf is provided in the Snort download directory. The user must customize this file for his site.

When Snort is run in NIDS mode, by default, it places the output of events of interest triggered by the rules in various files. Snort allows an *action* to be assigned to each rule, indicating what to do when the rule is triggered. An action of *alert* means to write the offending packet to a file named alert, which is created in /var/log/snort on many UNIX hosts, by default. On Windows hosts, the alert file is created in the *log* subdirectory in the current directory from which Snort is run. Here is an example of a Snort alert file entry:

```
[**] NMAP TCP ping [**]
03/21-13:33:51:880120 1.2.3.4:1029 -> 192.168.5.5:80

TCP TTL:46 TOS:0x0 ID:19678
******A* Seq: 0xE4F00003 Ack: 0x0  Win: 0xC00
```

There is an identifying message associated with the alert that the user can assign when the rule is created. This is optional; however, it informs the analyst of the perceived problem. The message for the preceding alert is "NMAP TCP ping". On the next line, there is a date and timestamp followed by source IP address (1.2.3.4) and port (1029), direction of the traffic (source to the left of the arrow and destination to the right of the arrow), and the destination IP address (192.168.5.5) and port (80) of the offending packet. The third line indicates that the traffic is TCP, it has an arriving time-to-live value of 46, a type of service value of 0, and an IP identification number of 19678. The final line lists the TCP flags set; the A signifies that the acknowledgement flag is set. It is followed by a hexadecimal representation of the TCP sequence number, the acknowledgement number, and the TCP window size. All of these fields can provide more details about the packet that triggered the alert.

This alert appeared because there is a rule that examines TCP segments with an acknowledgement flag set but an accompanying acknowledgement value of 0. Most of the time when this is observed, it is a telltale sign of nmap attempting to discover a live host. If the acknowledgement is allowed to reach the destination host, the host should respond to the unsolicited acknowledgement with a reset, regardless of whether the port is listening or not. That is why the message accompanying the alert is "NMAP TCP ping."

The alert action causes the activity to be logged as well. There is a separate action, log, which only logs the triggered activity. When activity is logged, it is recorded in a human readable format that can provide more verbose information about the packet, such as the payload. The logged packets are written to files and directories based on the IP addresses in the packet being logged. These are further segregated by the transport layer protocol and source and destination ports involved in the connection. Look at the contents of FTP activity that was logged:

```
[**] Attempted anonymous ftp access [**]
04/24-12:11:08.724441 192.168.143.15:3484 -> 192.168.143.16:21
TCP TTL:64 TOS:0x10 ID:30124  DF
*****PA* Seq: 0x93EE0AB7   Ack: 0xB8352E61   Win: 0x7D78
TCP Options => NOP NOP TS: 112024246 27551686
55 53 45 52 20 61 6E 6F 6E 79 6D 6F 75 73 0D 0A   USER anonymous..
```

The logged output contains the same information that the alert does, but it also has the payload if the decode (-d) command-line option was supplied. This message indicates that we have a rule to inspect ftp command-line traffic to destination port 21 for a user of anonymous. We will examine how this is accomplished in Chapter 14, "Snort Rules—Part II," but the payload from the previous output indicates that there was an anonymous user attempt. The hexadecimal representations of the ASCII values in the payload are also included in the logged packet.

The log and alert files can be a cumbersome way of analyzing output from Snort, so it allows you other options via configuration file changes. Activating available output options can enable writing output or alerts to spool files via a backend known as Barnyard, or directly to a database, to name a few of the possible options.

Snort Rules

Snort supports both header and payload inspection methods, allowing you to fully specify in a single rule what is considered a suspect packet. This flexibility allows you to build rules customized to your site that greatly aid in minimizing false positives, but in a format that is very readable. Remember all the heartache and toil involved in writing TCPdump filters, especially one to inspect a packet for a particular TCP flag setting? Well, writing an identical rule in Snort is almost trivial, as you will soon see.

As a short but important digression, what qualities does one look for in a good NIDS? There are many, but one of the most important is the capability to inspect and alter signatures. Believe it or not, there are NIDS available that do not allow the user to see the active signatures or alter them in any way. This blindsides the analyst and does not allow her to distinguish between false positives and real alerts. When an alert appears, it is presented as an irrefutable statement that a problem has appeared, and there is no way to validate it using the NIDS alone. If the analyst can examine the signatures and the packet that caused the alert, there is a better chance that a more accurate assessment can be made.

Additionally, signatures that allow an analyst to look at any field, either header or payload, from different perspectives potentially improve the quality of the NIDS. In other words, if a NIDS only allows the analyst to create rules that inspect packets for a given IP or port or protocol, it lacks the range to examine payloads or header fields on a more granular level such as TCP flag settings. Perhaps the analyst is interested in inspecting the payload for specific contents when the acknowledgement flag is set. Because other flags may be set along with the acknowledgement flag, it would be handy for the signature to allow for this specification as well.

The capability to inspect just about any field in a packet is an area in which Snort excels. There are many options available to configure a rule to specify just about any field in the packet and examine the value of that field in a variety of ways. And, the few fields that cannot be inspected via current Snort rule options can always be examined by supplying a filter at the end of the command line or by resorting to a command-line switch (-F) that allows Berkeley Packet Filters (BPF) to be specified in a file. Berkeley Packet Filters are what we have been calling TCPdump filters, which can be used to select the desired field. For instance, Snort doesn't have an option to examine the IP version field found in the high-order nibble of the zero byte offset of the IP header. Snort might be run to examine packets off the wire or from a binary file of captured TCPdump data using a BPF filter to find any packets with an IP version that does not equal 4. Here is the command that would perform this inspection reading packets from the network:

```
snort -v 'ip[0] & 0xf0 != 0x40'
```

As explained in more detail in Chapter 12, "Writing TCPdump Filters," this will mask out the low-order nibble of the zero byte offset of the IP header and look for a value of 4 in the high-order nibble of that field and write the output to the screen (-v).

Another benefit of using Snort is that it comes with a very large set of rules. It is not recommended that all of the rules be used on installation because the more active rules used, the slower the traffic inspection becomes. The analyst must decide which rules are appropriate for the site. And, amazingly, new Snort rules are released sometimes as soon as hours after a new exploit is discovered. This is by virtue of having so many savvy users and developers of Snort who respond almost instantly to develop and test new rules for these exploits.

However, a word of caution must be added about some Snort rules. Just because a rule becomes available shortly after an exploit is released, doesn't mean that it is a good rule—that is to say, just because a rule matches a given compiled version of an exploit's output doesn't mean that it is necessarily a rule that may find variations of the exploit from making minor changes in the source code. It is imperative that the rule writer understands not only the exploit code and output, but also the protocol against which it runs.

A good rule anchors on fields and values that must remain static for the exploit to succeed. For instance, if there is some kind of DNS exploit that generates a DNS identification number of 0xBEEF, this is not a good field or value to use in the rule. It is trivial to change this in the source code, and the exploit will most likely succeed regardless of the value of the DNS identification number.

Hidden Signatures

As a contractor for a client, I once had the opportunity to visit a commercial NIDS vendor about integrating output from its NIDS to some kind of correlation tool. Frankly, I believed the output from the NIDS wasn't worth trying to correlate since there was no way to validate if the generated alerts were real because there was no access to either the signatures or the packets that caused the alert. Why synthesize garbage? But, the client had requested my presence at the meeting, so I dutifully attended.

While there, I asked if there was any way that we could get access to the signatures. The vendor rep balked and asked why I would ever need to see the signatures. "Well, I want to know if we have a real detect or false positive," I politely responded. The rep replied that if I believed we had seen a rare false positive, I could call the support line and ask for help. With the number of false positives generated by the vendor's NIDS, I could only imagine that it had stock in the Baby Bells to answer so foolishly. Indignantly, I pressed on and asked the rep what the problem was with releasing his signatures. The response was that if I could see the signatures, so could the hackers! Honest to goodness, that was the best dog-ate-my-homework excuse he could come up with. More than anything, I suspect it was that he feared that the competition might pirate his product's signatures, but he didn't have the spine to say that. How are you supposed to take these guys and their proprietary signatures seriously? Okay, so we're not all blessed with the power to either make or influence the decision of which NIDS to buy. What if you happen to work at a site where you have a NIDS that has either a limited or no view of the signatures and traffic—do you throw in the towel? Well, if lobbying for a better NIDS fails, you can become resourceful! You can always run TCPdump in the background mode either alone or as part of Shadow. Or, you can try to do correlation with other sources of information such as firewalls, routers, or host logs. This is not ideal, but it prevents you from being totally blind.

We were running Shadow along with the deficient NIDS mentioned previously. An analyst called me to report that the NIDS was alerting on a Loki attack and asked if I could examine the TCPdump output to discover whether this was a real alert or not. I knew that Loki had a telltale signature years ago of a value of 0xf001 or 0x01f0 in the ICMP sequence number. The analyst was able to give me the source and destination IP numbers for the suspected Loki traffic. I searched the TCPdump records and discovered ICMP packets that matched the signature; however, this was just a case of coincidental use of those values in the ICMP sequence number in an innocuous ICMP echo request/response pair. This was an awkward and time-consuming way of dealing with this false positive, but it was better than putting full trust in the NIDS.

Snort Rule Anatomy

An individual rule is broken into two general parts. The first part, the rule header, defines who must be involved in order for the traffic to be considered by the rule options. The second part, the rule options, defines what must be involved. This includes packet header information (such as TCP flag settings) or the contents of the payload.

Generally speaking, both sections are used for most rules. It is possible to specify rules with only a rule header so that the given action can be taken for the provided hosts and ports. This is typically the case where pass rules are used to ignore traffic between specific hosts and ports, such as port 53 traffic coming from a site's DNS servers.

All conditions specified in both the rule header and the rule options must be true in order for an alert or some other kind of action to be triggered. It is also important to understand the Snort rules are stateless. In other words, each rule inspects one and only one packet. The rules themselves have no way of knowing what activity occurred in a packet preceding or following the current one. Snort attempts to build in functionality for state using a preprocessor such as IP defragmentation or TCP stream reassembly, but there are limits to what can be discovered when not examining traffic statefully.

Also, Snort triggers on the first rule that a packet matches and does not examine the remaining rules. The order that rules are listed in the rules files is important, but Snort does some ordering of its own. By default, Snort orders all rules by their action value in the following order: alert, pass, and log. This can be overridden by a command-line option that will be discussed later in the section, "The Action Field." However, Snort does some further ordering by grouping identical headers that is beyond the scope of this chapter. For more information, see www.snort.org/docs/faq.html#3.13.

Look at Figure 13.1 to see a sample Snort rule.

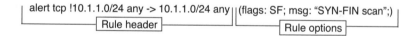

Figure 13.1   The anatomy of a Snort rule.

You see a rule header that gives the details of the action to be taken if the rule triggers and the information pertaining to the who values in the packet. In this rule, we alert when TCP traffic is observed that originates from a network that is not 10.1.1.x from any source port destined for network 10.1.1.x to any destination port. We assume that our internal network is the 10.1.1.x network, so this rule triggers when an outsider attempts to make an internal TCP connection.

If you turn your attention to the rule options, we further specify the what of the packet attributes. In this instance, the anomalous TCP flag pair of SYN and FIN is sought, and if found, a message of "SYN-FIN scan" is associated with the alert. The rules keywords will be described more thoroughly in the following sections.

Rumor has it that the rules syntax will change radically when Snort version 2.0 makes its debut. So, if you are reading this chapter after the release of Snort 2.0, it is best to refer to Snort documentation because the information presented here might be obsolete.

Rule Header Fields

As briefly mentioned, the rule header is responsible for specifying the action used to respond to a triggered rule, as well as specifying the protocol and source and destination addresses and ports. These who conditions must be met if the rule options are to be examined. Rule options will be explored in Chapter 14.

The Action Field

The first field in the rule header is the action field. This field instructs Snort on what to do if the rule is triggered. The valid values for the action field are the following:

- **Alert.** This value instructs Snort to create an entry in the alert file and to log the packet as well. The alert file is a single file that contains all detects that were made. The information written to this file in the default alert mode consists only of the packet header information. For the log entry, the same information (optionally including the payload if the -d command-line option is specified) that is written to the alert file is written to individual files found in a directory that usually has the name of the hostile IP number.

- **Log.** This value instructs Snort to only make a log entry. No record of the traffic is made in the alert file when the log action is used. The log files might have data from the application payload if the command-line option to decode the application (-d) is used.

- **Pass.** When a rule is triggered that has pass specified as the action, Snort does no further packet inspection—essentially dropping the packet from the detection engine. This is useful, for example, if you want to monitor anonymous ftp attempts on your network to non-anonymous ftp servers. You would write a pass rule to ignore anonymous ftp attempts to your valid anonymous ftp server. You would then use a second, normal, alert rule to log all other anonymous ftp attempts.

- **Activate.** These rules, when triggered, not only alert, but are also used to turn on other rules (dynamic) that remain idle until turned on.

- **Dynamic.** These remain idle (do not trigger) until turned on by an activate rule. After they are turned on, their behavior is the same as log rules.

Note that the activate and dynamic actions are being replaced by the tag option, which is found in the rule options. The tag option allows dynamic capture of packets for a given amount of time or a specified number of packets after the rule triggers.

It's also possible to define your own action types, which can be used to route rule output to various destinations. This sophisticated usage is not covered here, but can be explored at Snort's web site (www.snort.org). As briefly mentioned, the default order in which rules are processed is alert rules first, pass rules second, and log rules last. To change this default behavior, you must specify the -o command-line option when running Snort, which changes the order the rules are processed. Using the -o option changes the rule processing order to pass rules first, alert rules second, and log rules last. This was done when Snort was developed for public use to avoid having an errant pass rule accidentally disable every alert and log rule in the system. The −o option was developed as an expert mode for people after they understood how the rules system worked.

The Protocol Field

The protocol field in the rule header tells Snort which protocol to examine. Snort currently supports four different types of network traffic: TCP (Transmission Control Protocol), UDP (User Datagram Protocol), ICMP (Internet Control Message Protocol), and IP (Internet Protocol). Additional protocols may be added in the future such as ARP, RARP, GRE, OSPF, RIP, and IPX. Snort understands only IP version 4, though it will note that it has seen an IP version 6 packet. And, Snort is not IPSec aware, so it cannot decode unencrypted fields of those packets.

The Source and Destination IP Address Fields

The source and destination IP address fields identify where the hostile traffic is coming from and where it is going. It is possible to specify the IP addresses as a host, a subnet, or multiple hosts or subnets. The IP addresses are specified in classless inter-domain routing (CIDR) notation, an easy to write and under-stand format. This format includes as much of the address as needed, along with the number of bits in the network mask. Let's examine the format and some examples of IP addresses.

Format:

```
Address/netmask or any or
[address/netmask,address/netmask...]

Address = x.x.x.x
Netmask = bits of network mask
```

```
24.0.0.0/8 =           Class A
135.1.0.0/16 =         Class B
192.168.5.0/24 =       Class C
192.168.5.5/32 =       Host address
```

Special keywords:

```
any - match all addresses
!  -   negate address
$HOME_NET - variable defined elsewhere in rules file
```

CIDR notation details the base address and the number of bits of the base address that are associated with the network. For instance, the representation 24.0.0.0/8 means that this is a Class A address that has the first octet (24) allocated to the network and all the remaining octets associated with hosts on the network. Although the standard Class A, B, and C CIDR notations are seen in the previous examples, the beauty of CIDR notation is that the network bits don't have to fall on byte boundaries, so they might represent all network masks.

You can specify an IP address list by enclosing all IP addresses or networks between brackets ([ ]) and delimiting each of the list values by commas (but no spaces in between—the Snort rule parser doesn't allow spaces in the comma delimited list). If you want to examine traffic to destination host 1.2.3.4 or subnet 2.3.4.x, the following IP address list could be used:

```
[1.2.3.4,2.3.4.0/24]
```

A special keyword *any* can be used when any IP address is the matching criteria. And, as you've seen, the exclamation point (!) can be used to negate the IP address value when all IP addresses but the specified one are to be considered. Finally, to add more flexibility and portability to the rules, a variable can be used to indicate the IP address. The $HOME_NET variable is one that is used in many of the rules included with Snort to indicate the user's/analyst's home network. You can assign your internal network any variable name you want, but because many of the rules already reference $HOME_NET, it is best to use it. This variable must be defined in a rules file, the configuration file, or on the command line (-S) before it is referenced. Variables can be used in other fields in the rules as well.

The Source and Destination Port Field

The port fields are used to detail the source and destination ports of the traffic. The ports can be listed as a specific number, range of numbers, or the keyword *any*, which represents all possible source ports. Here are some possible port representations:

static port:	111
all ports:	any
range:	33000:34000
negation:	!80
less than or equal:	:1023
greater than or equal:	1024:

The first and most common port value is a static one, such as port 111, to represent the port associated with the Remote Procedure Call (RPC) portmapper. As with IP addresses, a generic port value can be supplied using the keyword any. A range of port numbers can be specified, such as ports 33000 through 34000 inclusive (33000:34000), which might represent UNIX traceroute UDP ports. Negation is also supported with ports as we are looking for any port but port 80 (!80) above. Ports can be indicated as a less than or equal to condition or a greater than or equal to condition. The ":1023" identifies that we want to look for all ports less than or equal to 1023 or the reserved port range. Finally, the "1024:" is used to say that all ports greater than or equal to 1024 should be considered—the ports typically found in the ephemeral source port range. You could also specify a port as a variable so long as you assigned a value to the variable before referencing it.

You might be wondering if you have to indicate a port for the ICMP protocol because it does not use ports like TCP and UDP. The rule syntax requires ports, so you must specify some kind of placeholder value. Although no port value makes sense, the value "any" is often used. Let's look at some possible port values.

Direction Indicator

The traffic direction field allows you to indicate the direction the packet must be traveling. Two options are available, allowing you to indicate a specific direction of flow, or that direction doesn't matter. Using the notation that looks like an arrow (->), the packet must be traveling from a source to a destination. The source information is specified to the left of the arrow, and the destination is to the right. The packet must be traveling in the listed direction; if it is traveling in the opposite direction, the packet will not pass the rule header test and will not be inspected any further against the rule.

If you use the notation that looks similar to a double-headed arrow (<>), the packet can be traveling to or from either address/port pair. For this notation, either side can represent the source or destination depending on the packet flow in the connection.

Summary

Snort provides a very good NIDS at no cost for the software. Understand that although it is free to use, there are costs associated with the hardware, as well as costs associated with customizing rules and making sense of the output. Snort is most useful when run in packet-sniffing mode where it compares the network traffic against a set of rules. This can be done either in real-time mode, or traffic can be captured in binary format and retrospectively analyzed later by feeding it back into Snort as an input file.

Snort rules provide a flexible and easily configurable means of specifying most header fields to inspect, as well as analyzing any data in the payload. The rules allow the user many different ways to indicate values for particular fields in addition to permitting the use of variables to represent values. Snort rules also provide the granularity necessary to be very explicit about the attributes of the packet that are to be inspected or ignored. The result is that there should be far fewer false positives and false negatives if the rules are properly configured for the site.

14

Snort Rules—Part II

THE PREVIOUS CHAPTER PROVIDED AN INTRODUCTION to Snort, in general, and Snort rules. As you will recall, a Snort rule is composed of a rule header, which was examined in detail in the previous chapter, and a rule option, which will be covered thoroughly in this chapter.

The rule header supplies the action that will be applied if the rule is triggered. It details the source and destination IP addresses and ports, the protocol, and the direction of the traffic flow. The rule header can be used alone to form a rule, but it is usually followed by a rule option to provide more detail about the packet attributes. Ironically, there are some commercial NIDS that only allow the same level of detail as a Snort rule header when specifying a signature. In other words, they don't allow the user to configure much more than the IP addresses, protocol, and TCP or UDP ports to define a signature. Obviously, this cannot be considered very robust in terms of rule or packet granularity. The rule options form the core of Snort's intrusion-detection capabilities.

Format of Snort Options

The rule options are separated from the rule header via required parentheses
(). Look at the following rule:

```
alert tcp !$HOME_NET any -> $HOME_NET any (flags: SF; \
msg: "SYN-FIN scan";)
```

The options portion is as follows:

```
(flags: SF; msg: "SYN-FIN scan";)
```

Each option is made up of an option keyword, and possibly a value for the
particular option keyword. In the preceding example, you find the option keyword flags paired with a value of SF and an option keyword of msg paired
with a value of SYN-FIN scan. The value that is associated with a given
option keyword depends on the option. Some options require numeric values
and others require text. Option keywords are separated from the associated
value via the colon (:), and individual options are delimited by a semi-colon
(;). A semi-colon must follow the final option as well or an error will be generated. Although most option keywords are usually followed by a value, there
are some options that require no value. One such example is the option
nocase that indicates a search for content in the packet's payload is to be case
insensitive.

Snort is pretty unconcerned and forgiving about the lack or abundance of
whitespace between delimiters such as ; and :. You don't have to supply spaces,
or you can supply multiple spaces between options, values, and delimiters. For
instance, the two following options should both work:

```
(flags:SF;msg:"SYN-FIN scan";)
(flags: SF   ; msg : "SYN-FIN scan"  ;)
```

The backslash (\) is a rule continuation character; rules can be continued on
separate lines if this character is supplied at the end of any unfinished line.
Speaking of special characters, the pound sign (#) is used as the comment
character for Snort rules.

Rule Options

Some of the most important and commonly used options will be discussed
now to convince you of the power of Snort rules. The entire list of burgeoning options will not be covered, but descriptions of all of them can be found
at www.snort.org by examining the online Snort Users Manual under the documentation link.

Msg Option

The msg option allows the user or analyst to assign an appropriate message to the output of a triggered rule. When you examine an alert or logged entry for the triggered rule, you will see the offending packet. You will not see the actual rule that triggered the alert in the output itself, so you need some descriptive way of associating the alert with the rule. If you assign an msg option value, it will appear before the offending packet output to give you a better idea of why the rule triggered.

Look at the following format, rule, and an associated alert that triggered from the rule:

Format:

```
msg: "<message text>";
```

Sample rule:

```
alert udp any any -> 192.168.5.0/24 31337 \
(msg:"Back Orifice";)
```

Sample output:

```
[**] Back Orifice [**]
04/24-08:49:21.318567 192.168.143.15:60256 -> 192.168.5.16:31337
UDP TTL:41 TOS:0x0 ID:49951
Len: 8
```

The Snort rule says to alert (and log) when a UDP packet from any source IP address or port goes to subnet 192.168.5 destination port 31337 and to assign it a message of "Back Orifice". When the rule is triggered, the alert is recorded with "[**] Back Orifice [**]" to describe the activity.

Logto Option

The logto option allows you to specify a filename to which to log the activity. This applies to rules with the alert or log action in the rule header only. A rule that is triggered with the alert or log action will normally write to a default directory (either /var/log/snort for UNIX hosts or, on a Windows machine, a subdirectory named log from wherever Snort is launched) or a directory speci-fied using the –l filename option on the command line. This assumes that the user hasn't changed the default logging to binary output (-b command-line option), to send the output to the syslog daemon (-s command-line option), or disabled logging altogether (-N command-line option).

The logto option can be used to send the output for a specific rule or class of user-chosen rules to a given file. Why might you want to use this option? Well, this is an excellent way to separate the truly dangerous or harmful kinds of alerts from those that are the garden variety. In the case shown in the exam-ple, if you suspect that you have some kind of trinoo distributed denial-of-service (DDoS) infestation or any other DDoS activity on the network, you can look directly at the DDoS file for signs of this. This will also be logged to the default alert file as well because the following sample rule uses the action alert.

Format:

```
logto: "<filename>";
```

The supplied filename should not include a path, only a filename. Including a path causes Snort to display an error message. You should place the filename in quotes, otherwise an initial space is sometimes added before the name.

Sample rule:

```
alert udp any any -> 192.168.5.0/24 31335 \
(msg: "trinoo port"; logto: "DDoS";)
```

Sample output:

If the rule is triggered, the output on this UNIX host will be found in /var/log/snort/DDoS:

```
[**] trinoo port [**]
04/24-09:07:41.320938 192.168.143.15:56881 -> 192.168.5.16:31335
UDP TTL:42 TOS:0x0 ID:4011
Len: 8
```

Ttl Option

The ttl option allows you to examine the arriving time-to-live field for a specific value. This option could be used for a variety of reasons. One reason to examine this field would be to look for a packet with a low arriving TTL value, which can be indicative of a UNIX host performing a traceroute or a Windows host performing a tracert. When the protocol is UDP and the port ranges are 33000 through 34000, it is most likely a UNIX traceroute. A Windows tracert is done via ICMP echo requests.

The following rule looks for UNIX traceroute traffic to the 192.168.5 network with a UDP port in the range 33000 through 34000 inclusive and an arriving TTL value of 1.

Format:

```
ttl: <number>;
```

Sample rule:

```
alert udp any any -> 192.168.5.0/24 33000:34000 \
(msg: "Unix traceroute"; ttl: 1;)
```

Sample output:

```
[**] Unix traceroute [**]
04/24-09:29:37.971353 192.168.143.15:40920 -> 192.168.5.16:33437
UDP TTL:1 TOS:0x0 ID:40923
Len: 18
```

Id Option

As you recall, the IP identification value is a 16-bit value that is found in the IP header of each datagram. Each new datagram is assigned a unique IP ID number that is typically incremented by 1 for each packet. This number becomes the fragment ID, which assists the destination host in reassembling fragments. The sample rule looks for an unusual IP ID value of 0. It now appears that Linux 2.4 kernels set the IP ID value to 0 when the Don't Fragment (DF) flag is set in the packet. The reasoning for this is that if the packet will never become fragmented, why bother to assign it a fragment ID?

Format:

```
id: <number>;
```

Sample rule:

```
alert icmp any any -> 192.168.5.0/24 any \
(msg: "Suspect IP Identification #"; ID:0;)
```

Sample output:

```
[**] Suspect IP Identification # [**]
04/25-09:21:36.371005 192.168.143.15 -> 192.168.5.16
ICMP TTL:64 TOS:0x0 ID:00
```

Dsize Option

The dsize option allows Snort to examine the size of the payload. You can inspect the payload size for an exact value, or a value less than or greater than a particular number. This can come in handy when you are creating a rule for buffer overflow attacks. These attacks might have a telltale signature of having a larger payload than expected. The following sample rule looks for ICMP packets with a payload size greater than 1,024 bytes.

Format:

```
dsize: [<|>] number
```

Sample rule:

```
alert icmp any any -> 192.168.5.0/24 any \
(msg: "Large ICMP payload"; dsize: >1024;)
```

Sample output:

```
[**] Large ICMP payload [**]
04/24-11:10:24.110169 192.168.143.100 -> 192.168.5.16
ICMP TTL:255 TOS:0x0 ID:5487  DF
ID:7564   Seq:0  ECHO
```

Sequence Option

The sequence option checks the value of the TCP sequence number. The Shaft distributed denial-of-service software is known to assign a fixed sequence number—hexadecimal 28374839—when a TCP flood is directed to a victim site. No doubt, this is something that is configurable in the source code, so this is not a failsafe method of identifying Shaft. Of course, a benign packet could coincidentally be using the same sequence number, too.

Format:

```
seq: <number>;
```

Sample rule:

```
alert tcp  any any -> any any \
(msg: "Possible Shaft DDoS"; seq: 0x28374839;)
```

Sample output:

```
[**]Possible Shaft DDoS [**]
04/25-07:19:58.582562 192.168.143.100:35680 -> 192.168.143.15:23
TCP TTL:255 TOS:0x0 ID:7705  DF
******S* Seq: 0x28374839  Ack: 0x0   Win: 0x2238
TCP Options => MSS: 1460
```

Acknowledgement Option

The acknowledgement option examines the value of a TCP acknowledgement number. The primary use for this currently is to detect nmap pings. As you discovered in the previous chapter, nmap sends a unique signature when it tries to assess if a host is alive. It sets the ACK flag on, and it sets the acknowledgement value of 0. This would be a rare setting to find in normal traffic because it would be indicative of an already established connection acknowledging that the previous TCP sequence number received was $2^{32} - 1$, and now the acknowledgement number is wrapping back to 0.

Format:

```
ack: <number>;
```

Sample rule:

```
alert tcp  any any -> any any \
(msg: "nmap TCP ping"; flags: A; ack: 0;)
```

Sample output:

```
[**] nmap TCP ping [**]
04/25-07:27:13.578488 192.168.143.15:63367 -> 192.168.143.16:80
TCP TTL:42 TOS:0x0 ID:26253
***A**** Seq: 0x16680003   Ack: 0x0   Win: 0xC00
```

Itype and Icode Options

The itype option is used to select a particular ICMP message type. The message type field is found in the zero byte offset of the ICMP message. Valid values for this and its partner option icode, which is used to represent the ICMP message code, can be found at www.iana.org/assignments/icmp-parameters. The icode option is often used in conjunction with the itype option. The ICMP message code is found in the first byte offset of the ICMP message. Many ICMP messages share the same type but are further delineated using the ICMP code field. For instance, an ICMP type of 3 has many different ICMP codes associated with it. If you are just interested in seeing ICMP port unreachable messages, you must qualify the rule with an itype value of 3 and an icode value of 3.

Format:

```
itype: <number>;
icode: <number>;
```

Sample rule:

```
alert icmp  1.1.1.0/24 any -> 192.168.5.0/24 any \
(msg: "port unreachable"; itype: 3; icode: 3;)
```

Sample output:

```
[**] port unreachable [**]
04/25-07:56:37.129338 1.1.1.16 -> 192.168.5.15
ICMP TTL:255 TOS:0xC0 ID:33569
DESTINATION UNREACHABLE: PORT UNREACHABLE
```

Flags Option

The flags option enables you to inspect TCP flag settings in many different ways. Starting from the least significant (rightmost) flag bit setting:

F: Finish flag set

S: Synchronize flag set

R: Reset flag set

P: Push flag set

A: Acknowledgement flag set

U: Urgent flag set

2: ECN echo flag set (formerly a reserved bit)

1: ECN congestion window reduced set (formerly a reserved bit)

0: No flag bits set

It's also possible to use one of three modifiers (+,★,!) to assist in examining flag combinations or negating a flag setting. For instance, the A+ flag setting indicates that the Acknowledgement flag must be set. It can be set alone, or any other flag might be set along with it. This could include an acknowledgement on push flag (meaning new data is being sent at the same time received data is being acknowledged to combine transfers into one packet), which is a common and legitimate combination. The ★ modifier is used when you have a combination of flags and any of those flags might be set. For instance, SFP★ says that any combination of the SYN, FIN, and PSH flags can be set—they can all be set; a lone SYN, FIN, or PSH can be set; or any pair in the trio can be set. Finally, the ! modifier specifies to negate the current flag setting. The flags option !S specifies that any TCP segment without the SYN flag set will be a candidate packet.

Format:

```
flags: <flag_settings>
```

Flag Settings:

F = FIN

S = SYN

R = RST

P = PSH

A = ACK

U = URG

2 = ECE

1 = CWR

0 = No flags set

See Figure 14.1 for a pictorial representation of Snort's TCP flag bits. Possible flag modifiers:

+ All, match if listed flag(s) set and any others set

★ Any, match if any combination of listed flag(s) set

! Not, match if listed flag(s) NOT set

Sample rule:

```
alert tcp  any any -> any any (msg:"Null Scan"; flags:0;)
```

Sample output:

```
[**] Null Scan [**]
04/25-05:49:51.914748 192.168.143.15:54746 -> 192.168.143.16:21
TCP TTL:51 TOS:0x0 ID:23446
******** Seq: 0x1CED3E2E   Ack: 0x0   Win: 0x1000
TCP Options => WS: 10 NOP MSS: 265 TS: 1061109567 0 EOL EOL
```

In the previous sample output, you see a string of eight asterisks (********). Snort changes an asterisk to its respective flag bit letter association (12UAPRSF) if the flag is set in the packet that triggered the alert. Because this is a null scan, no flag bits are set; hence, you see all asterisks.

CWR	ECE	URG	ACK	PSH	RST	SYN	FIN
1	2	U	A	P	R	S	F

Figure 14.1   Snort's view of the TCP flag byte.

Content Option

The content option is one of the most vital and potentially misused options. It provides a means of supplying payload content to search for in the packet. There are many ways to supply the content value and multiple different content values can be sought. This option is used liberally throughout the rules that are supplied in the Snort download, but the content option should also be used wisely. Seeking content in payload is considered to be computationally expensive—in other words, this can slow Snort down considerably if it is not done intelligently. Although the developers of Snort have maximized the efficiency of the algorithm applied to do content searches, it is a slow operation when compared with a more exact task such as a match of a header field value. This is because the header field value is, at most, four bytes long, yet payloads are often much longer, thus taking more time to search.

If at all possible, the content option should be qualified with other options as flags or those that will be discussed shortly, such as an offset into the payload where the content search begins, and depth into the payload where the content search ends. The content option is tested last even if it is listed first in the rule options. This is done to optimize the search by qualifying it with other options.

Content strings can be represented as text or a hexadecimal translation of binary data or a combination of text and hexadecimal. Text strings are enclosed in quotes ("") and matches are case sensitive unless the nocase option is used. Hexadecimal code is delimited with the pipe (|) characters. Multiple content options and values can be specified in a rule and all values associated with the multiple content options must be found in the packet. The content values associated with the multiple content options can appear in any order in the payload; in other words, they do not have to match the order in which they are listed in the rule. There is another available content option that will not be covered known as the content-list. This allows multiple content strings to be specified and if any of them match, the rule triggers. The Snort Users Manual found on www.snort.org discusses this option and gives an example.

Format:

```
content: <"value">;
content: <"value">; content: <"value">;
```

Sample rule:

```
alert udp $EXTERNAL_NET any -> $HOME_NET 53 \
(msg: "EXPLOIT BIND tsig Overflow Attempt"; \
content: "|00 FA 00 FF|"; content: "/bin/sh";);
```

Sample output:

```
02/22-15:33:19.472301 ATTACKER:1024 -> VICTIM:53
UDP TTL:64 TOS:0x0 ID:6755 IpLen:20 DgmLen:538
Len: 518

<lines omitted to condense output>

00 3F 90 E8 72 FF FF FF 2F 62 69 6E 2F 73 68 00  .?..r.../bin/sh.
0E 0F 10 11 12 13 14 15 16 17 18 19 1A 1B 1C 1D  ................
1E 1F 20 21 22 23 24 25 26 27 28 29 2A 2B 2C 2D  .. !"#$%&'()*+,-
2E 2F 30 31 32 33 34 35 36 37 38 39 3A 3B 3C EB  ./0123456789:;<.
07 C0 00 00 00 00 00 3F 00 01 02 03 04 05 06 07  .......?........
08 09 0A 0B 0C 0D 0E 0F 10 11 12 13 14 15 16 17  ................
18 19 1A 1B 1C 1D 1E 1F 20 21 22 23 24 25 26 27  ........ !"#$%&'
28 29 2A 2B 2C 2D 2E 2F 30 31 32 33 34 35 36 37  ()*+,-./01234567
38 39 3A 3B 3C EB 07 C0 00 00 00 00 00 3F 00 01  89:;<........?..
02 03 04 05 06 07 08 09 0A 0B 0C 0D 0E 0F 10 11  ................
D8 FA FF BF D8 F7 FF BF D0 7C 0D 08 04 F7 10 40  .........|.....@
22 23 24 25 26 27 28 29 2A 2B 2C 2D 2E 2F 30 31  "#$%&'()*+,-./01
32 33 34 35 36 37 38 39 3A 3B 3C EB 07 C0 00 00  23456789:;<.....
00 00 00 3F 00 01 02 03 04 05 06 07 08 09 0A 0B  ...?............
0C 0D 0E 0F 10 11 12 13 14 15 16 17 18 19 1A 1B  ................
1C 1D 1E 1F 20 21 22 23 24 25 26 27 28 29 2A 2B  .... !"#$%&'()*+
2C 2D 2E 2F 30 31 32 33 34 35 36 37 38 39 3A 3B  ,-./0123456789:;
3C EB 07 C0 00 00 00 00 00 00 00 FA 00 FF        <.............
```

This output provides the hex characters in the payload on the left side of the output, followed by the ASCII interpretation of those characters on the right side. The rule that was created looks for UDP traffic from outside the trusted network to destination port 53 on a host on the trusted network. Specifically, it looks for the existence of two strings—the first expressed in hexadecimal 00 FA 00 FF, and the second, the text /bin/sh. Both strings must appear in the payload in any order. This rule will be refined more after some other options are discussed.

Some rule options are used only as modifiers to a content option—in other words, they are meaningless and will generate an error message unless the content option is used. These options are: offset, depth, nocase, and regex. They follow the content option that they qualify and if multiple content options are given, the offset, depth, nocase, and regex options modify only the content option that they immediately follow.

To Push or Not to Push

If you examine the TCP rules supplied with Snort, you will discover that many of those with a content option include a flag option of A+. This means for the rule to trigger, the acknowledgement flag must be set and other flags can be set as well. This might seem odd because logically, you might be thinking, "Why isn't the flag setting P+?" After all, shouldn't Snort examine content when payload bytes are pushed in the packet?

That is absolutely true; it makes the processing more efficient by qualifying the rule to look at content when actual payload data is transmitted. According to the noted author, Richard Stevens, in *TCP/IP Illustrated, Volume 1*, many BSD derived stacks set the push flag any time data is transmitted; but other operating system stacks set the push flag when data is sent only if the sender empties its write buffer. This means that if the receiver advertises a small TCP window size and the sender doesn't empty its write buffer when transmitting data, only the acknowledgement flag is set. That is why the A+ flag setting is used, because it will match the condition regardless if the push flag is set or not. Although many packets with only the acknowledgement flag set do not have payload, they will be considered for examination.

Alternatively, an option of dsize > 0 could be used to make sure that there was payload in the packet before examining it. This would catch unusual traffic such as data on the SYN, which the A+ would not.

As an example of payload data sent in a packet with only the acknowledgement flag set, look at two TCPdump records from LaBrea version 2, as discussed in Chapter 9, "Examining Embedded Protocol Header Fields," that slowed the attacker by advertising an unusually small TCP window size and then effectively arrested data transfer by decreasing the TCP window size to 0. The first record shows the LaBrea host 10.10.10.155 pretending to be a web server and advertising an usually small TCP window size of 5. Host attacker.net sends 5 bytes of payload, yet you see there is no push flag set along with the acknowledgement flag because this amount of data was too small to empty attacker.net's TCP write buffer:

```
10.10.10.155.www > attacker.net.2045: S 998514038:998514038(0) ack 882335287
win 5
attacker.net.2045 > 10.10.10.155.www: . 1:6(5) ack 1 win 8576 (DF)
```

Offset Option

As mentioned, the content search is computationally expensive, but it can be made more efficient by starting the search at an offset into the payload if the location of the content is known to begin somewhere other than the first byte in the payload. By default, the content search starts at the first byte, which is considered to be offset 0.

Format:

```
offset: <number>;
```

Sample rule:

```
alert tcp any any -> 192.168.5.0/24 21    \
(msg: "Attempted anonymous ftp access";   \
content: "anonymous"; offset: 5;)
```

Sample output:

```
[**] Attempted anonymous ftp access [**]
04/24-12:11:08.724441 192.168.143.15:3484 -> 192.168.5.16:21
TCP TTL:64 TOS:0x10 ID:30124  DF
***AP*** Seq: 0x93EE0AB7   Ack: 0xB8352E61   Win: 0x7D78
TCP Options => NOP NOP TS: 112024246 27551686
55 53 45 52 20 61 6E 6F 6E 79 6D 6F 75 73 0D 0A  USER anonymous..
```

The text "anonymous" is found at the 6ᵗʰ byte in the payload, but because we begin the offset count at 0, it is found in offset byte 5.

Depth Option

The depth option is another useful option to help limit the amount of processing Snort must do on content searches. The depth specifies the number of bytes to search from the offset. If no offset is given, the offset is assumed to be 0. This option can drastically improve Snort's performance if packets have large payloads and the content being sought appears in well-defined areas of the payload.

Format:

```
depth: <number>
```

Sample rule:

```
alert udp !$HOME_NET any -> $HOME_NET 5632 \
(msg: "PCAnywhere Startup"; content: "ST"; depth: 2;)
```

Sample output:

```
[**] PCAnywhere Startup [**]
04/24-12:11:08.724441 192.168.143.15:3484 -> 192.168.143.16:5632
UDP TTL:64 TOS:0x10 ID:30124  DF
73 74 61 72 74 75 70   STARTUP
```

This rule is triggered if the characters "ST" are discovered two bytes from the default offset of byte 0.

Nocase Option

The nocase option makes the content search in the payload case insensitive. This means that Snort will match the content string being searched no matter what case is used. This is one of the few options that does not have an option value partnered with it.

Format:

```
nocase;
```

Sample rule:

```
alert tcp  any any -> any 21  \
(msg: "FTP warez snooping"; content: "warez"; nocase;)
```

Sample output:

```
[**] FTP warez snooping[**]
04/25-05:28:28.146374 192.168.143.15:3487 -> 192.168.143.16:21
TCP TTL:64 TOS:0x10 ID:30637  DF
***AP*** Seq: 0xE1977C8D    Ack: 0x452F7F9    Win: 0x7D78
TCP Options => NOP NOP TS: 118248207 33775174
43 57 44 20 57 61 52 65 5A 0D 0A              CWD WaReZ..
```

Regex Option

The regex option modifier of content allows wildcard characters to appear in the content string. Two wildcard characters are available: the ? specifies that a single character can be substituted in the position where the ? is found. The second wildcard character * indicates that any number of characters can be substituted where the * is found.

One excellent use of the regex option is looking for signs of buffer overflow characters. If a buffer overflow is successful on a UNIX host, the attacker might very well try to gain access to a shell such as the Bourne shell using /bin/sh. Yet, there are many other shells that can be used such as the C shell (csh), the Korn shell (ksh), and Bourne again shell (bash), to name a few. Therefore, specifying a proper string and wildcard character will find all of the various shells. Prior to the addition of the regex option, the only way to test for all different shells was to use different rules. Be warned that the regex option will not be fully functional until release 2.0 of Snort.

Format:

```
regex;
```

Sample rule:

```
log tcp any any -> 192.168.5.0/24 515/
(msg: "Attempted shell on lpd"; content: "/bin/*sh"; regex;)
```

Sample output:

```
[**] Attempted shell on lpd [**]
03/23-07:41:11.282960 1.1.0.1:1892 -> 192.168.5.55:515
TCP TTL:64 TOS:0x0 ID:63821 IpLen:20 DgmLen:60
***AP*** Seq: 0x32A77D55  Ack: 0x0  Win: 0x200  TcpLen: 20
2F 62 69 6E 2F 63 73 68 0A 00 00 00 00 00 00 00  /bin/csh........
00 00 00 00
```

The previous rule looks for shell access to destination port 515 known as the line printer daemon. The regex qualifier to the content value of /bin/*sh is used to find all the different types of shell access.

Session Option

The session option is used to capture user data from TCP sessions. It can provide a good forensics tool to see what a particular user is doing, especially if you suspect some kind of malicious behavior is taking place.

There are two available argument keywords for the session rule option: printable or all. The printable keyword only prints out data that the user would normally see or be able to type. The all keyword substitutes non-printable characters with their hexadecimal equivalents.

You should be aware that the use of the session option can degrade the performance of Snort, so it is best used retrospectively; capture the data in binary format (TCPdump files) and then run it through Snort. Also, note that typically when you use this option, you should use the direction operator that specifies both directions as shown in the example. Finally, it is best to use the –d command-line option to dump at the application level; otherwise, it doesn't make much sense to specify the session option.

By default, the session is recorded in the default log directory. The subdirectory beneath that is the IP number of the host initiating the activity. A file named SESSION:sourceport-destport, where sourceport and destport are the actual source, destination ports for the connection will be located in that directory.

Format:

```
session: [printable|all]
```

Sample rule:

```
log tcp any any <> 192.168.5.0/24 21 (session: printable;)
```

Sample output:

Assuming the source host for the session is 1.2.3.4 on port 1025, the following output will be in the log directory in subdirectory 1.2.3.4 file SESSION: 1025-21:

```
220 linux2 FTP server (Version wu-2.5.0(1) Tue Sep 21 16:48:12 EDT 1999)
ready.
USER jsmith
331 Password required for jsmith.
PASS snorty-the-p1g
230 User jsmith logged in.
SYST
215 UNIX Type: L8
QUIT
221-You have transferred 0 bytes in 0 files.
221-Total traffic for this session was 239 bytes in 0 transfers.
221-Thank you for using the FTP service on linux2.
221 Goodbye
```

Resp Option

The resp option allows an automated active response when malicious activity is detected. An active response attempts to disable a connection. There are many different combinations of active responses and multiple resp options can be given in a single rule.

TCP connections can be aborted by sending a reset to the sending host socket connection, the receiving host socket connection, or both hosts' socket connections. If the offending packet is UDP, different ICMP messages can be sent in an attempt to interrupt the UDP data flow. An ICMP network, host, or port unreachable message—or a combination of all three of these ICMP messages—can be sent.

The response option doesn't come automatically enabled with the source distribution. To enable it, you must explicitly configure Snort via the following command:

```
./configure --enable-flexresp
```

This includes the necessary code for compilation. It is also possible that your configuration of UNIX doesn't have a libnet.h include file required for this to compile. It is available from www.packetfactory.net.

No discussion of active response is complete unless the requisite caveats are offered. First, think smoking-brain hard before you decide to indiscriminately use active response. It should be used for situations where you perceive that unauthorized harmful access could occur such as a buffer overflow. Keep in mind that attackers can spoof source IP addresses, and you might end up using active response against an IP address or addresses that never sent you traffic to begin with. Think about the consequences of active response if someone spoofs a legitimate partner's IP addresses; it is possible for you to end up attacking a vital resource. Also, a false positive could cause a totally benign connection to be halted. This can cause a denial of service to legitimate users.

Another concern is timing issues. Many requests and responses are almost instantaneous, especially one such as a UDP DNS query–response pair. Attempting to actively respond to a perceived malicious DNS query might prove to be futile because by the time Snort reacts, the response has probably already been sent.

Format:

```
resp <resp_option[, resp_option…]>;
```

Available choices for the response are:

rst_snd	Send TCP RESET packets to sending socket
rst_rcv	Send TCP RESET packets to receiving socket
rst_all	Send TCP RESET packets to both sending and receiving sockets
icmp_net	Send an ICMP_NET_UNREACH to sender
icmp_host	Send an ICMP_HOST_UNREACH to sender
icmp_port	Send an ICMP_PORT_UNREACH to sender
icmp_all	Send all of the above ICMP_UNREACH packets to sender

Sample rule:

```
alert tcp any any -> $HOME_NET 21          \
(msg: "FTP password file retrieval";       \
flags: A+; resp: rst_all; content: "passwd";)
```

Sample session:

```
[root@verbo hping2-beta53]# ftp sparky
Connected to sparky.
220 sparky FTP server (SunOS 5.7) ready.
Name (sparky:root): jsmith
331 Password required for jsmith.
Password:
230 User jsmith logged in.
Remote system type is UNIX.
Using binary mode to transfer files.
ftp> cd /etc
250 CWD command successful.
ftp> get passwd
local: passwd remote: passwd
200 PORT command successful.
421 Service not available, remote server has closed connection
```

The previous rule calls for an active response to a connection to an ftp server that references the password file passwd. Snort resets both ends of the connection to interrupt this attempt because the resp option of rst_all was selected.

Look at the last line of the ftp session. You see that right after the attacker entered the command **get passwd**, the connection was actually closed. It is possible that the password file had already been transferred before the reset occurred.

Tag Option

The use of the tag option enables Snort to dynamically capture additional packets after a rule triggers. Without the tag option, only the packet that caused the rule to be triggered is recorded. This is an excellent way to see what transpires after the rule is triggered to get a better idea of the intent of the activity. This can also be useful for validating that some activity that triggered a rule is simply a false positive.
Format:

```
tag: <type>, <count>, <metric>, [direction]
```

- **type.** What traffic to record.
  - session. Record the packets from both sides of the connection
  - host. Record the packets from the host that caused the rule to trigger (must use direction modifier)
- **count**. Number of units specified by metric.
- **metric**. Number of packets/seconds to record.
  - packets. Record host/session for <count> packets.
  - seconds. Record host/session for <count> seconds.
- **direction**. Used only with "host" type to indicate host to tag.
  - src. Tag all traffic of source IP in triggered rule.
  - dst. Tag all traffic of destination IP in triggered rule.

Sample rule:

```
alert tcp any any -> any 21 (msg: "FTP passwd access"; flags: A+; \
content: "passwd"; tag: session, 10, packets;)
```

Sample output:

The alert file shows the abbreviated data from the miscreant connection to destination port 21:

```
[**] FTP passwd access [**]
03/21-20:31:05.610035 10.10.10.101:1454 -> 10.10.10.100:21
TCP TTL:128 TOS:0x0 ID:50697 IpLen:20 DgmLen:58 DF
***AP*** Seq: 0x17806739  Ack: 0x121C07E5  Win: 0x1FD3  TcpLen: 20
```

A directory named 10.10.10.101 was created with a file named TCP:1454-21 to record the session exchange of the attempted password file access and 10 subsequent records. Note that the command line used the –d option to capture and dump the data payload. This is an excerpt of the output:

```
03/21-20:31:05.610035 10.10.10.101:1454 -> 10.10.10.100:21
TCP TTL:128 TOS:0x0 ID:50697 IpLen:20 DgmLen:58 DF
***AP*** Seq: 0x17806739  Ack: 0x121C07E5  Win: 0x1FD3  TcpLen: 20
52 45 54 52 20 2F 65 74 63 2F 70 61 73 73 77 64    RETR /etc/passwd
0D 0A                                              ..


=+=+=+=+=+=+=+=+=+=+=+=+=+=+=+=+=+=+=+=+=+=+=+=+=+=+=+=+=+=+=+=+=


03/21-20:31:05.610731 10.10.10.100:21 -> 10.10.10.101:1454
TCP TTL:64 TOS:0x10 ID:1752 IpLen:20 DgmLen:109 DF
***AP*** Seq: 0x121C07E5  Ack: 0x1780674B  Win: 0x7D78  TcpLen: 20
31 35 30 20 4F 70 65 6E 69 6E 67 20 41 53 43 49    150 Opening ASCI
49 20 6D 6F 64 65 20 64 61 74 61 20 63 6F 6E 6E    I mode data conn
65 63 74 69 6F 6E 20 66 6F 72 20 2F 65 74 63 2F    ection for /etc/
70 61 73 73 77 64 20 28 36 37 39 20 62 79 74 65    passwd (679 byte
73 29 2E 0D 0A                                     s)...


=+=+=+=+=+=+=+=+=+=+=+=+=+=+=+=+=+=+=+=+=+=+=+=+=+=+=+=+=+=+=+=+=


<omitted boring records>


=+=+=+=+=+=+=+=+=+=+=+=+=+=+=+=+=+=+=+=+=+=+=+=+=+=+=+=+=+=+=+=+=


03/21-20:31:08.924038 10.10.10.101:1454 -> 10.10.10.100:21
TCP TTL:128 TOS:0x0 ID:52489 IpLen:20 DgmLen:58 DF
***AP*** Seq: 0x17806764  Ack: 0x121C0860  Win: 0x1F58  TcpLen: 20
52 45 54 52 20 2F 65 74 63 2F 73 68 61 64 6F 77    RETR /etc/shadow
0D 0A                                              ..
```

Putting It All Together

Now that you've endured the tedium to understand Snort rules, you might be wondering how you would write a rule for a new exploit that was released. Chances are that the user/developer population of Snort will have a new rule out for a current exploit very quickly. But, assume you have some code that professes to be an attack for which no Snort rule exists.

The first thing to do is to execute the exploit code in an isolated test network such as your home or a segregated lab environment at work. If the code works as advertised, record the packet exchange between the attacking and victim hosts. Then, look for unique and repeatable values in the packet that can be used to write a signature or rule. You might have to read some RFCs to become acquainted with the protocol used in the exploit to understand which are repeatable and which are modifiable values.

Suppose you downloaded some code that exploited a buffer overflow condition for DNS TSIG (transaction signature) records. This is an actual attack that was effective against unpatched versions of BIND from 4.x up to, but not including, 8.2.3. A TSIG record in DNS is another resource record type like an address or pointer record. It is used by resolvers and for dynamic updates to ensure the integrity of an exchanged DNS record using a cryptographic one-way hash and shared secret key.

Because the exploit attempts to get access to a shell at the privilege level that BIND (the "named" daemon) runs at, the captured traffic from the exploit should be examined for this signature. Here is the packet that contains the buffer overflow and subsequent attempt to get shell access:

```
02/22-15:33:19.472301 ATTACKER:1024 -> VICTIM:53

UDP TTL:64 TOS:0x0 ID:6755 IpLen:20 DgmLen:538
Len: 518

DE AD 01 80 00 07 00 00 00 00 00 01 3F 00 01 02  ............?...
03 04 05 06 07 08 09 0A 0B 0C 0D 0E 0F 10 11 12  ...............
13 14 15 16 17 18 19 1A 1B 1C 1D 1E 1F 20 21 22  ............. !"
23 24 25 26 27 28 29 2A 2B 2C 2D 2E 2F 30 31 32  #$%&'()*+,-./012
33 34 35 36 37 38 39 3A 3B 3C EB 0A 02 00 00 C0  3456789:;<......
00 00 00 00 00 3F 00 01 EB 44 5E 29 C0 89 46 10  .....?...D^)..F.
40 89 C3 89 46 0C 40 89 46 08 8D 4E 08 B0 66 CD  @...F.@.F..N..f.
80 43 C6 46 10 10 66 89 5E 14 88 46 08 29 C0 89  .C.F..f.^..F.)..
C2 89 46 18 B0 90 66 89 46 16 8D 4E 14 89 4E 0C  ..F...f.F..N..N.
8D 4E 08 EB 07 C0 00 00 00 00 00 3F EB 02 EB 43  .N.........?...C
B0 66 CD 80 89 5E 0C 43 43 B0 66 CD 80 89 56 0C  .f...^.CC.f...V.
89 56 10 B0 66 43 CD 80 86 C3 B0 3F 29 C9 CD 80  .V..fC.....?)...
B0 3F 41 CD 80 B0 3F 41 CD 80 88 56 07 89 76 0C  .?A...?A...V..v.
87 F3 8D 4B 0C B0 0B CD 80 EB 07 C0 00 00 00 00  ...K...........
00 3F 90 E8 72 FF FF FF 2F 62 69 6E 2F 73 68 00  .?..r.../bin/sh.
0E 0F 10 11 12 13 14 15 16 17 18 19 1A 1B 1C 1D  ...............
1E 1F 20 21 22 23 24 25 26 27 28 29 2A 2B 2C 2D  .. !"#$%&'()*+,-
2E 2F 30 31 32 33 34 35 36 37 38 39 3A 3B 3C EB  ./0123456789:;<.
07 C0 00 00 00 00 00 3F 00 01 02 03 04 05 06 07  .......?........
08 09 0A 0B 0C 0D 0E 0F 10 11 12 13 14 15 16 17  ...............
18 19 1A 1B 1C 1D 1E 1F 20 21 22 23 24 25 26 27  ........ !"#$%&'
28 29 2A 2B 2C 2D 2E 2F 30 31 32 33 34 35 36 37  ()*+,-./01234567
38 39 3A 3B 3C EB 07 C0 00 00 00 00 00 3F 00 01  89:;<........?..
02 03 04 05 06 07 08 09 0A 0B 0C 0D 0E 0F 10 11  ...............
D8 FA FF BF D8 F7 FF BF D0 7C 0D 08 04 F7 10 40  .........|.....@
22 23 24 25 26 27 28 29 2A 2B 2C 2D 2E 2F 30 31  "#$%&'()*+,-./01
32 33 34 35 36 37 38 39 3A 3B 3C EB 07 C0 00 00  23456789:;<.....
00 00 00 3F 00 01 02 03 04 05 06 07 08 09 0A 0B  ...?............
0C 0D 0E 0F 10 11 12 13 14 15 16 17 18 19 1A 1B  ...............
1C 1D 1E 1F 20 21 22 23 24 25 26 27 28 29 2A 2B  .... !"#$%&'()*+
2C 2D 2E 2F 30 31 32 33 34 35 36 37 38 39 3A 3B  ,-./0123456789:;
3C EB 07 C0 00 00 00 00 00 00 00 FA 00 FF        <.............
```

One obvious signature is the /bin/sh, which attempts to give shell access after a successful buffer overflow. Another signature of this output is that there must be some identification that a DNS TSIG record has been used.

The DNS type is a 2-byte field and a TSIG record will be assigned a value of 250 (0x00FA). There must also be a 2-byte DNS class associated with each different resource record type and the value assigned to a TSIG record is 255 (0x00FF)—to mean any class. Therefore, there must be an occurrence of 0x00FA00FF in the DNS payload for this to be a TSIG record. You would not find the occurrence of the string "/bin/sh" in a normal TSIG query, so looking for both of these values is likely to find malicious records without alerting on false positives. Although other values in this particular packet could be used for the rule, it is possible to alter the source code so that the exploit would still work, yet the DNS header or following TSIG records could change. Here is a rule that can detect the exploit:

```
alert udp $EXTERNAL_NET any -> $HOME_NET 53   \
(msg: "EXPLOIT BIND tsig Overflow Attempt";   \
content: "|00 FA 00 FF|"; offset: 12;          \
content: "/bin/*sh"; regex; offset: 12;)
```

The observed traffic uses UDP, and you want to look for attackers coming into your network from an outside host on any port to destination port 53. Two separate content options are used to find the multiple occurrences of strings that are in the signature. The option of regex is used in case a shell other than the Bourne shell is used. The regex option is a work in progress and doesn't always work as advertised in Snort version 1.8.3. In the previous example, it failed to work when included with the wildcard search of "/bin/*sh", but it will be fixed and should work in the upcoming version 2.x releases.

Also, the content strings are qualified using an offset of 12 indicating that the search is to begin at the 12th byte offset from the beginning of the DNS message. This is done for efficiency and accuracy because the DNS header takes up the first 12 bytes and the search to be performed is on the DNS payload, not the DNS header.

The TSIG Exploit

If you would like more information about TSIG, look at RFC 2845 titled, "Secret Key Transaction Authentication for DNS (TSIG)." More information about the exploit can be found at the Carnegie Mellon CERT site, www.cert.org, advisory CA-2001-02. There is a wonderful write-up of the exploit done by Paul Asadoorian, which can be found at www.sans.org/newlook/resources/IDFAQ/TSIG.htm. Many thanks to Paul for his discussion of the Snort rule and the attack output.

Summary

Snort rule options provide a wide range of attributes and ways to specify values to examine in a packet. The use of the options is quite intuitive and requires only some familiarization of the various options via experimentation or reading the Snort documentation. With virtually each new release of Snort, more options have been added, making Snort rules feature-rich and comparable or better than many of the commercial NIDS' signature writing capabilities.

To create a Snort rule for some exploit, run the exploit in an isolated environment and record the traffic either using Snort or TCPdump in a mode where the entire packet is captured for examination. Use any available Snort rule header fields or options to precisely identify the unique values and attributes of the exploit packets. Be aware that some aspects of the exploit source code can be changed to alter the packet content; so, attempt to extract the values or fields that are not likely to change when creating your rule. Selecting and qualifying appropriate fields and values to be used is not an easy thing to do because good signature writing is truly a practiced art that requires knowledge about the signature language, the exploit, and the protocol involved in the exploit.

IV

Intrusion Infrastructure

15

Mitnick Attack

IN THE FINAL SECTION OF THE BOOK, we will look at automated and manual responses, and architectural and organizational issues. We will use this chapter on the Mitnick attack to serve as a transition between this higher-level material and the more fundamental material that we have already covered. The Mitnick attack is one of the most famous intrusion cases to ever occur. If you are in the intrusion business, you should be aware of the techniques used by Mitnick to attack Tsutomu Shimomura's systems. In this chapter, we will also introduce many important issues, including reconnaissance and scanning for trust relationships. We will also consider perimeter and host defenses that are related to intrusion detection for our future discussions.

A primary source for this information is drawn from Shimomura's post on the Mitnick attack. If you want more information on the subject, or to get expanded versions of the quotations you see here, refer to `tsutomu@ariel.sdsc.edu` (Tsutomu Shimomura), comp.security.misc (date: 25 Jan 1995).

Exploiting TCP

The techniques Mr. Mitnick used were technical in nature and exploited weaknesses in TCP that were well known in academic circles, but not considered by system developers. The attack used two techniques: SYN flooding and TCP hijacking. Although SYN floods today can disable systems, the operating systems at the time of the attack, 1994, were far more susceptible to attack. The SYN flood kept one system from being able to transmit. Although it was in a mute state, the attacker assumed its apparent identity and hijacked the TCP connection. Mitnick detected a trust relationship between two computers and exploited that relationship. Surprisingly, few things have changed since then; for instance, computer systems are still set up to be overly trusting, often as a convenience to the system administrators or users.

IP Weaknesses

A number of reconnaissance, exploit, and denial-of-service attacks take advantage of flaws in the architecture or implementation of the Internet Protocol stacks. In Chapter 4, "ICMP," we discussed the use of broadcast ICMP in both network mapping and denial of service with Smurf. In Chapter 3, "Fragmentation," we discussed penetration of perimeters with fragments as well as malicious fragmentation with gaps and illegal offsets.

Some of these are older techniques, but new attacks based on programming flaws in IP implementations are being developed all the time. The following TCPdump trace is from the SNMP test tool PROTOS, released in February 2002:

```
18:49:54.519006 10.0.0.1.59108 > 10.0.0.2.161: GetRequest(33)
.1.3.6.1.2.1.1.5.0[len3<asnlen4294967295] (DF)
0x0000   4500 004c 0000 4000 4011 269f 0a00 0001
0x0010   0a00 0002 e6e4 00a1 0038 0efc 302e 0201
0x0020   0004 0670 7562 6c69 63a0 2102 0206 9202
0x0030   0100 0201 0030 1530 1306 082b 0601 0201
0x0040   0105 0044 84ff ffff ff02 0100
```

When we first ran this test against a Red Hat Linux 7.0 box, two interesting things happened: The SNMP server application on the Linux box crashed, and the Ethereal network analyzer also crashed. Why did they crash? If you notice the ASN.1 length in the square brackets at the top of the trace, you will notice it is four billion some odd bytes. That is a lot of free memory to try to allocate, and attempting to do so crashed the SNMP and Ethereal applications. As we work our way into the Mitnick attack, we will see that available memory was a major issue in that attack.

One simple way to exhaust memory that is used every day is intentionally not completing the three-way handshake. The weakness of TCP that Mitnick exploited comes from a design flaw in the early implementations of TCP stacks; however, this approach still does harm to some IP stacks.

TCP's Roots

When TCP was being developed, you couldn't purchase much memory for machines. If you could get 4 megabytes on a server, you were doing quite well. Therefore, the implementers of IP protocol stacks were very conservative.

The Internet is an outgrowth of a project from the 1970's by the US Department of Defense *Advanced Research Projects Agency* (ARPA). The ARPANET, as it was then called, was designed to be a non-reliable network service for computer communications over wide areas. In 1973 and 1974, a standard networking protocol, a communications protocol for exchanging data between computers on a network, emerged from the various research and educational efforts involved in this project. This became known as TCP/IP or the IP suite of protocols. The TCP/IP protocols enabled ARPANET computers to communicate irrespective of their computer operating system or their computer hardware.

For further information and the source of this quotation, see www.ie.cuhk.edu.hk/~shlam/cstdi/history.html.

Let's take a closer look at this memory exhaustion problem. To an application program such as ftp or telnet, sockets are the lowest layer, a programming interface to networking hardware. IP is another layer and is above sockets. TCP sits on top of IP. Because TCP is connection oriented, it has to keep state information, including window and sequence number information. A typical Internet protocol stack contains information relating to sockets. TCP is connection oriented (or stateful), so the server must keep track of all condition states and sequence numbers.

The C code below came from my Unix workstation. It can be thought of as a database record with a number of fields. The key point is that each of these fields consumes memory.

```
    struct ip {
#if defined(bsd)
                u_char  ip_hl:4,            /* header length */
                ip_v:4;                        /* version */
#endif
#if defined(powerpc)
                u_char  ip_v:4,            /* version */
                ip_hl:4;                       /* header length */
#endif
        u_char  ip_tos;            /* type of service */
        short   ip_len;                /* total length */
```

```
        u_short ip_id;                           /* identification */
        short   ip_off;                          /* fragment offset field */
#define IP_DF 0x3000                     /* dont fragment flag */
#define IP_MF 0x4000                     /* more fragments flag */
        u_char  ip_ttl;                     /* time to live */
        u_char  ip_p;                       /* protocol */
        u_short ip_sum;                 /* checksum */
        struct  in_addr ip_src, ip_dst;  /* source and dest address */
};
```

The preceding header file fragment is taken from an IP header file on a
SunOS 4.1.3 system. A struct—in this case, `struct ip`—can be thought of as a
database record and the items inside as fields for that record. Every time a new
connection is processed, these structs have to be created for socket, ip, and
other protocol information. That takes memory, and lots of it. After a server
replies to a SYN, it has committed memory and must keep it committed until
the timer, usually set at about sixty seconds, allows the memory to be released
if the connection is never established. Because memory is finite, the designers
of stacks have set limits. The SYN flood attack exploits the queue size limit of
the number of connections that can be simultaneously waiting to be established for a particular service. Though some modern operating systems are
more resistant to these SYN flood attacks today, many are not. An unpatched
Solaris 2.5 with a GB of memory will still be DoSed after 32 SYNs.

SYN Flooding

In a modern SYN flood, the goal is simply to throw hundreds or thousands of
packets per second at a server to exhaust either system resources, as we have
discussed, or even network resources when the rate is high enough.

    When an attacker sets up a SYN flood, he has no intention to complete the
three-way handshake and establish the connection. Rather, the goal is to
exceed the limits set for the number of connections waiting to be established
for a given service. This caused IP stacks in the 1994 era to be unable to establish any additional connections for that service until the number of waiting
connections dropped below the threshold. Until the threshold limit is met,
each SYN packet generates a SYN/ACK that stays in the queue (which
was generally between 5 and 10 total connections), waiting to be established.
Today, queues can be much larger; ranges between 100 and 1000 are
reasonable.

SYN Floods Five Years Later

SYN flooding was in the news in February 2000 with the famous DDoS attacks that were used against Yahoo! and other high-profile Internet sites. In the intervening years since the Mitnick attack, there have been some improvements in system networking stacks and perimeter defenses. The answer of the attackers has been simple: raise the number of SYNs by several orders of magnitude. The SYN flood described here is fairly elegant; the ones common to the Internet today are pure brute force.

Each connection has a timer, a limit to how long the system waits for connection establishment. The hourglass in Figure 15.1 represents the timer, which tends to be set for about a minute. After the time limit has been exceeded, the memory that holds the state for that connection is released and the service queue count is decremented by one. After the limit has been reached, the service queue can be kept full, preventing the system from establishing new connections on that port with about 10 new SYN packets per minute.

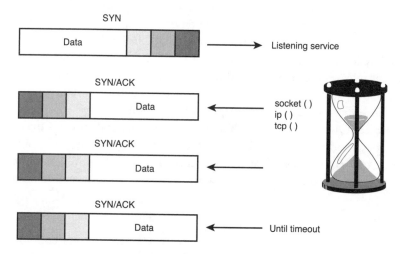

Figure 15.1 Getting down to it.

Covering His Tracks

Because the only purpose of the technique is to perform a denial-of-service attack, it doesn't make sense to use the attacker's actual Internet address. The attacker is not establishing a connection; he is flooding a queue, so there is no point in having the SYN/ACKs return to the attacker. The attacker doesn't want to make it easy for folks to track the connection back to him. Therefore, the source address of the packet is generally spoofed. The following IP header is from actual attack code for a SYN flood. At the very bottom, notice the dadd and sadd for destination and source address, respectively:

```
/* Fill in all the IP header information */
        packet.ip.version=4;            /* 4-bit Version */
        packet.ip.ihl=5;               /* 4-bit Header Length */
        packet.ip.tos=0;               /* 8-bit Type of service */
        packet.ip.tot_len=htons(40);   /* 16-bit Total length */
        packet.ip.id=getpid();         /* 16-bit ID field */
        packet.ip.frag_off=0;          /* 13-bit Fragment offset */
        packet.ip.ttl=255;             /* 8-bit Time To Live */
        packet.ip.protocol=IPPROTO_TCP; /* 8-bit Protocol */
        packet.ip.check=0;             /* 16-bit Header checksum (filled in
below) */
        packet.ip.saddr=sadd;          /* 32-bit Source Address */
        packet.ip.daddr=dadd;          /* 32-bit Destination Address */
```

As the following code fragment shows, this technique even uses an error-checking routine to make sure the address chosen is routable, but not active. When the attacker enters an address, the attack code pings the address (notice the slickping line in the following code fragment) to ensure it meets these requirements. If the address is active, it sends a RESET when it receives the SYN/ACK for the system under attack. When the target system receives the RESET, it releases the memory and decrements the service queue counter, rendering the attack ineffective. From an intrusion-detection standpoint, these bogus packets assembled for the purpose of attacking and probing can be called *crafted packets*. Quite often, the authors of software that craft packets make a small error at some point, or take a shortcut, and this gives the packet a unique signature. You can use these signatures in intrusion detection. When you detect evidence of a crafted packet, you know the sender is up to something. Take a look:

```
case 3:
                                     if(!optflags[1]){
                                        fprintf(stderr,"Um, enter a host
                                        first\n");
                                        usleep(MENUSLEEP);
                                        break;
                                     }
                                          /* Raw ICMP socket */

    if((sock2=socket(AF_INET,SOCK_RAW,IPPROTO_ICMP))<0){
                                        perror("\nHmmm.... socket
                                        problems\n");
                                        exit(1);
                                     }
                                     printf("[number of ICMP_ECHO's]-> ");
```

```
fgets(tmp,MENUBUF,stdin);
if(!(icmpAmt=atoi(tmp)))break;
if(slickPing(icmpAmt,sock2,unreach)){
        fprintf(stderr,"Host is reachable...
        Pick a new one\n");
        sleep(1);
```

Now you have a technique to use as a generic denial of service. You hit a target system with SYNs until it cannot speak (establish new connections). Systems vulnerable to this attack can be kept out of service until the attacker decides to go away and SYN no more. In the Mitnick attack, the goal was to silence one side of a TCP connection and masquerade as the silenced, trusted party.

What would attackers use today to accomplish the same thing? Any good current denial-of-service tool—for instance, an attack against Windows computers that has been pretty effective is jolt.c, based on malicious oversize ICMP messages.

Identifying Trust Relationships

So how did Mitnick identify which system to silence? How did he confirm a trust relationship existed? It turns out that many complex attacks are preceded by intelligence gathering techniques, or *recon probes*. Here are the recon probes detected by TCPdump, a network-monitoring tool developed by the Department of Energy's Lawrence Livermore Lab and reported in Tsutomu's post.

"The IP spoofing attack started at about 14:09:32 PST on 12/25/94. The first probes were from toad.com." (This information was derived from packet logs.)"

```
14:09:32 toad.com# finger -l @target
14:10:21 toad.com# finger -l @server
14:10:50 toad.com# finger -l root@server
14:11:07 toad.com# finger -l @x-terminal
14:11:38 toad.com# showmount -e x-terminal
14:11:49 toad.com# rpcinfo -p x-terminal
14:12:05 toad.com# finger -l root@x-terminal
```

Each of the commands shown—finger, showmount, and rpcinfo—can provide information about UNIX systems. If you work in a UNIX environment and haven't experimented with these commands in a long while, it might be worthwhile to substitute some of your machine names for target, server, and x-terminal to see what you can learn. Here is the information you can glean from the following commands:

- finger tells you who is logged on to the system, when they logged on, when they last logged on, where they are logging on from, how long they have been idle, whether they have mail, and when their birthday is (well, scratch the birthday). The analogous command for Microsoft Windows systems is **NBTSTAT**.

```
finger Example:
[root@toad /tmp]# finger @some.host.net
[some.host.net]
Login      Name            TTY        Idle    When      Where
chap  Bill Chapman x1568  pts/6      3:11 Tue 17:26  picard
chap  Bill Chapman x1568  console    8:39 Mon 14:44  :0
[root@toad /tmp]#
```

- showmount -e provides information about the file systems mounted with *Network File System* (NFS). Of particular interest to attackers are file systems that are mounted world readable or writable—that is, available to everyone.

```
showmount Example:
[root@toad /tmp]# showmount -e some.host.net
Export list for some.host.net:
/usr        export-hosts
/usr/local  export-hosts
/home       export-hosts
[root@toad /tmp]#
```

- rpcinfo provides information about the remote procedure call services available on a system. rpcinfo -p gives the ports where these services reside.

```
rpcinfo  Example
[root@toad /tmp]# rpcinfo -p some.host.net
  program vers proto    port
  100000    3   udp     111   rpcbind
  100000    2   udp     111   rpcbind
  100003    2   udp    2049   nfs
  100024    1   udp     774   status
  100024    1   tcp     776   status
  100021    1   tcp     782   nlockmgr
  100021    1   udp     784   nlockmgr
  100005    1   tcp    1024   mountd
  100005    1   udp    1025   mountd
  391004    1   tcp    1025
  391004    1   udp    1026
  100001    1   udp    1027   rstatd
  100001    2   udp    1027   rstatd
  100008    1   udp    1028   walld
```

```
100002   1   udp   1029   rusersd
100011   1   udp   1030   rquotad
100012   1   udp   1031   sprayd
100026   1   udp   1032   bootparam
```

These days, most sites block TCP port 79 (finger) at their firewall or filtering router, but it might be a good idea to try this from your home ISP account—get permission *first*! Again, hopefully your site blocks TCP/UDP port 111 (portmapper), but this is worth testing as well. In recent years, so-called secure portmappers have become available either from vendors or as an external package developed by Wietse Venema, available from the Coast archive at `ftp://coast.cs.purdue.edu/pub`.

Examining Network Traces

In the case of the Mitnick attack, however, none of these ports were blocked and toad.com acquired information that was used in the next phase of the attack. The following quotation is from Tsutomu's post:

> We now see 20 connection attempts from apollo.it.luc.edu to x-terminal.shell. The purpose of these attempts is to determine the behavior of x-terminal's TCP sequence number generator. Note that the initial sequence numbers increment by one for each connection, indicating that the SYN packets are not being generated by the system's TCP implementation. This results in RSTs conveniently being generated in response to each unexpected SYN-ACK, so the connection queue on x-terminal does not fill up.

As you examine the following TCPdump trace, note how it is in sets of three packets—a SYN from apollo to x-terminal, a SYN/ACK (step two of the three-way handshake), and a RESET from apollo to x-terminal to keep from SYN flooding x-terminal.

How to Read TCPdump Traces

```
Timestamp        Source host.Source Port   > Dst host.Dst Port: TCP FLAG(s)
14:18:25.906002 apollo.it.luc.edu.1000   > x-terminal.shell: S
SEQ NUM: ACK NUM        TCP Window Size
1382726990:1382726990(0) win 4096
```

The following traces begin "flooding" x-terminal. Note that the +++s have been added to emphasize the packet triplets:

```
+++
14:18:25.906002 apollo.it.luc.edu.1000 > x-terminal.shell: S
1382726990:1382726990(0) win 4096
```

```
14:18:26.094731 x-terminal.shell > apollo.it.luc.edu.1000: S
2021824000:2021824000(0) ack 1382726991 win 4096

14:18:26.172394 apollo.it.luc.edu.1000 > x-terminal.shell: R
1382726991:1382726991(0) win 0
+++


+++
14:18:26.507560 apollo.it.luc.edu.999 > x-terminal.shell: S
1382726991:1382726991(0) win 4096

14:18:26.694691 x-terminal.shell > apollo.it.luc.edu.999: S
2021952000:2021952000(0) ack 1382726992 win 4096

14:18:26.775037 apollo.it.luc.edu.999 > x-terminal.shell: R
1382726992:1382726992(0) win 0
+++
```

Notice the bolded value in the preceding trace. This is the sequence number if we take the second set of packets and focus on the sequence number in x-terminal's SYN/ACK; it is **2021952000**. The sequence number in the preceding set's SYN/ACK is **2021824000**. If you subtract 2021824000 from 2021952000, the remainder is 128,000. Does this represent any value? Yes, if it is repeatable. Check one more set of packets:

```
+++

14:18:27.014050 apollo.it.luc.edu.998 > x-terminal.shell: S
1382726992:1382726992(0) win 4096

14:18:27.174846 x-terminal.shell > apollo.it.luc.edu.998: S
2022080000:2022080000(0) ack 1382726993 win 4096

14:18:27.251840 apollo.it.luc.edu.998 > x-terminal.shell: R
1382726993:1382726993(0) win 0

14:18:27.544069 apollo.it.luc.edu.997 > x-terminal.shell: S
1382726993:1382726993(0) win 4096 "

14:18:27.714932 x-terminal.shell > apollo.it.luc.edu.997: S
2022208000:2022208000(0) ack 1382726994 win 4096

14:18:27.794456 apollo.it.luc.edu.997 > x-terminal.shell: R
1382726994:1382726994(0) win 0
```

Again, 2022208000 − 2022080000 = 128,000. So it is repeatable, or perhaps a better word is *predictable*. We know that anytime we send a SYN to x-terminal, the SYN/ACK will come back 128,000 or higher, as long as it is the next connection. With the ability to silence one side of the TCP connection and trust relationship and the ability to determine what the sequence number will be, we are almost ready to take over the trust relationship and the connection. Figure 15.2 shows the basic approach.

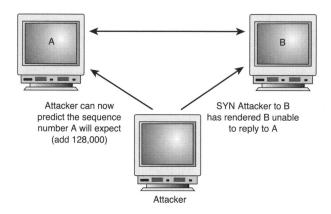

Attacker can now
predict the sequence
number A will expect
(add 128,000)

SYN Attacker to B
has rendered B unable
to reply to A

Attacker

Figure 15.2 Ready for the kill.

Setting Up the System Compromise?

How can this attack on a trust relationship be possible? Surely the computers would notice that the attacker has the wrong IP address. Well, the IP address is spoofed, so there would be no chance of seeing that. The time-to-live (TTL) might be a bit odd, but that is in the IP layer, and all the work is occurring at the TCP layer. The route to the system changes, so potentially it would be possible to detect something is wrong at some point in the route. However, no one is using IP options like record route, so this would never be detected. Instead, the primary focus is the sequence number. If you send a packet with the wrong sequence number, the other side sends a RESET and breaks off the connection. This is why it mattered that in the Mitnick attack, x-terminal had a predictable sequence number. So, now we can silence one party (server) and make the other party (x-terminal) believe we are that party (server). What happens next? Again, we return to Tsutomu's post:

> We now see a forged SYN (connection request), allegedly from server.login to x-terminal.shell. The assumption is that x-terminal probably trusts server, so x-terminal will do whatever server (or anything masquerading as server) asks. x-terminal then replies to server with a SYN-ACK, which must be ACK'd in order for the connection to be opened. As server is ignoring packets sent to server.login, the ACK must be forged as well.

Normally, the sequence number from the SYN/ACK is required to generate a valid ACK. However, the attacker can predict the sequence number contained in the SYN/ACK based on the known behavior of x-terminal's TCP sequence number generator, and therefore can ACK the SYN/ACK without seeing it.

You can see this in the section below. In the first line x-terminal is stimulated by server to open the connection. Server never sees the SYN/ACK so that is why it is missing from the trace. However, he knows to add 128,000 plus 1 to the initial sequence number that x-terminal proposed when sending the SYN/ACK. After the lone ACK, the connection is open.

```
14:18:36.245045 server.login > x-terminal.shell: S 1382727010:1382727010(0)
win 4096
14:18:36.755522 server.login > x-terminal.shell: . ack 2024384001 win 4096
```

Here, Mitnick exploits the trust relationship between x-terminal and server. The SYN packet is sent with a spoofed source address. The attacker sends this packet blindly; there is no way for the attacker to see the reply (short of a sniffer planted on x-terminal or server's network). Because Mitnick has used a fake source address, that of server, the SYN/ACK is sent to server. Server knows that it never sent a SYN packet, a request to open a connection. The proper response for server is to send a RESET and break off the connection. However, that isn't going to happen. As shown here, 14 seconds before the main part of the attack, the server's connection queue for the login port is filled with a SYN flood. The server cannot speak.

```
14:18:22.516699 130.92.6.97.600 > server.login: S 1382726960:1382726960(0)
win 4096
14:18:22.566069 130.92.6.97.601 > server.login: S 1382726961:1382726961(0)
win 4096
14:18:22.744477 130.92.6.97.602 > server.login: S 1382726962:1382726962(0)
win 4096
14:18:22.830111 130.92.6.97.603 > server.login: S 1382726963:1382726963(0)
win 4096
14:18:22.886128 130.92.6.97.604 > server.login: S 1382726964:1382726964(0)
win 4096
14:18:22.943514 130.92.6.97.605 > server.login: S 1382726965:1382726965(0)
win 4096
```

The r-Utilities

You would think that both telnet and r-utilities would have been completely replaced by a secure shell by now, but this simply is not the case. Both are still in wide use. The login service is also known as *rlogin*, and shell as *rshell*. These remote "convenience services" allow access to systems without a pesky password, which can get old if you have to enter it often. On UNIX computers, you can generally create a trust relationship for all users except root, or super user, by adding the trusted system and possibly the trusted account in a file called /etc/hosts.equiv. A root trusted relationship requires a file called /.rhosts. The r-utilities are obsolete and should not be used anymore;

> the secure shell service is a far wiser choice because it is harder for the attacker to exploit. In either the /hosts.equiv or the /.rhosts file, the plus sign (+) has a special meaning, that of the wild-card. For instance, a /.rhosts file with a "+ +" means to trust all computers and all users on those computers.

With the real server disabled by the SYN flood, the trusted connection is used to execute the following UNIX command with rshell: **rsh x-terminal "echo + + >>/.rhosts"**. The result of this causes x-terminal to trust, as root, all computers and all users on these computers (as already discussed). That trace is as follows:

```
14:18:37.265404 server.login > x-terminal.shell: P 0:2(2) ack 1 win 4096
14:18:37.775872 server.login > x-terminal.shell: P 2:7(5) ack 1 win 4096
14:18:38.287404 server.login > x-terminal.shell: P 7:32(25) ack 1 win 4096
```

At this point, the connection is terminated by sending a FIN to close the connection. Mr. Mitnick logs on to x-terminal from the computer of his choice and can execute any command. The target system, x-terminal, is compromised:

```
14:18:41.347003 server.login > x-terminal.shell: . ack 2 win 4096
14:18:42.255978 server.login > x-terminal.shell: . ack 3 win 4096
14:18:43.165874 server.login > x-terminal.shell: F 32:32(0) ack 3 win 4096
```

If Mitnick were now to leave the computer named server in its mute state and someone else were to try to rlogin, he would fail, which might bring unwanted attention to the situation. Therefore, the connection queue is emptied with a series of RESETs.

We now see RSTs to reset the "half-open" connections and empty the connection queue for server.login:

```
14:18:52.298431 130.92.6.97.600 > server.login: R 1382726960:1382726960(0)
win 4096
14:18:52.363877 130.92.6.97.601 > server.login: R 1382726961:1382726961(0)
win 4096
14:18:52.416916 130.92.6.97.602 > server.login: R 1382726962:1382726962(0)
win 4096
14:18:52.476873 130.92.6.97.603 > server.login: R 1382726963:1382726963(0)
win 4096
14:18:52.536573 130.92.6.97.604 > server.login: R 1382726964:1382726964(0)
win 4096
```

Detecting the Mitnick Attack

As we have mentioned, this chapter serves double duty: to tell the story of the Mitnick attack and also to set the stage for the final section of the book. As we complete this chapter, let's introduce the elements needed to detect and respond to an attack like this. The attack could have been detected by both host-based and network-based intrusion-detection systems. It could have been detected at several points, from the intelligence-gathering phase all the way to the corruption of /.rhosts file, when the target system was fully compromised. Intrusion detection is not a specific tool, but a capability, a blending of tools and techniques. In fact, a number of vendors, including NAI and ISS, offer hybrid systems that can perform log file analysis and packet analysis at the host system. As you read through the material in this book, you will see examples of detects by firewalls and by host-based and network-based intrusion-detection systems.

TCP spoofing is becoming harder all the time because many operating systems now randomize their initial sequence numbers, though Microsoft is a notable exception. With vulnerable operating systems, this is still a valuable technique for the more advanced attacker. SYN floods still work on many TCP stacks, although modern operating systems are much more resistant. And of course, even if a SYN flood will not work to take out one side of a trust relationship, there are denial-of-service attacks that can shut down an operating system. Much safer alternatives exist (secure shell, for example), but system administrators continue to use the r-utilities. If we cannot field a capability that enables us to detect the Mitnick attack, what can we detect? To restate, the Mitnick attack serves as an excellent indicator of intrusion-detection capability. Why make such a big deal of this? It turns out that almost a decade later, TCP hijacking is still almost impossible to reliably detect in the field with a single tool. Various products can demonstrate a detect in a lab, but the number of false alarms (false positives) in the field makes this system feature close to useless. The good news is most of the Mitnick attack was trivially detectable; so, let's look at some ways to accomplish this.

Network-Based Intrusion-Detection Systems

Network-based intrusion-detection systems can reliably detect the following entire recon probe trace. As an analyst, you will be tempted to ignore a single finger attempt, but the pattern in entirety really stands out and should never be ignored. Consider some of the ways network-based intrusion-detection systems might detect this recon probe:

```
14:09:32 toad.com# finger -l @target
14:10:21 toad.com# finger -l @server
14:10:50 toad.com# finger -l root@server
14:11:07 toad.com# finger -l @x-terminal
14:11:38 toad.com# showmount -e x-terminal
14:11:49 toad.com# rpcinfo -p x-terminal
14:12:05 toad.com# finger -l root@x-terminal
```

Trust Relationship

The scan is targeted to exploit a trust relationship. The whole point of the Mitnick probe was to determine the trust relationship between systems. There must have been some form of earlier intelligence gathering to determine which systems to target. If Mitnick could do this from a network, the site should be able to do the same thing, perhaps even better. Trained analysts who know their networks can often look at an attack to determine whether it is a targeted attack, but intrusion-detection systems don't currently have this capability.

Port Scan

Intrusion-detection systems can usually be configured to watch for a single attacker coming to multiple ports on a host. Port scans are a valuable tool for detecting intelligence gathering. You saw toad.com fire three probes to x-terminal. However, two of them (showmount and rpcinfo) will probably be directed at the same port (portmapper), which is at TCP/UDP 111. It is certainly possible to set the alarm thresholds to report connection attempts to two different ports on a host computer in under a minute. In actual practice, however, this would create a large number of false alarms. It wouldn't take long for the analyst to give up and set the threshold higher. Therefore, a network-based intrusion-detection system probably would not detect this probe as a port scan.

Host Scan

Host scans happen when multiple systems are accessed by a single system in a short period of time. In the example, toad.com connects to three different systems in as many minutes. Host scan detects are extremely powerful tools that force attackers to coordinate their probes from multiple addresses to avoid detection. In operational experience, we have found that one can employ a completely stupid brute-force algorithm (flag any host that connects to more than five hosts in an hour, for example) with a very acceptable false positive rate. If you lower the window from an hour to five minutes, connects to three or more hosts will still have a low false positive rate for most sites. If the intrusion-detection system can modify the rule for a host scan to eliminate the hosts or conditions that often cause false positives (for example, popular web servers, real audio, any other broadcast service), the trip threshold might be able to be set even lower than five per hour and three per five minutes. The host scan detection code in an intrusion-detection system should be able to detect the example recon probe.

Connections to Dangerous Ports

The recon probe targets well-known, exploitable ports. For this reason, the recon probe is very close to a guaranteed detect. Network-based intrusion-detection systems can and do reliably detect connects and attempted connects to SUNRPCs. On the whole, the attacker has some advantages in terms of evading intrusion-detection systems; she can go low and slow, and she can flood the system with red herring decoys and then go for her actual target. She probably has to go after a well-known port or service to execute the exploit, however, and this is where the intrusion-detection system has an advantage. SUNRPCs are a very well-known attack point and every intrusion-detection system should be able to detect an attempt against these services.

Host-Based Intrusion-Detection Systems

Because the attack was against a UNIX system, this review considers detecting the attack with two types of commonly used UNIX tools: TCP Wrappers and Tripwire. TCP Wrappers log connection attempts against protected services and can evaluate them against an access control list to determine whether to allow a successful connection. Tripwire can monitor the status of individual files and determine whether they were changed. When considering host-based intrusion-detection systems, you want at least these capabilities. Using tools such as PortSentry and LogSentry from www.psionic.com, you can achieve an even greater level of detection and protection by watching the logs and the packets addressed to the host system.

TCP Wrappers

TCP Wrappers or xinetd would detect the probes or attacks at the host level. For TCP Wrappers to work, you must edit the /etc/inetd.conf file to wrap the services that were probed, such as finger. It is also a good idea to add access control lists to TCP Wrappers. If a system is going to run a service such as finger, you can define which systems you will allow to access the finger daemon. That way, both the access would be logged and the connection would not be permitted. The following *fabricated* log entry shows what three TCP Wrappers finger connection events might look like on a system log facility (syslog):

```
Dec  24 14:10:29 target in.finger[11244]: refused connect from toad.com
Dec  24 14:10:35 server in.fingerd[21245]: refused connect from toad.com
Dec  24 14:11:08 x-terminal  in.fingerd[11066]: refused connect from toad.com
```

One of the interesting problems with host-based intrusion detection is how much information to keep and analyze locally and how much to analyze centrally. This fabricated example shows that three different systems (target, server, and x-terminal) are reporting to a central log server. A single finger attempt logged and evaluated on the host computer might be ignored. Three finger attempts against three systems might stand out, however, if they were recorded and evaluated on a central or departmental log server.

An analyst would consider access attempts to portmapper higher priority than finger attempts. At the time of the Mitnick attack, secure portmappers were not widely available. This is no longer the case, and so it would be an indication of an archaic or poorly configured UNIX operating system if both logging and access control features were not available for portmap. Host-based intrusion-detection solutions should certainly detect attempts to access portmap.

Tripwire

You could not reasonably use Tripwire to detect the recon probes. This is because it basically creates and stores a high-quality checksum of critical files, so that if the file or its attributes change, this fact can be detected. Tripwire could detect the actual system compromise, the point at which the /.rhosts file was overwritten. Unfortunately, even if the alarm goes off in near real-time, it is essentially too late. The system is already compromised, and a scripted attack can do a lot of damage very rapidly. Therefore, early detects are the best detects. If you can detect an intruder in the recon phase of his attack and determine the systems the attacker has an interest in, your chance of detecting the actual attack improves.

Preventing the Mitnick Attack

Certainly, the attack could have been prevented at multiple points. A well-configured firewall or filtering router is remarkably inexpensive, easy to configure, and effective at protecting sites from information-gathering probes and attacks originating from the Internet. Even for its time, this site was left open to more services than was advisable.

If the recon probes and r-utilities had been blocked, it would have been much harder for the attacker, perhaps impossible. In general, a site should be blocking almost all incoming packets except for packets destined for ports that need to be open. A file that will point out some of the more dangerous ports, called the Top Twenty list, `www.sans.org/top20.htm`, will give you pointers on not just what to block, but also ports to watch attempts to connect to. As we will see in Chapter 16, "Architectural Issues," the perimeter is a core part of an intrusion-detection capability.

You have already read about host-based security and the use of access lists. Obviously, systems need to run services to accomplish their work efficiently, but it is often possible to specify which systems are allowed to access a particular service (for example, by using TCP Wrappers). In this case, the attacker must actually compromise a trusted host and launch the attack from that host. The Mitnick attack just had to spoof the identity of a trusted host, which is a lot easier than actually compromising the trusted host.

Even after the attack was launched, if it had been detected and responded to, it could have been stopped. In Chapter 18, "Automated and Manual Response," we will discuss ways to slow down, or even stop, an attack that is in progress.

Summary

When doing a post mortem on a successful system compromise or attack, you can often determine that the attack was preceded by intelligence gathering "recon" probes. The harder issue is to detect recon probes, take them seriously, and increase the defensive posture of a facility or system. Many times these recon probes are used to locate and investigate trust relationships between computer systems.

Attackers often exploit a trust relationship between two computers. Many times, system administrators use such relationships as a convenience for themselves, even though they are aware that this is a "chink in the armor" for the system.

The Mitnick attack deliberately did not complete the TCP three-way handshake to SYN flood one side of the trust relationship. Many attacks and probes intentionally do not complete the three-way handshake.

Crafted packets include packets with deliberately false source addresses. These often have a signature that allows intrusion detection to detect their use.

Checking things only once is a general problem in computer security. When designing software or systems, build in the capability to check and then recheck.

The signature of TCP hijacking is that the IP addresses change during a TCP session, while the sequence numbers remain correct for the connection. Reliable detection of TCP hijacking is still beyond the reach of single-tool systems in real-world environments.

Intrusion detection is best thought of as a capability, not a single tool. The Mitnick attack serves as an excellent test case. Intrusion-detection systems that cannot detect this attack on a real-world network with a real-world load (such as a busy T-1 or higher), just mislead their users into thinking they are performing intrusion detection when in fact they are blind. Even the best intrusion-detection system will be blind to an attack that it is not programmed to detect. Many intrusion-detection analysts prefer to use systems that enable them to craft user-defined filters to detect new or unusual attacks. The next chapter presents examples of user-defined filters.

16

Architectural Issues

THIS CHAPTER CONSIDERS SOME OF THE TRADEOFFS, capabilities, and issues facing intrusion-detection system users and builders. This is a bit more theoretical than some parts of the book, but I use real-world examples to try to keep the material useful and pragmatic. We invest some time talking about *events of interest* (EOI). This is an important concept because an analyst gets better results from an intrusion-detection system if she understands what she is searching for and tunes the IDS to find it, as opposed to letting the IDS tell the analyst what to look for. We also discuss severity. All incidents are not created equal and should not be treated so. There is a great debate, a religious war in intrusion detection, about whether the sensor should be placed inside or outside the firewall. This chapter covers this and other sensor-placement issues as well.

One of the great myths that have occurred in the industry is the need to work in *real-time*. I have even seen this specified in procurement documents. What marketers mean by real-time is that intrusion-detection analysts are supposed to respond to beeps and alarms. Real-time, of course, is almost impossible, at least for human reaction, because the packet is traveling at the speed of light. Figure 16.1 shows the detect occurring just after real-time. The illustration was added to the book in case you ever need to point this out to your management because they are overemphasizing response time. In fact, UNIX and Windows NT computer systems do not support either real-time or even deterministic delay. We discuss these issues in push versus pull architectures, which leads into a section on the analyst console. Moreover, as we will shortly discuss, the intrusion analyst will run filters through second and even third passes over the data looking for EOI.

Every intrusion-detection maker falls short in providing a really great analyst interface. This is currently the primary thrust of development of course, so we will take some time to discuss the interface. What exactly does an analyst need?

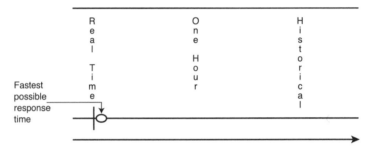

Figure 16.1   Time and ID response.

The next section discusses some of the tradeoffs, or "tuning knobs," that should be considered as you design or enhance your intrusion-detection capability. These include false positives and negatives and sensor focus.

Events of Interest

Chapters 13, "Introduction to Snort and Snort Rules," and 14, "Snort Rules-Part II," introduced events of interest in the sense that when you write a filter, you design it to find something you are interested in. For instance, if you are using the Snort rule content option to find the hex pattern 0xdead or 0xbeef, a pattern that has its roots as a test pattern but is sometimes used by attackers in their code, and you come across a packet with this pattern, this is potentially an EOI. There are three main issues surrounding the subject of EOI in intrusion detection:

- The balance between false positives and false negatives
- Targeting or focusing the sensor to ensure we detect EOI
- The effects of the limits of our system on our capability to detect

The false negative/false positive problem is a serious one in intrusion detection and a lot of our energy is invested in customizing filters to detect EOI and not to generate false alarms or false positives. On the other hand, false negatives would mean missing something we would have wanted to detect. I would like to illustrate what an analyst might do with a simple example. Attackers are known to use certain strings, numbers, and hex patterns in the software they create to do reconnaissance, denial of service, or direct exploits. Some of the classics are:

- The decimal patterns 31337 and 666
- The ASCII string, skillz
- The hex patterns 0xdead and 0xbeef

Suppose we create a filter looking for hex 0xdead as shown below:

```
alert icmp  any any -> 192.168.5.0/24 any       \
      (msg: "0xdead hex pattern seen";          \
       content: "|DE AD|";)
```

Would such a rule create false positives? Certainly it would. If the content of an ICMP packet happened to have these hex characters in this order, these simple content filters would alert. Would I want to run this rule in real-time? No, probably not. On the other hand, if we started seeing a lot of 0xdead 0xbeef, that could be significant. One of the lessons from the Shadow project was secondary analysis. Keep a couple of days of data and run programs to scrub the data looking for interesting events. I probably wouldn't even bother manually examining a single occurrence of 0xdead or 666 in a couple of day's worth of data, but if I saw a dozen, I would certainly think about pulling those connections and examining them.

The stories you learned about in Chapters 10, "Real-World Analysis," and 11, "Mystery Traffic," almost all have the same root. An analyst, looking at the data, saw something odd and said, "That's funny." When Judy and I were working together as active analysts for the Army and Navy respectively, we discovered a number of attacks for the first time. People would ask how we did it. I used to answer, "Pure, dumb luck." Now you know better. We would write scripts to slice and dice that data looking for those events of interest.

Another great classic script is to take a week or so of data and search for odd protocol activity as shown in the following .bpf filter:

```
not tcp and not udp and not icmp and not igrp and not igmp
```

You certainly would not want to run this in real-time; but, as a way to run through your data looking for events of interest that you might otherwise miss, this is obviously attractive. After you know your network and get your filter optimized, most likely you will rarely detect anything with this filter. I don't recommend that you run it interactively and watch the results, because you might get bored and quit running it. However, if you schedule the job to run once a week and only design the system to alert you if it finds results, you have a tool that might strike pay dirt one fine day. If you are shopping for these new correlation consoles or enterprise security managers, one feature you might want to look for is the capability to schedule and run scripts to examine your data.

Now we complete our study of EOI with a consideration of overall system limitations on the lower detect limit. Let's start with the bottom line: It is important to have a fairly clear understanding of what you are looking for and what events you are interested in, because you cannot collect or detect everything. Figure 16.2 shows both the data actually observable by your intrusion-detection system and the data you cannot observe.

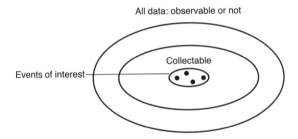

Figure 16.2 Sources of data.

Limits to Observation

As shown in Figure 16.2, the sensor or event generator might not be able to observe all events. This is often quite a surprise for folks who pay good money for an intrusion-detection system, and they slowly find out just how limited it is in practice. What kinds of things can't we observe?

- **Events on a different network.** Unauthorized "backdoor" connections into a network are very common; every machine with a modem has the potential to permit a backdoor. This issue shows up prominently in advertisements for host-based intrusion-detection systems because they can make the "we're here, we're there, we're everywhere" claim.

- **Sensor is not functioning.** Events that happen right in front of the IDS, but they are not observed because the IDS is brain dead. By brain dead, I mean anywhere between hard crashed like the blue screen of death, to pingable while not functioning. A good measure of IDS reliability might mean time between having to reboot the system, because that seems to be the fix for both Windows NT- and UNIX-based systems. I have personally experienced this joy multiple times with Shadow, NFR, NID, Snort, and RealSecure. Naturally, you only discover these systems need rebooting on rainy days when they are in a different building from your analyst console. Some systems are more robust than others, of course. What is the most effective Windows NT remote management tool? A car. If the sensor's disk fills up, this will also prevent collection.

- **No habla SNA or SS7.** Events in a protocol that the intrusion-detection system cannot decode are not observable. What if you need an intrusion-detection system that can decode Signaling System 7 or IBM's SNA? Is there a need for such a thing? For most of us, the answer is no; however, one fairly common event is when we detect a protocol we don't know. For instance, I know a number of people who have detected IP Protocol 54, NHRP (Next Hop Resolution Protocol), at their DMZs and have never seen an IDS decode this.

- **Exceeding bandwidth limit.** Events that occur above the sensor's maximum bandwidth-handling capability cannot be observed. At some point, the sensor has to start dropping packets and we enter what analysts euphemistically call statistical sampling. If you ask network-based IDS vendors what their upper limits of speed are, you get a lot of curious answers ranging from "80Mbps" to "it depends." *Hint:* Trust the person who says "it depends" more than the one who gives you a fixed number, especially a fixed number above T-3 speeds (45Mbps). The number of rules a sensor has to process is one primary factor in the sensor's upper detection limit for many systems, however the primary factor is the critical path. This is the longest execution path a given packet might cause the sensor to take. If a sensor is still processing one packet when another arrives, the packet will be dropped.

To recap what was just covered, intrusion-detection systems cannot look at every possible event. The reasons for this include the following:

- The event happened on another network.
- The IDS is dead.

- The IDS has no understanding of the protocol.
- The IDS has reached its maximum bandwidth limit, or has hit critical path on a given packet and has dropped packets that came later.

The bad news is there are events we can't even observe. The good news is that we find there are events that we can capture. Of all the packets that we can capture, some will match our filters in some way, and they are represented by the space of the inner circle. Finally, some of the total number of detects in the inner circle are valid and have value. We can refer to these as the EOI, the genuine, no-false-positive-about-it detects. They are the reason we go through all the trouble of deploying and operating intrusion-detection systems. Detecting an attack, especially a clever attack, is a lot of fun.

Low-Hanging Fruit Paradigm

Today, the primary standard in intrusion detection is the Snort ruleset. There used to be two major rulesets, but with the present legal troubles of Max Vision, his ruleset is no longer available. It has been inspiring to watch the community come and work together to build the rules, improve the port list, and explain the vulnerabilities. In some sense, I feel like a heel saying a single word against this worthy effort, but there is a risk to us that we at least need to be aware of. We have already discussed the basic issues of false positives and negatives when we covered signatures and filters to detect signatures. Now we need to consider the effect of the low-hanging fruit paradigm on false negatives. What do we mean by the low hanging fruit?

I live on the island of Kauai. Many things are in short supply, but we certainly have enough banana trees and free range chickens. After a hurricane seven years ago, many of the chicken coops were blown apart freeing the chickens. There are no natural predators, so now the island is overrun by chickens. My neighbor recently had a bumper crop of bananas in his garden. I have never stopped to think about just how many bananas can grow on one of these trees, but it can be more than one hundred pounds. As the tree began to bend a bit with the weight of the bananas, they came in range of the chickens, at least the lower ones. They would line up under the banana tree and jump/partially fly and nip at the exposed bananas. It was quite a sight to watch and many a banana was ruined as its bottom was nipped off. So, the low hanging fruit is the easily harvested, vulnerable fruit that any one or any thing can reach.

Suppose a number of intrusion-detection vendors were secretly download-ing the Snort ruleset and using this as a foundation for their own rules. What if their other major process was to go to a couple of well known sites for attack code to download the exploits to their labs, run the exploits, determine their signatures, build effective filters to detect these exploits, and then load these filters in the intrusion-detection systems we all use? If this were to hap-pen, we would begin to establish a lowest common denominator. At first blush, that sounds like a good thing; as a consumer, you could expect any IDS to meet at least a minimum standard defined by the Snort ruleset and the most available attacks (most of which are covered in the Snort ruleset, of course). The problem is that an attacker can then analyze the Snort ruleset and craft small changes to her attacks to make them evade the IDS. If a number of commercial vendors copy these rules, this becomes an interesting problem. It allows them to treat the ruleset, a tremendous asset to the community, as low hanging fruit.

Although the preceding paragraph is partially true, there are lots of ways to mitigate the problem. Many intrusion-detection vendors and researchers culti-vate contacts with the computing underground and have access to a larger library of attacks than those commonly published. Several research efforts attempt to collect attacks and exploits and to define vulnerabilities. The prob-lem is they use different names and descriptions. Mitre (`http://cve.mitre.org`) manages a project called the *Computer Vulnerabilities and Exposures* (CVE), , which enjoys broad industry support. Their goal is to develop a common nam-ing system, primarily to serve as a thesaurus for vulnerability descriptions, but also to support IDS development.

Also, it is sometimes possible to write a general filter to detect a family of exploits. We have already examined a general filter to detect web server attacks. During the discussion of that filter, you learned about a number of CGI-BIN attacks against web servers that attempt to acquire the system's pass-word file for offline decryption. The most famous is the phf attack. Several hundred others exist, however, including php and aglimpse. In the past, each of these had cgi-bin and /etc/passwd files somewhere in the packet, so it was possible to write a general filter to detect each of these and their cousins as well. Today, with the advent of shadow password files, we do not see many attacks against /etc/passwd; however we commonly see the following string:

```
id;uname -a; w
```

The command **id** gives you your effective userID; the semicolon delimits dif-ferent commands; **uname –a** gives the exact operating system and patch level;

and finally **w** tells you who is logged on to the system. It is also possible (and very advisable) to write general filters that detect odd events (things that just shouldn't happen) and to report them. A TCP packet with all flags set, or no flags set, and packets with unknown IP protocols are examples of these kinds of filters. Although you can increase the sensor-detection capability in many ways, the bottom line should be somewhat sobering: If an IDS depends on signatures and doesn't have a filter to look for that signature, how will it make a detect?

Human Factors Limit Detects

Another factor that limits the EOI we can detect and report is that people are part of the system. A typical day as an operator of an intrusion-detection system includes the recording and possible reporting of some number of detects. If you were to examine a year's worth of detects from a site, you might find that the detects cluster as 12 IMAPs, 5 portmaps, 25 ICMP ping sweeps, 30 Smurfs, 8 mscans, 4 portscans, 5 DNS zone Xfer attempts, 4 WinNukes, and so forth. If you check the site's Computer Incident Response Team (CIRT), you find that yup, these are the kinds of things being reported by those sites that do bother to report. So what's wrong with this picture? Not only does the IDS fail to report many events of interest because it does not have a signature for them, many times the analyst chooses not to report many of the events that are detected.

If you were to spend a day or two on the Internet doing web searches, you could easily collect a hundred different software implementations of exploits. Some won't compile easily, and others have limited documentation. Still others are variations on a theme. The simple fact remains, however, that you can easily collect more attacks than are commonly being detected and reported. So what's the problem? One part of the problem is the signature issue previously discussed. If the design of the system relies on signatures and a filter doesn't exist, the box cannot make the detect. Other factors that limit the detect capability of the system as a whole relate to the intrusion-detection analysts and the CIRTs to which they report.

Limitations Caused by the Analyst

Part of the reason for missed detects has to be laid at the feet of the intrusion-detection analyst. There are several issues here. Sometimes, an analyst might mentally evaluate an intrusion attempt and decide it isn't worth investigating. I have been guilty of this multiple times. Here is a classic example: Code Red is still active, because some people don't have the gumption to patch their IIS boxes. On a given day, I see a number of detects on port 80, but I do not tend to evaluate them in depth. I just figure it is Code Red. However, in February 2002, when the Apache PHP vulnerability was reported, I had to suddenly change my ways. After all, I run Apache.

Does an analyst report something he doesn't understand? Unknown patterns are challenging and require a significant understanding of TCP/IP and computer system processes to run to ground. What if the analyst doesn't trust her intrusion-detection system? It takes a lot of faith to sign a report based on a little picture on a console telling you such and such just happened. It takes even more faith to do this when the same IDS reports two email Wiz attacks (Wiz is a very, very old email attack) per day and six SYN floods per hour (and these are obviously false positives). Therefore, analysts are most certainly a weak link in the system. The reasons for this include the following:

- Failing to report what the IDS detects
- Lack of training needed to investigate new attack patterns
- Lack of understanding about TCP/IP, protocols, and services
- Lack of trust in the IDS itself

Limitations Caused by the CIRTs

Could part of the problem of missed detects be the CIRTs? If your CIRT gets a report for an IMAP, portmap, ICMP ping sweep, Smurf, mscan, portscan, DNS zone Xfer, WinNuke, or whatever, no problem. They have a database pigeonhole to put it in, and everyone is happy. If the CIRT gets a report saying, "Unknown probe type, here is the trace, whatever it is it turns my screens blue," what do they do with that? The person getting the report is probably entry level and so there is a hassle because a database pigeonhole doesn't exist. The advanced analysts have a lot of work to do, and the seasoned CIRT workers have been burned by a false positive or two and aren't that likely to take action unless they get a similar report from a second source. In intrusion time, this can be a serious problem. From the moment I first heard about the klogin vulnerability in May 2000, it was less than eight hours before we were dealing with our first compromised system.

This is a serious issue because the CIRT is almost certainly understaffed. Real people are on the phone begging for help because their systems are compromised and their organization never had the funding to take security seriously. Real people screaming for help with compromised systems has to take priority over unknown probe types that turn screens blue. At the end of the month or quarter or whatever, the CIRT puts out their report: We logged this many portmaps, ICMP ping sweeps, Smurfs, mscans, portscans, DNS zone Xfers, WinNukes, and so forth. The new analyst who reported the unknown probe type sees that the report makes no mention of the unknown probe, shakes her head, and silently decides, never again. The analyst doesn't know whether the CIRT thinks she is nuts or whether the CIRT just doesn't care. This is why we made a conscious choice with Incidents.org, an all volunteer CIRT and analysis organization, to be willing to post a new pattern before the whole world and write as our commentary, "We have no idea what this is, can anybody help us?" More than once I have been embarrassed by the answer, because it was a pattern I should have known. Over time, that has led us to act more like a conventional CIRT, to be cautious about what we post, to wait until we know more. This keeps the word from getting out, and may allow an attack more time before we understand it well enough to detect it and defend against it. We know we shouldn't clam up, but it is hard to fight human nature.

A brief recap of EOI is now in order. We cannot observe every event. Of the things that we can observe, some are dismissed as unimportant when in fact they are attacks—these are the false negatives. Others are flagged as attacks when they aren't—these are the false positives. The goal of the system designer and intrusion-detection analyst should be to maximize the events that can be observed while minimizing the false positives and negatives. A number of systems and program design issues arise here, but there are also human issues to consider. Although complete efficiency might never be achieved, you should accept nothing less as your goal.

Severity

Several schools of thought propose ways to reduce severity to a metric, a number we can evaluate. This section discusses some of the primary factors that should be used to develop such a number. Let's start, however, with a basic philosophical principle: Severity is best viewed from the point of view of the system (and its owners) under attack. This is an important principle because the further removed the evaluator is from a given attack, the less severe it is (at least to the evaluator).

It Happens All the Time

The intrusion-detection team that I worked with for several years was once invited to spend the day with a very large CIRT. The CIRT had an analysis team that had just accepted delivery of a spiffy new intrusion-detection capability, an analyst interface that could watch a large number of sensors. We all thought it might be interesting to sit with the Shadow team analysts at this CIRT's workstations and see how effective they could be with the new spiffy interface. Within four minutes, one of the Shadow analysts had found a signature indicating a root-level break-in to one of our sister sites. She wanted to call the site and tell them, but the CIRT workers laughed and said, "It happens all the time." No doubt that was true from their perspective. These folks operate well over a hundred sensors of their own in addition to all the reports they receive. They probably deal with more compromises in a year than I will experience in my entire working career. The trip still seems odd to me, however, because I know how much trouble and pain a compromised system can be to the system owners and those who have to assist them. Severity is best viewed from the point of view of the system under attack and its owner(s).

Although we do want to keep the human element in mind as we discuss the severity of attacks, we need to be able to sort between them so that we can react appropriately. At every emergency room, there is an individual in charge of triage, making sure that care is given to those who need it the most. This way, a patient with an immediate life-threatening injury doesn't have to wait while the medical personnel attend to a patient with a stubbed toe. In a large-scale attack response, resources become scarce very quickly, so an approach to triage for computer assets is required. Figure 16.3 introduces this concept at a high level.

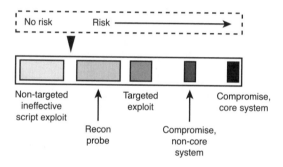

Figure 16.3 Severity at a glance.

Are nontargeted exploits for vulnerabilities that do not exist within your computer systems actually no-risk? When you study risk more formally, you will learn that part of the equation is your level of certainty; how sure are you that none of your systems have the vulnerability? I tend to be on the conservative side. In the examples that follow, I consider nontargeted, nonvulnerable exploits to be of no risk only if they are also blocked by the firewall or filtering router. In fact, there is a sense in which this is negative risk. The attacker using a nontargeted script exploit against a well-secured site is at a higher risk than the site because the attack will be reported. If the attacker succeeds in breaking in and doing damage somewhere else, the odds are at least fair that he can be tracked down.

What might be a reasonable method to derive a metric for severity? What are the primary factors? How can we establish an equation? How likely is the attack to do damage? And, if we sustain damage, how bad will it hurt? Clearly, these are all factors.

Criticality

How bad will it hurt is one of the most important issues to consider in risk management. I was giving a talk in Washington, DC and wanted to make a point about anti-virus and personal firewalls so I asked, "How many of you travel multiple times a year?" Most of the hands went up, which makes sense for a government headquarters crowd. Then I asked, "How many of you carry Cipro?" Cipro is the antibiotic that was prescribed during the Anthrax attacks. Because there had not been an anthrax attack since October 2001, nobody was thinking about that. However, I can just imagine what would happen if I were in a strange city and started feeling the worst case of the flu in my entire life. How would I get access to top-quality medical care? At home, I have my doctor, who knows me, and a medical record and friends that are doctors. In Houston, or Seattle, or New York City, the answer is go to the emergency room. Do you know that it is not impossible to wait 12 hours just to be seen in an emergency room? How bad will it hurt? This is the question that should drive us. Now, just so you don't think I am totally off my rocker for carrying Cipro, I also travel internationally a lot, and though I try not to drink the water and to cook it, peel it or forget it, having something like Cipro is an important tool if things go wrong. What does any of this have to do with anti-virus or a personal firewall? If you don't have these things and you are exposed, you are in a heap of trouble, just like anthrax and no Cipro.

It would be bad for me to be poisoned with anthrax, but it would be so much worse for the President of the United States to be poisoned with it. The major determinant for "how bad will it hurt?" is how critical the target is. If a desktop system is compromised, it is bad in the sense that time and work might be lost. Also, that system could be used as a springboard to attack other systems. If an organization's *domain name system* (DNS) server or email relay is compromised, however, a much more serious problem exists. In fact, if an attacker can take over a site's DNS server, the attacker might be able to manipulate trust relationships and thereby compromise most or all of a site's systems. When developing a metric, we need a way to quantify criticality. We can use a simple five-point scale, as follows:

5 points	Firewall, DNS server, core router
4 points	Email relay/exchanger
2 points	User UNIX desktop system
1 point	MS-DOS 3.11

Lethality

The lethality of the exploit refers to how likely the attack is to do damage. Attack software is generally either application or operating system specific. A Macintosh desktop system isn't vulnerable to a UNIX tooltalk buffer overflow, or an rcp.statd attack. A Sun Microsystems box running unpatched Solaris might quickly become the wholly owned property of Hacker Incorporated if hit with the same attacks. As an intrusion-detection analyst, I get nervous when an attacker can go after a specific target with an appropriate exploit. This is an indicator that the attacker has done his homework with recon probes and that we are going to have to take additional countermeasures to protect the target. Again, a five-point scale applies:

5 points	Attacker can gain root across network.
4 points	Total lockout by denial of service.
4 points	User access (via a sniffed password, for example).
1 point	Attack very unlikely to succeed (Wiz in 2002, for example).

The last example, 1 point for Wiz, introduces a really important point when calculating severity, and that is the effect of time. This is known as the lethality curve. The attackers have a term they call zero day, and it references an attack that works before it is publicly known. The exploit works fine, but it is tightly held by a fairly small number of people who are breaking into systems with it. This is a time of extreme lethality, but the number of uses is fairly low. Eventually, the attack is discovered and published. Now the community knows about it and so do the attackers. We enter a race condition—attackers race to get the exploit, learn to use it, and attack our systems. Defenders rush to apply patches, download new IDS signatures, or implement other countermeasures. During this phase, the attack is still pretty lethal, but the lethality is dropping; however, the incidence of attack attempts goes way up. Finally, we reach the crest of the wave. More and more defenders are patching their systems and applying other countermeasures, and over time, the attack becomes less and less destructive.

Countermeasures

What about firewalls or system patches or operating systems running from CD-ROMs? Countermeasures certainly affect severity and can logically be divided into system countermeasures and network countermeasures.

The five-point scale for system countermeasures is as follows:

5 points   Modern operating system, all patches, added security such as TCP Wrappers and secure shell

3 points   Older operating system, some patches missing

1 point   No TCP Wrappers/allows fixed unencrypted passwords

The five-point scale for network countermeasures is as follows:

5 points   Validated restrictive firewall, only one way in or out

4 points   Restrictive firewall, some external connections (modems, ISDN)

2 points   Permissive firewall (The key question is this: "Does the firewall allow the attack through?")

Calculating Severity

Analysts trained in the GIAC approach to intrusion detection use the following formula to calculate severity:

```
(Criticality + Lethality) - (System + Net Countermeasures) = Severity
```

Take a look at a couple examples. These are taken from the practical project required to achieve GIAC Intrusion Analyst certification. To put the examples in context, the entire analysis process is shown, even though the current focus is on severity.

The approach described here helps reinforce that attacks vary in severity. This discussion examines some of the factors that affect severity. You can cite these factors to help others understand when they ask, "What is it about? This attack that has you spun up?" Having a method to calculate severity can be handy when the handler is in the situation of having to triage, or choose how to deploy finite defensive assets. To the system owner, his system is the most important one in the world (much like everyone's own child is the cutest kid). You can use a severity-grading technique like this one to explain why you applied defensive assets to one owner's system rather than to someone else's.

Scanning for Trojans

This first example comes from a trace that David Leaphart selected for use in his practical. To help get you started, the first trace is saying that on March 24 at 1:54 A.M. source host computer 24.3.57.38 connected from source port 11111 to destination host computer 24.3.21.199 on destination port TCP 12345:

```
Mar 24 01:54:58 cc1014244-a kernel: securityalert: tcp if=ef0 from
24.3.57.38:11111 to 24.3.21.199 on unserved port 12345
Mar 24 03:14:13 cc1014244-a kernel: securityalert: tcp if=ef0 from
171.214.113.228:2766 to 24.3.21.199 on unserved port 1243
Mar 24 04:45:01 cc1014244-a kernel: securityalert: tcp if=ef0 from
208.61.109.243:3578 to 24.3.21.199 on unserved port 1243
Mar 24 04:45:06 cc1014244-a kernel: securityalert: tcp if=ef0 from
208.61.109.243:3832 to 24.3.21.199 on unserved port 27347
Mar 24 05:40:42 cc1014244-a kernel: securityalert: udp if=ef0 from
24.24.100.172:2147 to 24.3.21.199 on unserved port 137
Mar 24 14:56:08 cc1014244-a kernel: securityalert: udp if=ef0 from
63.17.79.40:4294 to 24.3.21.199 on unserved port 137
Mar 24 17:20:44 cc1014244-a kernel: securityalert: tcp if=ef0 from
62.6.100.45:1828 to 24.3.21.199 on unserved port 27374
Mar 24 20:50:47 cc1014244-a kernel: securityalert: tcp if=ef0 from
194.27.62.179:4857 to 24.3.21.199 on unserved port 27374
```

Analysis

The following questions prove very useful for determining the severity of any intrusion. Here they have been applied to the trace preceding identified:

- **Evidence of active targeting?**

  Yes. The traffic from the source is detected at the host's interface.

- **Identify the history?**

  No. Previous traffic from the source address was noted in the detect report.

- **Identify the technique?**

  TCP and UDP packets were directed at a specific host. The SYN packets were directed at TCP ports 12345, 1243, 27347, and 27374. The UDP traffic was directed at UDP port 137. The sources are hoping for a SYN-ACK, or no response in the case of UDP. The port scan is coming from different sources over a number of hours. All the source addresses are active on the Internet and do not appear to have been spoofed.

- **Evidence of intent?**

  This detect is a port scan of the victim looking for various vulnerabilities. These can be summarized as follows:

Port 12345	Netbus and also the TrendMicro listening port
Port 1243	SubSeven and Backdoor-G Trojans
Port 27374	SubSeven 2.0
Port 27347	Possibly a typing error for port 27374
Port 137	NetBIOS

The analyst needs to check the victim for evidence of Trojans and ensure that NetBIOS is not a problem.

- **Identify hostile individuals and groups?**

  Based on Whois, these source addresses came from various locales. They appear to be unrelated both in geography and time. The last address is of a little more concern, however, because it originates in Turkey. These scans appear to be hostile, but the victim seems to be rebuffing the scans.

Severity

I would assess the severity of this breach as follows:

- **Criticality.** This is a 2, presuming this is not a critical server.

- **Lethality.** This is a 4, because these exploits can be damaging.

- **Countermeasures.** This is a 5, assuming that the OS is fully patched.

- **Net countermeasures.** There doesn't seem to be a firewall, so this is a 0.

Host Scan Against FTP

Consider one more example. Eric Brock submitted Table 16.1. He used a FireWall-1 firewall to collect the information he used for his practical.

Table 16.1   **Example of Data Gathered on a Host Scan Against FTP**

ID	Date	Time	SourceIP	Source Port	DestIP	DestPort	Protocol	Info
661530	21Feb2000	9:09:24	195.243.30.140	4858	10.10.1.1	FTP	TCP	len 60
661531	21Feb2000	9:09:24	195.243.30.140	4857	10.10.1.0	FTP	TCP	len 60
661532	21Feb2000	9:09:24	195.243.30.140	4860	10.10.1.3	FTP	TCP	len 60
661533	21Feb2000	9:09:24	195.243.30.140	4859	10.10.1.2	FTP	TCP	len 60
...	...	...	...	...	...	...	...	...
661632	21Feb2000	9:09:25	195.243.30.140	1144	10.10.1.252	FTP	TCP	len 60
661633	21Feb2000	9:09:25	195.243.30.140	1145	10.10.1.253	FTP	TCP	len 60
661634	21Feb2000	9:09:25	195.243.30.140	1146	10.10.1.254	FTP	TCP	len 60

Analysis

So as we analyze the attack, we want to begin with the fact the packets came to our DMZ; you could call this active targeting. It is important to determine the history. In the list below we consider it only from our DMZ's perspective, but by using Dshield (http://www.dshield.org/ipinfo.php) we can also look at the history of the source IP address at other sites. We describe the technique that was used and then make are best assessment as to the purpose of the packets, the intent, the reason we saw these packets, and begin to make our final analysis conclusions.

- **Existence.** Someone claiming to be IP address 195.243.30.140 is visiting us.
- **History.** There is no history of this address visiting our network.
- **Techniques.** The visitor is sending one FTP packet to each address in our subnet. They are being sent extremely fast.
- **Intent.** The visitor is attempting to find hosts on our network that will respond on the FTP port.
- **Targeting.** Our entire network is being targeted, but no specific servers are being targeted.
- **Analysis.** This visitor is performing a scan of our network, looking for ftp servers. The visitor could be planning a denial-of-service attack against an ftp server, or he could be looking for an anonymous ftp server to see what he can download from it, or to see what he can upload to it.

Severity

Severity is made up of a number of dimensions, the criticality of the target, how lethal the attack is, and any system or network countermeasures that might mitigate the attack.

- **Criticality.** This is a 3, because no specific servers are targeted.
- **Lethality.** This is a 4, because there are many known ftp vulnerabilities.
- **System countermeasures.** This is a 2, because all operating systems are running the latest patches, but some are listening on the ftp port.
- **Network countermeasures.** This is a 4, because the firewall blocks all incoming ftp.
- **Severity score.** This severity score is 1. The formula is this:

```
Severity = (Criticality + Lethality) - (System Countermeasures + Network
Countermeasures)
```

Sensor Placement

A network-based intrusion-detection system isn't going to work unless there is a sensor. It will not work optimally if the sensor is not placed correctly. Generally, somewhere in the vicinity of the firewall is a good location for the sensor.

Outside Firewall

Usually, intrusion-detection sensors are placed outside the firewall in the DMZ (as shown in Figure 16.4). This allows the sensor to see all attacks coming in from the Internet. However, if the attack is TCP and the firewall, or filtering router, blocks the attack, the intrusion-detection system might not be able to detect the attack. Many attacks can be detected only by matching a string signature. The string is not sent unless the TCP three-way handshake is completed.

Although some attacks cannot be detected by a sensor outside the firewall, this is the best sensor location to detect attacks. The benefit to the site is that analysts can see the kinds of attacks to which their site and firewall are exposed. One of the reviewers of the book puts it this way: "Outside the firewall is *attack* detection, and inside it is *intrusion* detection." Well put!

During late 1997 and early 1998, a large number of sites detected attempts against the portmapper port (TCP/UDP 111). Sites with active portmappers are likely locations for rpc.statd. I ran a vulnerability scanner internally at two locations to see whether any risk existed. The scan turned up more than 50 systems that would answer an rpcinfo –p request (which means an unsecured portmapper) and further analysis showed that they were running statd. The firewall at both locations blocked the attacks, both via portmapper, and any attempt to directly access statd. Having information that sites I was concerned with protecting were under a concerted attack and that there was an internal exposure redoubled my efforts in the never-ending battle to get those portmappers secured and see whether patches were available from vendors for statd. For more information, refer to `www.cert.org/advisories/CA-97.26.statd.html`.

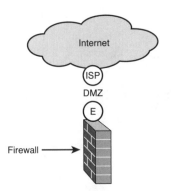

Figure 16.4 A sensor, or event detector, is used to instrument the DMZ.

DMZ (demilitarized zone) is the area between an ISP and the outermost firewall interface.

Sensors Inside Firewall

A school of thought says that sensors should be placed inside firewalls. Several reasons compel this placement. If attackers can find the sensor, they might attack it so that there is less chance of their activities being audited. Systems inside firewalls present less vulnerability than systems outside firewalls. If the sensor is inside the firewall and exposed to less noise, it might generate fewer false positives. Also, inside the firewall, you can detect whether a firewall is misconfigured (if attacks get through that are supposed to be stopped, for example).

It is certainly true that well-configured firewalls stop most low-end exploit attempts. It is also true that far too much attention is devoted to detection and analysis of these low-end attacks.

Both Inside and Outside Firewall

More is better. Best of both worlds. You have heard both of these slogans. For me, they are more than mere slogans. I deploy sensors on both sides of the firewall. If your organization can afford a sensor both inside and outside the firewall, this has certain advantages, such as:

- You never have to guess whether an attack penetrated a firewall.
- You might be able to detect insider, or internal, attacks.
- You might be able to detect misconfigured systems that can't get through the firewall so that you can help the system administrator.

If your organization is using an expensive IDS solution, this is not worth the cost and effort. If you do deploy dual sensors, the sensor on the inside of the firewall is the one to set up to page you in an emergency.

Misconfigured Systems

Intrusion-detection systems and their analysts should be able to troubleshoot the network. When I was involved in deploying Shadow, we usually spent the first week or two helping the site fix problems with the network. This is just as true today. Below are some of the common problems:

- localhost 127.0.0.1 or 127.0.0.2 broadcasting to an internal subnet.

- Misconfigured DNS files. These read from right to left; so if your site's network ID is 172.20.0.0/24 and you detect a host (172.20.30.40) doing a broadcast to 255.30.20.172, that could be a clue that someone didn't get the word that domain files read right to left.

- Incorrect subnet mask. Broadcast to 172.20.255.255 rather than to 172.20.30.255.

- Backdoors. When you see a packet coming from the Internet to 172.20.30.255 (using the network ID from the preceding example), there is a pretty good chance your network has sprung a leak—that is, a packet should not be coming from you, to you, outside your firewall.

Additional Sensor Locations

The most common place for a sensor is outside the firewall, but it is certainly not the only place that benefits an organization. Many intrusion-detection systems can be used to support the organization in a variety of additional locations, including the following:

- Partner networks, to which you have direct connections to customers and suppliers often inside your firewall.

- High-value locations, such as research or accounting networks.

- Networks with a large number of transient employees (consultants and/or temps, for example).

- Subnets that appear to be targeted by outsiders, or that have shown indications of intrusions or other irregularities.

A final issue in sensor placement is what the sensor is connected to. Networks today operate almost exclusively on switched VLAN environments. Sensors *can* operate in these environments. If the switches' spanning ports are not configured properly, however, intrusion detection is all but impossible. One thing to be aware of is that spanning puts a load on the switch. If a sensor is to be operated in a switched network, the implementation must be tested. TCP is a duplex protocol, and the analyst should ensure that the sensor is receiving both the source and destination side of the conversation. The sensor should also be tested to ensure that it sends data reliably from the switched location. It might be necessary to configure the sensor with two interface cards. The first can monitor in promiscuous mode (listening to all packets regardless of whether they are addressed to the sensor) attached to a spanning port. The second interface would be placed on a separate VLAN to communicate with the analysis station. Of course, throwing money at the problem is always a handy trick in intrusion detection. If you are having load and configuration problems, here are a couple of options:

- Consider a network tap. These are connected directly to the media and allow the sensor to see the data that passes by the tap.

- TopLayer, `www.toplayer.com`, has a switch designed to copy data from the network to an IDS.

- Cisco Catalyst 6000 switches can support an optional Policy Feature Card that allows you to control the data copied to the IDS in about the same way the TopLayer does.

Push/Pull

Now that you have determined where you want to place your sensor, how will you extract the data from it? The preferred behavior, at least when you first deploy a sensor or event generator, is to *push* events to the analysis system as they occur. When the sensor detects an event, it creates a packet with the pertinent data and shoots it to the analysis station. An obvious protocol for this would be something like an SNMP trap. Most commercial products have their own proprietary protocol for communications between the sensor and analysis station. The number-one feature potential customers look for when they compare intrusion-detection systems is "real-time" response.

Pushy Intrusion-Detection Systems

One of the more interesting selling points for intrusion-detection systems is how obnoxious they can behave. It seems like a good idea when looking for a system that the IDS will beep the console, send us email, page us, or call our cell phones. It usually takes only a couple weeks to turn off these handy real-time notification features. Even the most dedicated analyst will accept only so many false alarms at three o'clock in the morning.

Real-time is *not* possible until the intrusion-detection capability exists in the network switch fabric and computer system operating system and programs themselves. Even so, prospective customers of intrusion-detection systems want the event-detection information available to them as quickly as possible, and that makes a whole lot of sense. Certainly then, push is the correct architecture for network-based intrusion detection, right?

Push-based architectures have one very severe flaw. If their behavior is such that they generate a packet in response to a detect, and if the sensor can be observed, it is fairly easy to determine how it is configured. Over time, this would allow an attacker to determine what the sensor ignores. This kind of effort and patience is unlikely with low-end script-kiddie attackers, but almost guaranteed behavior from the high end, such as high-value economic espionage. The obvious solution to this problem is to push out the events on a regular basis as a stream. This gives the same, just a little later than real-time response, capability and masks what the sensor detects. If there are no detects, the stream is just filled with encrypted null characters.

Figure 16.5 shows the differences in architecture between push and pull systems. On the whole, push is the better architecture for intrusion detection. One of the best applications for pull is a covert sensor, which can be employed in an investigation. It can be focused on a particular computer system. It can also just passively monitor communications until a key phrase occurs, and then it can be used to capture the communication stream. Most of the sniffers deployed by hackers to collect user IDs and passwords are pull-based systems. They collect data until the collected data is retrieved.

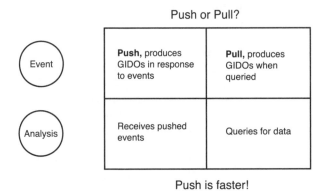

Figure 16.5   Push or pull?

Analyst Console

So, you have determined where to place your sensors and have selected between push, pull, or both paradigms to acquire the EOI information. Now you can finally get to work. The intrusion-detection analyst does her work at the analyst console. If an election was won with the mantra, "It's the economy, stupid," someone better tell the intrusion-detection vendors that, "It's the console, stupid." An organization typically looks for the following factors when shopping for an IDS:

- Real-time
- Automated response capability
- Detects everything (no false negatives)
- Runs on Windows XP/UNIX/Commodore 64 (whatever the organization uses)

That gets the box in the door, but will it stay turned on? I have visited several sites that deployed commercial intrusion-detection systems very early in the game, and although they are still connected to the network, the console has a thin layer of dust on its keyboard. After the organization has been using the system for several months, the feature set tends to be as follows:

- Faster console
- Better false positive management
- Display filters
- Mark events that have already been analyzed
- Drill down
- Correlation
- Better reporting

Most major commercial IDS system consoles were so bad that the Department of Defense funded a number of alternate designs. Several of these are now hitting the market as products in the Enterprise Security Console market. Most organizations can't afford to develop alternative interfaces; so if you are in the market for an IDS, this list might help you select one you can actually use. The following sections explore the console factors in greater detail.

Faster Console

The human mind is a tragic thing to waste, but that is exactly what happens when we put trained intrusion analysts' minds in a wait state. Here is what happens: The analyst has a detect, he starts to gather more information, he waits for the window to come up, he waits some more, and suddenly can't remember what he was doing.

I was working with the sales engineer of an IDS company recently and tried to point out that the interface was very slow. His answer of course was to buy a faster computer. (This was a twin 1.2Ghz Pentium IV with a gigabyte of RAM, which was still fairly current for January 2002.) One simple technique for improving the console performance is for the system to always query the information for any high-priority attack and have it canned and ready for the moment the analyst clicks on it. This way, the computer can wait for the analyst, rather than the other way around.

False Positive Management

False positives happen. Sometimes we can't filter them out without incurring false negatives, so we must ask: What we can do to manage them?

The Code Red web attacks serve as a good example. If we write a filter that dampens probes to port 80 (and most of us did), we stand the risk of a

massive false negative. If we don't use such a filter, we will cause a large
number of false positives (false positive in the sense that if we are not running
a vulnerable version of IIS, we don't need to be concerned with Code Red).
Because Code Red is a Windows problem, we could get part of the way
towards handling this problem with a better filter. If our filter language supports it, we could put in basic passive fingerprinting information for Windows
into our filter. For instance, a Windows system defaults to a TTL of 128 and
TCP window sizes between 5,000 and 9,000 for Windows NT and between
17,000 and 19,000 for Windows 2000; so if we see a TTL of greater than 128
and a window size that is not within spec, perhaps we could afford not to
display the detect. We still collect it, but we do not bother the analyst with it.
When the analyst selects any event in the potential false positive class, the console should display the regular normal information that it always does, but also
the additional data to enable the analyst to make the determination.

Responsibility for False Positive

IDS vendors' feet need to be held to the fire for better false positive management. The Snort ruleset is getting better and better about providing information in the help file that tells an analyst
whether there are possible false positives and what they are. But this is not good enough. Vendors
must be diligent in reducing them, because false positives are the biggest hurdle to successful incident management. Vendors should fix filters that cause too many false positives, make sure that
filters vulnerable to them are tunable, and delete filters that are useless and cause too many false
positives. If nothing else, they must carefully document exactly the traffic pattern triggering the
filters to report false positives.

Display Filters

The false positive management technique just discussed is used on some commercial IDS systems and should be considered a minimum acceptable capability. To reach a goal of detecting as many events of interest as possible, you have
to accept some false positives. Display filters are one way to manage these. This
is not a new idea; network analysis tools, such as NAI's Sniffer, have always had
both collection and display filters.

Mark as Analyzed

Unless you are a second-level (supervisor, trainer, or regional) intrusion analyst,
life is too short to inspect events that have already been manually analyzed.
After an analyst has inspected an event, it should be marked as done. This is
not rocket science. After all, the web browsers we all use mark the URLs we
have already visited. Ideally, this would be more like the editing functions on

modern word processors such as Microsoft Word—the event gets a tag with the date and time it was analyzed and the username of the analyst, and whether it was rejected as a false positive or accepted and reported.

Drill Down

We certainly wouldn't want to provide users an interface that intimidates them! When an organization first starts performing intrusion detection, it might be quite happy with the system displaying a GUI interface with a picture, the name of the attack, date, time, and source and destination IPs. The happiness often ends when the organization finds out that it has reported a false positive. At this point, the analyst starts to desire to see the whole enchilada and it should be available with one mouse click. Drill down is a very powerful approach. Analysts get to work with big-picture data, and then as soon as they want more detail, they just click. The analyst should not have to leave the interface he is using—that discourages research. Analysts certainly should not have to enter a separate program to get to the data—that is inexcusable.

Drill down is not possible unless the data is collected (and it certainly ought to include the packet headers). No analyst should have to report a detect he can't verify!

Correlation

Every analyst has seen a detect and scratched his head saying, "Haven't I seen that IP before?" Intrusion analysts at hot sites (sites attacked fairly often) frequently detect and report between 15 and 60 events per day. After a couple of weeks, that is a lot of IP addresses to keep track of manually. It also is not hard for the analysis console to keep a list of sites that have been reported and color those IP addresses appropriately.

Better Reporting

Two kinds of reports make up the bread and butter of the intrusion analyst: event-detection reports and summary reports. Event reports provide low-level detailed information about detects. Summary reports help the analyst to see the trends of attacks over time and the manager to understand where the money is going.

Event-Detection Reports

Event-detection reports are either done event by event or as a daily summary report. They are usually sent by electronic mail. The IDS should support flexibility in addressing and offer PGP encryption of the report. The reports might be sent to groups that specialize in collecting and analyzing this information such as Incidents.org or SecurityFocus or the organization's CIRT or FIRST team, the organization's security staff. If you are shunning the attacker or plan to take action, another powerful technique is to file the report as a memo to record. For every detect displayed on the console, the analyst should have the opportunity to report with a single mouse selection accepting the detect. The system should then construct a report, which the analyst reviews and annotates before sending.

If you are shopping for an intrusion-detection system or Enterprise Security Console, sit down at the console and see how long it takes you to collect the information needed to report an event and to send it via email (or other format such as XML) to a CIRT or FIRST team. If you can't access raw or supporting data, take your hands off the keyboard and walk away from the system. If it takes more than five to seven minutes and your organization intends to report events, keep shopping. If you can collect the information including raw or supporting data and send it in within two minutes, please send me email telling me about the product so I can get one too.

Weekly/Monthly Summary Reports

Management often wants to stay abreast of intrusion detects directed against the sites for which they are responsible. Event-by-event or even daily reporting might prove too time consuming, however, and doesn't help them see the big picture. Weekly or monthly reports are a solution to this problem. In general, the higher level the manager, the less frequently she should be sent reports.

Host- or Network-Based Intrusion Detection

The more information we can provide the analyst, the better chance she has of solving the difficult problems in intrusion detection. What is the best source of this information, host based or network based? If you read the literature on host-based intrusion-detection products, you might conclude that host based is a better approach. And, of course, if you read the literature of companies that are primarily network based, theirs is the preferred approach. Obviously, you want both capabilities, preferably integrated, for your organization. Perhaps the best way to consider the strengths of the two approaches is to describe the minimum reasonable intrusion-detection capability for a moderately sized organization connected to the Internet, such as shown in Figure 16.6.

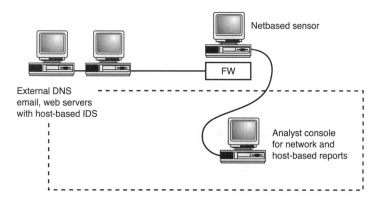

Figure 16.6   A common architecture for a moderately sized organization.

The sensor outside the firewall is positioned to detect attacks that originate from the Internet. DNS, email, and web servers are the target for about a third of all attacks directed against a site. These systems have to be able to interact with Internet systems and can only be partially screened. Because they face high overall risk, they should have host-based intrusion-detection software that reports to the analyst console as well. This shows the need for both capabilities, host and network based, even for smaller organizations. As the size and value of the organization increases, the importance of additional counter-measures increases as well.

This minimum capability does not address the insider threat. Much of the literature for (primarily) host-based solutions stresses the insider attack problem. I keep seeing studies and statistics that state the *majority* of intrusions are caused by insiders. This is beginning to change and most experts agree that the majority of attacks come from the Internet. Malicious code has become a huge problem, however, and in some sense Trojans and information-gathering viruses can be thought of as insiders after they are in your systems. If insider attacks are a primary concern for your organization, additional measures to achieve a minimum capability are required, such as the following:

- Use taps or spanning ports on network switches so that you are not blind on the inside.

- Configure the filters on your DMZ sensor so that they do not ignore your internal systems. You must keep tabs on outgoing traffic as much as incoming. This is especially true because malicious code has become such a major problem.

- Configure the filters on your border router or firewall to allow only outbound traffic if the addresses correspond to your assigned Internet addresses. This is called *egress filtering* and there is a how-to paper available at the Incidents.org web site (`http://www.incidents.org/defend/egress.php`).

- Deploy network-based sensors at high-value locations such as research and accounting.

- Deploy honeypot systems at juicy locations with files that appear to be anything you think insider attackers might be trying to steal.

- Place additional sensors from time to time on user networks as a random spot check.

- At the very least, you should deploy host-based intrusion-detection code on all server systems as well as corporate officers and other key personnel. Many personal firewalls are available for less than $75 a station, and they are easy to deploy (Tiny, ZoneAlarm, BlackIce, and Symantec Internet Security, for example).

- Establish a reward system for those who report on employees who misuse or steal from the organization.

Summary

Very often, the features that seem most desirable when searching for an intrusion-detection system don't prove to be all that important in actual use. The first one to go is usually the capability to send alerts to the analyst's pager.

For various reasons, intrusion-detection systems cannot even look at every possible event. Why? This chapter identified a few possible reasons: The event happened on another network. The IDS is dead. The IDS has no understanding of the protocol. Perhaps the IDS has reached its maximum bandwidth limit and dropped the packet. Further, the network-based IDS is limited to the capabilities of the spanning port on a switch, and encrypted packets prevent IDS identification.

An analyst gets better results from an intrusion-detection system if he understands what he is searching for and tunes the IDS to find it, as opposed to letting the IDS tell the analyst what to look for.

If you have only one sensor, place it outside your firewall.

When you have evidence that your site is under a targeted attack, and that the attacker knows the type of operating systems you have and is targeting them accurately, take additional countermeasures swiftly.

If possible, implement a balanced intrusion-detection capability with both network- and host-based solutions.

17

Organizational Issues

WHAT DOES RISK MANAGEMENT HAVE TO DO with intrusion detection? Every organization either consciously or subconsciously makes decisions about risk. Obviously, we decide how much risk we are willing to accept ourselves. The distributed denial-of-service attacks that became widely known in February 2000 and Code Red attacks in 2001 demonstrate clearly that we also decide how much risk we are willing to accept on others' behalf. The security of my site depends, at least in part, on the security of your site. This chapter lays the groundwork that will enable you to present a cogent argument to your management that intrusion detection is one tool for managing risk, or part of an overall security architecture. The highest and best purpose of a network intrusion-detection system is to identify the attacks being directed against our perimeter defenses so that we can ensure our systems are hardened to withstand these attacks. In other words, intrusion detection must serve as instrumentation that enables us to define the metrics we need to manage risk intelligently. This chapter also ties risk-management techniques and concepts directly to intrusion detection.

Organizational Security Model

To manage risk, we need a model, a way of describing the problem and what needs to be done from a process standpoint so that we can get our arms around the problem. A simple example of a model is the Top Twenty list. You can find one at www.sans.org/top20.htm. It lists the top twenty vulnerabilities that attackers exploit and how to fix them. Every major vulnerability scanner looks for evidence of these. This is a simple model, listing the twenty vulnerabilities most often exploited. Make sure there are tools to find these vulnerabilities, and describe the fixes so that all users can repair their systems. If a significant number of people do this, attackers will have a much harder time compromising systems, and everyone's risk is reduced. Alan Paller, a good friend of mine, created this model. Alan Paller is the Director of Research for the System Administration, Networking, and Security (SANS) Institute, and he developed another more complex model while on an international flight with some of the top security minds in the world. During the long flight to Australia, he continued to interview and question these individuals to develop a comprehensive security model.

While working with this model, I have been impressed with the results it gives after you take the time to implement it. As I reflect on the efforts and challenges of directing the startup effort that created the Global Information Assurance Certification (GIAC) certification and SANS Immersion training tracks, I am deeply thankful to have had a model like this to use. After twenty years of government service, adjusting to the speed we have to move at makes it hard to remember which way is up some days.

What to do? When I worked for the *Ballistic Missile Defense Organization* (BMDO), I used this security model to help me sort out the many contradictory priorities. In the government, everything is so ponderous that you need a roadmap to remember what you are trying to do. With SANS and the GIAC, everything is "practice what you preach." If we teach it, we do it. So, I am trying to implement the same model in a startup world where everything changes everyday. I did not develop this model; Alan Paller, Gene Schultz, Matt Bishop, and Hal Pomeranz did, but I have used it in the past and it has worked for me. I offer it to you in the hope that it helps you as well. As I describe it here, I will put an ID slant on the model, but you certainly can apply it in a more general way. Listing 17.1 shows the results of their work (courtesy of Matt, Alan, Hal, and Gene). Let's take a look at it. Instead of three steps (determine the top twenty vulnerabilities, scan or test for these vulnerabilities on your systems, and fix these vulnerabilities if they are present), this model has seven steps.

Listing 17.1 **The Seven Most Important Things to Do If Security Matters**

1. Write the security policy (with business input).
2. Analyze risks or identify industry practice for due care; analyze vulnerabilities.
3. Set up a security infrastructure.
4. Design controls and write standards for each technology.
5. Decide which resources are available, prioritize countermeasures, and implement the top priority countermeasures you can afford.
6. Conduct periodic reviews and possibly tests.
7. Implement intrusion detection and incident response.

Security Policy

Wait! Please don't close this book just because I wrote the words *security policy*. From my experience training analysts and teaching classes on intrusion detection, I know that the last thing an intrusion-detection analyst wants to do is write a security policy. When I teach, if I say "policy," I can see the eyes glaze over instantly. But applying filters to an IDS is kind of neat, right?

Consider that the filter rule set you upload to a sensor is called a policy. This is true for most other commercial systems, and it is well named because these filter sets *are* a security policy. A firewall is just an engine that enforces network policy. So let's recalibrate ourselves not to think of security policy as a pile of paper that took weeks to write and now sits gathering dust. For an intrusion-detection analyst, a security policy is a permission slip, the organization's approval to install dynamic and active policy in security engines, such as firewall and intrusion-detection systems. That's right, policy can serve as permission to do the right thing! At its heart, an IDS is a monitoring device and you should never monitor people without authorization. Policy is the umbrella that covers us when we execute the steps to actually use an IDS effectively.

Industry Practice for Due Care

Both risk and vulnerabilities are discussed further, so for right now, let's focus on due care, or *best practice*. Actually, I abhor the term best practice, perhaps we can use pretty good practice instead. Although every organization has pockets of expertise, no one group has all the answers. As you know, the technology rate of change is so high that none of us can keep up across all the subject areas. The best solution to this problem is to learn what people are doing and what is working for them. One of the greatest joys for me in being affiliated with the SANS Institute has been the consensus projects. Many of them are called *Step by Steps*, such as *Securing Windows 2000—Step by Step*. These are not the work of a single person, but many committed professionals who come together on a project to share their knowledge with others.

Security Infrastructure

Robert Peavy, the Director for Security and Counter-Intelligence for the BMDO, prepared a talk for the Federal Computer Security Conference titled, "Security as a Profit Center—How to Sell Protection to Your Leadership."

As much as anyone I have ever met, Robert Peavy understood that security, good security, requires people. This is at least as true in the intrusion-detection field as any other security domain. Intrusion-detection analysts are front-line troops. They often feel personally responsible for any attacks that penetrate an organization's defenses and compromise systems. They get burned out and there are some turnover issues, especially if they are double-hatted with incident response as well. They need training to remain aware of the latest attacks, but there is limited high-quality training available for them. What does all this mean? It means the wise organization has some depth for the role of intrusion-detection analyst and that takes a security infrastructure to accomplish.

Implementing Priority Countermeasures

As I am writing tonight, I have a great fear. I have run vulnerability scanners at a number of organizations that have both UNIX and now an increasing number of Windows 2000/XP computers. I am shocked by the number of systems that still have well known vulnerabilities as well as the number of systems that still have SNMP; and it has been two weeks since the CERT advisory on SNMP and the PROTOS test kit was released that searched for thousands of problems. Will this be the next rstatd?

Since 1997, an ever-growing number of Sun Solaris UNIX systems continue to be compromised using a buffer exploit against the rstat daemon. Several buffer-overflow exploits are available for DNS, so it certainly could happen. Last week, I scanned a UNIX system being placed outside a firewall. It had the Echo, Chargen, portmap, and r-utilities open. It reminded me of elementary school when we used to put those signs on our classmates saying, "Kick Me."

How do you know whether something is a priority countermeasure in a world where everything is the number-one priority? If an attacker can exploit a vulnerability from the Internet as easily as a hot knife slicing through butter, you have to decide whether you want to fix the problem before or after the system is compromised. I continue to be astounded by the number of organizations that do not have time to do it right, but they do have time to do it over.

Periodic Reviews

Wake up! If you are an intrusion-detection analyst, do not miss this! It is imperative that you review your filter set from time to time. When I worked on the Shadow intrusion-detection project, one of the things I forced myself to do every couple of months was to run the complement of our filter set against a week's worth of data and manually parse through the results looking for anomalies. We must strive to continue to enhance our filter sets to reduce false negatives. If this month's set of filters is picking up exactly the same attacks as three months ago, this is a bad sign.

So, besides setting filters to trap the things one normally ignores, how do we improve our filters? The bugtraq mailing list has proven to be an excellent source of information about new attacks, each of which might need new filters. Once again, if you can find another group doing intrusion detection and striving to do it well, and you can exchange information, as this is another excellent way to stay current.

Conducting periodic reviews is a more general security principle than just watching our filter set, of course. The intrusion-detection analyst also profits by examining the firewall filter set on a fairly regular basis. You might find what I call firewall creep. When the firewall was first installed, it had a fairly tight and orderly ruleset. As time goes on, however, this business interest and that new service become a set of exceptions, or modifiers, to the ruleset. As the rules grow, it becomes harder and harder to validate them. Also, from time to time, the firewall administrator might add in a special rule "just for testing" and forget that it is there. As an analyst you think, "No problem, we are blocking UDP port umpty clutch," when in fact you aren't. The real difficulty is tracking these changes; they happen when you least expect them and over a long period of time, a bit like a low and slow scan. I am starting to think that external scanning services with databases, so you can track what has changed, are a must. If you have never considered one of these, you might want to visit www.qualys.com.

Implementing Incident Handling

An exhaustive discussion of incident handing is beyond the scope of this book, but I want to touch on it as it relates to the model. Have you ever been certified to administer CPR? How confident would you feel if you had to administer CPR 3, 6, 12 months after your training? I call these "gulp" moments. I know I am qualified as an incident handler in some sense, but if I haven't handled an incident in a couple of months, I really feel the rust.

What does incident handling have to do with intrusion detection? A lot! The analyst is likely to be the one to raise the alarm. In organizations with structured incident-handling capabilities, the analyst might be assigned to provide network information to the handlers. In organizations without these structured incident-handling capabilities, the handlers are likely to be you and a system administrator or two. In the "Manual Response" section of Chapter 18, "Automated and Manual Response," read carefully and make notes concerning the things you know you need to do before you have to handle a serious incident. If you do this, it will really help when the gulp moment comes.

Defining Risk

What are the scariest three words an intrusion analyst is likely to hear?

We can't reasonably manage risk if we don't know what risk is. Risk occurs in the domain of uncertainty. If there is no uncertainty, there is no risk. Jumping out of an airplane two miles up without a parachute isn't risky; it is suicide. For such an action, there is a nearly 1.0 probability you will go splat when you hit the ground, or an almost 0.0 probability you will survive. However, there is also risk to jumping out of perfectly good airplanes with parachutes, as several skydivers discover each year.

Let's apply this concept to router protection filters. In many cases, these filters are connection events—that is, they are port number based. If we see a TCP connection at port 25, we identify it as sendmail and take whatever action is prescribed. However, any service can actually run at any port. There is the uncertainty; there is a risk that we will make the wrong decision. With the ephemeral ports (above 1024), this happens often. This uncertainty, coupled with the fact that an adverse action could be exploited (a service we intended to block could penetrate our site), leads to a risk. This is one reason many security professionals think that a filtering router does not serve as a firewall.

An intrusion-detection analyst needs to know the degree of uncertainty for specific filters. As an example, SYN flood filters often have a high degree of uncertainty. If an intrusion-detection analyst continues to report these, there is the potential for an adverse action. The CIRT might begin to trivialize this analyst's reports. Therefore, a filter's degree of uncertainty can result in risk to the analyst and the organization, especially in high-profile cases. Conversely, the expert analyst knows the conditions in which a filter is likely to perform well and also the conditions that lead to failure. These analysts develop the ability to "read between the lines."

Perhaps, the simple issue of reputation doesn't grab you. The same problem, uncertainty of filters, gets more interesting if a site employs automated response techniques.

I want to briefly mention one more potential adverse result of uncertainty with intrusion-detection filters. Several commercial IDS vendors provide lists of their filters. Sometimes, they rate their filters by their probability of producing a false positive and perhaps list conditions known to cause the false positives. This is a great service to the analyst. What if a company lists some of its filters as not having any chance of a false positive—that is, there should be no uncertainty, therefore there is no risk. Then, you dig in and find several of these filters do generate false positives. That realization can undermine your confidence in the company. I know; it happened to me. In fact, I started building test cases for the filters that according to the literature had no chance of a false positive and found several other filters had flaws. Well this really bugged me. Why say it doesn't error if it does? Then, I remembered that I had been issued a brain to keep my heart in check. Why get mad at this company when they have the most complete filter documentation of any commercial IDS? So, I just updated my copy of the filter documentation and sent them traces of my test cases. What do I get for my effort? I know a lot more about which detects to be uncertain about and the conditions likely to cause the filters to error and generate a false positive.

What about the Snort ruleset? It is open and can be examined and has been subjected to exhaustive public review—are these rules uncertain? To be sure, there are great advantages to public review (and you can bet that more than one or two of those rules finds its way into other IDS systems), but the fact that it is open means an attacker can be aware of it and modify the attack just enough to evade the rule.

Oh yeah, the scariest three words to an intrusion-detection analyst. They are when the gruff old decision-maker who has to make a hard call looks you in the eye and asks, "Are you sure?"

Risk

Risk happens. It is ridiculous to say I don't want any risk in a given situation. Rather, we manage risk. I heard on TV once that the space shuttle often has backup systems for its backup systems. A shuttle flight is an exercise in strapping yourself to a rocket and heading for space. Space is an environment where any number of things can kill you: radiation, heat, cold, vacuum, and finally the reentry. If you approach a reentry with too steep an angle, the mistake will crash you; and if your angle is too shallow, it will bounce you into space. That is a lot of risk, which is one of the reasons astronauts get all the free Tang they can drink.

If you really think it through, the whole process is nuts and no sane person would do it. NASA actually has go/no go criteria. If anything is wrong, they do not go ahead with the launch, even though there are backup systems. This is judged an unacceptable risk. Other risks are considered acceptable, like the bit about strapping yourself to a rocket. With any risk, we must decide how we will deal with risk. We have three options for dealing with risk:

- Accept the risk as is.
- Mitigate or reduce the risk.
- Transfer the risk (insurance model).

Accepting the Risk

If we don't install a firewall and we connect to the Internet, in some sense we are as daring as the men and women who bolt themselves onto rockets; what we are doing is risky and we've chosen to accept that risk. If we have information assets of high value and we don't do auditing on these hosts or use some form of intrusion detection, we are again choosing to accept the risk.

The concept of accepting risk is simple enough, but there is another aspect of this we need to consider. The elementary school bus driver who drinks a few too many beers before picking up the kids with his school bus is accepting risk all right, but he is accepting risk he does not have a right to accept. The firewall administrator who was just testing some service and mistakenly left it in the system might have caused the organization to accept a risk that it would not choose to accept. After all, why did it go through the trouble to buy and set up a firewall? One of the interesting problems of information security is that it is quite possible for an individual to accept a risk for an organization that he is not authorized to accept. I would like to illustrate this point with an intrusion-detection story.

Last week, we detected systems initiating file transfers from a site that we monitor. It was just odd enough that we decided to look into it a bit further. When we examined the payload of the ftps, it was clear each of these systems was sending a bit of information about itself. We weren't sure what the information was until we saw a couple instances of "Preferred Customer." It seemed like it had to be the registration field for Microsoft Office products. Our suspicions were quickly confirmed. A member of Human Resources had sent a memo as an attachment to an email message to all the senior managers of the organization. It was the fact they were senior managers that alerted me to further investigate the ftp sessions; these folks didn't even read their own email! They had a secretary screen their mail, print it, and put the important messages in their inbox. The email message sent by Human Resources was infected with a macro virus that sent information out of the organization. It apparently didn't do any serious harm. From an information warfare perspective, however, I was appalled, because it gives a clear potential infection vector into this organization, which could be exploited at a later time. This support employee, by just failing to maintain current virus software, accepted a high degree of risk for the entire organization. As Jimmy Kuo, a research fellow at NAI would say, "You are only as good as your last update." How about one more example?

The same week we detected many more systems initiating file transfers than usual from the same site we monitor. We found five in one day. When we pulled the payload, we found they were all going to the same IP address, the same user ID, and the same password. They were downloading files to the desktop systems. In this case, it turned out to be a shareware program, PKZip. Now, this is no Trojan; this is no sneak attack. A paragraph on the shareware web site stated that when PKZip was installed it came with a bonus component that downloaded ads. None of the five users gave a second thought to what they were actually doing; they just wanted PKZip. So what's the problem? Well, so long as the software is just downloading ads, there isn't a problem. However, keep in mind that many sites configure their firewalls so that if a connection is initiated from the inside, it passes through the firewall without any problems. This means there are several potential attacks from such a behavior.

Trojan Version

We have seen several examples of Trojan versions of legitimate software, such as the Trojan ICQs and Internet Relay Chat (IRCs). The user would not be aware that the program was actually uploading sensitive data from the system, or downloading tools that could be used to attack his organization's network from the inside.

In the same vein, what if the advertisement company hired a malicious individual, or an expert in economic espionage? Think about what he could accomplish with robot code that downloaded arbitrary files every time a system was booted! If this seems like science fiction, consider the use of netbugs (www.bugnosis.org) and spyware that is so common today.

Malicious Connections

There are a number of DNS attacks, but the idea in DNS cache poisoning is to manipulate the DNS system so that the client system goes to a malicious server rather than to the actual server. This is often done when a client answers a question, within a query.

The problem is complex; users of desktop Windows systems do not generally know what connections their systems are making. I honestly didn't know that software programs on my Windows system could connect to the Internet without me clicking on them. Several years back, I bought a software package, McAfee Office, primarily to get the Pretty Good Privacy (PGP) that comes with it, but decided to play with most of the software. One of the programs was called GuardDog, which is a security program for Windows systems. I installed it, and imagine my surprise when I booted my computer and it barked at me, to warn me that one of the programs on my system was trying to connect to the Internet. It was Real Audio; I didn't have the time to set up monitors and traps in my home lab to track it, so I just uninstalled it. Later, it turned out they were collecting information on users. Today, I use application-aware personal firewalls such as ZoneAlarm and Norton Internet Security.

We have gone through some important information, so let's take a second to summarize some points. In the preceding two examples, macro virus and PKZip, users' desktops initiated connections to the Internet without the users knowing about the connections. Both cases have the potential for harm to the organization, although mercifully the only real damage in these examples was my blood pressure shooting through 200. In both cases, one by inaction, one by action, the users make a personal decision to accept a risk that affects the entire organization.

Expanding Our View of Intrusion Detection

Neil Johnson, a researcher and faculty member at George Mason University, presented a really wonderful paper on intrusion detection and recovery against watermarked images at the SANSFIRE 2000 conference. If you spend a lot of time and money creating graphics, you might want to put a copyright seal on these graphics in some way. There are tools to do this. Then, it is possible to use World Wide Web worm technology to search the Internet looking for graphics to see whether your seal turns up on some server that didn't license the graphic. Neil explained this and demonstrated both attacks and the recovery techniques. Now, you might be thinking, what do watermarks have to do with intrusion detection?

As we continue our study of risk and its application in the field of intrusion detection, keep in mind that the dangerous enemy is not the one aimlessly running three-year-old canned attacks! The dangerous enemy is the one who knows what he wants and uses a hard-to-detect technique to get it. *USA Today* ran a story in the wake of 9/11/2001 that Bin Laden used steganography to send messages related to the attack. There are more pragmatic examples. In the case of a graphics company, its images are its crown jewels. To the company, this is the nightmare scenario: an attacker who can remove the proof that it is the owner of the images and possibly even brand the images under another company's name.

Mitigating or Reducing the Risk

What if we decide that even though it is risky to strap ourselves to a rocket, the end result of doing so is worthwhile? Perhaps our objective is greater than just a free drink of Tang; perhaps we have an opportunity to be the first human to set foot on Mars. The enterprise is still very risky, but we are certain that this is something we want to do. In this case, if we aren't foolhardy, what we do is try to find ways to make the endeavor less risky; we reduce the risk.

Have you ever thought about intrusion attacks against laptop computers? Most professionals carry them these days. They often have sensitive information about their organization on them. We have already mentioned information-gathering malicious code, but that can be directed against any system. How specifically are laptops vulnerable to attack? What can you do to mitigate their vulnerability?

Network Attack

If the organization uses Internet service providers (ISPs) to connect for email rather than secured dial-in, there is an opportunity to attack the organization's systems while they are on the net. They are outside the firewall and so the normal screening protections against NetBIOS and other Windows attacks that desktop systems enjoy inside the firewall are not available to them.

Snatch and Run

I really hate putting my laptop on the X-ray machine conveyor belt at airport security checks. If I don't make it through the metal detector, this is a golden opportunity for someone to steal it because I am physically separated from my briefcase in a dynamic, crowded environment. Worse, I only have one shoe on because thanks to the terrorist that tried to blow up the airplane with his shoes, mine are being inspected. Further, if someone does walk off with my laptop if I rush after them, I run the risk of getting shot by the National Guard with the M16s. There are also the situations when I get to my destination: Do I leave it in my hotel room when I go to dinner, or lug it?

I don't know whether you are worried about the information that professionals in your organization put on laptops. After all, it is just stuff such as your design and business plans, sales and marketing information, perhaps a bid work-up or two. I write this tongue and cheek, but if you interview the folks who lug these laptops around, you might find that they do not often perceive the information on them as sensitive and needing protection.

I do know my situation. In writing, teaching, and reviewing I often find myself working with proprietary information. I have signed several Non Disclosure Agreements and have always tried to be careful with that information. If a large security and network company decides I have not protected its information properly, I have to face its army of lawyers (alone). So I am inspired to do the best job I can to protect my laptop; I look for tools to mitigate the risk. Because I know that connecting to the Internet is risky, what are some of the tools that help protect my system?

I have looked at several tools. ZoneAlarm is free for personal use and works well. A lot of my friends swear by BlackIce, and the traces it creates have nice fidelity; but, it has steadily dropped in quality since the company was acquired. I have found the Norton Internet Security tool actually runs on XP, which is a plus. PGP appears to have a personal firewall, but my boss installed it on his XP and lost his ability to connect to the Internet. I went through that with Windows ME when I installed PGP. In both cases the culprit was the PGPNet product. With the ME computer, I thought about it for a while, I knew I needed PGP, but was pretty sure I didn't need ME so I just wiped out that system and rebuilt it as a Windows 2000 system. PGP also comes with PGPdisk that protects sensitive files should the laptop ever be stolen or suffer an intrusion, or you can use the Microsoft Encrypting File System on Windows 2000 and XP. Although PGP has a disk overwrite, data-destruction routine, I find BC Wipe from `http://www.jetico.sci.fi` to be a better tool for my purposes. There, that is my personal example of implementing countermeasures to mitigate risk.

Transferring the Risk

Last week, when I wasn't dealing with outbound ftps, I was dealing with flood damage. The toilet upstairs got stopped up (with a little help from my teenager). The chain that drops the stopper just happened to chink and not drop the stopper flush to seal the water. So, the water filled the toilet bowl and poured over onto the bathroom floor and began its journey in search of sea level. But wait, there's more! This happened to be the day the city decided to flush the fire hydrants, which stirs up all kinds of rust, so it wasn't clear water pouring through the house; it was blood red. When my wife got home, the water was pouring from the dining room chandelier like a fountain. The plaster ceiling had huge cracks and the wooden floor had already warped in two places. The water continued on, accumulating until the ceiling of my wife's sewing room collapsed, spewing rusty water and soggy ceiling tile on her machine and the projects below. My wife called me at work, asking where she should begin. "Turn off the water, move away from the dining room, I'm on my way," I answered.

I use the same incident-handling technique for everything. As I hung up the phone, it hit me that this had to be 20 to 30 thousand dollars worth of damage. I was very sad as I drove home and then busy as we tried to salvage what we could of my wife's sewing room. It wasn't until later at night that it hit me. I have insurance! In fact, I have insurance with a good company, one that has always treated me well. I always knew owning a home had risks that were beyond what I could financially accept. There just aren't good enough home firewalls to expect them to defend against toilets that get jammed and stuck on a day that the city is purging the fire hydrants. Like most homeowners, we had chosen to transfer the risk. So I called Travelers. They came over, were very sympathetic, and said they were going to take care of us. Sure enough, I was only out $100 for the deductible; and the job would have been done except that no one told my wife the five little words you never say to a contractor. Still, even after a "while you are at it," it only cost me an extra $2,500 and now I have crown moldings on the ceiling, something I am sure I always wanted.

So how does this notion of transferring risk apply to information assurance and intrusion detection? In the first place, there is a direct correspondence. Several agencies, including Lloyds and IBM, are now offering hacker insurance. They usually require the organization to do its part before insuring them, and their part is likely to include firewalls, vulnerability assessments, and intrusion detection, at least it would if I were offering such insurance.

We have discussed uncertainty and how it applies to risk. We have proposed that some risks we are willing to accept (whether or not we are authorized to do so), and other risks we are not willing to accept. In the last case, we need to either mitigate the risk or transfer it. Now, we need to deal with the issue of what agent is going to potentially do us harm; we call this the threat. Vulnerabilities are the gateways by which threats manifest themselves.

Defining the Threat

"Umm, I wouldn't go there if I were you".

"Why not?"

"Bad things will happen to you if you go there."

"What bad things?"

"Bad things."

This is not a compelling scenario, true? Most of us would not be persuaded by it. Imagine giving a similar pitch to management: If you don't fund an intrusion-detection system, bad things will happen to us.

We need to define and quantify bad things:

- What things?

- How bad?

- How likely they are to occur or repeat?

- How do you know?

- What support do you have for your answer?

So for each threat we can define and enumerate, we need to answer these questions.

How Bad—Impact of Threat

In the end, risk is evaluated in terms of money. This is true even if life is lost; in the case of loss of life, it might be a lot of money. For any threat we have defined, we take the value of the assets at risk and multiply that by how exposed they are. This yields the expected loss if we were to get clobbered by the threat. This is called the *single loss expectancy* (SLE) and the formula to calculate SLE is as follows:

```
Asset value × exposure factor = SLE
```

The exposure factor is an estimate, ranging from 0 percent to 100 percent of our loss of the asset. Consider the following calculation, the threat of a nuclear bomb exploding just above a small town whose total assets are worth 90 million dollars:

```
Example Nuclear bomb/small town ($90M × 100% = $90M)
```

Now let's bring it home. I have already mentioned that when I have conducted vulnerability scans of sites with UNIX computers I have found a number of systems with the tooltalk vulnerability. Can we apply this formula to these? First, we have to define the threat. Suppose we are a Class C site. The threat is a malicious attacker who gains root, exploits any trust models, encrypts the file systems, and holds the computers ransom for $250,000. The attacker scans the net and finds six vulnerable systems. The buffer-overflow attack quickly yields root. After exploiting the trust models of these systems, our attacker is able to root compromise four additional systems and therefore encrypt the disks of 10 UNIX workstations. So when the CEO of your organization comes in to work on Monday, his secretary finds the following in his email box:

```
To: John Smith, CEO
From: Dark Haqr
Subject: Rans0m
I 0wN U L^m3r  It wi11 c0st u a kwart3r Mi11i0n t0 g3t ur dAtA b^k.
```

What is our SLE at this point? We could say $250,000, but it might not be quite that simple. If there were backups, we might be able to restore from backups and just lose a day or two of work. If there aren't backups (please, please ensure there are always backups), we have a more interesting problem. At this point, we don't actually know if we will ever get the encryption key. The threat is that we will not. So, the value of the assets is the value of the data on these systems, plus the time to rebuild them from scratch, plus the loss from the downtime. How do we calculate the value of the data?

The value of data can be approximated by the burdened labor rate of the people who have been working on the system for the life of the project(s) on the system. To keep the numbers simple, we will consider each of the UNIX systems to be a professional's desktop. They are working on a single project that is two years along and they each make $60k, but their burdened rate (benefits, office space, and so on) is $100k. Ten people at $100k, for two years is $2 million dollars. What is our degree of exposure? It's 100 percent; the files are already encrypted. So, we quickly see that paying the quarter million and keeping our big mouths shut and not involving law enforcement is probably in our best interest. So in this scenario, we pay the money, get the key, and get back to work and everyone is happy. Now, what happens if we don't fix the vulnerability?

Frequency of Threat—Annualized

Annualized loss expectancy (ALE) occurs when a threat/vulnerability pairing can reasonably be expected to be consummated more than once in a given year. In a brief given to the Joint Computer Security Conference in March 2000, Dr. Gene Schultz postulated this might be an inadequate measurement. Given the nuclear bomb example in our small town, this can't happen; indeed, we drop as many bombs as we want on the town, but we aren't likely to cause any further damage. ALEs fit very well into models such as shoplifting, returns in the mail-order business, and defaults on loans. In a competitive environment (e-business, for example), however, how many ALEs events can you survive? Consider the case of distributed denial of service. If your web storefront is shut down four or five times in a month, some of that business goes to your competition. How do you recover from that? How do ALEs factor into information assurance and intrusion detection?

I mentioned earlier that intrusion-detection technology is easily applied to unauthorized use detection. I also think that this can be a waste of skilled intrusion-detection analysts. But, there is a powerful business argument that says this is a very wise use of the system and personnel. As we work through the following example, note that even though I kept the numbers ridiculously low, we still ended up with some serious money, enough to pay the burdened rate of those entry-level professionals the organization says it can't afford. Use the following formula to calculate ALE:

```
SLE x Annualized rate occurrence = Annual loss expectancy
```

This is nothing more than our SLE times the number of times it could be expected to occur in a year. This is why we ended the encrypted file system example with the question, "What happens if we don't fix the tooltalk vulnerability?" Dark Haqr takes our money, goes out and buys a Beamer, his friends inquire of the means of his sudden fortune, and we get to play the game again.

Let's do a common example: Web surfing on the job rather than working. First, we need to calculate an SLE. Say we have 1,000 employees, 25 percent of which waste an hour per week surfing:

```
$50/hr x 250 = $12,500
```

To calculate the ALE we observe, they do it every week except when on vacation:

```
$12,500 x 50 = $625,000
```

You can see why an organization might want to leverage its investment in intrusion-detection equipment and personnel to curb unauthorized use. Again, I kept the numbers much lower than what I have observed to be the case at many sites. Also, in the real world, the waste doesn't tend to be spread evenly across employees, but rather is localized in a small number of employees. If these employees can be identified and canned (after all, if they weren't working, they probably aren't really needed), there are a number of potential savings for the organization.

Recognition of Uncertainty

How reliable are the answers from these SLE and ALE calculations? If we are going to make decisions based on these calculations, we need to know how reliable they are. I spent a long afternoon with a gentleman who was trying to convince me to invest a lot of money in an intrusion-detection framework. This thing would do everything but wax your car: it had sensor fusion, automated correlation of vulnerabilities with incoming attacks, and even factored in virus reports in a very cool graphics display. "Best of all," he says, "it has an expert system."

He continued talking and I nodded from time to time, but I was already gone. I couldn't help but remember phrases from my artificial intelligence (AI) classes. How about this one, "The reason expert systems don't live up to their promise is that the rules we are putting in them aren't very good. The knowledgeable engineer interviews the experts in the field, but what we are learning is that the experts aren't very expert." Here is another, "One of the biggest problems with AI is when the system doesn't know what it doesn't know. In that respect, AI systems are exactly like people."

When we calculate SLEs and ALEs, we need to be sensitive to what we don't know, to the places we fudge the numbers, to the cases where the models just don't fit. "No problem," you might be thinking. "I have no intention of calculating SLEs." Umm, maybe you do something similar, but you do it in your head without a process or documentation.

I work in an organization that monitors networks, for instance, although I guess that doesn't come as a surprise. I was listening to a new employee briefing and they were told very clearly that pornography was forbidden and that if caught, the responsible employees would probably be escorted out the door and fired. Let's jump into the mind of one of these young new employees. Maybe he is curious to see whether the organization can detect him if he misspells a sexually oriented word on a search engine, or uses oblique references. The answer is probably yes. But then again, he might think, "Hmmmm, but I already know they don't have a sense of humor, the SLE is just too high." Well, maybe he wouldn't use those exact words, but you get my drift.

Might I share one more example of uncertainty in answers with you? In mid-February 1999, I attended a working group for *Presidential Decision Directive 63* (PDD 63). The goal was to get the 50 or so top researchers (and me) to consider four problem areas necessary for allocating approximately half a billion dollars in research money for intrusion detection and information assurance. One of the tracks was called anomalous behavior, which is Washington D.C. speak for the trusted insider problem. So, we all worked away and then presented our results. The anomalous group presented a finding that research had been funded 100 times more for detecting outsiders than insiders. Someone asked, "What study did you find that ratio in, and what was your source?" The answer from our distinguished scientists was "We made it up, but it's close."

Risk Management Is Dollar Driven

If you approach management and say you need $10,000 for an intrusion-detection system, they might want a bit more information. It is a good sign if they ask how much time it will take to run such a system; it shows they are listening and thinking clearly. A good manager knows the hardware and software costs are the tip of the iceberg and wants to get a handle on the whole picture. Managers want to understand how it fits into the business model. Risk management (and that includes intrusion detection) is dollar driven.

Whenever we are faced with a risk that is unsavory to us, we begin to wonder what can be done to reduce or mitigate the risk. As we pick our countermeasures, we should try to calculate what they would cost on a yearly basis. When you make a proposal to management, people really like it if you can give the cost breakdown and even an option or two. Remember those SLEs and ALEs; this is when they really come in handy. The countermeasure will cost some money, but look at the risk metrics!

Here is a very important aspect of pitching risk management to the organization's management: Don't nickel and dime. The bigger picture you can paint of all the risks, vulnerabilities, countermeasures, and get-well plans, the more receptive they are likely to be.

How Risky Is a Risk?

I really like to hear host-based intrusion-detection sales folks give presentations. It has always been an uphill battle, and in these days of personal firewalls where anyone that wants host protection can get it for $40 to $60, it is becoming comical! The sales people get going on the insider threat and play that issue like a harp with one string. They have to do this; they are fighting a perception problem, or perhaps it would be better to state this as an education problem. What they are trying to do is get the potential customer to rate one risk higher than another. If you think about it, this is a common sales tactic.

In Virginia, they don't get much snow, but at the beginning of winter, the auto ads are really pushing four-wheel drive vehicles. Never mind the fact that they cost more, are more mechanically complex, and get fewer miles per gallon than two wheel drives; if you buy one, you don't have to be afraid of the snow. We can learn two things from this: to consider as many risks as possible and to keep things in perspective. We want to be able to rank risk. There are two basic approaches to ranking risk: the quantitative and qualitative approach.

Quantitative Risk Assessment

The goal of this approach is to figure out what the risk is numerically. The most common way to do this is asset valuation using our friends the SLEs and ALEs. This is not worth doing for each desktop system in your organization! It can be a very effective tool at the organization level, however, and the numbers are not that hard to dig up. To calculate asset value (AV), use this formula:

```
AV = Hardware + Commercial software + Locally developed software + Data
```

Your comptroller should be able to produce your organization's hardware and software budget and actuals in a matter of minutes. The value of locally developed software is usually a bit trickier. You have to take the burdened cost of everyone paid to develop software for your organization for some number of years. Data is where it gets interesting! Isn't it true that almost everyone in your organization uses a computer? If so, the value of the data is what your organization has paid to keep those people in front of computers for whatever is a reasonable life cycle for the data. (I usually use three years.) This is going to be a big number! It shouldn't take longer than an hour to hammer out a reasonable value for your organization's information assets. This can be a really good thing to have available if you need to persuade management to fund something, or to quit doing something really risky.

Qualitative Risk Assessments

You can also apply a checklist approach to ranking risk. Generally, you have a list of threats, and you rank each item as a high, medium, or low risk. This works much better at the system level than the organization level. There are examples of a modified quantitative method and several checklist style qualitative method risk assessments at http://www.nswc.navy.mil/ISSEC/Form/AccredForms/index.html.

The accreditation "part II" forms at the web site are for the various architectures (Windows 95, NT, Macintosh, UNIX) are the qualitative method examples. The SCORE checklists at www.sans.org/SCORE are another resource. Finally, the Center for Internet Security www.cisecurity.org has a number of tools that you can run to assess your security posture. These tools pretend to be quantitative because they give you a numeric score; but if you look under the hood, you will quickly realize they are qualitative.

Why They Don't Work

In theory, both approaches to risk assessment work fine. In practice, they do not work so well. This is because we have a natural tendency not to tell the truth, because if we do show there is a vulnerability with a high risk, we have to do something to fix it. Therefore in practice, people who are performing a qualitative assessment come up with numbers that are really big. They know they cannot afford that much risk, so they do the assessment on smaller and smaller chunks until they get it down to the single desktop system, and that is silly! Guess which box (high, medium, or low risk) folks doing a quantitative assessment tend to pick. And if everything is a low risk, why bother?

Summary

From the time of the Cuban Missile Crisis to the fall of the Berlin Wall, if you were in the Department of Defense and you wanted money, the strategy was to go to Congress and say, "The Russians are coming." Despite the way TV and the movies portray the legislative branch, those folks aren't dumb and a lot of them have been on the hill for a long time. So at some point, they start pointing out that they funded this and they funded that all because the Russians were coming. Why hasn't that fixed the problem?

Now, we are doing it all over again to stop terrorism, or for the purposes of this book, to stop cyber-terrorism. If you don't need your year's worth of food and water and your thousand rounds of ammo for each gun to survive hackers, you certainly are going to need these things to survive the coming cyber-war. Sigh. This will work to extract money and attention for a season, but it is poor practice. This chapter has covered a sound organizational security model. We have looked at tools to assess and prioritize risk. We have a foundation for discussing what we do and why we do it with management. The next chapter discusses responses to attacks and system compromise. When we have these tools solidly in hand, we can discuss how the hackers are coming and how to survive a cyber-war in a reasonable manner.

18

Automated and Manual Response

WHEN WE WERE LEARNING HOW TO ANALYZE network traces, we discussed stimulus and response in detail. Now, we use the same concept but apply it at the organizational level as we consider the defensive responses available to us. The stimulus will generally be a "successful" attack or attack attempt. A successful attack, if detected, invokes an incident-handling procedure. How do we define a successful attack? In the vein of "any landing you can walk away from is a good one," we can say "any attack that causes us to take action above our normal filtering is a successful attack." Do you agree? If not, keep in mind that if we respond in any non-automated, non-normal way, it has to cost us resources. What I would like to do is offer three attack examples. Take a look at each of these and consider whether they are successful attacks:

- **Ping sweep.** A series of ICMP echo requests from a party conducting reconnaissance. Ping sweeps are usually launched from outside our intranet or autonomous systems to internal subnet broadcast addresses. They might be detected by a sensor such as a firewall or intrusion detection system.

- **Disk-based survey.** An employee receives a letter with a disk. If he places the disk in his computer, answers all the questions, and mails the disk back, he receives a free T-shirt.

- **TCP port 53 connections.** An Internet company that produces banner ads for web pages is observed pinging systems that have gone to these web pages and attempted to initiate connections to TCP port 53 on these systems.

What do you think? I would say that if your perimeter router or firewall blocks ICMP echo requests, the ping sweep is not a success. I have heard folks assert that this is just a reconnaissance probe, not an attack; but the question is, does it cost you resources? I was looking at a network trace recently in which the attacker was going after only actual live systems. It is kind of scary when they know what they are looking for.

The disk-based survey? Certainly, this is a successful attack. Most employees would never know which files were scanned or added to their system, but it is certainly true the attacker gets the benefit from the information the employee types into the survey—and your organization is footing the bill. As a security professional, you should inform your organization's employees to throw these disk-based surveys straight into the trash, or if they must, take them home to fill them out.

The simple DNS lookups? DNS queries happen all the time, and it is hard to determine which queries might be reconnaissance as opposed to the function call **gethostbyaddr** that occurs whenever someone is web surfing. However, the HTTP protocol headers contain a lot of information about the client that is web surfing. Some of the fields include the following:

- Host operating system.
- Version of the browser being used.
- The last web server visited. This is the referrer field.

Web servers routinely collect this type of information for marketing purposes. The collected data helps the webmasters tune the look and feel of the pages as well as phrases that web clients are looking for. However, this information can also be used to collect information about the web clients. If you add DNS, and possibly netstat type information, you begin to compile an incredible amount of information about a given IP address, or IP address range.

You might notice that I did not use any "gulpers" for the examples (with the possible exception of the ping sweep; however, these are not script kiddie examples either). I am very impressed with the philosophy of Escrima, a martial art. The idea is to take whatever targets your adversary offers and cut them apart (literally, knives are the primary weapon) a piece at a time. This is a fundamental principal of information warfare. Folks are constantly employing a wide variety of techniques against your organization, taking whatever is vulnerable. This is why a sound protection scheme, including defense in depth and automated response, is so important.

Automated Response

This section examines architectural issues of automated response, mechanisms available to us, and the most popular implementation—PortSentry—as well as the automated response capability of personal firewalls. Obviously, the cheapest and easiest response is the automated response. This form of incident handling should be widely practiced and, if done wisely and with care, is safe. There are a couple of gotchas we will address from the start. Because intrusion-detection systems have a problem with producing false positives, you might err and respond against a site that never attacked you. The good news is that you could take a number of passive defenses. These passive responses I describe do not cause harm. You would have to have rocks in your head to hit a suspected attacker back with an automated exploit due to the potential for error from IP spoofing and false positives.

The other problem is that if your attacker determines that you have automated response on, he might be able to use this against you. Imagine setting up the equivalent of an Echo-Chargen feedback loop involving two sites' auto-responding intrusion-detection systems and a couple of spoofed addresses. Or, at a major deadline, the attacker could target a site with spoofed attacks from its partner/customer/supplier addresses and cause the firewalls to isolate from one another so that the deadline cannot be met.

Architectural Issues

Because network-based intrusion-detection systems are generally passive, just tapping the bit stream, they do not usually respond to an attacker's stimulus. However, many commercial implementations of intrusion detection have the capability to connect directly to the firewall and this combination allows for automated response. In fact, hogwash, a firewall implementation based on Snort, actually integrates the two functions, and there are similar commercial products under development. The DMZ or Internet connection is an obvious place to implement automated response, but there are other very effective options that include internal firewalls and the host systems themselves.

Response at the Internet Connection

The closer to your site's Internet connection that you apply automated response, the more effective it will be; but the risk of harm to the organization coming from spoofing and manipulation also rises quickly. A primary reason for this is that your Internet connection is generally unfiltered—that is, after all, where you put your firewall and filtering router. This means these devices can be hit with any possible address (spoofed or not), 65,535 TCP ports with any number of flag and options combinations, 65,535 UDP ports again with options, ICMP, fragmentation, and all of the IP protocol types. This is a lot of space to defend against. Now a "deny all that is not specifically allowed" policy will prevent the overwhelming bulk of these possibilities from penetrating your perimeter, but the risk comes when we try to interpret all this using an automated policy. The bottom line, though, is that in the face of a rapidly increasing threat, and with the need to respond in the time it takes to evaluate a single packet, automated response is probably going to be widely implemented. And because you get the biggest bang for your buck by putting the capability near the Internet connection, we will probably continue to see solutions like hogwash and Tippingpoint's UnityOne (`www.tippingpoint.com`).

Internal Firewalls

Automated response using internal firewalls is much safer because the traffic an internal firewall receives generally is at least partially filtered. Also, you know your policy better. If you are defending five machines or so with your internal firewall, you have a pretty good idea with whom those hosts should be talking and on what ports. Of course, the catch is the automated response covers a lot less area. And there are cost issues both for hardware and software and also administration. The good news is a number of appliance and near-appliance devices need almost no configuration. The DSL and cable modem revolution has created a huge market for these, and there are a number of options including appliance products from Cisco, Linksys, Netgear, and Symantec. I really like the little $500 PIX, but try putting your hands on one; they seem to be permanently sold out. Because Network Address Translations (NATs) are so effective at preventing attacks and the lower end devices run about $250, there is no reason not to deploy them throughout your organization. If people do widely deploy boxes like that, I might have to find a new line of work. In fact, I am already working on my delivery: "Would you like a hot apple pie with that order?"

Host-Based Defenses

Automated response on the host is clearly where you get the minimum bang for the buck, but this is widely practiced, and the risk from spoofing is much lower than a perimeter solution. The industry trend is twofold: internal appliance type firewalls and host-based firewall defenses. A number of people, especially in university environments, depend entirely on software such as Psionic's PortSentry for their UNIX systems. PortSentry blocks an offending host from making any further connections and even drops the route so that the host cannot get back to try again. The PC world has a large number of personal firewall solutions. Because this is an automated response chapter, we should mention the amazing BackOfficer Friendly, www.nfr.com/products/bof/index.html. This is far more than a personal firewall! Perhaps we could consider it a honeypot or even an active defense solution. If you have a Windows system and want to get started learning about automated response, download this and give it a look. The only downside is that it hasn't really been updated as the threats increase. Imagine what would have happened if they had managed to incorporate LaBrea technology early in the Code Red days! The good news is these host-based defense systems are very effective, becoming more prevalent, and are fairly easy to install, configure, and maintain. Why do people depend so heavily on these programs? Often, they are security-conscious administrators at sites with no filtering from the Internet whatsoever! There are four main sources for unfiltered addresses:

- Cable modems and DSL
- Commercial organizations that don't care
- Universities in the name of academic freedom
- Connecting while on travel such as at an Ethernet equipped hotel

The cable modem and DSL world is going to be an ever-increasing threat to site defenders, so maybe I don't have to worry about pushing hot apple pies on the fast-food drive-through after all. I have instrumented a number of cable modem connections and tend to receive between about 5 and 20 probes per day. Hundreds of people are hooking up to cable and DSL everyday, and most of them have unprotected systems. This is something we became very aware of in 2001 with Code Red, nimda, and Leaves. Most cable modem style defenses such as NATs and host-based firewalls do not implement automated response; but it isn't a bad trade: intrusion protection for intrusion detection.

Commercial organizations that are inept or don't care and connect to the Internet will not survive the transition to an information economy. Yet, a surprising number of sites either do not have a firewall or have inadequate perimeter protection. When you connect your organization to the Internet, you will be probed and tested. If your systems are not combat ready and can be seen from the Internet, they will fall. If you are lucky, you get the playful sorts of attackers, but even then your system will likely be used to attack and probe others. A commercial organization with a compromised system could share a far worse fate if the attackers decide to use it to acquire corporate secrets. As we suggested earlier, if I were in business, in addition to a main firewall, I would strongly consider the use of internal appliance type firewalls. After you get inside the perimeter of many facilities, they have neither detection nor protection capability. Key hosts would do well to have system level protections.

The interesting battleground that I have been watching for several years is the university world. Many of these sites have no firewalls or filtering at all. Already, I have seen departments set up their own firewalls in universities that don't want to put one at the front door. And, system protections are popular with proactive administrators. A fully open Internet connection is an archaic and brain-dead throwback to academic freedom, and I doubt the practice will survive another four years. It will be fun to watch. The academics that claim all packets must be free to travel the Internet will probably back down soon enough. Just wait until their department's budget suffers a 50 percent cut due to the university losing a major lawsuit brought by a dot.com that lost significant revenue when the university's systems were compromised and used in an attack.

Connecting while on travel requires a bit of thinking. I often carry a small Linksys router hub with me, so that I have two layers of defense: the NAT and my personal firewall. Also, it allows my wife and I to be online at the same time; when you are used to being online for 14 hours a day, you aren't very good at taking turns to check your mail. The NAT allows me to mitigate the risk to my relationship and my important documents—what could be sweeter?

I understand that you might have reservations about implementing automated response. I try to set things up in class and show a number of intrusion detects from December 24 and 25 and comment that Christmas is a special time of the year. Then, when we come to the automated response discussion, I point out that during the Christmas and Easter vacations people are normally not around, but systems are still up. This can be an excellent time to experiment with automated response at the Internet connection. Because very little work is getting done, especially at Christmas, this is a fairly low-risk time to take your automated response systems out for a spin and see what they are capable of.

Next, let's work through our response options. It is a good idea to keep in mind the previous discussion about where the analysis and response functions are best accomplished.

Throttling

This is a smart response to port scans, host scans, SYN floods, and mapping techniques. The idea is to begin to add delay as a scan or SYN flood is detected; and if the activity continues, continue increasing the delay. This can frustrate several script-driven scans such as ping mapping to 0 and 255 broadcast addresses because they have to rely on timing for the UNIX/non-UNIX target discrimination. Enterasys and Cisco both have rate limiting. In fact, any device you can interface with that supports Quality of Service should be usable in this fashion.

Throttling can also be done at the protocol level. For UDP, the IDS could forge a source quench. For TCP, if the traffic goes through a proxy firewall, the outbound interface could send a small window size. I would avoid using the LaBrea trick of a window size of 1. Attackers will be looking for that next time around, but 5, for instance, will drastically slow down the attack.

Drop Connection

Dropping the connection is straight out of the string-matcher handbook. When I say "connection," of course I am talking TCP primarily, but the same general effect for UDP can occur using a shun (as discussed in the next section).

The attacker establishes a connection to an active port. Then he sends the packet, or packets (for intrusion-detection systems such as Cisco Secure IDS or Snort with packet re-assembly capability), that contains the attack string, or exploit. This is the point of great danger for a vulnerable system. The IDS detects the string and orders the firewall to drop the connection. Now, you might have a compromised system, but the attacker can't make use of the compromise directly. In the case of a buffer overflow, the victim computer is now running whatever code was beyond the command length and is probably running it as root. If it is a grappling hook type program (a small telnet daemon running on some predefined port), dropping the connection might only buy you a few seconds.

Shun

I am going to continue the attack just described with the shun technique, and then discuss why shun might be one of the most important automated and manual techniques at your disposal.

As the attack progresses, you have a new process running as root that has opened up a telnet daemon or sent back an X Window or whatever open door into our victim system the attacker has chosen. Dropping the connection does not help, because he is already planning to initiate another connection; or in the case of an X Window, you have initiated the connection to him from our side. Shunning might buy some relief. When you shun, you do not accept any more traffic to or from the offending IP address. This is a good technique and can be executed on just the offending host or on its subnetwork. A capability to look for whether you want to implement shun is a "never shun" file (also called a white list); you can place the addresses of your customers and suppliers in this file. This protects you from an attacker being able to spoof these addresses with some obvious script kiddie attack just to isolate you from the systems you do business with.

Shunning does not help you if the attacker is using two address families, which is fairly common. My friend Pedro Vasquez sent me a trace from Brazil with a DNS buffer-overflow coordinated attack that did exactly this. The attack came from one host and the X Window was displayed to another host. Just because shunning does not help you in every case, however, doesn't mean you shouldn't employ the technique.

Proactive Shunning

It turns out that a number of Internet service providers and even whole countries cannot, or will not, manage their hosts. Over time, as you have been doing intrusion detection, you come to realize that an incredible number of the attacks that you and your friends deal with (you are sharing data, right?) come from the same network addresses. Why play with fire? Eventually, they will find a way to burn you! Block them. Let me take this a step further: be willing to block them at the two octet or 16-bit mask. Be willing to block a whole country. Nobody is getting arrested for hacking, and it doesn't look like that is going to change any time soon. If countries that will not control their "research networks" start to be marginalized and are unable to reach large parts of the Internet, however, they will have to come to the table and talk turkey.

We have been experimenting with this on the SANS web server, and one single ISP that has open proxies has been the source network of more attacks than any other address group. We shunned them for about two months; they wrote and made promises, so we let them back into the site and within a day, we were attacked again. We are considering a permanent ban at this point.

Islanding

Islanding is the auto-response of last resort. The idea is, if a sufficient number of attacks occur over a time period (usually during time periods during which no analyst is on duty), the intrusion-detection system sends a command to an X10 or similar logic-controlled relay and drops the power to the router. The result of this is isolation of the site from the Internet. Although there is serious potential for a denial-of-service condition, this can be a reasonable strategy for three-day weekends at high-security sites. This capability can be hacked together with a few lines of code with any intrusion-detection system that issues SNMP traps. On second thought, maybe that SNMP trap idea is not so smart. Automated response does have a risk of self-inflicted denial of service. Only do something like this if you are willing to have the deadfall occur on any given "red-alert" alarm condition.

SYN/ACK

Suppose the intrusion-detection system knew the ports that a site blocked with its firewall or filtering router. Further, suppose that every time the IDS detected a TCP SYN packet to one of these blocked ports, it answered back with a forged SYN/ACK. The attackers would think they were finding lots of potential targets; however, all they would be getting is false positives. If you think about it, the latest generation of scanning tools has caused a lot of problems for the intrusion-detection community with their decoy capabilities. This would be a great way to answer back. I finally got to see this in action. Some friends of mine got a Raptor firewall. This works great. The attacker completes the three-way handshake and thinks he has a victim. He even sends data with the lone ACK, so you can see what he is up to.

Reset

This is the so-called Reset kill or as the Snort folks say, session sniping. I have serious reservations about this technique. The Reset kill can tear down someone else's TCP connection, and I have seen commercial IDS systems fire these kills based on false positives. The idea is if you see a TCP connection that has been established and the IDS detects a signature that requires action, you forge two Resets and send one to both sides to blow off the connection. It used to be possible simply to smack the initiating host, but attackers are learning to ignore Resets. This isn't used all that often, although it is available in Snort and commercial intrusion-detection systems.

Honeypot

An advanced site, in conjunction with throttling, can use its router to direct the attacker to a specially instrumented system called a honeypot. The honeypot could be used as a stand-in for the targeted host. We also have used honeypots with static addresses as stand-ins for internal hosts that have become "hot."

Every once in a while, a host that you are protecting will suddenly stir up a lot of interest and you will keep seeing probes and exploit attempts directed to it. In such a situation, a fun course of action is to change both its name and IP address and install a honeypot in its place. However, the most common use we have at www.incidents.org for honeypots is to figure out what the attackers are doing by catching their attack in a honeypot. I have tried three types of honeypots: a proxy system, the *Deception Tool Kit* (DTK), and an "empty" computer, the Honeynet approach.

Proxy System

During 1996 and 1997, I did a lot of research into hacker technology. The goal of the project was to collect as many exploit tools as possible. I took a Sun computer running SunOS 4.1.3, patched it as best I could, and installed the TIS toolkit. The system was named cray3. I copied an /etc/motd from a Unicos system and did everything I could to make it look like a cray. Thank goodness this was before TCP fingerprinting.

I used the TIS toolkit for the target services, ftp, telnet, SMTP, and so forth. Finally, I compiled Internet Relay Chat (IRC). The idea was to spend time on the hacker IRC channels, exchange code, get people to attack my system, and collect the techniques they used. There was only one small problem. I had never been on IRC! I knew that if I didn't do it right that I would show up like I had five legs and a tail. So what to do? I decided to start in a channel other than #hack. So I tried #thirtysomething. I have never been good at flirting, so I ended up wasting hours watching words fly by on the screen.

Next, I decided to try #Jesus. I figured church people would be nice to me. BZZZZT, they kicked me off within 10 minutes. I was really crushed!

Finally, in frustration, I signed on to the #abortion channel because that was what was about to happen to my project. They were some great folks, although strongly polarized on both sides of the issue. Best of all, they were willing to let a newbie learn to chat. After a week or so practicing my social graces, I entered #hack, but there was just one last little hitch. We had agreed that any hint of entrapment was outside project parameters and because I was doing this for the DoD, I found myself on #hack with a .mil source address. Well, that brought back memories of elementary school and "Kick Me" signs taped to my back; kick me they did.

However, I won a TCP trivia challenge or two, and after a while, we managed to get things going. It was a lot of fun, and they couldn't resist attacking the .mil system, so we were able to collect a lot of fun data.

DTK

The Deception Tool Kit was authored by Fred Cohen and is available at `http://all.net/dtk`.

It is written in a combination of Perl and C and emulates a large number of services. DTK is a state machine, can emulate virtually any service, and comes ready to do so out of the box for a number of them. It used to be pretty easy to compile and set up. As it has been improved to be more realistic, however, it has started to become a bear to build.

This state machine approach is essentially what BackOfficer Friendly is, and as I write this Marcus Ranum is writing another honeypot for SANS students to try.

Empty System

Nothing looks more like UNIX than UNIX, or Windows NT than Windows NT. So in some sense, the perfect honeypot is just a system that is a little older and slower and has a smaller disk (the smaller the better, in case you loose the bubble). Then, you instrument the heck out of the system and collect information as folks try to exploit it. This has been taken to near science by the Honeynet team. Incidents.org is a member of the Honeynet alliance and has a vmware-, www.vmware.org, based Honeynet with a firewall, intrusion detection system, and a couple of running operating systems all running on a single machine. Vmware is the closest thing to magic I have ever seen. Lately, there have been some troubling indications that some of the honeypots and Honeynets on the Internet have been identified and their IP addresses are being passed around in the underground so that they avoid these systems.

Honeypot Summary

Honeypots are an advanced technique. They can be low yield for the effort one has to expend. On the other hand, if you block with your firewall or filtering router, you never get to collect the attack if you filter. A honeypot enables you to collect the attack. If you don't have a hot system, the best thing to do is set your honeypot up as either your DNS, web, or email relay system. These systems are routinely added to attackers' shopping lists. The good news is you can collect attacks; the bad news is you collect the same attacks over and over again.

Manual Response

Intrusion-detection analysts often serve a double role as lead for incident handling, or as a handling team member. *Please* get one thing straight in your head right now: You are going to take a hit. Between the outsider threat from the Internet, the insider threat, and the malicious code threat, you are definitely going to take a hit. Analysts sometimes get in a mindset that they are responsible to protect the organization. You can't! We don't expect rescue-squad workers to ensure no accidents occur on I-95, right? We just ask them to help in a professional manner after the accident has occurred. Consider what I have said carefully. I have led a large intrusion-detection team with many sites and have seen several analysts develop a mindset that they are personally responsible to make sure no attacks get through.

If we are going to take a hit, a system compromise can't be the end of the world. Rather, the point is to deal with it as effectively and efficiently as possible. Because there might be some stress involved, we want a clear, well-defined process to follow. Think about CPR; they have their pithy acronym, ABC. The ABCs of CPR are as follows:

- **Airway.** Make sure it is clear.
- **Breathing.** Are they?
- **Cardiac.** Beating or not beating?

I found the following six-step process in a government publication in 1995. I have been working to refine this model ever since. The six steps are as follows:

- Preparation
- Identification
- Containment
- Eradication
- Recovery
- Lessons learned

This chapter doesn't discuss preparation or identification; after all, most of this book is devoted to preparation and identification.

Containment

In incident handling, you learn to maintain a reasonable pace; if you hurry, you make mistakes and that can be costly. There is one place to really move out, however, and that is containment. It is better to deal with two affected computers than four and better to deal with one compromised workgroup than a whole Windows domain. Good incident-handling teams can work in parallel. This is really important in cases in which multiple systems might be involved. As soon as the data has come in, I just make a copy, circle the addresses I need a team member to handle, and hand him the paper. Usually, I don't have to say more than my trademark "take good notes people, good notes."

The first thing to do in containment is to start reducing network connectivity.

Freeze the Scene

My first course of action is to pick up the phone and call the person nearest the system console. The language in the following section has been developed over years of hard-knocks experience. You are a technical person; the person you are calling on the telephone might not be. Also, as he realizes there is a problem, he might be under some stress. Of course, you will develop your own scripts and techniques, but I call the individual with a suspected problem and say:

Please take your hands off the keyboard and step away from the computer.

Thank you. Now, in the back of the computer there is a network connection, please find it and remove it from the computer.

My name is Stephen Northcutt, what is your name?

Pleased to meet you _____, and where is your office?

Sure, we know where that is. _____, can I get your phone number and any other office phones that you know?

You have done a fantastic job. We'll be right there; now do you have a fax machine? Great; while the team is on its way, I am going to fax you a set of instructions. _____, we need your help and I would appreciate it if you would start as soon as your receive the incident-handling guide. Can you tell me what operating system the computer is?

These are critically important lines. The trick is to say as few words as possible to get the point across. However the "noise" or non-content words such as please, thank you, and fantastic, are very important; we need to de-stress the situation if possible. Despite the attackers, I keep learning the hard way that our biggest danger is what we do to our evidence and ourselves. I am also working on my voice inflection. I don't have a really commanding, powerful voice, so I try to speak with authority, slower than my normal pace, and try to project kindness and empathy.

Sample Fax Form

Security Office @UR Organization
On Site Computer Incident Response Form
Revision 2.1.1
Date: Time: Printed Full Name:

Thank you for notifying the security department of this incident and
agreeing to help. Please do not touch the affected computer(s) unless
instructed to do so by a member of the Incident-Handling Team. In
addition, please remain within sight of the computer until a member of
the team gets there and ensures that no one touches the system. Please
help us by detailing as much information about the incident as possible.
We need a list of anyone who directly witnessed this incident; please list
their names below. If you need more space, please continue on a separate
sheet of paper:
Witnesses:
1)
2)
3)
What were the indications that you observed that led you to notice the
incident. Please be as specific and detailed as possible.
Incident indicators:
This next section is very important. Please be as accurate as possible.
From the time you noticed the incident to the time you called the
Incident-Handling Team, or help desk, please try to list every command
you typed and any file that you accessed.
Commands typed and files accessed:
Signature:_____

On-Site Containment

Whenever possible, we suggest two people be dispatched to the scene. One
handles the site survey, and the second team member, the more experienced,
should work at containing the computer system.

Site Survey

The survey member should use a portable tape recorder and describe the
scene. Record the names of everyone in the vicinity, if possible. Order everyone in the vicinity who was not there when the incident occurred, does not
normally work in the area, or isn't the system owner, to leave. While the on-
site handler is setting up the backup, interview the individual who phoned in

the incident. Determine the indications of the incident. Work with the employees in the area to check the other computer systems to see whether there are indications of compromise on these systems. Be certain to continue to record what you are seeing, or if you can't use a recorder, make sure to take good notes. Every few minutes, shoulder surf the incident handler and make a time-stamped notation of what you observe her doing; two records are better than one.

System Containment

The handler should try to get the normal system administrator for this system to ride shotgun. Ask him to help you take good notes. One of your primary goals is to make a backup of the system if at all possible.

Experienced handlers often have their own privileged binary applications and this includes backup programs. If you do not possess your own forensic-type backup and seizure tools, such as safeback, it might be wiser to copy all history files and log files to removable media before taking any other action. Incident handlers are supposed to write the contents of memory to removable media as well; while easily said, however, this has proven to be hard to do in practice. The best backups are bit-by-bit backups. If this option is not possible, the next question to answer is how critical the system is and how time pressing the incident is. If criminal activity is suspected and there is reason to believe that this actually is an incident, it might be best to do as follows:

- Power down the system
- Pop the drive
- Seal it in an envelope with a copy of your notes and the notes from the person who called in the incident
- Store the drive in an evidence safe or locked container with limited access

Hot Search

If it is a critical system and criminal prosecution is not a priority, you might have to search the system hot to find the problem. This is where a tool such as Encase or The Coroner's Toolkit (TCT) can really come in handy. Both tools are available for both old Windows (FAT) and more modern Windows (NTFS) file systems. Before running either tool, I like to run Tripwire on both the search drive and my host operating system before I start. That way, if something goes horribly wrong, I have an idea where to look for the problem. There used to be a forensics tool called Expert Witness, but it died in a lawsuit. I was doing a hot search of a drive that was infected with a virus and the next thing I knew I was infected with a virus. Now of course, the forensics tool sales representative is going to tell you this could never happen with his tool and he is probably right, but why take the chance?

In any case, your goal is to determine whether the evidence on the system reasonably supports the reported indications. This is known as validating the incident, and it is not limited to the information on the suspect hard drive. A good team doesn't leave a handler all alone; hopefully, someone is working the intrusion-detection system's records and other sources of data looking for information about the affected system while you are focused on the suspect system's hard drive.

Eradication

Sometimes, it is possible to examine the situation and remove the problem entirely; other times, it is not. With eradication, we need to pause for an upwardly mobile career observation about incident handling. If folks in an organization have suffered one compromised computer or six, they are usually pretty scared. If your team comes in and you are courteous and professional and get the job done, they really appreciate it. When they see you in halls and staff meetings, they nod and kind of say thanks with their eyes—it is a good thing. You are sort of a hero.

I used to have this really cool job in the U.S. Navy where I flew around in helicopters waiting for jets to go smacking into the water. Then we would hover over the ejected pilots and I would jump out and swim up to them, hook the crew up to a cable hoist, and we would pull them out of the ocean. You want to know what they always said when I swam up to them? Whenever I ran into them on the ship after the rescue, there was that same nod and saying thanks with their eyes.

However: If you show up and do your work and the problem comes back the next day, you are not a hero; you are an incompetent idiot. It is critical that you succeed in eradication, even if you have to destroy the operating system to do it. Repeat after me, "Nukem from high orbit." See, that isn't hard to say. Or, "Total eradication is too good for 'em."

I have tried to inject a little humor, because we must deal with a serious issue. As an incident handler, you need to be pre-authorized to contain and destroy to save your organization. Please take the preceding sentence very seriously. The incident-handling team needs to have a very senior executive in the organization as its sponsor or champion. The handler must be able to look that very young, very successful program manager droid, who has axed many a promising technical person on a whim, in the eye and say, "Yes, I know how important this system is. We will save as much of the data as your people have properly backed up, but the operating system is toast." Many times, the only way you can be certain the problem has been eliminated is to scrub that puppy to bare metal.

Oh yeah, when I swam up to these navy pilots, they always wanted to know "what happened?" They asked their questions in such a way that it was clear they wanted to know exactly one thing: Was it their fault? Might I suggest that when you handle an incident, the folks you come in contact will be very concerned that the incident was their fault. Why our culture is so bent on blaming the victim is beyond me! Be gentle and comforting when you speak. Don't come to conclusions early. Many times, running an incident to ground is like peeling an onion a layer at a time. Even if you know in your very bones it is their fault, be kind and supportive during the incident. The time to deal with what happened comes soon enough!

Recovery

The purpose of the incident-handling process is to recover and reconstitute capability. Throughout the process, we try to save as much data as we can, even if the system hadn't been backed up in a long time. Often, we can mount a potentially corrupted disk as a data disk and remove the files we need from it. This is another good application for Tripwire. Before mounting a suspect disk on your field laptop, make sure you have a very current Tripwire running so that you can be certain malicious code doesn't get on your computer.

Emergency medical technician (EMT) trainers use scenarios to drive home the academic points taught. One of the important lessons to teach EMTs is not to become a victim, because this makes the rescue even more problematic. If you see someone prostrate on the ground draped over a cable, for instance, don't run up to him and touch him. What if the cable is the reason they are lying there dead? What will happen to you when you grab someone connected to a high-voltage cable? The point is to use situational awareness and take a few seconds to think about the circumstances that caused the computer to be compromised. In the exact same way that failing to eradicate the problem makes the incident handler look stupid, we do not want to put the system back in business with the same vulnerability that caused it to be compromised.

This is an important point, because we will probably alter the system in some way. In fact, many times, the system owners will want to use this as an unexpected opportunity to upgrade the system, or freshen the patches. I find it amusing when the same manager who looked me in the eye during the containment phase and said things like, "Do you know how critical this system is? You can't shut it down," suggests that we upgrade the operating system before returning to service.

It is all well and good to freshen the operating system. However, what happens when an outsider makes a change to one of our systems? I oversaw the installation of a firewall once at a facility that didn't have one. For the next five years, every time someone couldn't connect to something, or their software didn't work right, I would get phone calls and/or email. "Is it the firewall?" This is a career risk vector to the incident handler. Remember our very young, very successful, hell-bent-on-rising-to-the-top executive? If anything goes wrong, he might use that to deflect attention from the fact that a system in his group was compromised. What countermeasures can we take?

During the incident-handling process, I like to keep the system owners informed. As long as they are in danger, they are very interested. As soon as they can see they are going to make it, they usually turn their attention to something else. It is imperative that early in the cycle, while the adrenaline is still flowing, to pull them aside and say something like this:

> Sir, our primary objective is to get you back in business with as little downtime and as few problems as possible. I am sure you understand that because the system was compromised, we will have to make at least some minor changes to the architecture, or it is likely to happen again. To ensure that the changes we make do not impact your operations, we need a copy of the system's documentation, especially design documents, program maintenance manuals, and most importantly, your system test plan. We will be glad to work with your folks to execute your system test plan before we close the incident.

Now, you and I both know that maybe five computers on the planet earth have an up-to-date, comprehensive test plan. There is no way on God's green earth that our slick young manager is going to be able to produce it. Time to invoke the power of the pen. We produce our preprinted incident closure form. It has blocks on it for the system administrator, primary customer, and system owner to state that they have tested the recovered system and that it is fully operational. So you say something like this:

> No test plan? Ummm, well sir I can't close an incident out unless the system has been certified as fully operational. Tell you what, if you will get your people to run the tests they use to certify your systems and document those tests and sign the form, tonight, we can get this incident closed. I am willing to stay as long as it takes because as you know, the CIO's goal for incident handling is for downtime to never exceed one day, and we can't clear this system for operation until it has been tested.

I invested a couple of paragraphs making this public safety announcement. It is really a bummer when a promising young incident handler gets blamed for system problems after pouring her heart out to save a compromised system. Now that you know the risk, practice safe incident-handling procedures.

After a system has been compromised, it might become a hacker trophy. The attacker might post his exploit in some way. I have seen several instances in which after a system is compromised, recovered, and returned to service, the attackers come out of the woodwork to whack it again. Use your intrusion-detection capability to monitor the system closely. It might be possible to move the system to a new name and address and install a honeypot for a few weeks.

Lessons Learned

At first, the incident was exciting and everybody on the planet wanted to get involved. There was the hunt for the culprit, sifting through clues to find the problem, and reconstructing the chain of events that led to the incident. Then comes the slow process of recovery and testing. This is less fun and folks are leaving, saying things like, "I guess you guys can take it from here." Finally, we are done. The problem is contained, eradicated, and the system is recovered. We are all drained and possibly a bit punchy. The last thing in the world you want to hear is, "the job ain't finished until the paperwork is done."

Two disciplines distinguish the professional from the wannabe: The pro takes complete and accurate notes every step of the way and does a good follow up. Both of these are disciplines; they do not come naturally. Every time you handle an incident, mistakes will occur. Mistakes also had to occur or the incident could have never happened. But that is a touchy subject, so tread lightly. Things could always have been done better. It is okay to make mistakes, just make new ones.

"Lessons learned" is the most important part of the process when approached with the correct mindset. It should never be a blame thing, rather an opportunity for process improvement. Here is the approach that has worked for me.

The incident handlers are responsible for documenting the draft of the incident report. As soon as they finish it, typos and all, they send a copy to each person listed as a witness, primary customer, and system owner. Anyone can make any comment he wants, and his comments will be part of the permanent record. The handlers make the call whether to modify the report. Within a week of the incident, a mandatory meeting should be held. Book the room for exactly one hour and start on time. The only order of business at the meeting is to review the final incident report's recommendations for process changes. One-hour meetings are not good places for the consensus approach. Just tally the votes for each item. The final report goes to the senior executive who is the sponsor of the team.

The most important section of an incident report is the executive summary. This is where you document why having a crack incident-handling team saved your organization a lot of money.

Summary

We face risks with every user or program we add to our systems and with every service we open on our firewall. Effective response, both automated and manual, is an effective mitigation technique. It enables your organization to move a bit faster and a bit more aggressively in this fast-paced world. Some of the automated responses include throttling to slow down the attack, dropping connections, shunning the attacker if he attempts to reconnect, islanding from the Internet in serious attacks, protocol tricks such as sending SYN/ACKs even if the host or service does not exist, and Reset kills.

Every organization has an incident-handling team; some just haven't formalized one. A formal team following the six-step process of preparation, identification, containment, eradication, recovery, and lessons learned will probably be more effective than an ad hoc response. The intrusion-detection analysts should always be members of the team and often are excellent choices for leading it.

One security model, time-based security, states that the time that we are protected is primarily based on the time it takes us to detect and react to an attack. As we tune our automated and manual responses, we train to react faster and hopefully better, increasing the protection we provide for our respective organizations.

19

Business Case for
Intrusion Detection

"WHERE DO I START? WHAT IS THE best ID tool to use?" A student asked
this question after he had just completed the most advanced class we teach on
the subject of intrusion detection, our hands-on, immersion curriculum. I was
more than a little surprised by that question. We had spent the past six days
and evenings hands on, learning about covert channels, malformed packets, and
TCP fingerprinting within a connection. We had worked and worked to show
the students why there is no silver bullet, why every IDS needs to be backed
up by a network recorder that captures all the traffic. I decided to answer with
a question. To the questioner, I must have sounded like someone from Oz, but
what I said was, "If your organization doesn't currently have an intrusion-
detection capability, why should they acquire one now? What's changed?" If
your organization doesn't currently have an intrusion-detection capability, it
will often be an uphill effort to champion one. To paraphrase Newton, an
organization at rest tends to remain at rest.

We are coming to the close of this book and before we move to our final
chapter, the future of intrusion detection, I would like to consider the business
case for intrusion detection. This is an important subject. The chapters that
precede this one give the sense that the knowledge required to be an analyst is

very technical, but fun. Also, I am sure you have a sense that the job of the intrusion-detection analyst with new detects and live attacks is exciting and challenging. Everyone that I know in the field is having a great time, but that isn't a good reason to deploy intrusion detection in your organization. If you made it past the first half of the book, you probably have a technical bent; so do I. But that isn't enough. Three of my heroes in intrusion detection, Ron Gula, Marcus Ranum, and Marty Roesch, have all started to say, "As a businessman…." Each of us is in business in some sense. This is still true if we work for the government, a university, or a not-for-profit. If you are even thinking about intrusion detection, your organization probably is fairly well funded. We have taken pains to develop a technical and architectural framework, but also to consider the business issues of risk management. If your ID capability does not fit in your organization's business model, it will be a source of friction. Let's work together to develop the strategies and processes needed to package intrusion detection for an organization.

This chapter was written for security professionals who:

- Don't currently have an intrusion-detection capability and are considering the merits of acquiring one

- Have a rudimentary capability and are considering a follow-on procurement or upgrade

- Have an existing capability and the organization is downsizing or restructuring and is in the process of evaluating this job function

In these cases, you aren't going to succeed by "wowing 'em" with technology. Appeals to duty or alarmist cries, "The hackers are coming, the hackers are coming," will not suffice to keep this project funded for the long haul—although it might well shake loose money for an additional purchase.

This chapter lays out a three-part plan that shows the importance of intrusion detection. The first part of the plan covers management issues, what I call the "fluffy stuff." Part one isn't technical, but it serves as the backdrop to allow management to support the intrusion-detection plan.

Part two of the plan answers the question "Why intrusion detection?" This is where you discuss the threat and the vulnerabilities; this is where you draw heavily on what you have learned about risk.

Part three offers your solutions and tradeoffs. The goal is to create a written report that serves as the project plan and justification. I have tried to lay this out so that it makes a nice presentation as well, because that is how one normally briefs senior management these days. Each item in a bulleted list is a suggestion for a PowerPoint slide. For extra credit, cut and paste the appropriate material from your written report into the notes section of the PowerPoint slides and suggest they be printed with notes pages showing. Few people take the time to do notes pages, so this will show you have it together.

All presentations and reports to management should start with an introduction called an Executive Summary. This is where you sum up the three most important points you are going to make. When you brief senior management, always be prepared to have your time cut short. "Can you do it in five minutes?" is not an unheard of request. In that case, you will show exactly three slides: your Executive Summary, Cost Summary, and Schedule. The Executive Summary is followed by a Problem Statement, in which you define the problem you are trying to solve. You probably want to extract a nice sound bite from the information in part two of the report for this. Your third slide is a roadmap where you define the structure of the presentation.

Part One: Management Issues

Your goal is to show management that this is part of an overall integrated information-assurance strategy that has tangible benefits to the organization. The key to doing this is to show that your proposed solution has the following characteristics:

- Bang for the buck.
- The expenditure is finite and predictable.
- The technology will not destabilize the organization.
- This is part of a larger, documented strategy.

Bang for the Buck

You need to be realistic. Intrusion detection is fairly costly. You need two fast computers ($2.5k each). If you choose commercial intrusion-detection solutions, the software license ($10k, to start), means that it costs $15k just to say *intrusion detection*. The network might need to be altered and there is the __ work-year salary and overhead for the intrusion-detection analyst; you could easily be talking $100k. But wait, there is more, bandwidth is increasing, so you need six sensors and a Top Layer switch just to watch the web farm, add another $100K. You need a database to search for slow speed scans and a correlation engine with a hardware RAID to hold all this data, add another $150K easily. In an environment focused on cost reduction, you are going to have to show a significant benefit to justify this expense.

The good news is that you can do exactly that. Risk is part of the business equation. In fact, there are markets that buy and sell denominated risk every day. Did you skip over the risk chapter? What is one way an intrusion-detection system helps reduce the *annualized loss expectancy* (ALE)? By observing the attacks against your organization, the analyst can assist the organization in fine-tuning its firewall and other defenses to be resistant to these attacks. Is that worth $100k - $350k? If not, here is another way an intrusion-detection system helps reduce loss. To conduct business, you might find that certain applications, or situations, require that some vulnerabilities need to be left on systems. A common example is that when you apply the recommended security patches to a system, it breaks some application. The intrusion detection can be focused on that particular vulnerability. In fact, this is an ideal opportunity to use that Reset kill you have been itching to try. There is a bang for the buck using intrusion-detection systems. You can show it, and you can quantify it.

Intrusion Detection Using Firewalls

One of the incredible changes on the market has been firewalls that log full binary data. OpenBSD's IPFilter and the commercial Raptor firewall can log data in BPF format. This binary logging allows you to run Snort or TCPdump filters against this information. This is incredible! I have already mentioned hogwash and UnityOne, firewall appliances with an IDS capability built in. My personal preference is to use two devices—if one fails the other continues to run.

Also, firewalls that do not have a binary logging capability can still be used in intrusion detection. As an example, Dshield (www.dshield.org), the technology that powers incidents.org, uses firewall data for its large-scale intrusion-detection capability. Firewalls certainly can be sensors. To be sure, firewalls that do not log most of the TCP header field values, such as TCP flags, only allow for very limited analysis. If you have a firewall with the fidelity of a Linux firewall (such as IPtables, for example), however, you can do a lot of the traffic-analysis techniques you have learned in this book.

If you do not have an IDS available, you can and should begin to apply what you have learned from this book by reviewing your organization's firewall logs. Needless to say, get permission first and be slow to raise alarms!

The Expenditure Is Finite

You know the old adage about a boat being a hole in the water you throw money into. I was reading a Sunday paper column recently titled, "Ten Tips on How to Increase Your Personal Wealth." One of the tips was don't buy a boat; if you have a boat, sell it. I am not so interested in wealth that I am ready to ditch my boats, but they do keep costing money (and they are mostly sea kayaks).

Here is one more house story that will help you understand a senior manager's concerns about containing expense. One day, I realized that everything I
did was done on a small fleet of laptops and a cell phone with a trillion
monthly minutes. In that moment, I realized I could live anywhere I want as
long as the area has cell towers and DSL or better. My wife and I settled on
Hawaii, and as luck would have it, DoD called the next day and asked me to
do two weeks of consulting on an IDS visualization project on Oahu, so
Kathy and I flew down to the islands. Two weeks later, we bought a dream
house on Kauai on the rim of a canyon overlooking the Wailua River halfway
between the rainforest and the beach. A month after we moved in, the dream
house became a nightmare house as it suddenly settled into the soft earth of
what had formerly been a pineapple field. A parade of insurance agents came
through claiming it was not covered, followed by structural engineers saying
they had never seen this before. Finally, a wise local pointed me to the best
contractor on the island, Luis Soltren—truly the best contractor I have ever
seen—but the house was totaled. Luis, like anyone who is the best at what he
does, is not cheap. It was the money pit, (never watch that movie if you are
remodeling), up close and personal. Every time they pulled a piece of
sheetrock or a tile, we would find more problems. Luis would shout for one of
us and we would look and shudder. I did remodeling in college, have built a
house, and roofed dozens, so I know a bit about the trade, and Luis was spot
on—these were all must-do repairs. The bill kept getting higher and higher.
When it crossed, no joke, $200k, I was sick to my stomach, and it kept going.
We are finally done, and I learned a very important lesson. The phrase total
cost of ownership is very popular in information technology, and I never really
considered it until I was caught in a project, my house, where it wasn't possible
to calculate what the final costs were going to be; they just kept going up.

Now, let's apply what we have learned from this story to intrusion detection
and your organization's senior management. Keep in mind that good managers
treat every dollar as if it is their own, and uncontrollable costs make them feel
the way my house made me feel.

When it comes to intrusion detection, management might well be willing
to pay the $100k or whatever, but management needs to be shown why the
expenses you propose in your plan are probably correct and that you aren't
going to have to come back for more and more money. For instance, a classic
error is to plan on using older, last-generation PCs for the intrusion system. I
propose the opposite. Buy the latest-generation PCs for intrusion detection,
and after six months to a year, roll them out as desktop machines.

Management will appreciate this as an honest and workable approach. It gives the organization the best possible intrusion-detection capability and the hardware upgrades are essentially free because buying new desktops is part of the computing life cycle.

Technology Used to Destabilize

The signature line of the hymn "Amazing Grace" is "I once...was blind, but now I see." This is what an intrusion-detection system does: It helps an organization go from a blind state to a seeing state. Time and time again, students who take the intrusion-detection curriculum we teach at SANS go back and start looking at their data and they realize they really need to change the way they do business. This is a good thing! However, it is a change, and people are suspicious of and resistant to change. When you propose intrusion detection, you must be sensitive to the potential for organizational change and make every effort to show that the IDS will "fit in." Some of the potential impacts to the organization are the configuration of the network, the effects on behavior of employees, and the need for additional policy support.

Network Impacts

We have discussed the challenges of deployment on switched networks. This needs to be carefully coordinated with the network operations people before the purchase order for the IDS is cut. The best thing to do is to get the spanning port working with a protocol analyzer; most network operations groups have one or more protocol analyzers. If the spanning port is difficult for your networks operations people to configure and maintain, network taps should be considered for the listening ports on the IDS. Many people feel that good practice for an IDS sensor is to be provisioned with multiple interface cards:

- Listening ports in promiscuous mode but without IP addresses. This makes it hard for attackers to find the sensor's listening ports.

- One interface, with an IP address, is used to communicate with the sensor.

The IDS will almost certainly require a firewall modification. Commercial vendors all seem to think that writing their own proprietary protocol for communications among their IDS consoles, sensors, and databases sets them apart from their competition. And of course, they are literally correct. Do your homework and research what ports need to be opened. If the IDS can be modified to use an existing hole in the firewall, use that. Even proxy-based firewalls often have a pass-through hole; a "suck-and-spit" proxy with no protocol knowledge already running to support some application or another. It will be great when the Intrusion

Detection Working Group (IDWG) finishes its work and there is a standard transport protocol based on beep (`www.beepcore.org/beepcore/docs/profile-idxp.html`) for intrusion-detection systems.

IDS Behavioral Modification

Behavioral modification is another aspect of running an IDS. You already know that I have concerns about using the IDS as big brother, even though many organizations are losing a lot of money to wasteful activities. The IDS is a data collection and analysis tool, however; so even if you aren't looking for trouble, you might still find it. You need to be prepared as an organization to deal with what you find now that you are no longer blind to network traffic. Let's use an IRC server as an example scenario.

You turn the IDS on and soon realize that a bright young kid in the computer operations department has set up one of your internal systems as an IRC server. How did you find this out if you weren't monitoring for IRC? We have discussed the fact that DNS, web, and email servers draw a lot of fire. That is nothing compared to the fire IRC servers draw! What the analysts see is a ba-zillion attacks and probes directed at a system in computer operations. When you look into it further, you find out the rest of the story. Obviously, the organization wants to turn this around and get the problem cleaned up. The wise analyst and organization will have established policy before the IDS was powered on to handle these things.

The Policy

I suggest that the organization consider an initial amnesty policy. By this, I mean the first 10 or so violations of the organization's acceptable-use computer policy be dealt with quietly and in a lenient fashion. A memo can be sent out that doesn't name anyone, but lists some of the examples and warns that in the future these activities will not be tolerated. I know of organizations that have turned on their shiny new IDS and examined their traffic for the first time. Imagine their surprise when they see things they do not approve of entering and leaving their network. They are now at an important decision point. If the organization reacts in a knee-jerk fashion and walks the employee straight to the door, the IDS will always be viewed with suspicion and hatred. Be especially careful with the way you deal with systems and network administrators; they are used to doing whatever they want. If you walk someone from the computer or network operations group to the door because they broke an acceptable-use policy you just started enforcing, your IDS might break down or suffer blindness caused by loose cables a lot in the future!

Management knows all about firestorms—hate and discontent and the interactions between folks with strong personalities. Managers deal with this kind of stuff every single working day. If your implementation plan shows that you are sensitive to the other players in the organization and that the IDS is not guaranteed to produce Excedrin headache number 36, they will be far more supportive of your plan.

Part of a Larger Strategy

This book is focused on helping the analyst of a network-based intrusion-detection system. However, we have also talked about system security, risk, vulnerability scanners, unauthorized use, incident handling, and now, business issues. You need to always be ready to show how intrusion detection fits in as part of the organization's information-assurance program.

To be honest with you, when I was younger, I didn't get it. I thought my mission in life was to implement the best technology at the most affordable price possible to help the research lab that I worked for be "world class." Phrased that way, it even sounds like a laudable mission. I would approach my boss with a technology and its technical tradeoffs and he would say, "Yes, but show me the big picture." It used to drive me crazy. I was convinced he was a total idiot with a personal goal of being named Luddite of the year. Fifteen years later, I am just starting to really understand. You can't play a song on a harp with one string. Any technology, no matter how wonderful, is useless unless it complements the existing business processes of the organization. When you brief management on the spiffy IDS you want to buy, be sure to include the hooks to system security, risk, vulnerability scanners, unauthorized use, incident handling, and business issues in your plan. Please allow me to do a quick repeat from Chapter 17, "Organizational Issues" (see Listing 19.1)

Listing 19.1 **The Seven Most Important Things to Do If Security Matters**[1]

- Write the security policy (with business input).
- Analyze risks, or identify industry practice for due care; analyze vulnerabilities.
- Set up a security infrastructure.
- Design controls, and write standards for each technology.
- Decide what resources are available, prioritize countermeasures, and implement top-priority countermeasures you can afford.

[1] Courtesy of Matt Bishop, Alan Paller, Hal Pomeranz, and Gene Schultz

- Conduct periodic reviews and possibly tests.
- Implement intrusion detection and incident response.

If your intrusion-detection proposal is written against a process like this, it will be obvious to management that it is part of a larger strategy. Senior management does not have the time to accept information piecemeal; it is responsible for broad business strategies. Take a bit of your time to make its job easier.

We have spent considerable time on the four issues that management needs to see in an intrusion-detection plan. If we do not cover these bases, their paradigms will not let them even consider the plan. Again, they are as follows:

- Bang for the buck.
- The expenditure is finite and predictable.
- The technology will not destabilize the organization.
- This is part of a larger, documented strategy.

Now we can move on to the technical stuff; this will be part two of your plan or proposal.

Part Two: Threats and Vulnerabilities

The second part of the plan is where you lay out the threats and compare them to your vulnerabilities and the value of your assets. The purpose of this is to answer the question, "Why do we need additional security measures?" I think that the highest and best purpose of network intrusion detection outside the firewall is to help assessment of the attacks directed against your organization and to ensure the internal hosts are hardened against these attacks. But before you have an IDS, how do you assess these threats? You want to examine the problem, the threats, and the vulnerabilities before you offer intrusion detection as the solution. Chapter 17's focus on risks gave the foundation you need to approach this section of the plan. Part two's elements are as follows:

- Threat assessment and analysis
- Asset identification
- Valuation
- Vulnerability analysis
- Risk evaluation

Threat Assessment and Analysis

A risk assessment purist would say you need a dictionary that enumerates all possible threats, and then you need to analyze each threat. For a plan to support an intrusion-detection system that is designed to be readable by management, this is a bad idea. Your goal is not to show all possible threats, but rather a sampling of probable treats. Management and the intrusion-detection analyst would do well to focus on what is likely to happen to it and how it is going to happen. I cover these in reverse order. The following list is my take on how these attacks are going to arrive. The primary threat vectors are as follows:

- Outsider attack from network
- Outsider attack from telephone
- Insider attack from local network
- Insider attack from local system
- Attack from malicious code

Threat Vectors

Let's just take a second to be sure of the term *threat vector*. If you go to the restroom of a restaurant, there is often a sign saying, "Employees Must Wash Their Hands Before Returning to Work." It has been well established that skipping this sanitary step is a disease vector. The dirty hands are the pathway, the conduit that allows the food poisoning.

A network-based intrusion-detection system might be able to detect outsider attack from the network, insider attack from the network, and possibly attack from malicious code (remember the Macro virus and PKZip examples from Chapter 17).

A host-based intrusion-detection system with an active agent might be able to detect all five vectors.

Threat Determination

Your goal for the purposes of establishing a business case for intrusion detection is to list well-known, probable threats as opposed to all threats. How do you find these threats? Sources might include the following:

- Newspaper or web articles on attacks at other places. If it happens to them, it could happen to you.
- Firewall/intrusion-detection logs for specific threats.
- System audit trail logs.
- Demonstration of an intrusion-detection system.

Many commercial intrusion-detection vendors allow you to take their systems for a test drive, with a 30-day trial or something similar. If you are serious about wanting to implement an IDS capability, I can't stress how important this is to do. It gives you a list of actual attacks against your network; this is helpful for establishing the threat. It helps establish the groundwork for part three of the plan when you show why you recommend an intrusion-detection system as opposed to, say, another firewall. And, it gives you experience with a couple commercial offerings. All too often, folks make their decision either based on something they read or on how friendly the salesperson is. If you have tried a few "loaner" IDSs, in part three of the plan, you can make honest statements about the tradeoffs between various systems.

If you can find the time to do it, interviews with folks in various parts of your organization can be a rich source of threats and vulnerabilities that you might otherwise have missed. I have had people tell me about shockingly bad practices when I ask them what they consider the largest dangers to the organization's information assets to be. Yet, they never came forward with the information on their own. As they say in Alabama, "Whaay-el, you never asked."

Asset Identification

Chapter 17 discussed asset valuation. Now, you focus on the concept a bit more. The huge value is the investment in data. If most of your workers use computers most of their workday, the value of the data on the computer is the cost of putting that worker in front of the console. The threats to that data are that it will be copied, destroyed, or modified.

We have touched on this throughout the book. So that we are really clear, however, I will reiterate: The most probable threat to that data is destruction from the system owner. As my Catholic friends would point out, this could be by a sin of commission, or a sin of omission. By commission, I mean an overt act, deleting the data accidentally, or on purpose, and never telling anyone so that it can be recovered. By omission, I mean the failure to back up the data properly, and that includes off-site backup. At least for the things that are within your power to change, work to ensure your data is backed up.

It turns out to be an almost impossible task to ensure that all the data throughout the organization is protected from being copied, destroyed, or modified. In the same way, making sure every data element is backed up, on and off site, is beyond the capabilities of any organization that I know of. This is a great lead-in to the notion of crown jewels, or *critical program information* (CPI) as they say in security texts.

Valuation

All your data is not of the same value. In fact, a small portion of the information that exists in your organization is what distinguishes you from your competition. Although all your data has value, crown jewels are the information that has critical value and must be protected.

You reflect this in the threat section of your plan. Find as many of the crown jewels as possible. Consider the threat vectors, and the known common threats, and use these as the examples of threats and vulnerabilities in part two of your intrusion-detection business plan.

In part three, you will discuss countermeasures to protect these clusters of high-value information. These might include the following:

- Host-based IDS software on the critical systems.
- Honeypot files. If your organization has sensitive documents, you can add special tagged strings into the document. One way to do this is invent acronyms that do not actually exist. Then you can program your IDS watch for these with a string, or content matching rule. This would tell you if these files are entering or leaving your network.
- Instrumenting internal systems with personal firewalls. (Technically oriented employees often enjoy doing this.)
- Network-based IDS in high-value locations.

Vulnerability Analysis

Vulnerabilities are the gateways by which threats are made manifest. All the threats in the world don't matter if there are no vulnerabilities.

Were you disappointed because I didn't give a long list of vulnerabilities from which to work? Well, they change almost daily so you need a pointer to a current list, not a static one that will be obsolete before the book is even printed. I like the Computer Vulnerabilities and Exposures (CVE) project (cve.mitre.org) the best because it cross-indexes a number of great vulnerability lists such as bugtraq and ISS's X-Force. However, you do not need to do this manually. Getting your general threat list as well as an assessment of your vulnerabilities is a fairly simple matter. A number of good vulnerability assessment tools are available. These tools test for specific threats, and they find potential vulnerabilities. Let's consider three classes of tools: system-vulnerability scanners, network-based scanners, and also phone-line scanners.

Tools such as COPS, SPI, tiger, and STAT are examples of system-vulnerability scanners. They work within the system looking for missing patches, incorrectly set file permissions, and similar problems.

Tools such as nmap, nessus, saint, ISS' Internet Scanner, and Axent's NetRecon are examples of network-based scanners. These are fairly fast and effective and scan the network looking for unprotected ports or services.

While conducting vulnerability assessments, you might also want to assess your risk from the attackers who scan your phone lines looking for active modems. Toneloc, available from fine hacking sites everywhere, is the most used tool for this. Phonesweep from http://www.sandstorm.net is a commercial tool with some additional features.

If at all possible, your vulnerability assessment should offer three views:

- **A system view.** Taken from selected systems with system scanners.

- **A network view.** Done from an internal scan of your network.

- **An Internet view.** Done from outside your firewall and, if possible, a phone scan as well.

Of course, you want some juicy vulnerabilities to spice up your report, but please also scan your firewall, DNS, mail, and web servers, as well as systems related to your crown jewels. These are the systems that your organization depends on.

Whew! Sounds like a lot of work, doesn't it? Correct, it is a lot of work and vulnerability assessments are not something that should be done only once. Why does it make sense for the intrusion-detection analyst to be involved in vulnerability assessments? It keeps you aware of specific problems and where in the organization your vulnerabilities are located.

Risk Evaluation

You have a lot of data. What do you do with it? Just because you collected it, do not stuff it all in your report, even as labeled appendixes. On the other hand, you do want it organized and available. Whenever you brief senior management, you want at least one supporting layer of data available—that is, if your slide says 12 systems are deemed to contain CPI, you darn sure want to be able to list those systems and explain the rationale for choosing them and not others.

Okay, we have answered the question of what you are not going to put in the second section of the report. What *should* you provide?

- A top-level slide with the value of the organization's information assets. Suppose you have 100 computers with a five-year life cycle, for instance. The hardware, software, and maintenance costs are $200k/year with information valued at $1 million.

- A network diagram that defines the boundary you are trying to protect.
- A basic description of the threat vectors.
- A general summary of your general vulnerability assessment.
- A description of the crown jewels: where they are, their value, and so on (include the firewall, DNS, mail, and web servers).
- Specific threats against the crown jewels.
- Specific vulnerabilities of the systems that host the crown jewels.

This should exist as a written report as well as a view-graph presentation. If you are doing a PowerPoint presentation (which is recommended), expand each of the preceding bullets to be a PowerPoint slide with three to five bullets each.

Part Three: Tradeoffs and Recommended Solution

Finally, you get to pitch your intrusion-detection system! You can hardly wait to get behind the console of that shiny new intrusion.com special and smell that new IDS smell. Slow down a little longer. You need to offer some tradeoffs, and also remember, you are going forward with a package. Intrusion detection by itself is a hard sell. From a risk-assessment, textbook standpoint, the next thing you are supposed to do is establish risk-acceptance criteria. This approach is put management on the spot and have it define what levels of risks it is willing to accept. Then, you go back and design comprehensive countermeasures for all risks greater than what management is willing to accept. Good luck!

Therefore, you should do the following:

- Define an information-assurance risk-management architecture.
- Identify what is already in place.
- Identify the immediate steps you recommend.
- Identify the options for these countermeasures.
- Produce a cost-benefit analysis.
- Implement a project schedule.
- Identify the follow-on steps illustrating where you want to go in the future.

Define an Information-Assurance Risk-Management Architecture

This sound like a hard chore, but it is really simple. You have defined the threats. You know the primary countermeasures. It could be as simple as implementing the following:

- Firewall from the Internet
- Network-based IDS outside the firewall
- Internal firewalls for crown jewels
- Network-based IDS covering crown jewels
- Host-based IDS on crown jewels' platforms
- Tagged honeypot files on crown jewels' platforms
- Basic hardening for all systems, antivirus programs, patches, and good configuration management to prevent silly file permission settings
- Organizational network-based backup with off-site storage
- Scanning of the internal network for vulnerabilities quarterly
- Certificate-based encryption for transmissions over the Internet with customers and suppliers as well as home and off-site workers
- Strong authentication for dial-ins
- Disk encryption and personal firewalls for laptops

This list might not be completely appropriate for your organization, but this is my view of the big picture for information assurance.

Identify What Is in Place

Every briefing or report to senior management should include a status slide, something that defines where you are now. If you follow your definition of your information-assurance architecture with your current status, it is a nice set up for the things you want to do next.

Identify Your Recommendations

Finally, you get to pitch the intrusion-detection system of your dreams. You want the pitch to be balanced. It is perfectly reasonable to pitch an intrusion-detection system and a vulnerability scanner (or whatever is appropriate for your organization) at the same time. For the pitch to be solid, it should include options, cost, and schedule information.

I just cry when I see someone take an hour of a senior manager's time to brief him on a problem and possibly recommend a solution when the presenter doesn't have the cost and backup information. The senior executive doesn't think she has enough information to make a decision, so she puts the matter off. What happens, however, is a very subtle characteristic of human nature. When you first hear about a scary problem, you are shocked and might well be moved to action. If you do not act, however, you have been inoculated against the problem. The next time you hear about it, you are less scared and less moved to action. Therefore, you need to be prepared to sell your project the first time!

Identify Options for Countermeasures

I hate doing this! I know what I want! I have done a market survey. Why should I have to justify the product I have selected? Well, if you didn't know this before, I'll let you in on a potential "gotcha." The commercial intrusion-detection system vendors aren't dumb! They are trying hard to reach the CIOs and other top executives of your organization with non-technical, high-level issues-oriented briefings. For instance, the host-based companies are pushing the insider threat really hard. Therefore, if you come marching into your CIO with your report and it doesn't mention the insider threat or consider host-based systems as options, you might be one down instantly.

> **Personal Firewalls**
>
> If you are facing management and the issue of the insider threat comes up, keep in mind that internal firewall and personal firewall data can come in very handy. In some sense, these serve as burglar alarms and can alert you to internal problems. Before asking senior management who is responsible for the organization's risk management, funding, and support, it is a good idea to know as much about the probable risks as possible.

Take the time to list at least one optional approach and to consider at least one alternative product for your recommended procurements. You don't have to pitch these slides; in fact, you shouldn't pitch these slides. But you do want them in case the issue comes up. While you are at this point, you need to take a second for an integrity check. Are you trying to buy a toy and help get the job skills to enhance your career or are you trying to secure your organization? Have you really taken the time to examine those firewall logs? If they have good fidelity, and you are honestly more concerned about your organization's security, perhaps you should consider spending the time and money on a different aspect of your information-assurance architecture.

Cost-Benefit Analysis

The cost aspect of this section is more important than the benefit section. This is where you give management a warm, fuzzy feeling that you know how much the recommended countermeasures are going to cost. As a program manager, when I hear something that I know I want to do, I really don't need a lot more information—just tell me what it will cost and when I can have it. Earlier, we talked about the case of having to present the whole package in five minutes. In that situation, you would use three slides: the Executive Summary, the Cost Summary, and the Schedule.

Why Cost-Benefit Matters

Cost-benefit analysis doesn't sound sexy to an intrusion analyst, but going through the exercise for even a one-page financial analysis is really worth the time. I used to have an employee who was very bright, but she had an uncanny knack for coming up with the projects guaranteed to fail. Because she was so smart, when she would suggest that we ought to do something, I would think, "Yeah, that makes sense, let's do it." The next thing I knew, it was crash and burn time, and I would look silly again in front of senior management. Then what do you suppose happened? She came up with one of those, "I think we should...." My heart started pounding, my brain racing. I could feel my stress level go up. A wiser manager would have sat down with her and taught her to calculate the cost, the risk, and the potential benefits of a course of action. It is easy after you have done it once. Not me, though. I just reminded her of the failures, and in so doing, probably lost any chance of hearing another idea from a brilliant software engineer.

Not all benefits are tangible and that is important, but this is where you want to support your bang-for-the-bucks slide. This is the point where you list the costs. In the written report, you should list all the costs; in a presentation, you should present only the summary costs. If there are questions, refer management to the written report.

Have you ever given a pitch and had a member of the management team challenge you? And just out of the blue, they say, "I don't think that is going to work." They don't even give a reason. They might have a double-digit IQ, but the spotlight is on you! This is where it really helps to be prepared. Let me make it plain for you: There is a better-than-even chance management will ask the following questions, and you will have to give the answers shown. Will an intrusion-detection system:

- Actually stop attacks? No.
- Detect everything? No.
- Cost a significant amount of money in equipment and salary? Yes.

So you see, you really do want to be prepared! As backup material, I strongly recommend you have at least one ALE (annualized loss expectancy) or SLE (single loss expectancy, as explained in Chapter 12, "Writing TCPdump Filters") calculation for what you think is the biggest general threat against the organization. You should also have a couple examples of specific threats against crown jewels if possible. Select your cases carefully so that they support your choice of countermeasures. If you end up needing these slides, your pitch is in trouble; so do a good job on them.

Business Plan

I am a passionate, vision-driven person and I need to be honest with you about something. I am physically incapable of labeling anything I write a "cost-benefit analysis." Let's be careful here, 9 out of 10 consultants would agree that is the correct title and form for what you should take to management for a final approval of a project. It is probably what decision-making management expects. So, after telling you plainly that I am outside the normal and customary in this regard, please let me share what I do. I produce a business plan, often it is only a couple of pages long, but it helps me focus on the issues. It has the same basic content as a cost-benefit analysis. I deal with costs, advantages, tangibles, and intangibles, but there is one added factor: It will help advance the business. It seems to me that anything you do should serve two purposes: It should solve the problem at hand, and it should advance the business. The energy and capital you invest should help your organization achieve or maintain the lead in your field. "Oh come on Stephen," you might say, "intrusion detection is an overhead function; you can't make money on it!" Wanna bet? Baseball, I mean intrusion detection, has been very, very, good to me, and to many of my friends as well. Don't shortchange yourself and skip learning the material in this chapter. Learn to write a business plan or a cost-benefit analysis. This skill might literally pay off for you.

Project Schedule

I have written software (badly) for 15 years or so, but I have also managed some pretty skilled coders. I try to get estimates from them so that I can pass up milestone information on future deliverables. Depending on the person, I either double or triple their estimates. Software people invariably think something is a simple matter of a few lines of code until they get into the problem.

The point I am trying to make is that managers develop a radar, a sixth sense for bogus schedules. You are on the next-to-last slide of your presentation, or next-to-last section in your report. You do not want to blow it here.

If you are not experienced at project management, here are some gotchas with fudge factors of items that will take longer than you probably estimated:

- Procure anything and everything (2×)
- Compile and run any free software (2×)
- Get management approval for any policy (5×)
- Install the software and test it (2×)

- Get the sensor to work on a switched network (5×)
- Get the analysis station to connect to the sensor through the firewall (3×)
- Get clearance to install host-based intrusion-detection software on production systems (5×)
- Sweep your phone lines for vulnerabilities (5×)
- Fix problems you find with a network vulnerability sweep (5×)

The preceding list was partly done in fun, but I also am serious. If these items are part of your critical path, you might want to give your schedule a second look.

Follow-On Steps

At this point, you have finished everything we need to do to pitch your solution. We have defined and quantified both the problem and the solution with options. What could possibly be lacking? Will installing this solution solve all the organization's problems? If not, you should identify some of the next steps. If you are recommending a network-based intrusion-detection system, for instance, your next steps might be as follows:

- Host-based perimeter defenses for critical systems
- Database for trend analysis, especially with the emergence of enterprise security modules that allow you to consider data from NID, HID, firewall, router, and system log files
- Internal network-based IDSs for high-value locations
- Organization-wide host-based perimeter defense deployment

Each of these steps should include a high-level estimate for timeframe and cost. Taking the time to show the next steps helps management in two important ways. It shows you have technical vision—that there really is a well thought out plan. Also the budget planning cycle for capital purchases at many organizations is done several years in advance. By presenting the follow-on steps, financial planners can use your information as budget "wedges" for future years.

Repeat the Executive Summary

You know the drill. Tell them what you are going to tell them, tell it to them, and then tell them what you told them. This is an excellent time to repeat your Executive Summary points.

Summary

I hope this chapter and this book have been helpful to you. This chapter was tailored for security professionals who don't have an intrusion-detection capability, want to upgrade their capability, or have these job positions under scrutiny. In much of the book, we try to give you a bit of insight into the enemy. In this chapter, we have tried to give you insight into management and business processes.

The most important thing to keep in mind, both for yourself and when you brief management, is that intrusion detection should be an integral part of your organization's information-assurance strategy. In fact, intrusion detection should be a part of every nation's information-assurance strategy. The events of this coming year with massive IRC bot driven distributed denial-of-service attacks, SNMP/ASN.1 exploits, and polymorphic attacks will prove this to be true. You don't need an IDS to detect a DDoS attack, but it will help you find the compromised hosts before they can be used to hurt someone. Now, let us take some time to discuss the future of intrusion detection in our final chapter in this book.

20

Future Directions

P ROGNOSTICATION IS DANGEROUS. HAVE YOU SEEN THE studies on the accuracy of newspaper and tabloid predictions? How will we do better? It is time to discuss the leading edge, the emerging tools and trends in intrusion detection. I am asked to speak on the future of various information assurance topics a couple times a year and try to stay abreast of trends, hold focus groups, and so forth. None of that ensures that I will be right about anything; so, consider what you read in this chapter with care. With that, here is my read on the future for intrusion detection.

In terms of broad trends, we will discuss the emerging threat, cyber-terrorism, the ease by which attackers are able to install and run malicious code on our systems, the improvements in reconnaissance and targeting, skills versus tools, defense in depth, and large-scale intrusion detection. Finally, we'll close with some short takes on emerging trends.

Increasing Threat

One of the drivers that fuels the continued interest in intrusion detection is the increasing threat. The progress in attacker tools over the past year has been incredible. I am not talking about Code Red so much as Leaves and the IRC *bot* (robot programs) nets that reached a significant level of sophistication in mid-2001. Attackers have the firepower to knock almost any site off the Internet. They can coordinate a fast scan, blowing through half of a class B in about five minutes from 2,500 or so discrete source hosts. They can also scan very slowly, modulating the technique to be almost undetectable. Many of these attackers are also security practitioners by day, a disturbing fact, and they are not planning to stop writing attack code.

Cyber-Terrorism

"Have you seen any evidence of increasing attacks, anything significant?" No less than five of my friends that work for the government had asked me that question by noon on 9/11/2001. Suddenly, we started hearing about cyber-terrorism and, with Executive Order 13231 filed after the attack, we see the US Government preparing defensive mechanisms against cyber-terrorism. Although we have tried to detail the increasing threat, and to be sure there is a lot of firepower out there, I do not see any evidence that cyber-based terrorism is a near-term threat. There are hints and glimmerings of it, but the emphasis of terrorism seems to remain fixed on bombs and guns. Is cyber-terrorism a credible threat? In some sense, it has to be. Much of the infrastructure is computer controlled, and the computers are certainly vulnerable. The main thing that seems to be holding cyber-based terrorism back seems to be the attacker's apparent lack of skill and motivation. In other words, the committed terrorists still seem to prefer bombs and guns to laptops for now.

With that said, we do need to consider the implications of the large attack networks that have been formed in the past year. One reason we have not seen more damage is that many of the people involved in creating these attack networks are not really malevolent.

An interesting trend that is as true today as it was when I first learned about it in 1997 is that a main theme of all this advanced denial of service is Internet Relay Chat (IRC). Groups of hackers fighting for control of IRC chatrooms developed the denial-of-service tools. As long as people were content to clobber IRC servers, who cared? Now the genie is out of the bottle and it cannot be put back. It is interesting that the latest attack networks are IRC bots, but they are certainly not constrained to IRC targets. If a group bent on terrorism was to gain control of one of these networks, it could certainly do significant damage, especially financially. If you could keep the top ten Internet businesses offline for a week, what would the potential financial damage be? It is more than just the lost revenue; it would include the weakened state of the companies and potentially a serious effect on the stock market, especially the technology rich NASDAQ exchange.

The bottom line on terrorism, cyber or not, is that your organization should have a contingency plan. Right after 9/11, there was a bit of concern about creating and updating business continuity plans, but it seemed to pass quickly, even while the site of the World Trade Center was still smoking. The main thing is to make sure you have an alternative way of doing business in case the net infrastructure gets severely perturbed at some point.

Large-Scale Compromise

Trojan horses, logic bombs, and software vulnerabilities are incredibly rampant. The bad news is that it is essentially impossible to secure modern operating systems. One of the reasons for this is their complexity. Take a look at your active processes, ps –ax or ps –ef on UNIX and Ctrl+Alt+Del on Windows. Ask yourself if you would recognize if something changed on anything that is shown. These are high-level listings, not the function calls and .dlls themselves. If someone were able to plant a malicious routine on one of your systems, you would probably not be able to find it except with a tool like anti-virus software. So how do these backdoors and such get planted on your systems?

A huge vector for Windows systems in the past two years has been browser related problems. A number of vulnerabilities in Microsoft's Internet Explorer have been reported that allow attackers to run arbitrary programs on systems when the browser downloads web pages with specially formatted strings. This is on top of the previous trend of creating attacks based on vulnerabilities in the Outlook mail program. Granted, these attacks are at the bottom of the food chain in some sense—PCs—many of which are on dial up connections and cannot do that much damage; but just as many are inside government facilities, corporations, educational institutions, and homes with broadband connectivity. On UNIX systems, a variety of buffer overflows have been found and exploited that allow attackers to accomplish the same thing. In addition to the techniques that attackers use to break into systems, they are also becoming more adept at finding systems to break into.

Improved Targeting

In this book, you have learned a lot about the various reconnaissance techniques attackers use. Multiple organizations are involved in Internet mapping efforts. Some of the aspects of advanced targeting include the following:

- Techniques to maximize results using broadcast packets when possible. If a site allows broadcast packets to enter its network from the Internet, this allows the attackers to get significant results with a fairly low number of stimulus packets. Scanning is actually fairly slow going; this is the reason nmap and other tools default to an echo request first. If they get a reply, they invest in scanning for open ports and protocols.

- Avoidance of dangerous IP address ranges, based on lists of honeypots and sites that are known to be alert and active in reporting to CIRTs and law enforcement.

- Sharing reconnaissance data between scanning organizations minimizes the footprint. If two groups have different techniques and they share the results, it is harder to detect them in action, especially if they both use distributed scanning.

Because the reconnaissance has been going on for a long time, we are now seeing the results of long-term mapping efforts. When you see a few probes, they might be validating that the site map the attackers hold is still fairly up-to-date. As new vulnerabilities are found, the attackers will have the capability to launch precision attacks.

How the Threat Will Be Manifested

The fact that systems are vulnerable and attackers are perfecting their techniques for finding vulnerable systems is not news. What changed in late 2001 and early 2002 was the scale. Large-scale, successful attacks such as Leaves SubSeven scans, Code Red and nimda against IIS, and the SNMP/ASN.1 and Apache PHP attacks in early 2002, left attackers with networks of thousands and thousands of compromised zombie systems, and they had primitive, but workable command and control systems to manage these networks.

This much firepower has a couple of uses. You can threaten to blow almost any site off the Internet. By February 2002, two years after the original distributed denial-of-service (DDoS) attacks against high-end web sites like CNN and Yahoo, attackers were going after ISPs. In February, when the SANS Institute was funding a webcast about a free new Cisco router security configuration tool, the ISP streaming the webcast, Digital Island, reported it was hit with a denial-of-service attack disrupting the webcast. And, the attackers continued to explore their firepower. As March of 2002 opened, we were seeing test attacks where sites were knocked off the Internet by doing a traceroute, determining the routers the site needed to connect to the Internet and leveling them. They were also beginning to experiment with TCP port 179, BGP. As I write this, I cannot know the future, but from the close of February 2002, my way-out-on-a-limb guesses would be that two things seem likely:

- The attackers are not going to be able to resist testing out this firepower. Some will just be in it for the money and will try extortion, threatening to disrupt e-business sites like eBay or Amazon. Others will be more interested in a grand stunt, probably against the two exposed services on the Internet, routing and DNS; and if you can take out routing, DNS falls naturally. Our best analysis says you cannot take down the entire Internet, because it is made up of too many independent parts.

- The government is going to do the only thing it can do—make it a serious criminal penalty to run these kinds of attacks. This has already started with the laws that passed after 9/11, but if the attackers do pull a bold stunt, lawmakers around the globe will probably have to respond.

This is not to say that all is gloom and doom—far from it. The threat might be reaching its highest point in a few months, but there appears to be some natural limits to the growth.

Defending Against the Threat

There are countermeasures and limits to the increasing threat. In this section, we will first discuss the natural limits and then consider the development of skills and tools for defenders. Also, the community is making progress in understanding and implementing defense in depth. We are also deploying intrusion detection in a large-scale mode to be able to see the trends quickly. The good news is they are about ready to hit some limits that ought to slow them down a bit. What limits?

- The current DDoS type attack tools like Leaves and litmus have their command and control via Internet Relay Chat. This is both their strength and weakness. At some point, the community is going to wise up and start blocking this type of protocol. There are countermeasures that the attackers can and will take, but these can and will be contained.

- A large number of scans depend on public addresses. Every time an organization switches to a NAT and private addresses, it becomes just a little bit harder for attackers.

- Many of the attack networks we are currently facing are a result of the Leaves (via SubSeven), Code Red, and SNMP/ASN.1 bonanzas of mid-2001 and early 2002. OK, this is where I go so far out on a limb. It isn't funny, but a large number of these machines are Windows, and lately there has been some evidence that Microsoft really cares. I think that seeing 180,000 IIS web servers switch to (mostly) Apache in the months after Code Red really got their attention.

- Follow the money! The money is primarily going into the defensive side of the house. The attacker community is demonstrating a lot of ingenuity, but as lower cost, easy-to-configure security appliances come on to the market, and security training that really works becomes available, there will be less low hanging fruit. Attacking will become less fun and less common, and it will be easier to shun sites that do not stop bad behavior.

Money really is the interesting question. It seems logical to assume that if you are investing in security, it will make a difference. However, February 13, 2002, the United States Office of Management and Budget (OMB) released a report 2002-05, http://www.whitehouse.gov/omb/inforeg/fy01securityactreport.pdf, on federal information security. The report, to no one's surprise, outlined a number of shortcomings including the following:

- Inadequate senior management attention
- Ineffective security education and awareness
- Improper security practices by outside contractors
- Inadequate detection and reporting of vulnerabilities

However, the most significant finding in the report was there was no detectable correlation between the amount of money invested in information security and the results. Further, they did not even consider the importance of good tools other than in some discussion about capital expenditure. In the near future, if we are able to invest the money we have available wisely on skills development and apply some good process when deciding which tools to purchase, I think we will make some significant forward progress.

Skills Versus Tools

The interest in the topic of intrusion detection is still on the rise. SANS offered the first Intrusion Detection Immersion Curriculum in March 2000 and not only was it sold out, would-be analysts really turned to some high-end social engineering trying to get a seat. Today, we offer the current hands-on, six-day intrusion-detection track somewhere in the world every week. That is a demonstration of the demand, and it is fueled by a desire to learn how to do intrusion detection. Would-be analysts are learning all the things that you learned in this book: bit masking, basic analysis skills, and how to write filters, all the atomic skills that prepare one to do intrusion detection.

At the same time, companies are working to build better and better tools. It is fairly clear at this point that you cannot build an IDS that does not require a skilled operator. The one commercial company that tried to make an easy-to-use GUI as number one priority gets a lot of sales, but many companies that buy their products are replacing them a year later. As we move forward, it looks like the balance will swing to tools designed to allow an analyst to use her skills.

Analysts Skill Set

Intrusion-detection systems have the same problem as anti-virus software: New attacks are not detected because there is no signature for them. But the problem is worse because so few signatures have been defined for NIDS, still less than 2,000 decent signatures, compared with the 30,000 or more for anti-virus. There are natural limitations of signature-based network intrusion-detection systems, and to be effective, I recommend coping strategies like a box recording all traffic. That way, it is possible to go back after the NID alerts and examine the stimulus that lead to the activity reported by the NID. I also like to keep a cache of at least several days of raw data, so if I get lucky and detect something I have a way of checking to see if there was previous activity. Today, an analyst needs the ability to write a filter to run these types of searches. In the future, as console solutions are fielded, it might be possible to do much of this with canned searches, but even with relational databases, an analyst might have to be able to describe the search he needs in SQL.

Companies are realizing they need skilled people. Even in the economic downturn of 2001, SANS was still running class after class and most of the classes were full. Companies are even requiring certification when they are looking to hire. At first, this was laudable, but depressing, "IDS Analyst needed, must be able to write IDS rules, interpret hex, and hold a current CISSP certification." Arrrg, please do not interpret this as a slam against the Certified Information System Security Professions (CISSP), but the CISSP certainly does not certify a person to run an IDS or configure a firewall or to do any other technical task. However, companies are learning fast, and recently the Foote survey echoed the earlier Gartner survey that showed Global Information Assurance Certifications (GIAC) certifications contributed to a higher salary and a higher chance of employment. The tools are getting better, but for the next few years at least—and I expect forever—nothing replaces a skilled analyst.

The rapid emergence of personal firewalls is already a major defensive force, although we need to find easy ways to harness this data. They range from the load-and-forget Symantec Internet Security, which combines anti-virus with lightweight protection and detection, to BlackIce, which can log packets for analysis. These folks have essentially solved that old host-based problem, the effort of deployment! Security conscious employees take it on themselves to install personal firewalls at work and at home; if they bother reporting, they become valuable sensor inputs. There are automated tools like Dshield, `www.dshield.org`, to take the data from these systems and examine it for trend information. Network-based NIDS are still being deployed at a good rate as well. It is easier to get someone to stick two boxes on her network than to get her to even think about adding a nonproduction, cycle-consuming, software layer to all the hosts in her network. When I analyze what it takes to do a really effective job of intrusion detection, the advantages of personal firewalls on the host computers of security-aware employees are enormous and really add to the network-based data. So, it is no surprise that we are coming to the age of the console, the database driven system that normalizes NID data with firewall, personal firewall, anti-virus, and potentially other data such as syslog reports, and gives us a better view of what is going on in our networks defensively than we have ever had.

Improved Tools

These new consoles have a number of forms. Some of them are advanced log watchers like Big Brother (`www.bb4.com`) and NetIQ (`www.netiq.com`); content analysis tools like SilentRunner (`www.silentrunner.com`); and correlation engines tools like netForensics (`www.netforensics.com`), ISS SiteProtector (`www.iss.net`), and Intellitactics NSM (`www.intellitactics.com`). This is just the tip of the iceberg. I know of a number of companies that are racing to unveil products including the Sourcefire OpenSnort console (`www.sourcefire.com`) that uses the high performance database tool named barnyard that was developed by Andrew Baker. As they start to really compete and we go through the rounds of reviews and bakeoffs, we should end up with some very usable tools. The good news is that there are factors that should serve to slow the rate of improvement for attacker tools.

Companies have been buying tools all along, but they are not getting the kind of quality they deserve for the money they spend. We mentioned a commercial IDS earlier that many companies, a year after they install it, are replacing. What is wrong with this picture? Obviously, the company has a world class marketing program, but how have we as a community allowed a sensor that doesn't even record the TCP code bits to exist for so many years, to waste so many organizations' time and money? The good news is it looks like the next release will be credible, but we need to demand tools that work.

The competition in the network intrusion detection arena is funny. You don't have to be an industry insider to quickly realize that Ron Gula with Dragon, Robert Graham with BlackIce, now RealSecure and Marty Roesch with Snort are not just brilliant, they are really invested mentally and emotionally in their products. In the background is the very capable Kevin Zeise on the Cisco team. He might not be as visible as the others in the field, but he is the kind of guy that runs four miles in the morning, eats two pieces of key lime pie for breakfast, rolls out a new product line by lunch, and then saves the world from the latest cyber catastrophe before retiring for the evening. He is fully capable of running with the IDS pack. The various mailing list and conference battles are great entertainment, but they also serve a purpose. In a world of marketing and lies, these three folks, at least for now, are seriously committed to building the best tool they can. Who will win? It isn't something one person can do, it will be the best team. So in the spirit of predicting the future, back out onto a limb I go:

- Enterasys is having some problems right now with the SEC and has had cash flow problems for a while. Stock options aren't as much of a motivator when you drop from 11 to 4 in a single day, so watch for some bailouts of brainy engineers that want another shot at making a million dollars. I like Dragon and particularly like some of their network gear but don't think I want in for more than a 100 shares—too likely to become wallpaper. So, I think Dragon could have been a contender, but the SEC probably banged them too hard for them to compete in this neck-and-neck field.

- ISS and Robert Graham have to be the odds-on favorite in early 2002. The ISS management team is good, the marketing team better, and the X-Force side of the house has been solid for years. There were a lot of things I liked about BlackIce that Robert could build into RealSecure in his sleep. There is no doubt in my mind that, short of burning out or getting hit by a bus, Robert will produce a sensor to be reckoned with. The question is whether they will be able to build or integrate with a great console. As I write this, SiteProtector is just too new to be evaluated, but it has to work for ISS to shine because they have bet heavily on entering the managed services market, and they need this tool to do it. My prediction is that the answer will come down to the skills versus tools argument. If they build their console so that it helps a skilled worker be all she can be, I think ISS can win against everyone except Cisco. If they build a console that has a philosophy of "sit here and if you see a red triangle, call me," I think they will lose any chance at market credibility.

- Cisco developed a strategy years ago of moving intrusion detection into the network. The Catalyst 6000 and the Policy Feature Card is going to give TopLayer, the darling of the gotta go fast intrusion analyst, a serious run for the money. This call is a no brainer. High-end sites with high-value assets are going to go Cisco. My money is where my mouth is too; when their stock dips, we pick up another chunk whenever we can.

- Sourcefire, led by Marty Roesch, just received two million dollars in round one venture capital. I need to be honest; I am hardly objective. When the company started and I was given an opportunity to fund the startup, I jumped at it. So read what I say with more than a bit of salt and I will try to stick to the main issues. The facts are simple: Snort is the most widely deployed sensor on the planet and the Snort ruleset and language are the most commonly read and written. This is without debate. However, that is free Snort, and I have watched from the sidelines as my friend Gene Kim and Tripwire have tried to make the transition from free software to commercialware and it is not an easy task. Moreover, Marty is not the only one with the idea of commercializing Snort. My guess is that he has entered the market at the best of times. At a time when it is harder and harder to find a decent stock value, ISS and Enterasys have plummeted, reducing their value, this is now a great opportunity for the tiny Sourcefire.

The bottom line, my guess, is that by the time this book gets into your hands, Cisco and Sourcefire will be stronger, ISS holding its own, Enterasys on the ropes, and NFR, no closer to an IPO than they ever were. Will Tippingpoint, the new Swiss army knife of information security, even be in the running? Probably not, it is most likely still a year or two before users will be ready for integrated firewalls/NIDs, but we will see. The fact that cannot be argued is that the significant competition and innovation is driving the bar up and we all win because of that. One reason that I am so focused on this new generation of consoles is they are the foundation for analysts to maintain situational awareness and one of the most important tools for building active defense in depth.

Defense in Depth

Military history teaches us to never rely on a single defensive line or technique. We have tried to teach you not to rely on your NID alone. When a filter fires, it might be necessary to determine why it fired and the network activity that preceded it. We have been trying to teach you to rely on your ability to decode a packet in addition to using your NID as a tool. This is one small example of defense in depth.

The firewall serves as an effective noise filter, stopping many attacks before they can enter your network. Within your internal net, the router or switch can be configured to watch for signs of intrusion or fraud. When a detect occurs, the switch either can block the session and seal off the host or just send a silent alarm. You can improve your model further by adding the host-based layer of defense. Here, you can detect the insider with a legitimate login (whether or not it is really his) accessing files he shouldn't. Toss in a couple more network-based intrusion-detection systems, including a few stealthy ones, and you have an architecture sufficient to counter the increasing threat. Sadly, this architecture seems to be more likely found in a Jetsons cartoon than real life. So what is possible today and in the near future to implement defense in depth?

The five perimeter rules of the road are the first steps, the ones you should put into practice today if you are not already doing them. Please do not start with a lot of talk about a crunchy perimeter and a soft chewy inside; we will get there soon enough. The five rules are all covered in the book and the appendix, but this is the final chapter and needs to be the summary chapter as well as a discussion on the future of intrusion detection. The five rules of the road are as follows:

- **Squelch all outgoing ICMP error unreachable messages.** You might choose to stop other outgoing ICMP error messages, but do not fail to stop these. Doing this will reduce your site's vulnerability to reconnaissance.

- **Split horizon DNS.** You might call this by a different name, but the concept is simple. The DNS server(s) that can be reached from the outside should only know about a few of your hosts including your mail server, web server, and you fill in the rest of the blanks. Otherwise, this DNS server can be used for reconnaissance against your site.

- **Proxy when possible.** Not only are proxies available on your firewall, but they can also be put between the Internet and your Internet facing devices.

- **Network Address Translation (NAT).** If your site can find the backbone to give up those evil public addresses and move to private addresses, you will instantly find a tenfold benefit in your resistance to attack.

- **Implement auto-response.** Yes, really. The anti-junk mail world has been doing it for years. The Raptor firewall with its active defense and BackOfficer Friendly haven't melted down the world. There is a place for auto-response and you need to get in the game (as they say in the movie *Zorro*), as safely as possible.

Defense in depth doesn't stop with the perimeter, of course. It includes configuration management, personal firewalls, anti-virus, content scanning at the perimeter, operating system patches, and an active vulnerability scanning program.

Large-Scale Intrusion Detection

One of the most fascinating trends in 2001 was the emergence of three large-scale intrusion detection efforts: Aris by SecurityFocus.com, MyNetWatchman (www.mynetwatchman.com), and Dshield (www.dshield.org). Each of these works by providing reporting software to hundreds or even thousands of clients. These clients range from Check Point firewalls and Linksys cable routers to personal firewalls. The data is sent to a central site that allows it to be examined for trends.

The aggregation of this much data from all over the world is a powerful tool. Dshield, for instance, was adding about six million records per week. Although there are significant issues with normalization, within the first year of Dshield's operation, the technology was used to discover the Ramen, Lion, and Leaves worms. For instance, the CERT advisory on widespread vulnerabilities with SNMP and ASN.1 was released on February 12, 2002, and you could see the increase in scanning as the month progressed, as shown in Figure 20.1.

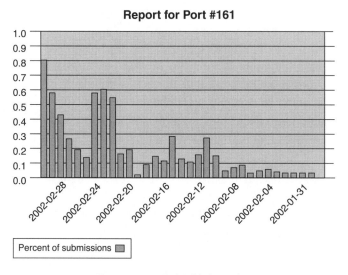

Figure 20.1   Dshield data plot.

These are new implementations, and the community is still trying to learn how to make the best use of the tools. Distributed intrusion detection systems like Dshield is such a profoundly significant concept that a number of people I talked with found it hard to understand why it hadn't been done earlier. One of the reasons is that a subtle shift in attitude took place after the turn of the century, and people were willing to share data.

Sharing

I asked the Incidents.org community if anyone wanted to contribute a sidebar for the second edition of the book. It is no less true today, so we will keep it in this edition. The following was submitted by Richard Bejtlich, a skilled intrusion analyst, and I decided to place it here primarily because of the fourth question below.

"I make optimum use of my network intrusion detection system (NIDS) by asking four questions:

- What could cause suspicious traffic to be generated?

- What events could my NIDS miss?

- How does real Internet behavior differ from textbook descriptions?

- Should I share events with the security community?

The first question suggests that packets can be forged, manipulated, and unwillingly solicited, in addition to being routed directly. The second question requires me to understand my NIDS' limitations, and remember it might not explain or even capture every related packet. The third question implies that traffic not matching the norms of RFCs or technical studies is not always malicious. The last question encourages intrusion detectors to share their questions and discoveries with the security community, whether through www.sans.org or forums like the securityfocus.com Incidents list."[1]

[1]Richard Bejtlich

In addition to detection, these large-scale intrusion detection networks also play a crucial role in response. As they collect data and the information passes a certain threshold, they can create automated or semi-automated reports and send them to the responsible party for an IP address. For instance, on February 28, 2002, IP address 217.128.207.17 from the abo.wanadoo.fr domain was detected sending 33,995 packets. Now, that certainly warrants sending a note, though sending a note to Wanadoo asking them to quit ftp scanning is a bit like sending a note to Bin Laden asking him to stop terrorism—at best, they don't care. However, many people do care, and the note from Dshield might be the first hint a system administrator gets to help him realize he has a problem. Below is a note from another satisfied customer:

> "Thank you for the notification of illicit activity coming from a computer in the University of XXXXX XXXXXX domain. This was a faculty member's computer that was found to have the "mummy" virus when the eSafe virus scanner was ran on the computer. We have attempted to disinfect this computer to prevent the unauthorized intrusions to your and other networks. Again thanks for the notification; and if there is anything else we can do, please let me know."

By the way, I am a bit skeptical about the particulars in the report. The mummy virus is an MS-DOS Jerusalem variant, so this sounds like an excuse to cover some mischief, but as long as the behavior changes, it is another win for these new defense systems. To date, only Aris has a business model to support what it is doing, so it is not clear that these first implementations of large-scale intrusion detection will survive long term. I certainly hope they are an emerging trend. I would like to close the chapter and the book with a quick review of the anti-virus industry, a discussion of hardware-based and program-based intrusion detection, and finally, some of the changes in auditing.

Emerging Techniques

Current intrusion-detection systems are fairly limited. Network-based systems are not well suited to detect the insider threat, mobile code, intelligence-gathering viruses, modem-based attacks, or runs along the trust model. Host-based systems can detect these attacks, but they suffer from two big problems: the cost of deployment and the system overhead "tax." There is a lot of money to be made by the company that can build and market the better mousetrap. The enterprise security consoles we have discussed are one technology poised to collect some of this money—after all, what security guy is not going to want a cockpit? Curiously, the market sector that appears to have snatched defeat from the jaws of victory is the anti-virus arena.

Virus Industry Revisited

I have watched in amazement as NAI and Symantec, two companies in exactly the right place to take advantage of the gap between the increasing threat and existing response, have failed to take total control of the host-based intrusion detection market. Even if anti-virus makers do not want anything to do with the intrusion-detection market sector, they are already intersecting with it. These Trojans all have a network signature, SubSeven, and netbus and all the rest. Anti-virus companies can detect all of these and remove them as well! Well, maybe not. The first clue I had that anti-virus could be evaded was when one of my students realized he had accidentally downloaded a Trojan when he saw "notepad.exe" go by after having clicked on a download page. After some investigation, he determined it was QAZ. And yet, his anti-virus didn't pick it up. But how is this possible with a well known Trojan? Well, it turns out that the attacker community can "pack" the Trojan with any number of tools. For more information on this, go to http://rr.sans.org/malicious/trojan_war.php.

However, do not count out the anti-virus industry. It can detect the work of many of the more popular packers and certainly can detect the Trojan when it becomes active on the network if you also have a personal firewall packaged with your anti-virus. Well, you can if the malicious code doesn't disable the firewall and/or anti-virus software as one of its first orders of business, but the companies are working on defending against this as well.

Symantec's Internet Security product that combines anti-virus with a personal firewall is not a bad product, but it could have been a killer application. Anti-virus companies are poised to be the 800-pound gorillas in intrusion detection. An anti-virus company could excel in this industry because of the following eight reasons:

- No security tool has better desktop penetration than anti-virus software.

- Intrusion-detection tools often have fewer than 500 signatures; virus software can detect more than 20,000.

- Virus software comes with implementations for firewalls, server systems, or the desktop.

- These tools can identify, contain, eradicate, and recover with minimal user intervention.

- Anti-virus companies have fully solved the issue of updating a user's signature table with a variety of painless options.

- Many large organizations have site licenses with these software companies and are pretty satisfied.

- Anti-virus companies are already oriented to very fast turnaround of a signature table when a new exploit is detected.

- These software companies often have companion products with security capabilities.

The match is so perfect that I cannot understand why we aren't seeing these products dominate the industry. It would be so easy to make the changes to the NAI or Symantec personal firewalls to let them serve as network intrusion detection systems, but with every software release, they seem to move further and further away from providing a tool that is industrial strength.

Next, we will discuss intrusion detection in hardware. Cisco, more than any other company, has been intentionally pursuing putting intrusion detection in the network itself, so that you have hardware-based intrusion detection solutions.

Hardware-Based ID

There are three serious challenges to network-based intrusion detection:

- Encrypted packets that foil string matching
- Fast networks beyond the speed of the sensor
- Switched networks

We discuss intrusion detection in the switch shortly. Encryption is an interesting problem. It is good if your organization is doing it and having the key escrowed. Encryption is a bad thing if someone is using it to evade your detection system. How do you know if a bit stream is encrypted? You test for randomness, of course. This is easy to do, but expensive in terms of CPU cycles. There is an argument that this should be done in hardware. I am not sure this is valid; general-purpose computers keep getting faster and faster. With that said, there are places where applying hardware to the problem makes a lot of sense. One of the best applications is faster nets.

The perfect place for Cisco SecureIDS is on a card placed in a Cisco router or switch. This, however, is just a toaster without a power supply. The really interesting advances come by doing limited intrusion detection as a software process in the router or switch. This is a desperately needed future trend. One advantage of this is that you finally achieve real-time, or wire speed. In all other solutions (except intrusion detection in the firewall), you detect the intrusion right after the packet has flown by. In this case, you can literally stop it or divert it to a honeypot. The capability to do this seems to be at hand with the Policy Feature Card that is available for the Catalyst 6000 switches. I am not sure why they built the card, perhaps to provide a product to compete with TopLayer, the application layer switch that well-funded intrusion detection analysts turn to when they have the need for speed. Perhaps they project advances in the QoS market that I just do not see on the horizon. However, the ability to filter, mark a packet, application switch, or failover switch inside the network fabric at the rate of 5 million packets per second at layer 3—much more at layer 2—opens a number of possibilities for detection and protection. This would include many of the auto-response capabilities such as dropping a connection, rate limiting, copying traffic to a more powerful IDS or binary logger, or switching the connection to a honeypot. Like large-scale intrusion detection systems, it will be a while before we really know what to do with tools like this, but learning should be a lot of fun.

Program-Based ID

I just cannot get over the size of programs today. I used to own a computer called a Commodore 64. The 64 stood for the amount of RAM, 64K. The implication is that the programs had to load and run in that memory space. There is an important lesson to be learned by comparing the functionality of the Commodore 64 to my 400Mhz Pentium II with 1024MB of RAM. The applications that ran on the Commodore had about the same functionality as my Microsoft Office suite. However, these programs are huge! If we are going to tolerate bloatware, and it is clear we will, we might as well start asking for some security in the programs.

At the seminal conference for intrusion detection SANS' ID'99, I was fortunate enough to break away for an hour to have lunch with Simson Garfinkle, who is writing software designed for special-security applications. A lot of security software, especially vulnerability-testing programs, can be used for malicious purposes. He wants to protect his intellectual property from intrusion (software piracy), and he also wants to ensure the software cannot be misused without it being clear and obvious which copy of the software is the origin.

Can software prevent or detect that it is being copied or misused? For a while, this was a big issue for computer games, at least the copy-protection aspect. It doesn't seem to be such a hot topic today. None of the games my son has bought require a dongle. One of the forensics tools I use, Expert Witness, has some degree of license protection built in with a hardware dongle. Microsoft must have some scheme with its strange orange sticker on the CDs, the long pin numbers, and its techniques for phoning home and inspecting the network for license violations. Simson, however, was taking the issue a lot more seriously than any of these companies appear to be. He was proposing a series of countermeasures, including encrypting segments of the programs and chaining checksums.

Let's take this a step further. Could a critical program detect that it is under attack? Suppose sendmail or Bind had a static library of security functions. The program could then detect an unauthorized entity is trying to access it, or that the input it is receiving is actually binary code. It could then block the attack and raise an alarm. Programs could even develop profiles about their uses so that they can detect that someone "out of profile" is accessing their files and take some preprogrammed action. Still another way to do intrusion detection at the program level is to put a wrapper around the program, which is most certainly an emerging trend.

The first wrapper was Wietse Venema's TCP Wrapper program, which was a wonderful security tool for years—although perhaps xinetd with ICMP support is more appropriate today. But, the concept has been extended. You might want to check out immunix (`www.immunix.org`). I would expect that, for Internet facing applications, this will be an emerging theme to the point that eventually, sound practice will be to chroot it, wrap it, or both.

Smart Auditors

This emerging trend was in the book the first go around and it didn't happen. I put it in again in the second edition and there was some progress—not enough for me to get hired by Miss Cleo—but I am sticking with this as an emerging trend! According to Alan Kay, the best way to predict the future is to invent it, and by the time this book is in your hands, SANS should be engaged in helping to establish pragmatic tools and resources for auditors. Auditors are already smart—that is why they do the auditing and you do the sweating. Auditors are starting to understand security technology and practices at a rapid rate. The days are gone and will not return when they ask whether you have a firewall, nod when you say "yes," and then walk away.

I think the emerging trend is for auditors to understand security-assessment tools and to be able to operate them. Auditors can visit your site, plug in, and, while they are interviewing you, run an assessment tool. They can then compare your answers against the assessment—cheerful thought, eh?

Although it will be a pain for system administrators when we are audited, knowledgeable, equipped auditors could be one of the most effective countermeasures against the increasing threat. Hackers, trusted insiders, and malicious code authors are not really that smart; we are just a bit lazy, careless, and naive. So when we make a mistake or get sloppy, it leaves a hole that attackers find and exploit. If we are held accountable, we actually do the things that we know we ought to do and the organization benefits.

Summary

All data that I have indicates that the future looks good for the intrusion-detection analyst. We will have plenty of work to do, and we should be able to get decent pay for our work. Good analysts are in extreme demand, and that should not change in the near term. Companies are starting to understand that the skills component is important and are asking for GCIA certifications, or demonstrated ability for higher paying jobs. Tools, techniques, and training are being developed to counter the threats, and some of these will make our lives easier.

Thank you for reading this book. I have enjoyed teaming with Judy and Marty on this update, and I thank them for their skills and insights. Truly this is becoming an analyst's handbook.

Please grant me one closing note, one more minute of your precious time.
The `www.incidents.org` resource depends upon the involvement of the community and may well have to close at some point. While it is there, your book
comes with a warranty, a way to stay up-to-date, a forum to discuss anything
you don't understand or disagree with, and most important, a place for you to
share your insights. Please get involved. We welcome every nation, every point
of view, and detects from every brand of intrusion-detection software.
Intrusion detection is in its infancy and needs to improve. That can only
happen if you get involved. See you on Incidents!

V

Appendixes

Exploits and Scans to Apply Exploits

IN THIS APPENDIX, WE WILL EXAMINE a number of network traces. Each has a story to tell. Most of these traces are in the TCPdump format. This format is consistent with the traces in the book *TCP/IP Illustrated, Volume 1: The Protocols*, by Richard Stevens (published by Addison Wesley, 1994). This reference should be at the fingertips of any serious intrusion-detection analyst

False Positives

This appendix starts with some of the errors analysts are prone to make. Although the *Computer Incident Response Teams* (CIRTs) hire some top-notch analysts, the errors in this first section are just subtle enough that they might slip by them as well. On the surface, many CIRTs say that they prefer that you report liberally, even if you are afraid it might be a false positive. I agree, to a point, although I think that if you are not sure what something is you should say so right in the report! In the final analysis, you (as the analyst) are closest to the data. You see the network traffic on a daily basis. To steal a line from America's second-favorite bear, "Only you can prevent false positives."

All Response, No Stimulus

The following trace is the classic pattern commonly mistaken for a backdoor. Before going too far, however, take a look at some of the characteristics of the trace so that you don't miss anything. At 7:17, the sensor observed a packet from mysystem, the source port was echo (or 7), the packet was addressed to target1 destination port 24925, and the size was 64 bytes:

```
TIME                 SRCHOST  SRCPORT >   DSTHOST DSTPORT  Proto Size
07:17:09.615279      mysystem.echo   > target1.24925:     udp   64
```

The first time I saw this, my blood pressure went through the ceiling; I just knew I was dealing with a backdoor. Why, you might ask? Well I *knew* that my site blocked incoming echo at the firewall, so it was not possible that someone was bouncing echoes off of mysystem. Therefore, my reasoning was that I was either dealing with some form of malicious code, a UDP flooder of some sort that had a signature of source port 7, or there was a backdoor. Now, that was bad reasoning because no one in his right mind would write malicious code that used 7 as a source port—it would be too likely to draw attention.

When I searched for the stimulus traffic, however, I could not find it, and that is what confused me. In truth, the network perimeter had changed over the weekend and someone really was bouncing echoes off of mysystem. Why didn't I see the stimulus traffic? The two most likely possibilities are asymmetric routing and a misconfigured spanning port. Some older implementations of switched networks in spanning mode only span one direction of the traffic, which can cause a false positive. Here is the trace:

```
07:17:09.615279 mysystem.echo > target1.24925: udp 64
07:17:10.978236 mysystem.echo > irc.some.where.40809: udp 600
07:17:11.001745 mysystem.echo > irc.some.where.14643: udp 600
07:17:11.146935 mysystem.echo > irc.some.where.49911: udp 600
07:17:12.254277 mysystem.echo > irc.some.where.28480: udp 600
07:17:12.350014 mysystem.echo > irc.some.where.20683: udp 600
07:17:12.835873 mysystem.echo > target1.5134: udp 64
07:17:13.266794 mysystem.echo > irc.some.where.16911: udp 600
07:17:13.862476 mysystem.echo > target1.32542: udp 64
07:17:14.032603 mysystem.echo > irc.some.where.32193: udp 600
07:17:14.579404 mysystem.echo > irc.some.where.24455: udp 600
07:17:14.619173 mysystem.echo > irc.some.where.5120: udp 600
07:17:14.792983 mysystem.echo > irc.some.where.47466: udp 600
07:17:14.879559 mysystem.echo > target1.16878: udp 64
07:17:15.308270 mysystem.echo > irc.some.where.12234: udp 600
```

Spanning Ports

Switched networks are a major challenge for network-based intrusion detection. A sensor with a single network interface, one that listens in promiscuous mode and also reports to the analysis station, might upset some switched network configurations.

If your network operations folks want you to add a second interface to the sensor, you should try to accommodate them. Use one interface to listen in promiscuous mode; it doesn't even need an IP address. The other interface can be for communication with the sensor. In fact, this is pretty much the best practice for running a network intrusion-detection sensor these days as it helps protect the sensor from attackers and makes it harder to detect.

If the preceding trace is not caused by a misconfiguration of a spanning port on a switched network, what else could cause it? A backdoor connection or malicious code could certainly cause this pattern, but make that your second guess.

This trace is titled "All Response, No Stimulus." IP communications generally have a stimulus and a response. When analysts encounter traces they don't understand, their job is to determine what the stimulus was. This determination helps answer the questions about what is going on. This trace stands out because you can tear through all the traffic, but you cannot find the stimulus; this is all the sensor sees. The event of interest in this case is the packets being sent to mysystem's echo port.

What else can you learn from this trace? For starters, what is this echo thing, and what does it do? The echo program reads a string and repeats it. Think of it as an automated liberal arts undergraduate student. Now that you know the expected behavior of echo, it is possible to fill in the blanks for what the traffic should have looked like (if the sensor is misconfigured, for example, or if we are dealing with a backdoor connection).

The simulated, reconstructed traffic is as follows:

```
07:17:09.527910 target1.24925 > mysystem.echo: udp 64
07:17:09.615279 mysystem.echo > target1.24925: udp 64
07:17:10.823651 irc.some.where.40809 > mysystem.echo: udp 600
07:17:10.978236 mysystem.echo > irc.some.where.40809: udp 600
```

So what does that show? It shows target1 and irc.some.where sending a string to mysystem and getting the string echoed back. Now why would they do that? The answer is they probably wouldn't. Even if one system was to use echo for testing or to troubleshoot, two using it simultaneously stretches coincidence past the breaking point. This is probably a denial-of-service with target1 and irc.some.where as the intended victims. A wise rule of thumb is to turn off any network service on a computer system you don't actually need. If the system administrator for mysystem had commented echo out of /etc/inetd.conf, this trace would have never happened. If this hasn't convinced you to turn echo off yet, that's okay—additional traces later on show more fun with echo.

This trace has yet another problem. The destination ports include 24925, 40809, 14643, 49911, and so on. Because these are echo replies, we assume they were the source ports from the sending system. The range is more random than normal for source ports, however; generally, you can expect to see 24925 followed by 24926 and so forth. Therefore, these are probably replies to crafted packets. Mistaking a trace for a "backdoor" pattern (when it is, in fact, a misconfigured switched network) can happen, but it is not that common.

Take a look at one final example of "All Response, No Stimulus" before moving on. At first glance, this too might be perceived to be an attack of some sort:

```
11:38:54.010000 masker.com > 192.168.133.127: icmp: address mask is 0xffffe00
11:39:43.180000 masker.com > 172.16.33.116: icmp: address mask is 0xffffe00
11:53:37.780000 masker.com > 192.168.58.105: icmp: address mask is 0xffffe00
11:56:43.690000 masker.com > 172.16.178.85: icmp: address mask is 0xffffe00
12:15:52.550000 masker.com > 172.16.121.67: icmp: address mask is 0xffffe00
12:25:41.800000 masker.com > 172.16.247.72: icmp: address mask is 0xffffe00
12:45:07.470000 masker.com > 172.16.110.69: icmp: address mask is 0xffffe00
12:45:31.530000 masker.com > 172.16.167.73: icmp: address mask is 0xffffe00
12:58:23.350000 masker.com > 192.168.214.116: icmp: address mask is 0xffffe00
```

Remember the ICMP address mask request? It asked a host to respond with the subnet mask of the network on which it resided. Although the TCPdump output does not have the word *reply* in it, you do see the words *address mask* and a hexadecimal number. These are replies to address mask requests. All the hosts receiving these replies are nonexistent hosts, however, so they could not have initiated the request.

Again, it appears that the culprit is spoofing the 192.168 and 172.16 IPs and firing them at masker.com. Why would someone most likely do this? An educated guess is some kind of flooding attempt to masker.com using a different delivery mechanism than an ICMP echo request. Truthfully, it really doesn't matter what kind of activity you direct at a target host if flooding and perhaps a denial of service are the intent. Now, take a look at a false positive that has fooled many beginning analysts.

Scan or Response?

Take a look at the following detect that appeared on Shadow's hourly web wrap-up. Shadow is configured to look for traffic destined for UDP port 1080, which is the socks proxy server. There are some associated exploits, so we want to be alerted when someone shows interest in the socks port. Here it is:

```
18:20:12.080000 dns.com.53 > myhost.com.1080: 5 NXDomain* 0/1/0 (128)
18:20:12.300000 dns.com.53 > myhost.com.1080: 6 NXDomain* 0/1/0 (119)
18:20:12.410000 dns.com.53 > myhost.com.1080: 7* 1/0/0 (48)
```

But, look carefully at what is going on in this output. Does anything look vaguely familiar to you? Concentrate on the notation after the 1080. Is that your final answer, or perhaps maybe you want to use a lifeline to the audience? What about the source port? A correct response does not yield a million dollars or help ratings during TV Sweeps month, but isn't this reminiscent of some kind of DNS activity? Yes, it appears to be a response from dns.com to myhost.com for multiple DNS queries that were issued. The identification numbers for the queries are 5, 6, and 7, and query number 7 received one resource record, no authority records, and no additional records.

Because this smacks more of response than scan, you need to look at out-bound traffic from your network to see whether this was a DNS query initi-ated by myhost.com. Sure enough, the following output puts this all in perspective:

```
18:20:11.870000 myhost.com.1080 > dns.com.53: 5+ (50)
18:20:12.090000 myhost.com.1080 > dns.com.53: 6+ (41)
18:20:12.310000 myhost.com.1080 > dns.com.53: 7+ (32)
```

The explanation is that myhost.com requested resolution of queries 5, 6, and 7 from dns.com. The client selected ephemeral source port 1080 on which to issue these queries. When the responses came back from myhost.com, they were directed to destination port 1080. Shadow cannot correlate what we just did, however, and so blindly fires any time a scan is detected on its signature filters. The bottom line is that this is a false positive. One of the most common false positives, however, is the SYN flood.

SYN Floods

As an analyst, one of the scary calls for me to make is a SYN flood. It is very easy for an intrusion-detection system to be wrong about this when, in fact, this detect actually is a false positive. If the SYN flood comes from a known hostile address, or if other hostile activity is associated with the connection, or if it is very obvious (50 or more connection attempts in less than a minute, for example), I might report the activity. Otherwise, I tend to sit on it and watch for further activity.

Valid SYN Flood

The following trace shows an actual SYN flood:

```
14:18:22.5660 flooder.601 > server.login: S 1382726961:1382726961(0) win 4096
14:18:22.7447 flooder.602 > server.login: S 1382726962:1382726962(0) win 4096
14:18:22.8311 flooder.603 > server.login: S 1382726963:1382726963(0) win 4096
14:18:22.8868 flooder.604 > server.login: S 1382726964:1382726964(0) win 4096
14:18:22.9434 flooder.605 > server.login: S 1382726965:1382726965(0) win 4096
```

```
14:18:23.0025 flooder.606 > server.login: S 1382726966:1382726966(0) win 4096
14:18:23.1035 flooder.607 > server.login: S 1382726967:1382726967(0) win 4096
14:18:23.1621 flooder.608 > server.login: S 1382726968:1382726968(0) win 4096
14:18:23.2284 flooder.609 > server.login: S 1382726969:1382726969(0) win 4096
14:18:23.2825 flooder.610 > server.login: S 1382726970:1382726970(0) win 4096
14:18:23.3457 flooder.611 > server.login: S 1382726971:1382726971(0) win 4096
14:18:23.4083 flooder.612 > server.login: S 1382726972:1382726972(0) win 4096
14:18:23.9030 flooder.613 > server.login: S 1382726973:1382726973(0) win 4096
14:18:24.0052 flooder.614 > server.login: S 1382726974:1382726974(0) win 4096
```

Did that look familiar? Maybe this will help:

Source: tsutomu@ariel.sdsc.edu (Tsutomu Shimomura), comp.security.misc
Date: 25 Jan 1995

"About six minutes later, we see a flurry of TCP SYNs (initial connection requests) from 130.92.6.97 to port 513 (login) on server. The purpose of these SYNs is to fill the connection queue for port 513 on server with 'half-open' connections so it will not respond to any new connection requests. In particular, it will not generate TCP RSTs in response to unexpected SYN-ACKs."

False Positive SYN Flood

After you compare the preceding excerpt from the Mitnick attack with the following trace, you might wonder what the heck the difference is. Well, the differences are quite subtle. The source port increments in both traces, as does the sequence number. The TCP window size is the same: 4096 bytes. Clearly, there are two TCP retries with four packets each shown below, note the static source port and static sequence number and the 3, 6, 12 time interval. The arrival times of the packets are very similar. So how do we sort this out?

```
14:02:22.5166 host.2104 > server.25: S 1382726960:1382726960(0) win 4096
14:02:25.5669 host.2104 > server.25: S 1382726960:1382726960(0) win 4096
14:02:31.7447 host.2104 > server.25: S 1382726960:1382726960(0) win 4096
14:02:42.8311 host.2104 > server.25: S 1382726960:1382726960(0) win 4096
14:02:58.8868 host2.3311 > server.25: S 2382927964:2382927964(0) win 4096
14:03:01.9434 host2.3311 > server.25: S 2382927964:2382927964(0) win 4096
14:03:07.0025 host2.3311 > server.25: S 2382927964:2382927964(0) win 4096
14:03:19.1035 host2.3311 > server.25: S 2382927964:2382927964(0) win 4096
```

What a difference a small change, email rather than a different service, makes! Email is expensive, at least to mail relays. If the email relay cannot push the mail out the first time, the relay must try again an hour later. If you notice the time, you get a hint of what is to come. The "victim" of the denial–of–service attack here is not a victim at all, it is a mail server and it is down. The mail is queued up all over the world trying to send it the mail. Every hour these systems, all over the world, try again, often near the top of the hour. So, we have this false *SYN flood* condition.

Another very common false positive is Microsoft Internet Explorer visiting a web page. It creates a connection for each GIF, JPEG, HTML, and so forth, up to a limit of 32. As a rule of thumb, therefore, do not report a SYN flood on TCP 25, TCP 80, or TCP 443.

Even better, as a general rule, be very slow to believe your IDS or to report a SYN flood (especially because you are just beginning your journey as an analyst). Most commercial intrusion-detection systems produce false positives on SYN floods so often that you have to set their counters to a very high number, which means they will never detect a real SYN flood. The good news is that more modern operating systems can resist SYN floods of low numbers of SYNs, so it is becoming safer and safer to ignore them. The SYN floods that do affect modern systems are very high volume and difficult not to detect.

Although SYN floods in low volumes might be safe to ignore, the Windows Trojan horses (such as Back Orifice) certainly are not. These programs can give an attacker total control over an infected computer. When dealing with a high-risk problem such as Back Orifice, the analyst should not turn that filter off on the intrusion-detection system even if the filter generates false positives.

Back Orifice?

Trojan horses and scanning for Trojans accounts for a large number of the attacks between mid-1997 and the present. Back Orifice and Netbus were the original frontrunners in late 1998 or early 1999, and then SubSeven became a major force in late '99 and early 2000. The default port for Back Orifice is 31337 UDP, and 12345 TCP for Netbus (port 12346 as well, although I have never seen this in actual use). Most Trojans can be configured to operate at other ports of course, which can make it harder to locate them. Further, 31337, like 666 and the hex patterns dead beef are often of hacker activity. We saw this following trace twice in a single day; I just had to chuckle:

```
11:20:44.148361 ns1.com.31337 > ns2.arpa.net.53: 38787 A? arb.arpa.net. (34)
11:52:49.779731 ns1.com.31337 > ns1.arpa.net.53: 39230 ANY? hq.arpa.net. (36)
```

This is a great time to mention that TCPdump has a desire to be helpful. Although this is a UDP trace, it does not say UDP like the first echo example of this chapter. Instead, TCPdump uses this opportunity to tell us more about the packet because it knows DNS (UDP port 53), because DNS has its own format. Our client system ns1.com is doing a name lookup on the DNS server ns*.arpa.net. So what are the 31337s doing there?

As an analyst, this was the question I wanted to answer when I saw the trace. We pulled the packet, printed it in hex, ran it through tcpshow, and compared it to other DNS lookups. It was normal.

Before BIND 8, the expected, although not required, behavior from a name server doing a UDP lookup is that the source port is 53 as well. Sometimes, I have seen the source port as 137, indicating that the client is a Windows system. Why 31337?

Like all of us, I was busy at work, so I forgot about it until an analyst at another site flagged the same pattern to my attention. I picked up the phone and started working my way through this corporation until I finally found the bright young chap who managed the DNS server. I told him what I saw:

Northcutt: I am seeing source port 31337s coming to various DNS servers.

Young Chap: Uh, we've looked into it, and it is not Back Orifice.

Northcutt: I know that, but it sets off every intrusion-detection system that sees it.

Young Chap: You should fix your intrusion-detection system.

Northcutt: No. You fix your source port or my site will block you, and my friend's sites will block you; your company will lose its contracts, and you will lose your job.

He asked who I was again, and we started to make progress toward a solution.

So, we had a false positive in a sense; it was not an attack. Instead, it was just a young kid who figured that because he could configure a DNS system, he was "eleet." He just needed a bit of calibrating and everything was all right. Ignoring the traffic leads to some dangerous choices; an analyst should not disable an intrusion-detection system filter, for example, for a potentially dangerous attack signature. The analyst must verify that the detect is not a false positive before reporting it. Some people think I was overly harsh with the young chap. I would ask them to keep in mind the problems such activity could cause at the CIRT level. Remember, only you can prevent false positives.

Note that modern DNS servers running BIND 8 choose an unprivileged port above 1024, but they probably won't choose 31337 consistently.

This story also illustrates how important it is for your organization not just to report detects to your CIRT, but also to share with other intrusion-detection-capable organizations that have something in common with you. This is how I determined the 31337 wasn't just a fluke. Also, at times you might need to shun an Internet address block if they are being antisocial.

> **Shunning Works!**
>
> Once, a major Internet service provider was not providing support when its address block was being used to attack our sites. Time and time again we tried to reach its organization to get help. Finally, we blocked them (email, web, the whole nine yards). Within three weeks, they were screaming in pain because they were starting to lose money; corporate customers were pulling out. They agreed to be responsive in the future and to triple their Internet abuse staff. Who could ask for more?

This concludes the discussion about common false positives. Strictly speaking, the exploit is when the attacker goes for the kill and the software or technique exploits a vulnerability in a computer system. In actual practice, it is very difficult to distinguish between scanning for vulnerabilities and the actual attack. In fact, the current generation of attack tools do both; they scan to find vulnerabilities and they also attack. Therefore, this section contains a bit of mix and match, primarily considering vulnerabilities, but also touching on scanning for vulnerabilities when appropriate.

I am not the only one struggling with categorizing these traces in a nice organized manner. The research side of intrusion detection has been working on this problem for years and has not yet produced an accepted taxonomy of attacks. The *Database of Vulnerabilities, Exploits, and Signatures* (DOVES) project released a CD-ROM with its work on categorization in February 1999. For further information, contact Dr. Matt Bishop (bishop@cs.ucdavis.edu). Mitre has fostered the creation of the *Common Vulnerability Enumeration* (CVE). The CVE is probably the most significant effort and enjoys wide support from the vendor community; more than 2,000 vulnerabilities have been accepted by its editorial board at this time with an additional 1,700 candidates. For further information, check out CVE's web site at cve.mitre.org.

The following section examines traces from IMAP exploit attempts.

IMAP Exploits

No series of exploits has reaped as much havoc on the Internet as IMAP. Buffer overflows, such as the IMAP vulnerability, are not uncommon; several major problems have occurred with DNS buffer overflows as well. Because these programs run as root, the attack is potentially devastating, leaving the attacker with root access.

10143 Signature Source Port IMAP

The pattern here is the classic pattern of one of the most devastating buffer overflows ever unleashed on the Internet. Note that this scan contains two destination networks. Also note the time gap between packets. The gap is so large because this scan was targeting every Class B network on the Internet. This trace comes from mid-1997, and this particular signature is rarely seen now:

```
14:13:54.847401 newbie.hacker.org.10143 > 192.168.1.1.143: S
14:24:58.151128 newbie.hacker.org.10143 > 172.31.1.1.143: S
14:35:40.311513 newbie.hacker.org.10143 > 192.168.1.2.143: S
14:43:55.459380 newbie.hacker.org.10143 > 192.168.2.1.143: S
14:54:58.693768 newbie.hacker.org.10143 > 172.31.2.1.143: S
15:05:41.039905 newbie.hacker.org.10143 > 192.168.2.2.143: S
15:13:59.948065 newbie.hacker.org.10143 > 192.168.3.1.143: S
```

111 Signature IMAP

The following trace is another IMAP scan/exploit that has a repeatable signature. The fixed source port, the fixed sequence and acknowledgment fields with the 111, and of course the window size of 0 is a nice touch. From a signature-use standpoint, this one is particularly interesting. We started to see it in late 1998 following the large numbers of source port 0 and SF set scans, (these are shown next), and then it disappeared. In early 1999, this signature reappeared. I have no idea what the story behind this behavior is; it is as if the software got lost for a few months! Here is the trace:

```
00:25:09.57 prober.2666 > relay.143: S 111:111(0) win 0
00:25:09.59 prober.2666 > relay.143: S 111:111(0) win 0
00:42:50.79 prober.2666 > web.143: S 111:111(0) win 0
00:43:24.05 prober.2666 > relay.143: S 111:111(0) win 0
00:43:24.07 prober.2666 > relay.143: S 111:111(0) win 0
00:44:20.42 prober.2666 > relay2.143: S 111:111(0) win 0
00:44:42.62 prober.2666 > ns2.143: S 111:111(0) win 0
00:44:42.64 prober.2666 > ns2.143: S 111:111(0) win 0
00:44:42.67 prober.2666 > ns1.143: S 111:111(0) win 0
00:44:42.69 prober.2666 > ns1.143: S 111:111(0) win 0
```

Exploit Ports with SYN/FIN Set

One of the fascinating patterns to watch has been the various mutations of a pattern called SYN/FIN (or more commonly, SF). This is one of the most significant patterns in intrusion detection in the sense that an analyst will almost certainly have seen this and should be expected to know this pattern. The earliest instantiation I am aware of is the attack Jackal.c from late 1996, and the most recent variation I have seen was a buffer overflow against secure shell in December 2001. Attackers set SYN/FIN because it passes through a static packet filter, because they block on a SYN only. However, if a packet with SYN/FIN gets to either a Windows or UNIX system with that port open, they respond with a SYN/ACK. This is great from an attacker's point of view, because it penetrates the perimeter and still lets them compromise the system. Take your time with this section to look at some of the major variations of this pattern and to learn its history.

Source Port 0, SYN and FIN Set

The first clue I had about the following trace was a post to bugtraq in March 1998. I did not actually pick this trace up for another month. Here, the signature is source port 0, which is not logical; and both SYN and FIN flags are set, which is also not logical. An intrusion-detection system ought to be able to pick up this kind of trace! Note the random-appearing subnets 26, 24, 17, 16, 24, as well as hosts. This is possibly to make the scan less obvious. Also note the speed of the scan. Scan detectors should be able to detect five connect attempts to five different hosts in about a quarter of a second. Take a look:

```
13:10:33.281198 newbie.hacker.org.0 > 192.168.26.203.143: SF
     374079488:374079488(0) win 512
13:10:33.334983 newbie.hacker.org.0 > 192.168.24.209.143: SF
     374079488:374079488(0) win 512
13:10:33.357565 newbie.hacker.org.0 > 192.168.17.197.143: SF
     374079488:374079488(0) win 512
13:10:33.378115 newbie.hacker.org.0 > 192.168.16.181.143: SF
     374079488:374079488(0) win 512
13:10:33.474966 newbie.hacker.org.0 > 192.168.24.194.143: SF
     374079488:374079488(0) win 512
```

The preceding scan presents several interesting advantages. FINs might be allowed through filtering devices even if SYNs are not. This improves the probability of a response. Also, because the FIN signals connection tear down, some logging systems will potentially fail to report the connect attempt. SYN/FIN was a trademark of a scanning tool named jackal, which was purported to penetrate firewalls. The challenge with this signature is that more than one exploit/scan is believed responsible for creating it. A more current tool that can generate a similar signature is nmap, the most effective intelligence-gathering tool yet deployed by attackers.

Source Port 65535 and SYN FIN Set

The following trace is an interesting variant of the preceding trace. This was collected in November 1998. There is speculation that this pattern is probably the result of an attack tool that enables the user to select any source port she wants. Although I have no doubt that such a tool either exists or will exist in the near future, that does not begin to explain why intrusion-detection analysts have collected hundreds of examples with source port 0 and a large number with source port 65535. In the early days, before 1999, analysts had not yet collected any examples with any other source port and SYN/FIN set. The source port was hard-coded into the software and that the source port 65535 is a second-generation code branch from the original. The trace follows:

```
16:11:38.13 IMAPPER.65535 > ns2.org.143: SF 3794665472:3794665472(0) win 512
```

```
16:11:38.13 IMAPPER.65535 > ns2.org.143: SF 3794665472:3794665472(0) win 512
```

DNS Zone Followed by 0, SYN FIN Targeting NFS

Although IMAP has been an effective target of opportunity for attackers, it certainly isn't the only target. The following trace has similarities to the source port 0 and SYN/FIN set pattern. In this case, however, we are dealing with a double dipper. First, the attacker tries an attack against TCP 53, which is also DNS. The difference is you use TCP 53 rather than UDP 53 when you want a zone transfer—in essence, a host table of the site.

As previously noted, the 0 source port and the SF flag sets are a signature for a common IMAP exploit. This attack directed at NFS almost certainly shares code with that exploit. These code branches help to identify attackers who write, modify, or compile code as opposed to those who can run only existing exploits. What apparently has happened is that the attacker has bolted a different exploit onto an older delivery system.

Say what? Well, we make the case later that at least some part of what we are dealing with is warfare. In weapons, one often separates the warhead from the delivery system. For instance:

- Archers could use one tip for firing into infantry and a different arrowhead for launching flaming arrows at castles.

- Catapults could throw rocks to bust walls or dissuade charges, but could also throw flaming missiles if that was what was needed.

- Modern cruise missiles can carry conventional weapons and slip in the enemy's bedroom window (or so the Gulf War footage would have us believe) or they can carry nuclear warheads.

In each of these cases, a delivery system can fire multiple exploits (I mean warheads). You should not be surprised to see the same principle in information warfare. The arrowhead in the following trace is the NFS port, 2049. The signature of the delivery mechanism (source port 0 and SYN/FIN set) is shown in bold:

```
12:11:48 prober.21945 > ns1.net.53: SF 1666526414:1666526414(0) win 512
12:11:49 prober.21951 > ns2.net.53: SF 11997410:211997410(0) win 512

12:36:54 prober.0 > relay.net.2049: SF 3256287232:3256287232(0) win 512
12:37:03 prober.0 > web.net.2049: SF 3256287232:3256287232(0) win 512
12:37:05 prober.0 > relay2.net.2049: SF 3256287232:3256287232(0) win 512
```

This pattern has continued. One classic sighting was in February 2000; posters to GIAC were reporting source port 0, SF set to TCP port 109, the POP2 service. This pattern has most recently mutated to reflexive source and destination ports—for example, source port 109, SF set to destination port 109. A final note about the preceding trace: This individual is probably a rookie. If you hit a site with an exploit and do not get in, it is far wiser to move to a different IP address before trying again. Using the same IP address twice increases your risk of a knock on the door from federal agents. That said, this was the first time we saw the code branch to the NFS exploit. There are no easy answers. And, it is still going on. In December 2001, we picked up an attack against secure shell (TCP 22), source port 22, destination port 22, SF set.

Scans to Apply Exploits

This final section discusses a number of interesting patterns that, with the exception of discard and IP-191, tend to use well-known vulnerable ports. One challenge you face when sorting out the exploit tools from the scan tools is that because most sites use their firewall or filtering router to block risky ports, it becomes difficult to collect information. With TCP-based attacks, for instance, the three-way handshake never completes because the connection is blocked, which makes it all but impossible to know the intention of the attacker.

The first trace examined here is the mscan pattern, a favorite tool of attackers.

mscan

The following trace is representative of one of a very common attack pattern, mscan. The multiscan exploit code is widely available and does not indicate an "eleet" or well-connected attacker. That said, it gets its fair share of system compromises, because it scans for vulnerabilities present in a large number of systems connected to the Internet:

```
06:13:23.188197 bad.guy.org.6479  > target.mynetwork.com.23:   S
06:13:28.071161 bad.guy.org.15799 > target.mynetwork.com.80:   S
06:13:33.107599 bad.guy.org.25467 > target.mynetwork.com.143:  S
06:13:38.068035 bad.guy.org.3861  > target.mynetwork.com.53:   S
06:13:43.271220 bad.guy.org.14296 > target.mynetwork.com.110:  S
06:13:47.831695 bad.guy.org.943   > target.mynetwork.com.111:  S
```

AL-98.01 AusCERT Alert multiscan (mscan) Tool 20 July 1998,
`ftp://ftp.auscert.org.au/pub/auscert/advisory/AL-98.01.mscan`:

> "AusCERT has received reports indicating a recent and substantial increase in network scanning activity. It is believed that intruders are using a new tool called 'Multiscan' or 'mscan'. This tool enables the user to scan whole domains and complete ranges of IP addresses to discover well-known vulnerabilities in the following services: statd nfs cgi-bin Programs ('handler', 'phf' & 'cgi-test,' for example) X, POP3, IMAP, Domain Name Servers, finger."

So, you ask, "What is a scanner doing in the exploit chapter?" Sue me! The exploits for telnet, Web, IMAP, DNS, POP3, and Portmap are so numerous and so well known I thought it was appropriate.

Son of mscan

Of course, if one attacker has mscan, another has to do it one better. The following trace was first seen in November 1998. We can learn some things from this trace. The scan rate is on the order of 10 packets per second. That is no record, but it is fast. We would certainly hope our intrusion-detection system's port scan detect code would take note of 10 SYN packets to different ports on the same system in one second!

What are all those ports? Throughout the book, I use the Internet Assigned Numbers Authority (IANA) paper on ports (`ftp://ftp.isi.edu/in-notes/iana/assignments/port-numbers`) for services 1024 and below. Above 1024 is a mess, and we work through these ports carefully. If you have an Internet connection, you might want to download a copy of the port listing now. Another excellent source of information is an /etc/services file from a UNIX computer, the best being the one that ships with FreeBSD. However, I am learning more and more to use Google (`www.google.com`). You simply type **port 12345** or whatever and then read the discussions. Everyone knows 12345 is Netbus, but I didn't know that it is also a license manager. Nor did I know that Trend Micro uses this as a listening port. I would have never known about this if I had not queried Google. If you don't have access to one, or the time to go get one, refer to the service names at the beginning of each line for this trace:

```
Echo- 20:50:19.872769 prober.1454 > mail.relay.7: S 7460483:7460483(0) win
8192  (DF)
Discard- 20:50:19.881293 prober.1455 > mail.relay.9: S 7460502:7460502(0) win
8192  (DF)
Quote of the Day- 20:50:19.916488 prober.1456 > mail.relay.17: S
7460545:7460545(0) win 8192  (DF)
Daytime- 20:50:19.983115 prober.1457 > mail.relay.13: S 7460592:7460592(0)
win 8192  (DF)
```

```
Chargen- 20:50:20.026572 prober.1458 > mail.relay.19: S 7460646:7460646(0)
win 8192  (DF)
FTP- 20:50:20.118159 prober.1459 > mail.relay.21: S 7460745:7460745(0) win
8192  (DF)
Telnet- 20:50:20.215007 prober.1460 > mail.relay.23: S 7460845:7460845(0) win
8192  (DF)
Time- 20:50:20.415433 prober.1462 > mail.relay.37: S 7461008:7461008(0) win
8192  (DF)
DNS- 20:50:20.475574 prober.1463 > mail.relay.53: S 7461095:7461095(0) win
8192  (DF)
Gopher- 20:50:20.616177 prober.1464 > mail.relay.70: S 7461209:7461209(0) win
8192  (DF)
Finger- 20:50:20.675549 prober.1465 > mail.relay.79: S 7461295:7461295(0) win
8192  (DF)
HTTP- 20:50:20.766639 prober.1466 > mail.relay.80: S 7461396:7461396(0) win
8192  (DF)
TSMUX- 20:50:20.869773 prober.1467 > mail.relay.106: S 7461494:7461494(0) win
8192  (DF)
POP2- 20:50:20.983764 prober.1468 > mail.relay.109: S 7461608:7461608(0) win
8192  (DF)
POP3-20:50:21.040400 prober.1469 > mail.relay.110: S 7461645:7461645(0) win
8192  (DF)
Portmap- 20:50:21.125914 prober.1470 > mail.relay.111: S 7461746:7461746(0)
win 8192  (DF)
NNTP- 20:50:21.224194 prober.1471 > mail.relay.119: S 7461846:7461846(0) win
8192  (DF)
NetBIOS- 20:50:21.325783 prober.1472 > mail.relay.139: S 7461955:7461955(0)
win 8192  (DF)
SMUX- 20:50:21.415527 prober.1473 > mail.relay.199: S 7462046:7462046(0) win
8192  (DF)
REXEC- 20:50:21.483920 prober.1474 > mail.relay.512: S 7462096:7462096(0) win
8192  (DF)
RLOGIN- 20:50:21.543247 prober.1475 > mail.relay.513: S 7462194:7462194(0)
win 8192  (DF)
RSHELL- 20:50:21.577268 prober.1476 > mail.relay.514: S 7462199:7462199(0)
win 8192  (DF)
PRINTER- 20:50:21.581449 prober.1477 > mail.relay.515: S 7462203:7462203(0)
win 8192  (DF)
UUCP- 20:50:21.615331 prober.1478 > mail.relay.540: S 7462205:7462205(0) win
8192  (DF)
```

What is the (DF) at the end of each line in the trace? That is the spiffy Don't Fragment flag. The packets in this trace are supposed to arrive in one parcel or be thrown away.

Having examined the preceding trace, what operating system is being targeted? Most likely, UNIX is the target, because many of these services do not normally run on other operating systems. Of course, if the only answer back from the scan were port 139, the attacker would guess he had detected a Windows box. Could the 139 port be targeted at UNIX, even though 139 is normally associated with Windows systems? Yes, SAMBA allows UNIX systems to "speak" NetBIOS, and there are SAMBA exploits as well.

Broad-brush scans such as these are one reason I recommend the following:

- Turn off any service you are not actively using and wrap services you need with TCP Wrappers configured to deny all and only allow those with whom you want to communicate.

- Firewalls should be configured to block everything not needed to conduct an organization's business.

One last thing before moving on—did you notice the packet that was out of sequence? Notice how as time increases various fields, such as source ports and destination ports, also increase. Now on the fourth line down, one of the destination ports is out of sequence. No big deal; on the Internet, packets can arrive out of order. Now, check its source port. Interesting! This could potentially be a signature that enables us to identify this pattern.

Access Builder?

Look at one more multiscan. This is typical of several that appeared in the December 1998/January 1999 time frame. Note that the scan targets Back Orifice (actually, it targets 31337; to target Back Orifice, this should be UDP) and Netbus. One of the interesting things about this scan is that it hits the same machine on the same port twice. Also, note the attempt to access port 888. This port has an official meaning: It is 3Com's Access Builder and is also used for a database:

```
13:05:02.437871 scanner.2577 >
192.168.1.1.888: S 922735:922735(0) win 8192  (DF)
13:05:02.442739 scanner.2578 >
192.168.1.1.telnet: S 922736:922736(0) win 8192  (DF)
13:05:03.071918 scanner.2578 >
192.168.1.1.telnet: S 922736:922736(0) win 8192  (DF)
13:05:03.079767 scanner.2577 >
192.168.1.1.888: S 922735:922735(0) win 8192  (DF)
13:05:03.680841 scanner.2577 >
192.168.1.1.888: S 922735:922735(0) win 8192  (DF)
13:05:04.274991 scanner.2578 >
192.168.1.1.telnet: S 922736:922736(0) win 8192  (DF)
13:05:04.278967 scanner.2577 >
192.168.1.1.888: S 922735:922735(0) win 8192  (DF)
13:05:05.391873 scanner.2575 >
192.168.1.1.12345: S 922734:922734(0) win 8192  (DF)
13:05:05.392074 scanner.2576 >
192.168.1.1.31337: S 922734:922734(0) win 8192  (DF)
13:05:06.079211 scanner.2575 >
192.168.1.1.12345: S 922734:922734(0) win 8192  (DF)
```

Single Exploit, Portmap

The following trace is fairly simple. In this case, a system is targeting multiple sites looking for portmapper. An interesting thing about this scan is that the attacking host comes from a U.S. Government lab. Despite the way the government is portrayed by the *X-Files* and in various movies, this probably is not a covert plot. Instead, when you get attacked by government computers, it is an opportunity to make a difference: That system is probably compromised.

When I called that lab, the fellow in charge of security was so thankful for the tip that he was willing to send me the attack code and data files from the attacker. The attack code was targeting rpc.statd. The data files had two names: XXX.domains and XXX.results, in which XXX was the target of the attack such as mil.domains and isp.domains. This is called the shopping list. The results file was a listing of systems that had systems with active, unprotected portmappers. These results files were presumably the shopping lists for the next stage of this attack, the actual exploit. The sensors in this case were TAMU netloggers, an interesting but obsolete network-logging software package and their trace is shown below.

```
12/03/97 02:35:53 EB419A7E muon.phy.nnn.gov    994 -> relay.nnnn.arpa.net
sunrpc
12/03/97 02:35:56 EB419A7E muon.phy.nnn.gov    994 -> relay.nnnn.arpa.net
sunrpc
12/03/97 02:36:02 EB419A7E muon.phy.nnn.gov    994 -> relay.nnnn.arpa.net
sunrpc
12/03/97 02:36:08 F94110F6 muon.phy.nnn.gov    995 -> ns1.nnnn.arpa.net
sunrpc
12/03/97 02:47:46 C4AF4C22 muon.phy.nnn.gov    954 -> 192.168.16.7
sunrpc
12/03/97 02:47:52 C4AF4C22 muon.phy.nnn.gov    954 -> 192.168.16.7
sunrpc
12/03/97 03:09:26 A63222B3 muon.phy.nnn.gov    861 ->
gw1.havregrace.arpa.net sunrpc
12/03/97 03:09:29 A63222B3 muon.phy.nnn.gov    861 ->
gw1.havregrace.arpa.net sunrpc
12/03/97 03:09:35 A63222B3 muon.phy.nnn.gov    861 ->
gw1.havregrace.arpa.net sunrpc
```

Port 111 TCP is an attempt to access portmapper. This trace was particularly interesting because for several years access attempts on TCP 111 were fairly rare, although UDP 111 attempts were quite common. This particular attempt was a harbinger of things to come. Note that the source ports are all below 1024, which indicates the process running on the government system is running as root. This system is compromised! By March 1998, this exploit was mowing down a large number of Sun Solaris systems, many of which were the DNS, web, or mail servers for their sites. This is particularly interesting because the vulnerability was widely known and the fix was widely available, as shown here:

- Computer Emergency Response Team (CERT) put out a warning in December 1997 at `http://www.cert.org/advisories/CA-97.26.statd.htm`.

- More and more UNIX operating systems were shipping with "secure" portmappers.

- Wietse Venema's code to protect portmapper was available at `http://coast.cs.purdue.edu/pub/tools/unix/portmap`.

rexec

The following trace is just a variety of rexec attempts. The interesting thing about rexec is that it does expect a password for authentication. So, why don't the attackers use rlogin instead? They are probably trying default passwords, because rexec does not tend to log. Also, SGI systems shipped for a long time with a guest account with a password of guest. An attacker could then use this at least to get reconnaissance information and probably to also begin privilege escalation. An attacker has a low chance of being detected unless the site has either network- or host-based intrusion detection.

The following trace represents how many attempts?

```
21:30:17.210000 prober.1439 > 172.20.18.173.512: S 334208000:334208000(0) win
61440
21:30:22.720000 prober.1439 > 172.20.18.173.512: S 334208000:334208000(0) win
61440
21:30:46.720000 prober.1439 > 172.20.18.173.512: S 334208000:334208000(0) win
61440
21:31:02.170000 prober.1449 > 172.20.18.173.512: S 340608000:340608000(0) win
61440
21:31:07.720000 prober.1449 > 172.20.18.173.512: S 340608000:340608000(0) win
61440
21:31:31.720000 prober.1449 > 172.20.18.173.512: S 340608000:340608000(0) win
61440
```

Two attempts. Observe the source ports 1439 and 1449—each is retried two times. Also, note the sequence numbers: 33420... for the first three packets and 34060... for the second set of three packets. You need more data to make an educated assessment, but notice that the two sequence numbers end in 08000. Given two distinct TCP sequence numbers, it is very unlikely that they would have this pattern. This might indicate some kind of crafting of the sequence number. Look at other TCP sequence numbers referenced in the book, and you will discover that most are fairly unique and do not show such patterns.

POP3

Here, we have a fast scan with nicely uniform arrival times. If this doesn't set off our scan detect code, nothing will! A number of POP buffer exploits exist, so the target is easy to understand.

What is odd about this trace is the host selection. The scan is targeting a particular subnet, number 14. But what is the deal with the hosts? If you were the analyst on duty and you saw this, what would you check for?

```
20:35:25.260798 bad.guy.org.4086 > 192.168.14.101.110: S
20:35:25.279802 bad.guy.org.4129 > 192.168.14.119.110: S
20:35:25.281073 bad.guy.org.4141 > 192.168.14.126.110: S
20:35:25.287761 bad.guy.org.4166 > 192.168.14.128.110: S
20:35:25.290293 bad.guy.org.4209 > 192.168.14.136.110: S
20:35:25.295865 bad.guy.org.4234 > 192.168.14.141.110: S
20:35:25.303651 bad.guy.org.4277 > 192.168.14.146.110: S
20:35:25.317924 bad.guy.org.4302 > 192.168.14.173.110: S
20:35:25.319275 bad.guy.org.4378 > 192.168.14.171.110: S
```

(If my answer differs from yours, it's okay.) I would want to know whether these were actually active hosts on the 14 subnet. If they are, the attacker already clearly has some information about us from a previous intelligence-gathering effort. If they are active hosts, and also run popd, it is past time to consider increasing the countermeasures for that subnet!

Targeting SGI Systems?

The following trace shows a port scan, but it is pretty specific and it looks like a UNIX system is the target. This is believed to be targeted at SGI UNIX systems due to port 5232, part of their distributed graphics. Unless the intrusion-detection system is weighting the IMAP and telnet port (and most do), this scan could easily be missed because it is only three packets:

```
21:17:12 prober.1351 > 172.20.4.6.imap: S 19051280:19051180(0) win 512 <mss
1460>
21:17:12 prober.1352 > 172.20.4.6.5232: S 12879079:12879079(0) win 512 <mss
1460>
21:17:12 prober.1353 > 172.20.4.6.telnet: S 42734399:42734399(0) win 512 <mss
1460>
```

Discard

When Discard gets a packet, it throws it away. When we detected this, we joked that it must be a student of Richard Stevens (because he uses Discard for many of the examples in his book). In this case, four SYNs were attempted to each host in the scan before moving on to the next host in the scan:

```
08:02:35 dscrd.net.268 > 192.168.160.122.9: S 1797573506:1797573506(0) win
16384  (DF)

08:02:38 dscrd.net.268 > 192.168.160.122.9: S 1797573506:1797573506(0) win
16384  (DF)
```

Three-Port Scan

I added this scan primarily because the added latency of the HTTP portion of
the scan. It is much slower than the rest of the trace. And as an added bonus, I
bet you haven't seen a daytime scan before! Most likely, this is a benign network mapping effort out of Bell labs called Netsizer—of course, if the source
address happens to be your primary competitor, you might want to look into
this further! Here it is:

```
20:50:04.532822 prober.54934 > myhost.domain: S 2118852885:2118852885(0) win
8760 (DF)
20:50:08.028023 prober.54934 > myhost.domain: S 2118852885:2118852885(0) win
8760 (DF)
20:50:14.432349 prober.54934 > myhost.domain: S 2118852885:2118852885(0) win
8760 (DF)
20:50:27.226116 prober.54934 > myhost.domain: S 2118852885:2118852885(0) win
8760 (DF)
20:50:52.824148 prober.54934 > myhost.domain: S 2118852885:2118852885(0) win
8760 (DF)
20:53:26.414741 prober.54944 > myhost.http: S 2144702009:2144702009(0) win
8760  (DF)
20:53:29.913485 prober.54944 > myhost.http: S 2144702009:2144702009(0) win
8760  (DF)
20:53:49.111043 prober.54944 > myhost.http: S 2144702009:2144702009(0) win
8760  (DF)
20:54:14.710959 prober.54944 > myhost.http: S 2144702009:2144702009(0) win
8760  (DF)
20:55:05.905554 prober.54944 > myhost.http: S 2144702009:2144702009(0) win
8760  (DF)
21:00:10.209063 prober.54968 > myhost.daytime: S 2196732969:2196732969(0) win
8760 (DF)
21:00:13.703247 prober.54968 > myhost.daytime: S 2196732969:2196732969(0) win
8760 (DF)
21:00:20.103798 prober.54968 > myhost.daytime: S 2196732969:2196732969(0) win
8760 (DF)
21:00:32.902480 prober.54968 > myhost.daytime: S 2196732969:2196732969(0) win
8760(DF)
21:00:58.500635 prober.54968 > myhost.daytime: S 2196732969:2196732969(0) win
8760(DF)
```

Weird Web Scans

This scan earns no speed records, but that is intentional. Is the attacker looking
for web servers? We could hypothesize they are and UNIX-based web servers

at that. Sending the packet to the 0 host address is an old-style BSD broadcast; Windows systems will fail to answer. The scan proceeds at a slower rate so that all the inputs can be processed.

Note the source port remains the same for each subnet:

```
18:45:06.820 b.t.t.6879 > 172.20.1.0.http: S 1025092638:1025092638(0) win
61440
18:45:09.356 b.t.t.7136 > 172.20.2.0.http: S 1041868014:1041868014(0) win
61440
18:45:12.626 b.t.t.6879 > 172.20.1.0.http: S 1025092638:1025092638(0) win
61440
18:45:14.375 b.t.t.7395 > 172.20.3.0.http: S 1059077568:1059077568(0) win
61440
18:45:15.184 b.t.t.7136 > 172.20.2.0.http: S 1041868014:1041868014(0) win
61440
18:45:16.790 b.t.t.7650 > 255.255.255.255.http: S 1075727476:1075727476(0)
win 61440
18:45:17.970 b.t.t.7905 > 172.20.5.0.http: S 1092175088:1092175088(0) win
61440
18:45:20.190 b.t.t.7395 > 172.20.3.0.http: S 1059077568:1059077568(0) win
61440
18:45:20.442 b.t.t.8160 > 172.20.6.0.http: S 1108940634:1108940634(0) win
61440
18:45:22.695 b.t.t.7650 > 255.255.255.255.http: S 1075727476:1075727476(0)
win 61440
18:45:23.648 b.t.t.7905 > 172.20.5.0.http: S 1092175088:1092175088(0) win
61440
```

TCP Broadcast?

Well, the 0 host ID looks like old-style broadcasts, and smells like old-style broadcasts, but here is a comment from one of the book's reviewers:

"First, there is no such thing as broadcasting using TCP. See *TCP/IP Illustrated, Volume I*, p. 169: 'Broadcasting and multicasting only apply to UDP, where it makes sense for an application to send a single message to multiple recipients. TCP is a connection-oriented protocol that implies a connection between two hosts (specified by IP addresses) and one process on each host (specified by port numbers).'

"In fact, to be sure I tried this out against our test network, which contains about 25 hosts—all different OSs and hardware, old software and new software—against several different TCP ports, using both the .0 and the .255 broadcasts...and no hosts will answer this request. The .0 or .255 address is interpreted as a unicast address and no other hosts on the net will pick up the packet. This further makes sense when we think about how TCP identifies connections according to the tuple (src ip, dst ip, src port, dst port). In the case of a broadcast address, there is no way to include that address in the tuple. The attacker cannot obtain a broadcast-type response from these SYN packets because there is no way to negotiate a three-way handshake using a broadcast address."

However, routers do not work at the TCP layer, they work at the IP layer; so this packet is not actually looking for web servers, it is doing reconnaissance hoping for ICMP error messages such as unreachables.

The following excerpt is another web-based scan, from the access_log of a
UNIX computer running the Apache web server code. This captured the contents of the traffic destined for the httpd port. By using both the network IDS
and the host-based logs, we can fuse what is happening. Apache is the most
popular web server software in use on the Internet. This trace is the result of a
popular web server multi-CGI-BIN exploit; whisker or the nessus tools are
famous examples. These are commonly in use. We cannot seem to go a day
without someone trying to run one of these against www.sans.org:

```
prober - - [11/Dec/1998:15:28:26 -0500] "GET /cgi-bin/phf/ HTTP/1.0" 404 165
prober - - [11/Dec/1998:15:28:26 -0500] "GET /cgi-bin/php.cgi/ HTTP/1.0" 404
169
prober - - [11/Dec/1998:15:28:26 -0500] "GET /cgi-bin/campas/ HTTP/1.0" 404
168
prober - - [11/Dec/1998:15:28:26 -0500] "GET /cgi-bin/htmlscript/ HTTP/1.0"
404 172
prober - - [11/Dec/1998:15:28:27 -0500] "GET /cgi-bin/aglimpse/ HTTP/1.0" 404
170
prober - - [11/Dec/1998:15:28:27 -0500] "GET /cgi-bin/websendmail/ HTTP/1.0"
404 173
prober - - [11/Dec/1998:15:28:27 -0500] "GET /cgi-bin/view-source/ HTTP/1.0"
404 173
prober - - [11/Dec/1998:15:28:27 -0500] "GET /cgi-bin/handler/ HTTP/1.0" 404
169
prober - - [11/Dec/1998:15:28:28 -0500] "GET /cgi-bin/webdist.cgi/ HTTP/1.0"
404 173
prober - - [11/Dec/1998:15:28:28 -0500] "GET /cgi-bin/pfdispaly.cgi/
HTTP/1.0" 404 175
prober - - [11/Dec/1998:15:29:50 -0500] "GET /cgi-bin/phf/ HTTP/1.0" 404 165
prober - - [11/Dec/1998:15:29:51 -0500] "GET /cgi-bin/php.cgi/ HTTP/1.0" 404
169
prober - - [11/Dec/1998:15:29:51 -0500] "GET /cgi-bin/campas/ HTTP/1.0" 404
168
prober - - [11/Dec/1998:15:29:51 -0500] "GET /cgi-bin/htmlscript/ HTTP/1.0"
404 172
prober - - [11/Dec/1998:15:29:52 -0500] "GET /cgi-bin/aglimpse/ HTTP/1.0" 404
170
prober - - [11/Dec/1998:15:29:52 -0500] "GET /cgi-bin/websendmail/ HTTP/1.0"
404 173
prober - - [11/Dec/1998:15:29:52 -0500] "GET /cgi-bin/view-source/ HTTP/1.0"
404 173
prober - - [11/Dec/1998:15:29:52 -0500] "GET /cgi-bin/handler/ HTTP/1.0" 404
169
prober - - [11/Dec/1998:15:29:53 -0500] "GET /cgi-bin/webdist.cgi/ HTTP/1.0"
404 173
prober - - [11/Dec/1998:15:29:53 -0500] "GET /cgi-bin/pfdispaly.cgi/
HTTP/1.0" 404 175
```

IP-Proto-191

To the very best of my understanding, this cannot be an exploit and probably isn't an immediate prelude to one. I wanted to include it, however, because IP protocol types that are not TCP, UDP, or ICMP are not that uncommon as scans.

What is ip-proto-191? Durned if I know. An 8-bit protocol field in the IP header was set to 191:

```
00:32:28.164183 prober > 192.168.0.255: ip-proto-191 48
00:32:28.164663 192.168.4.5 > prober: icmp:192.168.0.255 unreach
00:32:30.192825 prober > 192.168.1.255: ip-proto-191 48
00:32:33.203521 prober > 192.168.2.255: ip-proto-191 48
00:32:36.219821 prober > 192.168.3.255: ip-proto-191 48
00:32:36.220302 192.168.4.5 > prober: icmp:192.168.3.255 unreach
00:32:38.243973 prober > 255.255.255.255: ip-proto-191 48
00:32:41.254622 prober > 192.168.5.255: ip-proto-191 48
00:32:44.262961 prober > 192.168.6.255: ip-proto-191 48
00:32:47.276258 prober > 192.168.7.255: ip-proto-191 48
00:32:50.285609 prober > 192.168.8.255: ip-proto-191 48
00:32:50.286098 192.168.4.5 > prober: icmp:192.168.8.255 unreach
```

What is the origin of the ip-proto-191 notation? TCPdump tries to figure out the IP protocol by looking at the appropriate field in the IP header. TCPdump knows the common protocol translations. If it finds a 1 in this field, it labels it as ICMP in the output—6 is TCP, and 17 is UDP. If it is not a protocol that it knows about, however, it uses the ip-proto notation with the number that it discovered in the protocol field.

The preceding output also shows a response from 192.168.4.5. This response, in itself, supplies some reconnaissance about the network. Even if you do not get a protocol unreachable, you still have every chance of seeing a host unreachable.

Summary

Analysts make many common mistakes. These include SYN floods, misconfig-ured networks, and being too quick to match a signature. If possible, try to avoid sending false positives to your CIRT.

Some of the tricks attackers are using for either stealth or better penetra-tion, such as setting both the SYN and FIN flag, allow these packets to be trivially detected.

B

Denial of Service

IN FEBRUARY 2000, DENIAL-OF-SERVICE ATTACKS WERE the hot topic. With a network of more than 2,000 compromised systems, most of them via a DNS buffer overflow, attackers shut down major high-profile Internet sites such as CNN and eBay. Although the end of this chapter covers these attacks, they are the exception and not the rule for denial of service. In general, denial-of-service attacks groan on and on, doing little harm besides wasting people's time and bandwidth and occasionally crashing a system. In the vast majority of these attacks, the source address is faked or "spoofed." Please be very slow to phone the owners of the address space that you think just hit you with a denial of service and read them the riot act! One day it might be your address that is spoofed. This is a short chapter divided into two sections. The first section deals with denial-of-service brute-force attacks that are widespread and regularly detected even if they are not all that well known. The second section includes additional well-known attacks, but these are more elegant; in fact, they tend to be one-packet kills—that is, a single attacker packet that can freeze or shut down a system.

Brute-Force Denial-of-Service Traces

These brute-force patterns have reached a point that they are known by almost all Internet institutions. The curious thing is that I still find sites and systems vulnerable to these attacks. Keep in mind that one of the characteristics of many of the denial-of-service attacks is that the attacker can use one of your systems to cause harm to someone else. The fixes are well published and well understood; *please* implement them. Only you can prevent SYN floods, UDP floods, Smurf, and Echo-Chargen!

Smurf

The Smurf attack has no effect except to consume bandwidth. The most important thing to consider with regard to the effectiveness of Smurf is that for your site's Internet connection to run smoothly, you depend on the security policy of other people's sites. This is a very old attack, but you still see it deployed with the most current attack tools. Smurf is still deployed for exactly one reason: It still works. In the following case, `spoofed.pound.me.net` almost certainly did not really send the echo request to `192.168.1.255`. Instead, an outside computer interjects this into the network, as shown in Figure B.1. The poor spoofed addressee will potentially get hit with a large number of ICMP echo replies. If spoofed is on a slow Internet connection, this might be harmful; and if a large number of hosts reply to the Smurf, damage can be done to fast networks.

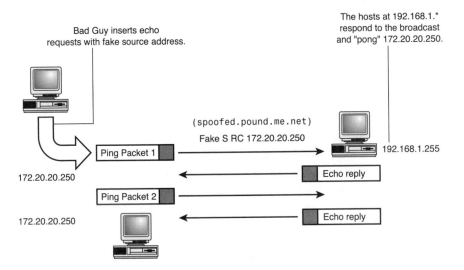

Figure B.1   ICMP denial of service.

Cisco published the following field notice titled "Minimizing the Effects of 'Smurfing' Denial of Service Attacks." The following quotation is from that document:

A Scenario: Assume a co-location switched network with 100 hosts, and that the attacker has a T1. The attacker sends, for example, a 768 kbps stream of ICMP echo (ping) packets, with a spoofed source address of the victim, to the broadcast address of the "bounce site." These ping packets hit the bounce site's broadcast network of 100 hosts. Each of them takes the packet and responds to it, creating 100 ping replies outbound. By multiplying the bandwidth, you see that 76.8 Mbps is used outbound from the "bounce site" after the traffic is multiplied. This is then sent to the victim (the spoofed source of the originating packets).[1]

[1]www.cisco.com/warp/public/707/5.html

I chose to reference a Cisco technical manual because Cisco routers—the most widely deployed routers in the world—are one of the primary keys to eliminating Smurf attacks. Let's examine how the attack works and then the countermeasures:

```
00:00:05.327 spoofed.pound.me.net > 192.168.15.255: icmp: echo request
00:00:05.342 spoofed.pound.me.net > 192.168.1.255:  icmp: echo request
00:00:14.154 spoofed.pound.me.net > 192.168.15.255: icmp: echo request
00:00:14.171 spoofed.pound.me.net > 192.168.1.255:  icmp: echo request
00:00:19.055 spoofed.pound.me.net > 192.168.15.255: icmp: echo request
00:00:19.073 spoofed.pound.me.net > 192.168.1.255:  icmp: echo request
00:00:23.873 spoofed.pound.me.net > 192.168.15.255: icmp: echo request
```

All for One

Many denial-of-service attacks and network-mapping probes use broadcasts, packets addressed to all members of a network, to accomplish their purposes. RFC 919 sets several standards for broadcasts, including the rule that 255.255.255.255 must not be forwarded by a router or routing host.

How did 255.255.255.255 come to be? The local network layer can always map an IP address into a data link layer address. Think about switched networks—that is exactly how they work. So, the choice of an IP "broadcast host number" is somewhat arbitrary. Something needed to be selected, and it seemed reasonable that it should be one that was not likely to be assigned to a real host. The number whose bits are all 1s had this property. Keep the idea of all 1s in mind; we will look at patterns where the broadcast is not 255.255.255.255 due to subnet masking, but the all 1s remains true.

The address 255.255.255.255 denotes a broadcast on a local hardware network, which must not be forwarded by a router or routing host. This address might be used, for example, by hosts that do not know their network number and are asking some server for it. A common case of this is a diskless workstation; as it is booting up, it broadcasts a request for help in finding its operating system. Its server hears the request and answers, providing the next step in the boot up process and then the customized files this system needs to do its job.

Therefore, a host on net 36, for example, might do the following:

- Broadcast to all of its immediate neighbors by using 255.255.255.255

- Broadcast to all of net 36 by using 36.255.255.255

(Note that unless the network has been broken up into subnets, these two methods have identical effects.)

If the use of "all 1s" in an octet of an IP address means "broadcast," using "all 0s" could be viewed as meaning "unspecified." There is probably no reason for such addresses to appear anywhere but as the source address of a bootp. bootp is one of the protocols used to help diskless systems and routers load their operating systems and configuration files. Although there is a legacy ICMP Information Request datagram, these are obsolete and should not occur in normal traffic. As a notational convention, however, we refer to networks (as opposed to hosts) by using addresses with 0 fields. For example, 36.0.0.0 means "network number 36," whereas 36.255.255.255 means "all hosts on network number 36."[2]

[2]www.library.ucg.ie/Connected/RFC/919/7.htm

Directed Broadcast

If you detect a pattern such as the following 255.255.255.255, the odds are that it was sent as a simple broadcast and has been expanded by your router, as shown here:

1. A packet originally destined for 172.20.4.255 assumes a netmask of 255.255.255.0, the size of a Class C network. This broadcasts to all hosts of the 172.20.4 network.

2. A router, possibly in your organization, has the 172.20.4 interface. When it copies the packet from the Internet and rebuilds it on the 4 interface, it expands the broadcast, thereby referencing all hosts served by that interface. Therefore, it rewrites to broadcast as 255.255.255.255.

In the following trace, the broadcast has been expanded. The all 1s broadcast is as described earlier, and the legacy all 0s broadcast has been expanded to the network portion of the netmask. Who answers these expanded pings? Every system that hears them! Therefore, one packet coming in from a spoofed address ends up being amplified to hundreds or thousands of packets. Sites that do not block incoming ICMP are known as *Smurf amplifiers*. You can find a listing of these, including the top 10, at www.powertech.no/smurf or www.netscan.org. (In this case, it is not a great honor to be in the top 10.) Take a look at the trace:

```
05:20:48.261 spoofed.pound.me.net > 192.168.0.0:      icmp: echo request
05:20:48.263 spoofed.pound.me.net > 255.255.255.255: icmp: echo request
05:21:35.792 spoofed.pound.me.net > 192.168.0.0:      icmp: echo request
05:21:35.819 spoofed.pound.me.net > 255.255.255.255: icmp: echo request
05:22:16.909 spoofed.pound.me.net > 192.168.0.0:      icmp: echo request
```

```
05:22:16.927 spoofed.pound.me.net > 255.255.255.255: icmp: echo request
05:22:58.046 spoofed.pound.me.net > 192.168.0.0:      icmp: echo request
05:22:58.061 spoofed.pound.me.net > 255.255.255.255: icmp: echo request
```

In terms of countermeasures, you can build perimeter defenses that are denial-of-service resistant. Instead of connecting a proxy or application gateway firewall directly to your Internet connection, you might want to have a router first. After all, they are more efficient at blocking high-bandwidth attacks simply because they are designed to operate at "wire speeds." You should also block outgoing packets that have a source address not from your network; this is known as *egress filtering*. You can find examples of egress filtering for a large number of routers and firewalls in the GCFW practical assignments at www.giac.org/cert.php. Many denial-of-service attacks use spoofed source addresses. If you do not let them on the Internet, you are being a good net-neighbor. Needless to say, if one of your systems is sending out spoofed addresses, that is a clue that this box might have been compromised.

Echo-Chargen

Echo-Chargen is another example of a classic brute-force attack that uses poorly defended sites and poorly configured systems as amplifiers. This attack mostly looks for UNIX systems as amplifiers, so it is not quite as potent as Smurf, which uses any system. You know how they depict the audiences of tennis matches on cartoons? Everybody's head goes back and forth following the ball. This pattern is just like that except that the heads would have to oscillate at just under the speed of light. Echo is UDP port 7; if it receives a packet it echoes back the payload. If you send echo an "a," it replies with an "a."

Chargen (character generator) is UDP port 19. If you send Chargen any characters, it replies with a pseudo random string of characters.

In the following trace, an outsider spoofs a number of connections to various hosts' Chargen ports. The hope here is that they will reply back to the echo port and a game of Echo <--> Chargen ping-pong will begin burning bandwidth and CPU cycles.

You can still detect this in actual use, but it is becoming more rare. You can help make it even more rare. There is no reason to allow packets addressed to these ports through your organization's firewall or filtering router. These services should be commented out of your UNIX system's inetd.conf files:

```
08:08:16.155354 spoofed.pound.me.net.echo > 172.31.203.17.chargen: udp
08:21:48.891451 spoofed.pound.me.net.echo > 192.168.14.50.chargen: udp
08:25:12.968929 spoofed.pound.me.net.echo > 192.168.102.3.chargen: udp
08:42:22.605428 spoofed.pound.me.net.echo > 192.168.18.28.chargen: udp
08:47:21.450708 spoofed.pound.me.net.echo > 172.31.130.93.chargen: udp
08:51:27.491458 spoofed.pound.me.net.echo > 172.31.153.78.chargen: udp
08:53:13.530992 spoofed.pound.me.net.echo > 172.31.146.49.chargen: udp
```

I studied martial arts for many years and eventually became an instructor. Twice a year we would have a black belt test. The school's master would invite other masters to form a panel for the test. Of course, it is customary to bow to these masters, and they bow back. I have a mischievous streak, and from time to time I would bow, they would bow, I would bow again, they would bow again, and so on, until they finally looked up with a pained expression and walked away. I cannot look at an Echo-Chargen trace without thinking about that little trick.

The example trace is UDP, but I have found you can make the oscillation with the TCP variant of these services as well, although I haven't figured out how to spoof the address and make it work. For fun, if you have Cisco routers, telnet to your router's Echo or Chargen port. For instance, $ `telnet myrouter` 7 accesses the TCP echo port. Many Cisco routers seem to have these open by default.

Elegant Kills

Brute-force attacks tend to rely on spoofed addresses to provide a bit of cover for the attacker. One packet kills can operate with a much lower footprint. They take advantage of flaws in the IP stack's capability to deal with illegal conditions, or even bad programming. The following sections look at several of these, including Echo-Chargen, Teardrop, Land, and a fun little attack against an adventure game called Doom.

Teardrop

Smurf and Echo-Chargen work by brute force; Teardrop works by finesse. It takes advantage of a simple fact: Network protocol stacks are not good at math. They are especially bad at negative numbers. This is another ancient attack, and although it is still in use, I do not see it that often. My intrusion-detection students must complete a practical assignment to achieve certification. The assignment varies in the details, but essentially it is to collect and analyze about 10 network traces. Quite often, they instrument their cable modems and collect data for a while, and Teardrop shows up on many of the practical assignments. Therefore, it is still being tried. The next question is this: Does it still work? Sure, but only on unpatched or older operating systems. The following is an example of a Teardrop trace:

```
10:25:48.205383 wile-e-coyote.45959 > target.net.3964: udp 28 (frag
242:36@0+)
10:25:48.205383 wile-e-coyote > target.net: (frag 242:4@24)
```

Because it has been a long time since Chapter 3, "Fragmentation," perhaps a reminder is in order. The top line shows a fragment named 242 with 36 octets of data for offset 0. The second line shows 4 more octets of data for offset 24. Therefore to service this packet, the operating system would have to rewind from 36 to 24. Negative numbers can translate to very large positive numbers, and so the operating system is likely to scribble all over some other program's section of memory. Try this a couple times and you kill the system.

The core problem is that many IP stacks do not know how to deal with negative, or illegal, numbers. I most recently saw this when the PROTOS toolkit was released along with a CERT advisory on February 12, 2002. HD Moore, a security researcher, was running the toolkit against a Red Hat, Linux 7 box and caused a segmentation fault. We tried to look at this packet with Ethereal, but it killed Ethereal. A TCPdump trace is shown here:

```
18:49:54.519006 10.0.0.1.59108 > 10.0.0.2.161:  GetRequest(33)
.1.3.6.1.2.1.1.5.0[len3<asnlen4294967295] (DF)
4500 004c 0000 4000 4011 269f 0a00 0001
0a00 0002 e6e4 00a1 0038 0efc 302e 0201
0004 0670 7562 6c69 63a0 2102 0206 9202
0100 0201 0030 1530 1306 082b 0601 0201
0105 0044 84ff ffff ff02 0100
```

Notice that, at the top of the trace, TCPdump is trying to tell us something about the Abstract Syntax Notation (ASN.1) length being over 4 billion bytes long. Even with modern systems, that is one heck of a lot of memory to allocate to a single packet. The `84ff ffff ff02` near the end of the hex dump is the value in the length field, if you were just dying to know that.

It is just a matter of time until someone finds another field in the IP stack to do this trick with.

Note that another characteristic of fragmentation is that it eludes some intrusion-detection systems that do not support packet reassembly.

Land Attack

The Land attack is famous for two reasons: It is a very elegant one- or two-packet kill, and it is the "hello world" of intrusion-detection filters. As soon as I heard about it, I wrote a filter to detect it—after all, you cannot ask for an easier signature. But we never captured an attack. I was afraid we had made some kind of silly error in the filter, so I downloaded the attack exploit and compiled it. Now what system could I run it against? I needed something that had intrusion detection running so that I could get a trace of the attack. At that time, we had only intrusion detection in the DMZ. What about the web server? It was in the DMZ. So, I put the web server's IP address into the exploit script, fired the exploit, and boom, the web server crashed as advertised. I hurried over to reboot the web server and never gave the experiment a second thought. Well, until our intrusion-detection analyst called. She was so excited because she had found an actual Land attack and had already reported it to our CIRT. I just kind of said, "Great job," and spent the rest of the day quietly whistling to myself. The detect she saw is shown in the trace below:

```
12/03/97 02:19:48        192.168.1.1        80        -> 192.168.1.1
80
12/03/97 02:21:53        192.168.1.1        31337 -> 192.168.1.1
31337
```

I hope the statute of limitations for this deed has passed by the time this book gets printed.

We're Doomed

I love the culture I live in. First, they convince my kid to play with dolls; they just call them action figures. When he finally gets too old to play with dolls, he trades his plastic action figures in for cyber action figures. Some of the great cyber action figures, complete with horns and everything, live in the game of Doom.

Doom is played on port 666. So what is going on in the following trace?

```
12/03/97 02:19:48        0 206.256.199.8        19 -> 192.168.102.3
666
12/03/97 02:21:53        0 206.256.199.8        19 -> 164.256.23.100
666
12/03/97 02:28:20        0 206.256.199.8        19 -> 164.256.140.32
666
12/03/97 02:30:29        0 206.256.199.8        19 -> 192.168.18.28
666
12/03/97 02:30:44        0 206.256.199.8        19 -> 164.256.67.121
666
12/03/97 02:34:47        0 206.256.199.8        19 -> 164.256.140.32
666
12/03/97 02:35:28        0 206.256.199.8        19 -> 147.168.130.93
666
12/03/97 02:36:56        0 206.256.199.8        19 -> 192.168.18.28
666
12/03/97 02:39:23        0 206.256.199.8        19 -> 147.168.153.78
666
12/03/97 02:41:55        0 206.256.199.8        19 -> 147.168.130.93
666
```

Apparently, some individuals are so bored that they are spoofing a bunch of addresses, such that if these attackers chance on folks playing Doom, the Chargen output might disrupt the game in some way (and a single packet can be enough to do the trick).

The following simulated reconstructed trace shows the cause and effect of such an action, finding a Doom server. Again, 147.168.153.78 in this case is spoofed, and the activity is being caused by an unknown IP address. Although Doom traffic is becoming more rare these days, a similar game called Quake still generates a packet or two. Here is the Doom trace:

```
12/03/97 02:39:22        0 147.168.153.78      666 -> 206.256.199.8
19
12/03/97 02:39:23        0 206.256.199.8       19 -> 147.168.153.78
666
```

Actually, I had not seen this trace in a long time and was going to remove it from the material; then the following variant showed up again in January 1999. Note that the intrusion-detection system did flag this. What tips us off and lets us know that?

```
17:58:13.725824 doomer.echo > 172.20.196.51.666: udp 1024 (DF)
17:58:13.746748 doomer.echo > 172.20.196.51.666: udp 426 (DF)
18:03:24.133079 doomer.echo > 172.20.46.79.666: udp 1024 (DF)
18:03:24.157238 doomer.echo > 172.20.46.79.666: udp 426 (DF)
21:05:22.503299 dns1.arpa.net.domain > doomer.domain: 42815 (44)
21:05:26.152327 doomer.domain > dns1.arpa.net.domain: 42815* 2/0/0 (98) (DF)
23:50:15.728480 doomer.echo > 172.20.76.2.666: udp 1024 (DF)
23:50:15.751821 doomer.echo > 172.20.76.2.666: udp 426 (DF)
```

Sure! The domain lookup is a big hint! We have already discussed Echo and Chargen, and we have seen them show up together. What is going on? The attacker is bouncing off an open echo port to cover his tracks, the receiving computer will see the system with echo port in the source address field, not the attacker. The attacker spoofs the address of the target machine to a machine, and then bounces traffic off these ports onto the game. The preceding signature is a tough one; 7 to 666 is also a classic signature of a UDP flood denial-of-service program called Pepsi. However, Pepsi scanners do not usually pause for a refreshing DNS lookup.

As this discussion shows, both brute-force attacks and elegant denial-of-service attacks take advantage of flawed site and system protection. How do they know which systems to take advantage of? In some cases, attackers simply try all the addresses, hoping to get lucky. In other cases, they perform reconnaissance. One of the best tools, bar none, to do this is nmap.

nmap

nmap is the most versatile scanner available at any price for Windows and UNIX (and the price is *free*). This software can create a large number of traces, and in early 1999 was being called the most potent denial-of-service engine available. Some of the best information about the denial-of-service effects of nmap was published by the National Infrastructure Protection Center

(NIPC). NIPC produces biweekly reports called CyberNotes. Electronic copies are available on the NIPC web site at `http://www.nipc.gov`. CyberNotes lists specific vulnerabilities that nmap exploits. Issue 99-2, for example, reports a scan on port 427 that causes the dreaded blue screen of death on Windows 98 systems running the Novell Intranet Client. I certainly do not disagree with NIPC, but if a piece of networking software dies because it receives a packet on a certain port, we should not blame the vulnerability scanner. Packets happen. In fact, in the years since nmap was first released, many stacks have crashed, but this has forced the manufacturers to fix their products because nmap is so prevalent.

nmap is a vulnerability scanner, but it operates in several powerful modes, including some that can knock out unpatched systems. These modes include the following:

- Vanilla TCP connect() scanning
- TCP SYN (half open) scanning
- TCP FIN, Xmas, or Null (stealth) scanning
- TCP FTP proxy (bounce attack) scanning
- SYN/FIN scanning using IP fragments (bypasses packet filters)
- UDP raw ICMP port unreachable scanning
- ICMP scanning (ping-sweep)
- TCP Ping scanning
- Remote OS identification by TCP/IP fingerprinting
- Reverse-indent scanning

nmap was integrated starting with Shadow 1.6. It is great. When the analyst sees a connection to a system from the Internet that causes concern, the analyst can scan the *internal* system. Shadow's default is to use the vanilla TCP connect, although all modes are available. The purpose is to quickly determine what services the internal system has available. And yes, from time to time when OS fingerprinting, I have crashed a system or two. I guess the good news is that it is really hard for the attackers to compromise the system if you crash it when fingerprinting it!

Mutant Packet Arms Race

In mid-1998, I was talking with the development team for Cisco's vulnerability scanner, Net Sonar. Members of the team were discussing the great pains they took to avoid crashing systems while scanning them.

Today, nmap has some serious competition from hping2 when it comes to generating some seriously funky packets. I hope that an arms race does not develop between the two of them to see which can do the most harm the fastest.

Distributed Denial-of-Service Attacks

Before the millennium rollover, I ran into a former coworker who, within the past five years, had retired from her computer-related job. After exhausting more pertinent topics, I asked her whether she planned to fly home to Nebraska for the Christmas holiday. Indeed, she was staying into the New Year. I was curious whether she had any fears about the possibility of Y2K computer problems and flying. She admitted no anxiety and asked me whether there was anything that she should be concerned about. I calmly mentioned a minor inconvenience of a massive denial-of-service against *all* infrastructure systems such as power grids, airlines, and banks continuing for days, weeks, or even years to assuage her nonexistent anxiety. Innocently enough, she replied, "What's a denial of service?" Believe me, this is a sharp woman, and I thought nothing less of her because of her question; I just realized that my fears were based on my exposures, and her peace of mind was based on her exposures.

I believe, however, that exposure for most of the rest of the media-connected world changed with the denial-of-service attacks against some of the major Internet players, such as Yahoo! and eBay, in February 2000. You could not help but hear on the nightly news or read on the front pages of the newspapers about these attacks that felled these giants of e-commerce. Months later, the media still buzzes about the lack of consumer confidence associated with these attacks much as years ago you couldn't read or hear about the Russian space station Mir without hearing the word "beleaguered."

The software responsible for these and many more attacks is known as *distributed denial of service* (DDoS) because it is a denial of service originating from many different source hosts. Thankfully for us as authors and perhaps unfortunately for you as readers, we haven't captured any traffic associated with these attacks. But, no discussion of denial of service today is respectable unless the distributed denial-of-service attacks are covered.

Intro to DDoS

Remember the powerful Smurf attack that used an intermediate site and all its responding hosts to amplify a denial-of-service attack? That is a drop in the ocean compared to the magnitude of some of the distributed denial-of-service attacks. If you look at the architecture of the Smurf attack, you will discover that there is really one hostile origin of the attack: A malicious user at one host crafts one or many ICMP echo requests to a broadcast address of the amplification site with a spoofed source IP of the target host. Many amplification hosts can magnify the intensity of the attack.

In a DDOS attack, many different "hostile" hosts enlisted are directed to attack a target site. These so-called hostile hosts are compromised hosts that have had distributed denial-of-service software installed on them. Maybe this new public awareness about these attacks will eliminate some of the naive attitudes of "why would someone want to break into my computer...it's got nothing worth stealing."

DDoS software comes in many different incarnations, each with different terminology and techniques. Among all, however, there is a notion of a controlling computer that directs the compromised hosts to attack a site. Therefore, you have multiple origins of hostile hosts simultaneously attacking the victim site. The intent is to clog the portals of the victim site by consuming the resources for handling legitimate traffic. The victim site has to figure out a way to block the DDoS traffic while still allowing the legitimate traffic.

DDoS Software

Historically, four different DDoS programs were known: Trinoo, *Tribe Flood Network* (TFN), TFN2K, and Stacheldraht (German for barbed wire). With each new release, they seem to have evolved into more complex packages with richer functionality. Most work on Linux or Solaris hosts, and TFN2K works on Windows NT hosts. Reports of new Windows-like DDoS are surfacing.

Some new terminology must be introduced. At the top of the DDoS attack, you have a host, usually known as the client, which is used by the person coordinating the attack. Next, at a layer below that, you have a host or hosts known by the term *master* or *handler*. The master controls subservient hosts to launch attacks. Finally, at the bottom, you have hosts known both as *agents* or *daemons*, which actually launch the attacks. The terminology gets tricky because it sometimes differs for the individual attacks.

Trinoo

This software uses controlling hosts known as masters, and attacking hosts known as daemons. The communications between the client and the masters and the masters and the daemons is done using TCP and UDP. There are standard ports, but these can be altered. Trinoo can send only UDP floods to random destination port numbers on the victim host. Communications between hosts in an unaltered configuration are as follows:

```
client   → master:   destination port TCP 27665
master   → daemons:  destination port UDP 27444
daemons  → master:   destination port UDP 31335
```

TFN

Chapter 4, "ICMP," discussed TFN. Basically, there are TFN masters and daemons, which again represent the controlling hosts and the attacking hosts. The communication between master and daemon is done via an ICMP echo reply. The ICMP echo reply can direct the daemon to send a UDP flood, TCP SYN flood, ICMP echo flood, or a Smurf attack. The master can manipulate the IP identification number and payload of the ICMP echo reply to identify the type of attack to be launched. TFN can also spoof the source IP to hide the origin of the attack.

TFN2K

TFN2K was the first of the DDoS programs to be transported to Windows. The communications between the master and agents can be encrypted and can be over TCP, UDP, or ICMP with no identifying ports. The master can spoof the source IP so that if it is detected, the real master cannot be identified. The agent can attack using a TCP SYN flood, a UDP flood, ICMP flood, or Smurf (as we saw with TFN). Additionally, the attacking agent can alternate among these types of attacks for any given attack. And, the agent-generated attack packets have a spoofed source IP by default.

Stacheldraht

Stacheldraht is a combination of Trinoo and TFN with encryption added to communications between the client and handler and the handler and the agents. Agents can generate TCP SYN floods, UDP floods, ICMP floods, and Smurf attacks against the victim. Default communications are as follows:

```
client    →  handler: TCP port 16660 or 60001
handler   →  agent:   TCP port 65000 or ICMP echo reply
agent     →  handler: TCP port 65000 or ICMP echo reply
```

Today, since the discovery of the leaves worm with the f.exe malicious code in June 2001, the main emphasis seems to be on controlling systems from IRC channels or using flooding IRC bots. If you see traffic entering or leaving your network on TCP 6667 (actually TCP 6660–6670) you probably should consider taking a close look at it, unless you are sure the owner of the system is actually using IRC to chat.

Summary

In denial-of-service attacks, the source address is probably spoofed. Please report them to your CIRT anyway. Many of the denial-of-service attacks are very old and well understood; this does not mean they aren't effective. Although there is nothing impressive about Echo-Chargen, I was just talking with a major Internet service provider that lost a T3 circuit for three hours to an oscillation.

As far as DDoS attacks, you can do little right now if you become a victim site. A document is available from www.incdents.org to guide you step by step if you think one of your UNIX hosts might be infected with one of these Trojans. A wise analyst will download and read this from www.incidents.org/react/trojan.php before she has to deal with an infected system. And, you certainly can take some measures for preventing your site from becoming a launching ground. First, make sure you have egress filtering that allows packets to leave your network only if they contain source IPs from your network. There is an excellent paper on egress filtering available from Incidents.org, www.incidents.org/protect/egress.php. This prevents source IP spoofing used by many of the attacks. Also, you can configure your intrusion-detection system to look for some of the signatures so that you have detection capabilities if you do become a launching site. And, as trite it sounds, you have less chance of a host compromise if you block unnecessary traffic into your sites and your hosts are well patched and maintained. This prevents the compromises necessary to install the DDoS software.

Detection of Intelligence Gathering

CHAPTER 16, "ARCHITECTURAL ISSUES," RAISED THE ISSUE THAT CIRTs have to focus primarily on compromised systems. And they do! How would you feel if you were on the phone with your CIRT trying to get information you need to deal with the latest nasty Trojan horse code and they said, "Sorry we are devoting all our resources to a new intelligence-gathering technique?"

Wise intrusion analysts devote a lot of attention to the prevention, detection, and reporting of mapping techniques. They know that recon is just part of the game. As attackers amass high-quality information about the layout of networks and distribution of operating systems, it enables them to specifically target their attacks. You do not want to allow your organization to get in a one-exploit, one-kill situation!

The line between exploit/denial of service and recon probe couldn't be thinner. Any exploit that fails (or succeeds) also provides intelligence about the target.

This appendix contains many traces showing information-gathering techniques and reviews some of the ways an attacker might map the network and its hosts. This appendix also briefly covers NetBIOS-specific issues because there are so many deployed Windows systems. The appendix concludes by examining some of the so-called stealth mapping techniques.

Network and Host Mapping

The goal of host mapping is just to determine what hosts or services are available in a facility. In some sense, the odds are in the analysts' favor; we are, after all, defending very sparse matrices. Suppose you have a Class B network, 172.20.0.0 (which is 65,536 possible addresses). There are also 65,536 TCP ports and 65,536 UDP ports possible per host. That means that the attacker has 23 trillion+ possible targets. Scanning at a rate of 18 packets per second, it would take a shade under 5 million years to completely scan the network. Because computers have a life span of between three and five years, the rate of change confounds the usefulness of the scan.

Now to be sure, attackers are coming up with smarter and faster scanning techniques. An attacker has no need to consider all possible port numbers. Fifty TCP and UDP ports account for the probable services, so the target space is something in the range of 163 million (which could be scanned in less than four months at 18 packets per second). Hmmmm, that is achievable! And if the site doesn't have intrusion detection, the site owners will probably never know whether the attacker's scan randomizes the addresses and ports a bit.

If the attackers can get an accurate host map, however, they can turn the tables on those of us who defend networks big time. Many address spaces are lightly populated. If the attacker can determine where the hosts are, they have a serious advantage. Suppose our Class B network is populated with only about 6,000 computers, for instance, and the attacker can find them. Now the attacker can scan the populated hosts on the network, at 18 packets per second, in less than 10 days—and there are still much more efficient ways to do the scan. In fact, if we allow ICMP echo request broadcasts, they can ping map our network with only 255 packets.

The point of the story is obvious. If attackers cannot get intelligence information about our site, they are forced to guess about a very sparse matrix. If we do let their intelligence-gathering probes succeed, they don't have to do much guessing at all.

So how can an attacker get such an accurate host map? Many sites still make a *host table* available for FTP download. Other sites allow DNS zone transfers. Or, perhaps the attacker has to work to discover this information with host scans.

Chapter 4, "ICMP," covered some of the more rudimentary ICMP mapping techniques. The crudest of them all tried to send ICMP echo requests to individual hosts and created a lot of noise doing so. We also saw the broadcast ICMP echo requests that attempted to map a network by sending the ICMP echo requests to the .0 and .255 addresses, possibly making the process more efficient and less noisy. This section describes another mapping attempt using the echo request and revisits the network-based broadcast in more detail.

Host Scan Using UDP Echo Requests

In the following trace, the attacker is targeting multiple network addresses. Two were detected by this sensor constellation, but it is very probable there were many more. By interleaving the scan, the attacker has managed to space the UDP echo requests far enough apart that the probe will not be detected by most scan detect codes. The scrambled addresses are also a nice touch. The udp 6 refers to UDP payload with 6 bytes of data. As discussed in the last section in this chapter, stealth in intrusion detection has a fairly specific meaning, but I consider the low and slow approach the best stealth technique. Here is the trace:

```
02:08:48.088681 slowpoke.mappem.com.3066 > 192.168.134.117.echo: udp 6
02:15:04.539055 slowpoke.mappem.com.3066 > 172.31.73.1.echo: udp 6
02:15:13.155988 slowpoke.mappem.com.3066 > 172.31.16.152.echo: udp 6
02:22:38.573703 slowpoke.mappem.com.3066 > 192.168.91.18.echo: udp 6
02:27:07.867063 slowpoke.mappem.com.3066 > 172.31.2.176.echo: udp 6
02:30:38.220795 slowpoke.mappem.com.3066 > 192.168.5.103.echo: udp 6
02:49:31.024008 slowpoke.mappem.com.3066 > 172.31.152.254.echo: udp 6
02:49:55.547694 slowpoke.mappem.com.3066 > 192.168.219.32.echo: udp 6
03:00:19.447808 slowpoke.mappem.com.3066 > 172.31.158.86.echo: udp 6
```

Instead of relying on the ICMP echo request to find hosts, this scan is seeing whether any host will reply on the echo port. The echo port echoes back (imagine that) any characters sent to it. Good system administrators should not have this port listening and good network administrators should not allow in traffic to this port.

A Word About Detecting Scans

Until some brilliant researcher comes up with a better technique, scan detection boils down to testing for X events of interest across a Y-sized time window. An intrusion-detection system can and should have more than one scan detect window. For instance, we have seen several scans that exceed five events per second. By using a short time window in the range of one to three seconds, the system can detect a high-speed scan and alert in near real-time, three to five seconds after the scan begins. Nipping such scans in the bud is one of the best uses of automated reaction. The next reasonable time window is on the order of one to five minutes. This detects slower but still obvious scans. The Shadow intrusion-detection system has had some success with a scan detect of five to seven connections to different hosts over a one-hour window.

I developed code that was enhanced by Bill Ralph that implemented a scan detect process designed to examine a 24-hour time window to investigate the TCP half-open scans and mildly low and slow scans. Now that most intrusion detection systems feed databases, a major focus of console development is detection of low and slow scans. Scans have been detected using database queries with rates as low as five packets from a single IP address over 60 days. A scan rate that low makes sense only if it is interleaved (executed in parallel from multiple source addresses) to the extreme. We have documented scans of about 2,500 hosts working together and the entire w32.leaves worm network was about 30,000 compromised hosts, so distributed slow scans are in the hands of attackers.

Netmask-Based Broadcasts

Which of the echo requests in the following trace are broadcasts? All of them! We all recognize the 0 and the 255, but they are all broadcast packets under the right conditions, and the point of this trace is to test for these conditions. What are these right conditions? They are networks that have a different subnet mask than the usual one. Take a look:

```
02:21:06.700002 pinger> 172.20.64.0: icmp: echo request
02:21:06.714882 pinger> 172.20.64.64: icmp: echo request
02:21:06.715229 pinger> 172.20.64.63: icmp: echo request
02:21:06.715561 pinger> 172.20.64.127: icmp: echo request
02:21:06.716021 pinger> 172.20.64.128: icmp: echo request
02:21:06.746119 pinger> 172.20.64.191: icmp: echo request
02:21:06.746487 pinger> 172.20.64.192: icmp: echo request
02:21:06.746845 pinger> 172.20.64.255: icmp: echo request
```

I once worked in a facility that charged for network addresses. A single host address was $50/month and a subnet with a netmask of 255.255.255.0, or 256 possible addresses, was $1,000/month. The facility had a Class B address space assigned to it, 172.29.0.0, which they broke up into subnets. It turns out that if we bought a router and leased a subnet from them, we could bring our address space tax way down. Here is how.

Rent one subnet 172.29.15.0 for $1,000/month. The expected subnet mask would be 255.255.255.0. That gives us 256 possible addresses, but 0 and 255 are not usable for hosts, so that leaves 254 usable addresses. At $50/month, that is $12,700/month; so getting the subnet for $1,000/month is already a big win. With our own router, however, we could make the subnet mask anything we wanted on "our" side of the router.

Suppose we could find three more small groups as cheap, er frugal, and ruggedly individual as we are. We could use 2 bits of our address space for internal subnets to create four subnets with 6 bits of address space each. 2^6 is 64. The netmask for this is 255.255.255.192, or in hex 0xffffffc0. We could each have our own subnet to do with as we please and split the $1000/month for just a little more than the price of five individual addresses. Great, but what is the broadcast value for a subnet mask of 255.255.255.192?

$255 - 192 = 63$, which is the broadcast value for an "all 1s" broadcast, which means 0 or 64 is the value for an "all 0s." If that is too easy, however, consider this:

```
c       0     in hex is
1100    0000  in binary.
^^            the two high order bits were lost to the NETID
  ^^    ^^^^  so we have 6 bits of host ID to play with
```

6 bits all set to 1s = 32 + 16 + 8 + 4 + 2 + 1 = 63.

Now, the pattern we see in the trace above is an ICMP echo request to 0, 64, 63, 127, 128, 191, 192, and 255.

Could 127 and 128 also be broadcasts? Sure, if we have a situation in which we need lots of subnets, but each one can have a lower number of hosts if we can steal 1 bit from the HOSTID space and use it for subnets. If we use 25 bits for the NETID (33,554,432 possible subnets) each with 7 bits of HOSTID space (128 possible addresses), this would be a subnet mask of 255.255.255.128. What is the broadcast address? 255 − 128 = 127. 127 is the "all 1s" broadcast.

Could 191 and 192 also be broadcasts? If we have a situation in which we need lots and lots of subnets, but each one can have a low number of hosts, we can use 27 bits for the NETID (134,217,728 possible subnets) each with 5 bits of HOSTID space (32 possible addresses). This is a subnet mask of 255.255.255.64. 255 − 64 = 191.

Of course if we allow ICMP in, they could just send one packet with an ICMP netmask request and be done with it! If the site answers a netmask request, it returns the network mask that it is using, eliminating the guesswork.

Port Scan

Time for an easier trace. The following trace is a basic port scan. After our attacker has found a host, he may want to scan it to see what services are active. This trace is TCP, and the scan counts down on the destination port. The skips in the source ports are interesting. This may be a very busy machine or more than one scan may be going on. This is a good example of a bursty trace; compare the arrival times at the beginning of the trace to the end. In the beginning of the trace, there is a lower number of packets per second arriving than at the end. Any number of factors can influence this. If we can correlate this trace to other traces from other sensor systems and they are also bursty, however, we can begin to make some assumptions about the source machine. The skipped source ports indicate the source of the burstiness may be the source computer and not the network in between. If we can match up the source ports of our detect with a detect from another sensor, we may be able to make assumptions as to whether multiple scans are occurring, or whether this scan is being initiated from a busy multiple-user computer. The trace follows:

```
09:52:25.349706 bad.guy.org.1797 > target.mynetwork.com.12: S
09:52:25.375756 bad.guy.org.1798 > target.mynetwork.com.11: S
09:52:26.573678 bad.guy.org.1800 > target.mynetwork.com.10: S
09:52:26.603163 bad.guy.org.1802 > target.mynetwork.com.9: S
09:52:28.639922 bad.guy.org.1804 > target.mynetwork.com.8: S
09:52:28.668172 bad.guy.org.1806 > target.mynetwork.com.7: S
```

```
09:52:32.749958 bad.guy.org.1808 > target.mynetwork.com.6: S
09:52:32.772739 bad.guy.org.1809 > target.mynetwork.com.5: S
09:52:32.802331 bad.guy.org.1810 > target.mynetwork.com.4: S
09:52:32.824582 bad.guy.org.1812 > target.mynetwork.com.3: S
09:52:32.850126 bad.guy.org.1814 > target.mynetwork.com.2: S
09:52:32.871856 bad.guy.org.1816 > target.mynetwork.com.1: S
```

Scanning for a Particular Port

So what service runs on TCP 7306? Durned if I know. As I mentioned in
Appendix A, it never hurts to ask www.google.com, because all of the port lists I
have looked at are incomplete. This trace was collected in late December
1998, which was the beginning of a number of interesting scans that all
seemed to be targeting strange ports. This scan is well crafted; there is no obvious signature.

The first and last packet in the following trace resolve to a host name; the
middle four don't, as is obvious from the fact that the Internet address is
shown for these rather than a name. This can indicate that the attacker is
"shooting in the dark," that he does not have an accurate network map. Often
a reason some names do not resolve is that they don't exist. Take a minute to
look at the last packet in the trace; source ports usually increase, but this
decreases by 22. Because the initial sequence number (49684211) is also lower,
this packet probably got lost along the way and arrived out of order:

```
09:54:40.930504 prober.3794 > lula.arpa.net.7306: S 49684444:49684444(0) win
8192  (DF)
09:54:40.940663 prober.3795 > 192.168.21.20.7306: S 49684454:49684454(0) win
8192  (DF)
09:54:41.434196 prober.3796 > 192.168.21.21.7306: S 49684945:49684945(0) win
8192  (DF)
09:54:41.442674 prober.3797 > 192.168.21.22.7306: S 49684955:49684955(0) win
8192  (DF)
09:54:41.451029 prober.3798 > 192.168.21.23.7306: S 49684965:49684965(0) win
8192  (DF)
09:54:41.451049 prober.3776 > host.arpa.net.7306: S 49684211:49684211(0) win
8192  (DF)
```

Complex Script, Possible Compromise

The next trace is comprised of multiple individual probes and attacks. It is
shown here in five parts. The accesses to portmap (SUNRPC) imply this
attacker is attempting a compromise or gathering intelligence. Further, the
system answers back, which is a bad thing. Portmap should be blocked by the
filtering router or firewall, and secure portmap code should be on any system
that runs SUNRPC. Note that these attacks are directed against two systems:

host 16 and host 17. From the ports accessed, I assume these are UNIX systems. It is quite possible that these two systems have a trust relationship so that if one falls, they both fall.

Then we see the access to TCP port 906, which is unassigned, and the target system answers back. This could well indicate that malicious code has been installed on the system. Instead of sending or receiving data, however, the attacker closes the connection. Two hours later, the attacker pings to see whether the systems are still there. Take a look:

```
00:35:33.944789 prober.839 > 172.20.167.16.sunrpc: udp 56
00:35:33.953524 172.20.167.16.sunrpc > prober.839: udp 28
00:35:33.984029 prober.840 > 172.20.167.17.sunrpc: udp 56
00:35:33.991220 172.20.167.17.sunrpc > prober.840: udp 28

00:35:34.046598 prober.840 > 172.20.167.16.906: S 2450350587:2450350587(0)
win 512
00:35:34.051510 172.20.167.16.906 > prober.840: S 1996992000:1996992000(0)
ack 2450350588 win 32768  (DF)

00:35:34.083949 prober.843 > 172.20.167.17.sunrpc: udp 56
00:35:34.089272 172.20.167.17.sunrpc > prober.843: udp 28

00:35:34.279472 prober.840 > 172.20.167.16.906: F 117:117(0) ack 69 win 32120
00:35:34.284670 172.20.167.16.906 > prober.840: F 69:69(0) ack 118 win 32768
(DF)

02:40:43.977118 prober > 172.20.167.16: icmp: echo request
02:40:43.985138 172.20.167.16 > prober: icmp: echo reply
```

The preceding trace is fairly significant, and as an analyst I would be concerned and recommend further investigation. Let's talk about response for a minute. We want to back up, investigate, contain, and clean. If these were my systems, I would direct the following:

- Take your hands off the keyboard and keep them off.
- Pull the network cable immediately; we will be right there.
- After you are on the scene, one of your top priorities is to back up the system(s).
- Treat the backup tape as evidence.

The port 906 bears further investigation. The easiest thing to do is bring a laptop and a small hub to the system you expect may be compromised. Plug the laptop and one of the possibly compromised systems into the hub. Then, load your own copies of system utilities (ls, ps, netstat, for example) into a directory on the suspect system and set your path to that directory, or get them from a CD that you have created. From the laptop, telnet to the possibly compromised system on port 906. Run your versions of netstat and ps and such on the suspect system to see what is active. Also, examine the .rhosts and /etc/hosts.equiv on the suspect system to see what other systems are trusted by our dynamic duo.

An Alternative Approach

There is no way I can do justice to incident handling in a few paragraphs. *Incident Handling Step by Step* is a collaboration of more than 90 incident handlers. It is available from www.sans.org. One best practice technique if the system is down, or must be rebooted, is to use a bootable CD-ROM. Then, you can mount the system disk as a data drive. If at all possible, keep the original hard drive as evidence.

When you are finally satisfied that you understand what is going on with port 906, unless you are totally certain the system was not compromised, the following is the best course of action.

Turn to the system owners and ask when the last full backup was made. Make sympathetic clucking noises as they say "never" or "two years ago" and nod your head sadly. Look them in the eye and ask whether any data absolutely must be saved. Back up data files only, format the hard drive, and tell them to be sure to install all the appropriate security patches before putting the system back in business. Hook your laptop to the local area network. Scan the local net for SUNRPC and also for systems that answer on port 906, whatever else you have learned. Continue nuking from high orbit until the infection is sanitized.

Does this sound draconian? The death of a thousand cuts is far worse. By the way, we have talked about Loki and distributed denial of service tools like Trinoo using echo requests and replies for other purposes. Perhaps you would want to take a close look at the content of that ping in the trace as well.

"Random" Port Scan

This scan was well on its way to setting a speed record. This is another example of scanning ports that don't make any sense. There is no detectable signature; the purpose of the scan is unknown:

```
11:48:42.413036 prober.18985 > host.arpa.net.794: S 1240987936:1240987936(0)
win 512
11:48:42.415953 prober.18987 > host.arpa.net.248: S 909993377:909993377(0)
win 512
11:48:42.416116 prober.19031 > host.arpa.net.386: S 1712430684:1712430684(0)
win 512
11:48:42.416279 prober.19032 > host.arpa.net.828: S 323265067:323265067(0)
win 512
11:48:42.416443 prober.19033 > host.arpa.net.652: S 1333164003:1333164003(0)
win 512
```

```
11:48:42.556849 prober.19149 > host.arpa.net.145: S 2112498338:2112498338(0)
win 512
11:48:42.560124 prober.19150 > host.arpa.net.228: S 1832011492:1832011492(0)
win 512
11:48:42.560824 prober.19151 > host.arpa.net.840: S 3231869397:3231869397(0)
win 512
11:48:42.561313 prober.19152 > host.arpa.net.1003: S 2435718521:2435718521(0)
win 512
11:48:42.561437 prober.19153 > host.arpa.net.6: S 2632531476:2632531476(0)
win 512
11:48:42.561599 prober.19165 > host.arpa.net.280: S 2799050175:2799050175(0)
win 512
11:48:42.563074 prober.19166 > host.arpa.net.845: S 2065507088:2065507088(0)
win 512
11:48:42.563115 prober.19226 > host.arpa.net.653: S 1198658558:1198658558(0)
win 512
11:48:42.563238 prober.19227 > host.arpa.net.444: S 1090444266:1090444266(0)
win 512
11:48:42.565041 prober.19274 > host.arpa.net.907: S 2414364472:2414364472(0)
win 512
```

Okay, we don't know the purpose of the scan, and that is frustrating. So as an analyst, what do we know about this? We know it is fast and we know that the source port behavior is unpredictable—sometimes it skips, and sometimes it doesn't. Why doesn't the trace make sense? Why in the world is someone scanning so many unknown ports? I am not sure that we will ever know these answers. In the past few years, there have been a lot of very odd scan patterns. The best guess I have is that someone was using nmap, hping2, isic, packetx, or a similar tool to craft scans that had no possible purpose, probably from spoofed source addresses. That answers how, but not why!

Here is a guess: to drive intrusion-detection analysts crazy; to see what they would report and what they wouldn't; to see whether the scanners could cause a CNN news report that the world was under some horrid new cyber attack. Granted, it is far fetched, but it is the best I can come up with. How should the analyst react to this trace and other unknown seemingly random scans? I do recommend reporting stuff like this, because you never know what piece of information will help your CIRT. If your firewall is set to deny everything not specifically allowed, and none of your hosts answer back, however, don't get stressed. The best idea is to create a directory named "Scans_From_Mars" and file these detects there.

Database Correlation Report

I am a strong fan of allowing analysts to "fire and forget"—that is, when they see a detect, just report it and move on. When we first started doing fairly large-scale intrusion detection (five sites, 12,000 computers or so), the analyst had to manually check all the sensors for a correlation of source port, source IP, destination port, destination IP, and so on. Back then, if you were looking for something like correlation of TTL field or some behavior of the sequence number, it might take days to sort it out.

Life is too short for that kind of madness. After a pattern has been detected and reported, the database looks to see whether any correlations exist. This is what such a report might look like. This report was generated by a military correlation system known as Dark Shadow. It is based on an Oracle database. When an analyst detects and reports an intrusion attempt, Dark Shadow checks for that pattern across its data window of X sensor locations for Y months. If it finds a match, it creates a correlation report. This is why the analyst can operate in a fire-and-forget mode.

Note that from the source port ranges, it appears that two processes are running (destination port 111 is contacted by source ports from 617–1023, and destination port 25 by ports 2294–29419) on scanner, one to check email and the other to check portmapper. The two processes are probably bound by a shell script and reading from a file of target IP addresses. The probability is very high that this scan is interleaved across many more addresses. Here it is:

```
06/04/98 03:20:25    scanner    622      172.20.1.41     111  t
06/04/98 04:02:35    scanner   21091      172.20.1.1       25  t
06/04/98 04:02:36    scanner    890       172.20.1.1      111  t
06/04/98 04:06:04    scanner   21242    172.20.10.114      25  t
06/04/98 04:09:15    scanner    617     172.20.10.114     111  t
06/04/98 07:24:47    scanner    2295    192.168.229.18     25  t
06/04/98 07:28:06    scanner    1017    192.168.229.18    111  t
06/04/98 07:28:21    scanner    2333      172.20.1.41      25  t
06/04/98 07:31:40    scanner    729       172.20.1.41     111  t
06/04/98 12:46:21    scanner   20553    172.20.48.157      25  t
06/04/98 12:49:40    scanner    1023    172.20.48.157     111  t
06/04/98 16:05:22    scanner   29276      172.20.1.1       25  t
06/04/98 16:08:33    scanner    803       172.20.1.1      111  t
06/04/98 16:08:52    scanner   29419    172.20.10.114      25  t
06/04/98 16:08:53    scanner    900     172.20.10.114     111  t
```

SNMP/ICMP

The *Simple Network Management Protocol* (SNMP), even before the exploits that followed the release of the PROTOS toolkit in early 2002, could provide an attacker with a lot of information about your hosts and network configuration. According to the RFC NSMP is port 161 TCP and UDP. I have never seen a TCP version of SNMP in practice, but for safety,) port 161 TCP and UDP should be blocked from the Internet.

It is amazing how many devices, such as micro hubs, x-terminals, and printers, have SNMP agents. By default, these devices are protected by a well-known password (community string), typically "public." Many security-conscious organizations change this password, usually to one of the following:

- Private
- Internal
- The name of the organization

Note: Forgive me if you thought I was serious. The choices of private, internal, or the name of the organization for SNMP community strings are not advised. Pick something hard to guess.

In the following trace, notice the use of broadcast for both SNMP and ICMP. This is a very effective mapping technique because the attacker doesn't have to send many packets to potentially collect a lot of information.

```
17:31:33.49 prober.1030 > 192.168.2.255.161: GetNextRequest(11)[¦snmp]
17:31:33.73 prober.1030 > 255.255.255.255.161: GetNextRequest(11)[¦snmp]
17:31:33.73 prober > 255.255.255.255: icmp: echo request
...
17:43:17.32 prober > 192.168.1.255: icmp: echo request
17:43:17.32 prober.1030 > 192.168.1.255.161: GetNextRequest(11)[¦snmp]
```

FTP Bounce

We have another trace courtesy of the correlation database engine. In this case, the analyst is searching for FTP-DATA (TCP port 20) without an initiating FTP (TCP port 21). This can be the result of FTP bounce. The advantage to the attacker of using FTP bounce is that his identity is hidden. This is just like using an open proxy server, except that the source port will always show as TCP 20 for FTP-DATA. To do this, they just log on to a vulnerable FTP server as anonymous and open up arbitrary ports to probe the intended victim. This is not usually a very serious threat, unless the FTP server is a trusted host by its organization. Then, an attacker may be able to use the FTP server to probe the organization. FTP bounce is the subject of a CERT advisory, which you can find at `www.cert.org/ftp/cert_advisories/` `CA-97.27.FTP_bounce`.

In some implementations of FTP daemons, the **PORT** command can be misused to open a connection to a port of the attacker's choosing on a machine that the attacker could not have accessed directly. There have been ongoing discussions about this problem (called "FTP bounce") for several years, and some vendors have developed solutions for this problem.

When we uncovered the traffic in the following trace, we went back to prober and it was an FTP server, it supported anonymous FTP, and we were able to use the **port** command as advertised. The interesting thing is this trace was detected long before going to unknown ports became a fad. The following trace represents all the connections from prober to the protected network (172.20.152):

```
date       time       source IP  src port  dest IP       dest port
04/27/98 10:17:31     prober     20        172.20.152.2  3062 t
04/27/98 10:27:32     prober     20        172.20.152.2  4466 t

05/06/98 06:34:22     prober     20        172.20.152.2  1363 t
05/06/98 09:12:15     prober     20        172.20.152.2  4814 t
05/06/98 09:15:07     prober     20        172.20.152.2  1183 t
05/06/98 10:11:30     prober     20        172.20.152.2  1544 t
```

NetBIOS-Specific Traces

This section examines some traces that appear to be targeted at Windows systems. NetBIOS uses 135–139 TCP and UDP. It is certainly true that other systems than Windows use NetBIOS (SAMBA, for example), but as a general rule NetBIOS traffic can be expected to be generated by and targeted against Windows systems.

A Visit from a Web Server

One of the characteristics of NetBIOS is that traffic to destination port UDP 137 is often caused by something a site initiates. If you send email to a site running Microsoft Exchange, for example, the site will often send a port 137 attempt back. The following trace turned up because we saw 137s and then we started searching for the cause factor. To find the answer, we pulled all traffic for jellypc and found the web access. Then, we did the same for jampc and it was the same pattern. Being able to pull all the traffic for a host is very valuable when doing analysis. If your IDS does not support this, beat on your vendor!

> **Public Safety Announcement**
>
> Although this section focuses mostly on NetBIOS, let me take a minute to mention that there are hostile web servers on the Internet. When a system from your site visits a web server, that server can collect a lot of information about you, including your operating system and browser version. If your site doesn't use *Network Address Translation* (NAT), the web server will have your IP address. It is often possible to extract the web client's email address. Some sites open a connection back to the client and perform what we believe is TCP stack analysis. (And we haven't even discussed cookies.)

The web server in the jellypc trace wasn't satisfied with just the information it could collect from the HTTP headers; the server wanted more, so another system from the same subnet comes back to the hosts that visited the web server to collect the information available from the NetBIOS Name Service.

Here is the pattern:

```
12/02/97 08:27:18   jellypc.arpa.net 1112 -> www.com       http
12/02/97 08:27:19          0 bill.com        137 -> jellypc.arpa.net       137

12/02/97 17:06:03   jampc.arpa.net 2360 -> www.com       http
12/02/97 17:08:10          0 bill.com        137 -> jampc.arpa.net       137
```

I got on the phone and had a great chat with a technical type who runs the network there. It turns out that they are using a piece of commercial software for marketing purposes that creates a comprehensive database of your likes and dislikes.

If you want to see what kind of information is available about a particular Microsoft Windows host, the command is called nbtstat and it runs on Windows NT systems. A Windows host that runs NetBIOS cannot refuse to answer an nbtstat. A sample trace is shown here:

```
C:\>nbtstat -a goo

NetBIOS Remote Machine Name Table

     Name              Type        Status
- - - - - - - - - - - - - - - - - - - - - - - - - - - - -
Registered Registered Registered
MAC Address = 00-60-97-C9-35-53

GOO              <20>   UNIQUE
GOO              <00>   UNIQUE
KD2              <00>   GROUP
KD2              <1C>   GROUP
KD2              <1B>   UNIQUE
GOO              <03>   UNIQUE
SRNORTH          <03>   UNIQUE
INet~Services    <1C>   GROUP
IS~GOO           <00>   UNIQUE
KD2              <1E>   GROUP
KD2              <1D>   UNIQUE
.._MSBROWSE_.<01>   GROUP
```

The NetBIOS name of my machine, Goo, can be picked up as well as my workgroup, KD2. The logon name I use on that machine is srnorth. It is also possible to determine that I have a master browser cookie.

Perhaps this application of the wildcard request doesn't concern you, but I have been able to use nbtstat queries to determine an entire organizational structure as well as most of the logon names.

Null Session

But wait, there's more. Null sessioning has been described as analogous to finger. In essence, it is logging on to a system as a nobody user. Although you cannot modify anything, you can learn about the system. A sample command string is as follows:

```
net use \\172.20.244.164\IPC$ "" /USER:""
```

This generates literally pages of information, a section of which is shown here:

```
2/18/98 1:39 AM - Jsmith - \\192.168.4.22
UserName

Administrator
   Groups,Administrators (Local,
Members can fully administer the computer/domain)
   AccountType,User
   HomeDrive
   HomeDir
   PswdCanBeChanged,Yes
   PswdLastSetTime,Never
   PswdRequired,Yes
   PswdExpires,No
   AcctDisabled,No
   AcctLockedOut,No
   AcctExpiresTime,Never
   LastLogonTime,11/20/98 3:24 PM
   LastLogonServer,192.168.4.22
   Sid,S-1-5-21-706837240-361788889-398547282-500
```

Null sessioning can be prevented on Windows 2000 and if you will give me a second, I will test it on Windows XP Professional. Yup, it works—Control Panel, Administrative Tools, Local Security Policy.

Stealth Attacks

The first time I heard the term *stealth* was in a paper by Chris Klaus titled "Stealth Scanning—Bypassing Firewalls/SATAN Detectors." He was describing what people now usually refer to as "half open"—that is, intentionally violating the TCP three-way handshake. There are a number of variations of half scans, and we are going to examine all the common ones. These are not all that hard to detect in and of themselves, but as you will learn in the discussion on coordinated attacks, they are getting some help. Nowadays, some folks use stealth to mean null flags (no flags or code bits set). The only approaches I

find actually stealthy are those based on either low and slow, or highly distributed, packet delivery. As time goes on, static packet filters continue to be less
and less common; half-open scans are less and less an issue. They certainly
should not be called stealth because they stand out like a sore thumb. The
Snort web page, www.snort.org, lists a number of effective rules to detect
these probes.

This is a season of advanced scans; attackers with the skill to type, make, and
actually compile software are using tools that give them the look and feel of
"eleetness." Three years ago it was jackal; at the turn of the century, hping and
nmap; and today, distributed scanners.

In the book, *Inside Firewalls* by Robert Ziegler (New Riders), I commented
that I continue to be astounded by the security provided by Network Address
Translation (NAT). My most important files are on a vmware version of Linux
7.2 on my Windows laptop, and the Linux system is behind a NAT. So, if
attackers can get through my home perimeter defenses, which also include a
NAT, and break into my XP laptop, they still have another NAT to go
through. With appliance firewalls available as cheap as $300, you can afford a
number of NATs in your organization, which will foil most of this scanning.
There is also a strong argument that nothing penetrates a well-configured,
proxy-based firewall (although we will dispute this in a moment). None of the
deception tools will elude a well-trained analyst with an IDS that collects all
the traffic and has a supporting database. If your site has chosen a lesser path,
you may be in for a wild ride.

> As we get ready to launch into some traces of stealth
> techniques, take a minute to read the opening comment
> from the original 1997 jackal.c source code. /* Jackal -
> Stealth/FireWall scanner. With the use of halfopen ports
> and sending SYNC (sometimes additional flags like FIN)
> one can scan behind a firewall. And it shouldnt let the
> site feel we're scanning by not doing a 3-way-handshake
> we hope to avoid any tcp-logging. Credits: Halflife, Jeff
> (Phiji) Fay, Abdullah Marafie. Alpha Tester: Walter
> Kopecky. Results: Some firewalls did allow SYN | FIN
> to pass through. No Site has been able to log the con-
> nections though during alpha testing. ShadowS shad-
> ows@kuwait.net Copyleft (hack it i realy dont care). */

It was a brilliant idea! If the filtering router tests for SYN, feed it a SYN/FIN.
However, the statement that jackal had never been logged by any site misses
the mark. In Appendix A, "Exploits and Scans to Apply Exploits," you saw the
IMAP traces with the SYN/FIN set, which were detected by the Shadow

system. Competent intrusion–detection systems were able to log and analyze anything sent by jackal (or hping or nmap). In fact, today when attackers set SYN/FIN, they make our job easy.

Explicit Stealth Mapping Techniques

The two well-known explicit mapping techniques are the SYN/ACK and the FIN scan. Both of these generate a RESET, if they hit an active host. They also get an ICMP error message back if the host is unreachable. Explicit stealth mapping is more efficient than inverse mapping (described later), but is possibly more obvious.

FIN Scan

I have never detected a FIN scan in the wild and have chosen not to simulate one. In the case of a FIN scan, one would detect a large number of packets with the FIN flag set where there was no three-way handshake ever established. We have already discussed using a database to find FTP bounce. A good intrusion-analysis system should provide the capability to look for spurious traffic such as FINs, to connections that were never established. I have seen ACKs only and have seen them penetrate a Check Point firewall.

Inverse Mapping

Inverse mapping techniques can compile a list of networks, or hosts, that are not reachable and then use the converse of that map to determine where things probably are. We will also show a DNS example of all replies and no queries. Before we go on, though, if you absolutely cannot do NAT and must use public IP addresses, make sure you do not allow ICMP unreachables out of your network. That will not stop all inverse mapping techniques, but it will quench a large number of them. As you look at the trace that follows, keep this in mind: the answers by router.mynet.net are doing all the harm:

```
02:58:05.490 stealth.mappem.com.25984 > 172.30.69.23.2271:
    R 0:0(0) ack 674719802 win 0
02:59:11.208 stealth.mappem.com.50620 > 172.16.7.158.1050:
    R 0:0(0) ack 674719802 win 0
02:59:20.670 stealth.mappem.com.19801 > 192.168.184.174.1478:
    R 0:0(0) ack 674719802 win 0
02:59:31.056 stealth.mappem.com.7960 > 192.168.242.139.1728:
    R 0:0(0) ack 674719802 win 0
02:59:42.792 stealth.mappem.com.16106 > 172.16.102.105.1008:
    R 0:0(0) ack 674719802 win 0
03:00:50.308 stealth.mappem.com.8986 > 172.16.98.61.1456:
    R 0:0(0) ack 674719802 win 0
```

```
03:00:58.939 stealth.mappem.com.35124 > 192.168.182.171.1626:
     R 0:0(0) ack 674719802 win 0
03:00:58.940 router.mynet.net > stealth.mappem.com:
     icmp: host 192.168.182.171 unreachable
```

Answers to Domain Queries

Another variation of inverse mapping is shown here. The probing computer sends answers to domain questions that were never asked. The goal is to stumble across a subnet or host that doesn't exist, which will generate an ICMP unreachable message. As stated earlier, this pattern tends to evade detection. It can be found with scan detect code if the attacker gets greedy and probes too many hosts too quickly. It can also be detected by retrospective analysis scripts or database searches for application state violations. Here is the example of inverse mapping:

```
05:55:36.515566 stealth.com.domain > 172.29.63.63.20479: udp
06:46:18.542999 stealth.com.domain > 192.168.160.240.12793: udp
07:36:32.713298 stealth.com.domain > 172.29.185.48.54358: udp
07:57:01.634613 stealth.com.domain > 254.242.221.165.13043: udp
09:55:28.728984 stealth.com.domain > 192.168.203.163.15253: udp
10:38:53.862779 stealth.com.domain > 192.168.126.131.39915: udp
10:40:37.513176 stealth.com.domain > 192.168.151.126.19038: udp
10:44:28.462431 stealth.com.domain > 172.29.96.220.8479: udp
11:35:40.489103 stealth.com.domain > 192.168.7.246.44451: udp

11:35:40.489103 stealth.com.domain > 192.168.7.246.44451: udp
11:35:40.489523 router.mynet.net > stealth.com:
                 icmp: host 192.168.7.246 unreachable
```

Because IP spoofing, usually part of a denial-of-service attack, is so common, you may be asking, "Why isn't the explanation for this IP spoofing of the 172.29, 192.168, and so forth addresses and directing them to stealth.com?" Couldn't this just be seeing the echoes of this activity directed back to our network? The problem is that this doesn't resemble normal DNS responses. It doesn't have any indications that some kind of DNS query was issued.

To investigate this further, you might try to find out whether stealth.com is really a DNS server. You use the **nslookup** command and change servers to stealth.com and try to resolve any address. If it works, you know that stealth.com is a true DNS server and the mystery intensifies. (Tragically, nslookup, at least on UNIX, is being deprecated by the more obscure dig program.) If it doesn't respond, chances are it is not a DNS server, and it really is the aggressor. It is also possible that it is a DNS server, but you might not have access to it.

Answers to Domain Queries, Part 2

The following activity is similar to what you just saw because both use source port of 53 or domain. This output is TCP and came from multiple different sources, however, unlike the preceding activity. Any guesses about what is going on here?

```
11:19:30.885069 host1.corecomm.net.53 > myhost1.com.21: S 7936:7936(0) win
1024
11:17:29.375069 host1.corecomm.net.53 > myhost1.com.139: S 7936:7936(0) win
1024
11:15:32.115069 host1.corecomm.net.53 > myhost1.com.23: S 7936:7936(0) win
1024
11:11:17.485069 host1.corecomm.net.53 > myhost1.com.43981: S 7936:7936(0) win
1024
11:09:12.945069 host1.corecomm.net.53 > myhost1.com.880: S 7936:7936(0) win
1024
12:01:05.060000 host70.corecomm.net.53 > pc112.com.880: S 1738:1738(0) win
1024
12:03:24.820000 host70.corecomm.net.53 > pc112.com.139: S 1738:1738(0) win
1024
12:06:12.620000 host70.corecomm.net.53 > pc112.com.21: S 1738:1738(0) win
1024
12:09:09.940000 host70.corecomm.net.53 > pc112.com.43981: S 1738:1738(0) win
1024
12:09:57.960000 host70.corecomm.net.53 > pc112.com.23: S 1738:1738(0) win
1024
```

This appears to be a scan of myhost1.com, pc112.com, and many other hosts not shown in this abbreviated output of some common destination ports such as 21 (FTP), 23 (telnet), and 139 (NetBIOS Session Manager). But, there are some funky destination ports along with those common ones that aren't readily identifiable, such as 43981 and 880. You can round up all the usual suspect explanations for the unconventional ports, but in this case, your analysis should concentrate more on the source port used.

TCP source port 53 might be allowed into many networks because this can be indicative of activity from a long DNS response. Remember from Chapter 6, "DNS," that UDP DNS responses of more than 512 bytes are reissued to the DNS server to destination port TCP 53. When the response returns to your network, the source port will be 53 and you need to allow that back in to receive that response. A smart network administrator qualifies this so that it is allowed back in only if it was established inside the network of origin, and only if the destination port is greater than 1023 (indicative of an ephemeral port), which is the case in the long DNS responses.

That is not the case in the preceding scan, but the scanner is banking on the packet-filtering device being open on source port 53 without any further qualification. This way, the scanner might circumvent a normally protective packet-filtering device.

It is interesting to note that the TCP sequence numbers you see in the scan are repeated for each of the same source-to-destination port scans. These should change for each new TCP segment created. Another forensics tidbit about this scan that is not obvious unless you look at many more records than are shown, gives some insight into the nature of the TCP sequence number crafting. The preceding scan shows two TCP sequence numbers: 7936 and 1738. Considering that the TCP sequence number field is 32 bits long, these are very small initial sequence numbers—quite unusual. All the TCP sequence numbers from this scan were lightweight, and when the activity was dumped in hex, the reason why was discovered. The high-order 16 bits of the TCP sequence number were always 0s. This is confirmation that some kind of sequence number manipulation was performed, and it becomes a signature of this activity.

Fragments, Just Fragments

Consider this final example of an inverse mapping technique. As you have already learned, only the first fragment chunk comes with protocol information. Attackers using this technique (along with some interesting variations) were able to penetrate older firewalls and filtering routers. The firewalls would assume that this was just another segment of traffic that had already passed their access lists. Needless to say, this has been fixed in most vendors' products.

In this case, however, the prober isn't particularly interested in firewall penetration. Once again, if one of the target hosts does not exist, the router sends back an unreachable message. The attacker can then compile a list of all the hosts that do not exist and, by taking the inverse of that list, has a list of the hosts that do exist. This is why this class of techniques is called inverse mapping. Take a look:

```
18:32:21.050033 PROBER > 192.168.5.71: (frag 9019:480@552)
18:32:21.109287 PROBER > 192.168.5.72: (frag 9275:480@552)
18:32:21.178342 PROBER > 192.168.5.73: (frag 9531:480@552)
18:32:21.295332 PROBER > 192.168.5.74: (frag 9787:480@552)
18:32:21.344322 PROBER > 192.168.5.75: (frag 10299:480@552)
18:32:21.384284 PROBER > 192.168.5.76: (frag 10555:480@552)
18:32:21.431136 PROBER > 192.168.5.77: (frag 11067:480@552)
18:32:21.478246 PROBER > 192.168.5.78: (frag 11579:480@552)
18:32:21.522631 PROBER > 192.168.5.79: (frag 11835:480@552)
```

Measuring Response Time

Lately, we've seen a lot of traffic coming from all over the place directed to DNS servers, but not for the purpose of querying for DNS information or ostensibly of malicious intent. What is happening is that companies have developed software that tries to deliver the best possible response time to web requests. It has been demonstrated that most users will tolerate about an eight-second delay in receiving responses and after that they might go to a competitor site with better response time. It has become a matter of e-business survival and profitability to offer good response time, and because necessity is the mother of invention, software has been created to accomplish the mission. The patterns explained in this section are from a product known as 3DNS.

One technique is to associate the user request with an authoritative DNS server for the user's host and find the response time to the DNS server. This assumes that the authoritative DNS server and the user's hosts are geographically close, which might not always be the case. Why not just find the distance to the user's host? Indeed, this seems more logical, but many sites are well protected, and access to the user's host is not always available. They figure there is a better chance of having some kind of access to the DNS server, which may or may not be the case.

There has been a lot of hue and cry from analysts who see their IDS fired because of the traffic generated by this software. Many sites feel violated because traffic is directed to the sacred DNS server, of all hosts. And, many more sites don't understand what is happening and perceive this activity to be an attack of some sort. The final objection is that this is unauthorized information gathering, regardless of whether it benefits the end user.

Let's take a look at some of the signatures associated with this type of traffic. One thing that you should keep in mind is that many different web sites use this software and so you will see many different source IPs. Because of the unique signatures generated from multiple source IPs, this has been mistaken for some kind of coordinated attack. As you will see, however, it really isn't.

Echo Requests

No surprise with the following TCPdump activity to measure response time to your DNS server. The echo request is issued and the response time is measured based on receipt of an ICMP echo reply, if there is one:

```
10:25:44.070000 216.32.68.13 > mydns.com: icmp: echo request
10:25:44.070000 216.32.68.13 > mydns.com: icmp: echo request
10:25:44.070000 216.32.68.13 > mydns.com: icmp: echo request
10:30:01.530000 216.32.68.13 > mydns.com: icmp: echo request
10:30:01.530000 216.32.68.13 > mydns.com: icmp: echo request
10:30:01.550000 216.32.68.13 > mydns.com: icmp: echo request
10:30:25.660000 209.67.29.8 > mydns.com: icmp: echo request
10:30:25.660000 209.67.29.8 > mydns.com: icmp: echo request
10:30:25.670000 209.67.29.8 > mydns.com: icmp: echo request
10:32:12.520000 209.67.78.200 > mydns.com: icmp: echo request
```

As you have learned, however, many sites block ICMP echo requests because ICMP has capability to map sites both actively with a ping, and also by eliciting error messages that give away the position of hosts and routers in a site. And, if this is the case, an attacker, or even a service provider using a tool like 3DNS might focus their reconnaissance on the DNS server.

Actual DNS Queries

If the user's DNS server didn't respond to the ICMP echo request and the server using the 3DNS probing software is configured to continue to try to make contact with the DNS server, more activity is sent, as shown here:

```
216.32.68.11.3200 > mydns.com.53: 0 [0q] Type0 (Class 0)?. (36)
mydns.com.53 > 216.32.68.11.3200: 0 FormErr [0q] 0/0/0 (12) DF
216.32.68.11.3201 > mydns.com.53: 256 [0q] Type0 (Class 0)? . (36)
mydns.com.53 > 216.32.68.11.3201: 0 FormErr [0q] 0/0/0 (12) DF
216.32.68.11.3202 > mydns.com.53: 512 [0q] Type0 (Class 0)? . (36)
mydns.com.53 > 216.32.68.11.3202: 0 FormErr [0q] 0/0/0 (12) DF
```

A real DNS query is not issued, but one is sent to UDP port 53 with a DNS message of all 0s. TCPdump performs some integrity checking of the DNS message and if it discovers what it considers to be noteworthy fields, it reports them. The 0q means that there were zero queries in the DNS message, for example. Normally, for types other than inverse queries there will be at least one query. That is why TCPdump reported it and all other 0-padded fields it considers to be odd. This elicits an error response from mydns.com, which is then used to compute the round-trip time.

Probe on UDP Port 33434

Here is yet a third type of activity directed at the DNS server if the others have failed:

```
209.67.78.203.3310 > mydns.com.33434: udp 36 [ttl 1]
209.67.78.203.3311 > mydns.com.33434: udp 36 (ttl 2)
216.32.68.10.3307 > mydns.com.33434: udp 36 [ttl 1]
216.32.68.10.3308 > mydns.com.33434: udp 36 (ttl 2)
216.32.68.10.3307 > mydns.com.33434: udp 36 [ttl 1]
216.32.68.10.3308 > mydns.com.33434: udp 36 (ttl 2)
209.67.78.200.3411 > mydns.com.33434: udp 36 [ttl 1]
209.67.78.200.3412 > mydns.com.33434: udp 36 (ttl 2)
```

This output is much like you might see with a UNIX traceroute. Traceroute has the signature of attempting a UDP connection to a high-numbered port in the 33000+ range, such as seen here. This is slightly different because the standard implementation of traceroute uses incrementing destination ports. These are to static UDP destination port of 33434. The anticipated response will be a port unreachable error, in which case response time can be computed when the 3DNS software receives the response. The incrementing TTL values can also be a signature of Traceroute, if the DNS server is inside the sensor that captured this activity.

3DNS to TCP Port 53

A final attempt to establish a connection to TCP port 53 is made if all others fail. This attempt differs from most SYN connections because you will see that 64 bytes have been included in the payload. Normal traffic has no payload until after the three-way handshake has been completed. The 64 data bytes are sent to approximate a reasonable-sized payload, one that is neither too small nor too large. The anticipated response will be either a SYN/ACK from a listening server or a RST/ACK from one that is not listening:

```
209.67.78.202.2202 > mydns.com.53: S 997788921:997788985(64) win 2048
209.67.78.202.2200 > mydns.com.53: S 869896644:869896708(64) win 2048
209.67.78.202.2201 > mydns.com.53: S 1386586413:1386586477(64) win 2048
216.32.68.11.3102 > mydns.com.53: S 765045139:765045203(64) win 2048
216.32.68.11.3100 > mydns.com.53: S 865977968:865978032(64) win 2048
216.32.68.11.3101 > mydns.com.53: S 565178644:565178708(64) win 2048
```

This approach seems destined to fail for many sites, especially if this is the final attempt when all others have failed because of blocked access to the other methods. The problem is that most security-conscious sites block access to TCP destination port 53 because that can be used to download the DNS maps that contain all registered hosts and their IP numbers. Therefore, if traffic is blocked, perhaps they could do the measurements from an ICMP unreachable received from the router blocking the access. What if the block was done by a router that has been silenced from delivering host unreachable errors? This is just as fruitless as the other failed attempts.

Worms as Information Gatherers

If all users at your site share a common mail server, and it is configured to examine mail for viruses that have been identified, many might be eliminated before they can infect the target host. But, users might not all use the same mail server; they might not run virus eradication software; and if they do, they might not update it frequently. This increases the risk of infection.

Viruses and worms have not been viewed conventionally as information gatherers. We are starting to see a new class of worm that acts as some kind of agent to harvest or seek information. This might involve attempting connections to other hosts after a host has been infected. If this is the case, and there is some kind of IDS at an egress point of the infected host, we can observe the activity. Two such worms are examined here: Pretty Park and RingZero.

Pretty Park Worm

I was reviewing an alert about outbound blocked activity at one of our sites and discovered that an internal host was attempting to connect to an Internet Relay Chat (IRC) port 6667 on many different destination IPs. This site had blocked outbound activity to many of the conventionally used IRC ports just because the site was hard pressed to find redeeming quality in many. I'm sure it can be argued that there are many reputable and upstanding chat rooms, but often times users gravitate to ones that aren't work related. And, every summer when the new crop of cyber-connected summer students arrived, this site usually saw a couple of them try to engage in IRC activity and fail.

It was late February, a Friday afternoon to be exact, and I was seeing this activity. I reported it to the appropriate contact, and he said that he had informed the owning administrator of the detected activity. I also dumped logs of the rejected outbound activity, but didn't give them much scrutiny. Had I been more thorough, I would have discovered that the host was attempting connections to IRC sites about five times a minute. This either reflects an obsessive-compulsive desire to connect or an automated program.

On the following Monday, I received another alert about outbound IRC activity—no big deal. I just thought it was the same host I had already identified trying once again. But, I searched the logs again and found four more hosts engaged in similar activity. The scary part was that they were all going to the same destination hosts, many of them in foreign countries. And, so the inevitable thought of horror arose in my paranoid analyst's brain: We had suffered multiple compromises using a common vulnerability, and the intruder was trying to contact her home base to report the triumph. Another, more comforting (compared to a compromise) thought occurred that maybe there was some kind of worm infection.

Sure enough, when my Windows-savvy coworker examined one of the infected hosts, he located some strange programs running (FILES32.VXD and PRETTY PARK.EXE) and identified this as the Pretty Park worm. Using netstat, he discovered that the host had sent a TCP SYN to destination port 6667. Apparently, Pretty Park is a worm that arrives via an email attachment and one of the duties of the worm is to go to these IRC sites in hopes of sending back information about the hosts—things such as passwords and details about the infected host. You can get a more thorough description of Pretty Park at http://vil.nai.com/vil/wm98500.asp.

Here is an excerpt of the activity captured by TCPdump. The destination port is 6667, and the destination hosts change:

```
09:30:34.470000 infected.com.1218 > ircnet.grolier.net.6667: S
662405:662405(0) Âwin 8192 (DF)
09:30:37.370000 infected.com.1218 > ircnet.grolier.net.6667: S
662405:662405(0) Âwin 8192 (DF)
09:30:43.370000 infected.com.1218 > ircnet.grolier.net.6667: S
662405:662405(0) Âwin 8192 (DF)
09:30:55.370000 infected.com.1218 > ircnet.grolier.net.6667: S
662405:662405(0) Âwin 8192 (DF)
09:31:04.050000 infected.com.1220 > irc.ncal.verio.net.6667: S
691990:691990(0) Âwin 8192 (DF)
09:31:06.970000 infected.com.1220 > irc.ncal.verio.net.6667: S
691990:691990(0) Âwin 8192 (DF)
09:31:12.970000 infected.com.1220 > irc.ncal.verio.net.6667: S
691990:691990(0) Âwin 8192 (DF)
09:31:24.970000 infected.com.1220 > irc.ncal.verio.net.6667: S
691990:691990(0) Âwin 8192 (DF)
09:32:34.130000 infected.com.1222 > mist.cifnet.com.6667: F
722101:722101(0) ack 1426589426 win 8680 (DF)
09:32:43.070000 infected.com.1224 > krameria.skybel.net.6667: S
782083:782083(0) Âwin 8192 (DF)
09:32:55.070000 infected.com.1224 > krameria.skybel.net.6667: S
782083:782083(0) Âwin 8192 (DF)
09:33:04.170000 infected.com.1226 > zafira.eurecom.fr.6667: S
812112:812112(0) Âwin 8192 (DF)
```

The lesson here is that the theory of fusing host-based and network-based software yields the best results.

On the host-based side, we would like to believe that worm-eradication software prevents infection, but this doesn't work for all hosts. Detection was network-based in this case because logging the denied traffic was what identified a possible problem.

RingZero

Another worm, a Trojan horse known as RingZero, that sent out network traffic was discovered in September 1999. The first identified traffic pattern associated with RingZero was a Shadow detect of a scan of many different hosts for TCP port 3128, the squid proxy server port. Here is a sample of the captured activity seen by Shadow:

```
12:29:48.230000 4.3.2.1.1049 > 172.16.54.171.3128: S 9779697:9779697(0) win
8192 Â<mss 1460> (DF) (ttl 19, id 9072)
12:29:58.070000 4.3.2.1.1049 > 172.16.54.171.3128: S 9779697:9779697(0) win
8192 Â<mss 1460> (DF) (ttl 19, id 29552)
12:30:10.960000 4.3.2.1.1049 > 172.16.54.171.3128: S 9779697:9779697(0) win
8192 Â<mss 1460> (DF) (ttl 19, id 39792)
12:44:54.9600001.2.3.4.3243 > 172.16.187.212.3128: S 356330349:356330349(0)
win Â8192 <mss 1460> (DF) (ttl 242, id 962)
12:44:57.930000 1.2.3.4.3243 > 172.16.187.212.3128: S 356330349:356330349(0)
win Â8192 <mss 1460> (DF) (ttl 242, id 11714)
```

```
12:45:03.930000 1.2.3.4.3243 > 172.16.187.212.3128: S 356330349:356330349(0)
win Â8192 <mss 1460> (DF) (ttl 242, id 22466)
12:45:15.930000 1.2.3.4.3243 > 172.16.187.212.3128: S 356330349:356330349(0)
win Â8192 <mss 1460> (DF) (ttl 242, id 33218)
12:46:13.070000 1.1.1.1.2262 > 172.16.99.110.3128: S 20315949:20315949(0) win
Â8192 <mss 1460,nop,nop,sackOK> (DF) (ttl 116, id 35676)
12:46:16.080000 1.1.1.1.2262 > 172.16.99.110.3128: S 20315949:20315949(0) win
Â8192 <mss 1460,nop,nop,sackOK> (DF) (ttl 116, id 46428)
12:46:22.070000 1.1.1.1.2262 > 172.16.99.110.3128: S 20315949:20315949(0) win
Â8192 <mss 1460,nop,nop,sackOK> (DF) (ttl 116, id 57180)
12:46:34.080000 1.1.1.1.2262 > 172.16.99.110.3128: S 20315949:20315949(0) win
Â8192 <mss 1460,nop,nop,sackOK> (DF) (ttl 116, id 2397)
```

Three hostile hosts (1.1.1.1, 1.2.3.4, and 4.3.2.1) scanned different internal 172.16 hosts for port 3128. When an additional investigation was performed, it was discovered that the scanning host also attempted connections to destination ports 80 (HTTP) and 8080 (alternate HTTP). Shadow filters don't look for those destination ports because they are likely to trigger a lot of false positives. A lot of sites saw similar activity, and it appeared to be coming from many different source hosts from all over the world with as many as a half dozen different scans per hour. Most of these scans hit destination addresses that didn't exist, indicating that no prior reconnaissance had been done or it hadn't been done well.

One theory concluded this was from one host that was just spoofing source IPs. In the preceding scan output that was executed with the TCPdump **–vv** option, (this is the reason you see the additional information in parenthesis), the TTL value is displayed. The **–vv** option also displays a field known as the IP identification number that appears as "id #." If this activity were all from one spoofed source IP, the arriving TTL value should have remained relatively constant unless it was being crafted.

When traceroutes were attempted back to many of the source IP addresses, the hop counts to get from my site back to the alleged source IP appeared credible. If you can estimate the initial TTL assigned by the source IP and figure out the difference between that and the arriving TTL, you can approximate the hop counts. The difficulty is guessing the initial TTL. If you look at the chart found at www.honeynet.org/papers/finger/traces.txt, most times you can figure out a reasonable initial TTL.

Not only were the hop counts believable, but all the source IPs appeared to be alive and pingable, something not typically found with randomly pirated source IPs. Finally, in the preceding scan, notice that the final scanning IP, 1.1.1.1, has different TCP options (nop, nop, sackOK) from the other records. This points more to the source's hosts being genuinely different and real, rather than a crafter taking the time to artificially introduce these differences.

In conjunction with a SANS call for help in determining the cause of these scans, a very astute network administrator, Ron Marcum of Vanderbilt University, discovered a PC on his network scanning hosts on other networks looking for ports 80, 8080, and 3128. The RingZero Trojan appeared to be the culprit. It looked for any hosts that were using open proxy servers found on ports 3128, 80, or 8080 and, at least for a while, collected ones it did find on an FTP site. There is value in knowing where an open proxy server is; it enables hackers to hide their true source IP identities. Open proxy servers enable you to tunnel through them and assume that IP number as the source IP. Some questions still remain about RingZero; it is not known how the Trojan infects a particular host, and it has not been determined what IPs the Trojan scans when downloaded.

Summary

The attacker community is investing an incredible amount of effort to scan the Internet. The single most important service for your site to block is ICMP echo requests. Reconnaissance probes should be taken seriously; if attackers can learn where your hosts are, they can make fairly short work of determining what services these hosts run. If they cannot determine which of the hosts in your network address space are active, they have a very sparse matrix with which to work. One great defense is to use RFC 1918 private address space instead of using public address space. If you have public address space and do not have split horizon DNS, attackers can just ask your DNS server where your hosts are with reverse lookups. Also, when possible, a NAT is a fantastic defense against probing. I recommend several layers of NATs. Finally, try to configure your perimeter not to allow ICMP unreachable error messages out of your network.

Also, with the new class of viruses and worms being released, infiltration of your well-guarded site might come from within. This is a natural evolution of information-gathering techniques because many sites have become more proficient at shunning reconnaissance from the outside.

Index

F

N

T

H O W   T O   C O N T A C T   U S

VISIT OUR WEB SITE

W W W . N E W R I D E R S . C O M

On our web site, you'll find information about our other books, authors, tables of contents, and book errata. You will also find information about book registration and how to purchase our books, both domestically and internationally.

EMAIL US

Contact us at: **nrfeedback@newriders.com**

- If you have comments or questions about this book
- To report errors that you have found in this book
- If you have a book proposal to submit or are interested in writing for New Riders
- If you are an expert in a computer topic or technology and are interested in being a technical editor who reviews manuscripts for technical accuracy

Contact us at: **nreducation@newriders.com**

- If you are an instructor from an educational institution who wants to preview New Riders books for classroom use. Email should include your name, title, school, department, address, phone number, office days/hours, text in use, and enrollment, along with your request for desk/examination copies and/or additional information.

Contact us at: **nrmedia@newriders.com**

- If you are a member of the media who is interested in reviewing copies of New Riders books. Send your name, mailing address, and email address, along with the name of the publication or web site you work for.

BULK PURCHASES/CORPORATE SALES

The publisher offers discounts on this book when ordered in quantity for bulk purchases and special sales. For sales within the U.S., please contact: Corporate and Government Sales (800) 382-3419 or **corpsales@pearsontechgroup.com**. Outside of the U.S., please contact: International Sales (317) 581-3793 or **international@pearsontechgroup.com**.

WRITE TO US

New Riders Publishing
201 W. 103rd St.
Indianapolis, IN 46290-1097

CALL/FAX US

Toll-free (800) 571-5840
If outside U.S. (317) 581-3500
Ask for New Riders
FAX: (317) 581-4663

New
Riders

W W W . N E W R I D E R S . C O M

Solutions from experts you know and tru

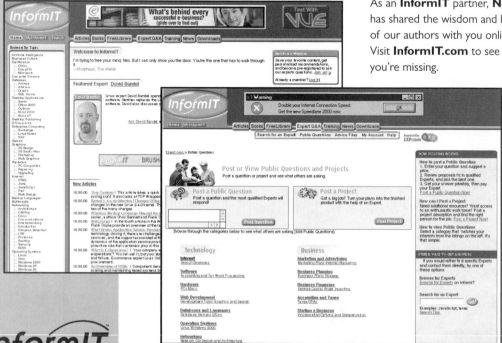

VIEW CART

search ⊙

▸ Registration already a member? Log in. ▸ Book Registration

Publishing the Voices that Matter

OUR AUTHORS

PRESS ROOM

| ⋮⋮ web development | ⋮⋮ design | ⋮⋮ photoshop | ⋮⋮ new media | ⋮⋮ 3-D | ⋮⋮ server technologies |

EDUCATORS

ABOUT US

CONTACT US

You already know that New Riders brings you the **Voices that Matter**.

But what does that mean? It means that New Riders brings you the

Voices that challenge your assumptions, take your talents to the next

level, or simply help you better understand the complex technical world

we're all navigating.

Visit **www.newriders.com** to find:

- ▸ **10% discount** and **free shipping** on all purchases
- ▸ Never before published chapters
- ▸ Sample chapters and excerpts
- ▸ Author bios and interviews
- ▸ Contests and enter-to-wins
- ▸ Up-to-date industry event information
- ▸ Book reviews
- ▸ Special offers from our friends and partners
- ▸ Info on how to join our User Group program
- ▸ Ways to have your Voice heard

WWW.NEWRIDERS.COM

Colophon

The image on the cover of this book, "Sunbeams in a Forest," was taken by Martial Colomb. Many of Colomb's photographs of well-known international sites are featured on travel and tourism web sites.

This book was written and edited in Microsoft Word and laid out in QuarkXPress. The fonts used for the body text are Bembo and Mono. It was printed on 50# Husky Offset Smooth paper at VonHoffman, Inc in Owensville, MO. Prepress consisted of PostScript computer-to-plate technology (filmless process). The cover was printed at Moore Langen Printing in Terre Haute, Indiana, on 12 pt., coated on one side.